T0236366

Lecture Notes in Computer Science   9572

Commenced Publication in 1973
Founding and Former Series Editors:
Gerhard Goos, Juris Hartmanis, and Jan van Leeuwen

More information about this series at http://www.springer.com/series/7409

Costas Lambrinoudakis · Alban Gabillon (Eds.)

Risks and Security of Internet and Systems

10th International Conference, CRiSIS 2015
Mytilene, Lesbos Island, Greece, July 20–22, 2015
Revised Selected Papers

 Springer

Editors
Costas Lambrinoudakis
University of Piraeus
Piraeus
Greece

Alban Gabillon
Université de la Polynésie Française
Faa'a
French Polynesia

ISSN 0302-9743   ISSN 1611-3349   (electronic)
Lecture Notes in Computer Science
ISBN 978-3-319-31810-3   ISBN 978-3-319-31811-0   (eBook)
DOI 10.1007/978-3-319-31811-0

Library of Congress Control Number: 2016934430

LNCS Sublibrary: SL3 – Information Systems and Applications, incl. Internet/Web, and HCI

Printed on acid-free paper

This Springer imprint is published by Springer Nature
The registered company is Springer International Publishing AG Switzerland

Preface

These are the proceedings of the 10th International Conference on Risks and Security of Internet and Systems (CRiSIS 2015). The conference brought together academic researchers and industry developers, who discussed the state of the art in technology for exploring risks and security issues in Internet applications, networks, and systems. Each year papers are presented covering topics including trust, security risks and threats, intrusion detection and prevention, access control, and security modeling.

The conference program included seven technical papers sessions that covered a broad range of topics from trust and privacy issues and risk management to cloud systems and cryptography. The conference program also included an invited talk by Dr. George Leventakis (Senior Security Expert, Center for Security Studies, Hellenic Ministry of Public Order and Citizen Protection) entitled "European Program for Critical Infrastructure Protection. Linking Policy, Research and Implementation" and a tutorial session given by David Espes (Lecturer and Researcher, UMR CNRS lab-STIIC and University of Western Brittany) on "Software-Defined Networking Security." The conference attracted many high-quality submissions, each of which was assigned to four Program Committee members for review and the final acceptance rate was 35 %.

We would like to express our thanks to the various people who assisted us in organizing the event and formulating the program. We are very grateful to the Program Committee members for their timely and rigorous reviews of the papers. Our gratitude also goes to the University of the Aegean and especially to Prof. Christos Kalloniatis, for supporting the organization of the conference. Finally we would like to thank all of the authors who submitted papers for the event and contributed to an interesting set of conference proceedings.

January 2016

Costas Lambrinoudakis
Alban Gabillon

Organization

General Chairs

Sokratis Katsikas   University of Piraeus, Greece
Frédéric Cuppens   TELECOM Bretagne, France

Program Committee Co-chairs

Costas Lambrinoudakis   University of Piraeus, Greece
Alban Gabillon   Université de la Polynésie Française, Tahiti

Tutorial Chair

Nora Cuppens-Boulahia   Telecom Bretagne, France

Local Organizing Chair

Christos Kalloniatis   University of the Aegean, Greece

Program Committee

Ayed Samiha	TELECOM Bretagne, France
Bonnecaze Alexis	I2M, Aix Marseille Université, France
Chaouchi Hakima	Telecom & Management SudParis, France
Chen Yu	State University of New York - Binghamton, USA
Cuellar Jorge	Siemens AG, Germany
Damiani Ernesto	University of Milan, Italy
De Capitani Di Vimercati Sabrina	Università degli Studi di Milano, Italy
Dewri Rinku	University of Denver, USA
Di Pietro Roberto	Bell Labs, USA
Dubus Samuel	Alcatel-Lucent Bell Labs, Greece
Fernandez José M.	Ecole Polytechnique de Montreal, Canada
Gamble Rose	Tandy School of Computer Science, USA
Gritzalis Dimitris	Athens University of Economics and Business, Greece
Gritzalis Stefanos	University of the Aegean, Greece
Guirguis Mina	Texas State University - San Marcos, USA
Jean-Louis Lanet	Inria-RBA, France
Kalloniatis Christos	University of the Aegean, Greece
Kotenko Igor	St. Petersburg Institute for Informatics and Automation of the Russian Academy of Sciences, Russia

Lopez Javier	University of Malaga, Spain
Martinelli Fabio	IIT-CNR, Italy
Mouratidis Haris	University of Brighton, UK
Mylonas Alexios	Athens University of Economics and Business, Greece
Panaousis Emmanouil	University of Brighton, UK
Panda Brajendra	University of Arkansas, USA
Pernul Günther	Universität Regensburg, Germany
Posegga Joachim	University of Passau, Germany
Rannenberg Kai	Goethe University Frankfurt, Germany
Ravindran Kaliappa	City University of New York, USA
Rieger Craig	Idaho National Laboratory, USA
Rizomiliotis Panagiotis	University of the Aegean, Greece
Rusinowitch Michael	LORIA – Inria Nancy, France
Samarati Pierangela	Università degli Studi di Milano, Italy
Shetty Sachin	Tennessee State University, USA
Soriano Miguel	Universitat Politècnica de Catalunya, Spain
Spanoudakis George	City University, UK
Stoelen Ketil	SINTEF, Norway
Tapiador Juan	Universidad Carlos III de Madrid, Spain
Xenakis Christos	University of Piraeus, Greece
Zhou Jianying	Institute for Infocomm Research, Singapore

Contents

Trust and Privacy Issues

Addressing Privacy and Trust Issues in Cultural Heritage Modelling

Michalis Pavlidis[1]([⊠]), Haralambos Mouratidis[1], Cesar Gonzalez-Perez[2], and Christos Kalloniatis[3]

[1] University of Brighton, Brighton, UK
{m.pavlidis,h.mouratidis}@brighton.ac.uk
[2] Institute of Heritage Sciences (Incipit),
Spanish National Research Council (CSIC), Madrid, Spain
cesar.gonzalez-perez@incipit.csic.es
[3] Cultural Informatics Laboratory,
Department of Cultural Technology and Communication,
University of the Aegean, Mytilene, Greece
chkallon@aegean.gr

Abstract. The management of cultural heritage information is an important aspect of human society since it enables us to document and understand our past and learn from it. Recent developments in ICT have significantly boosted research and development activities aimed at the creation and management of cultural heritage resources. As a result, information systems play an increasingly important role on storing and managing cultural heritage information and allowing preservation of the information in a digital way. To support such effort, a number of cultural heritage conceptual models have been developed and presented in the literature. However, such models they focus on the heritage entities and information, but fail to include issues such as privacy and trust. Our research has shown that these are important issues to consider in order to have a complete cultural heritage model. This paper presents the first work in the literature to include privacy and trust as part of a cultural heritage conceptual model. We demonstrate the applicability of our work using a real world case study from the Iron Age settlement of Castrolandin in Spain.

Keywords: Cultural heritage · Information systems · Privacy · Trust

1 Introduction

Heritage is anything that can be considered important to be passed to future generations and it is broadly divided into natural heritage and cultural heritage. Anything to which a social group attributes particular aesthetic, artistic, documentary, environmental, historic, scientific, social or spiritual values is commonly designated cultural heritage. Cultural heritage consists of tangible and intangible elements. Tangible elements include heritage sites, buildings and artefacts,

© Springer International Publishing Switzerland 2016
C. Lambrinoudakis and A. Gabillon (Eds.): CRiSIS 2015, LNCS 9572, pp. 3–16, 2016.
DOI: 10.1007/978-3-319-31811-0_1

while intangible elements include practices, representations, expressions, knowledge, and skills, or in other words elements that are embodied in people rather than in inanimate objects.

The management of cultural heritage information is an important aspect of human society since it enables us to document and understand our past and learn from it. Appropriate management is required for the effective identification, interpretation, maintenance, and preservation of significant cultural entities. It requires though having a deep and shared understanding of what cultural heritage is and what cultural heritage is composed of. Recent developments in ICT have significantly boosted research and development activities aimed at the creation and management of cultural heritage resources. As a result, information systems play an increasingly important role on storing and managing cultural heritage information and allowing preservation of the information in a digital way [1]. Having the information digitised also helps to make the information available on ways that was not possible before. For example, a number of archeological sites can be "visited" from anywhere in the world and visitors can view and receive information about artefacts like they are visiting the physical sites. However, this situation apart from the obvious advantages, introduces some privacy and trust issues. For example, part of digitised cultural heritage information may be private [2], and even though information might be personalised [3], still there have to be safeguards that will ensure there is no privacy violation.

On the other hand, many heritage entities, such as buildings, are tied to the land, which can be private property, and even some heritage entities are private property themselves. Local communities are fighting to preserve their way of life as part of their heritage. Travel and cultural institutions use this uniqueness to promote travel and tourism, and while this brings in revenue and exposure, cultural heritage sites that were preserved by virtue of their isolation are now being severely damaged and even destroyed. This situation introduces a wide range of cases where privacy issues must be respected by government organisations related to cultural heritage and other involved parties. For example, in some scenarios, the government can force the owner of a highly rated cultural heritage house to open it to the public a few days a month. However, this can result in a violation of the owner's privacy. Therefore, modelling explicitly the privacy requirements of such situations can contribute to the resolution of the aforementioned issues. Elements to model would include the details of privacy, what information is subject to what privacy levels, and who has access to what. In order to achieve this, it would be necessary to identify what actions must be carried out in order to protect the owners' privacy when cultural heritage entities are documented.

However, accomplishing this does not solve the uncertainty about whether the aforementioned actions related to privacy protection will be carried out or not. Without further analysis, they are just assumptions which may prove wrong and lead to violation of cultural heritage owner's privacy. The same situation exists when actions regarding the conservation and allowance of use of cultural heritage objects are considered. Such actions are assigned to agents but without further justification of whether the agents can be trusted to take them, they remain just assumptions. If the agents never realise the assigned actions, this will lead to a deterioration of the condition of the cultural heritage entity or inconvenience it. Therefore, further analysis is required in order to justify if the agents assigned with certain actions can be trusted to do so, or that there are appropriate control mechanisms in place to ensure that the agents will do so.

To address these issues this paper presents a conceptual modelling approach that makes use of works from the fields of cultural heritage, privacy, and trust. CHARM [4,5], PriS [6–8], and JTrust (Justifying Trust) [9,10], respectively, are adapted and combined in a single conceptual model to jointly address this problem area. The next section provides background about these three approaches. Section 3 presents our proposed conceptual model while Sect. 4 presents a methodological process for using the conceptual model. Section 5 demonstrates the applicability and usefulness of our proposed model using a case study. Section 6 discusses the related work, followed by the conclusion and future work.

2 Background Information

The Cultural Heritage Abstract Reference Model (CHARM) [4,5] is a wide and shallow conceptual model for cultural heritage, which includes over 160 classes representing very abstract concepts, such as Place, Material Entity, Agent, and Performative Entity. CHARM does not only represent the specific entities that might make up cultural heritage, but also other entities, which are necessary in order to describe and understand the former, such as documents, representations, and valorisations. These are the three major concerns that are captured in CHARM:

- Evaluable entities. An valuable entity is anything to which cultural value can be assigned. In other words, an evaluable entity is each of the individual things to which people can add cultural value. Evaluable entities comprise all the raw matter that may become cultural heritage, including tangible and intangible things.
- Valorisations. A valorisation is the discourse that adds cultural value to an evaluable entity. In other words, a valuation is the social and cultural vehicle that people use in order to produce cultural value.
- Representations. A representation is a persistent expression of one or multiple evaluable entities or valorisations.

The PriS method [6–8] is a requirement engineering methodology that incorporates the modelling and analysis of privacy requirements into the system development process. Privacy requirements are identified after the investigation of the implications that privacy goals have on ordinary organisational goals. PriS specifies the following eight privacy goals:

- Authentication
- Authorisation

- Identification
- Data Protection
- Anonymity
- Pseudonymity
- Unlinkability
- Unobservability

Furthermore, PriS specifies a set of rules to transform privacy requirements into implementation techniques through the use of privacy process patterns used for identifying system architectures, which support the privacy requirements.

JTrust [9,10] is a methodology for reasoning about trust relationships and it is founded upon the notions of trust and control as the means of confidence achievement. Any dependency on entities of an information system to carry out an action introduces an uncertainty about the fulfilment of that dependency. It can also constitute a vulnerability for the system in case the other entity does not behave as expected, i.e. fulfil the dependency. Therefore, appropriate ways of removing the uncertainties and building confidence in the dependences is accomplished with the identification of dependency resolutions. Such resolutions need to be found based on trust or/and control. Moreover, in case of trust there four types of trust resolution:

- Experiential trust
- Reported trust
- Normative trust
- External trust

JTrust provides a structured way of identifying explicitly trust assumptions that underlie the system analysis and can endanger the satisfaction of the system requirements.

3   Cultural Heritage Conceptual Model with Trust and Privacy

A conceptual model can be described as an abstraction of reality according to a certain conceptualisation. This abstraction usually consists of an abstract representation of specific aspects of domain entities, called concepts. When a conceptual model is represented as a concrete artefact, it facilitates the communication and analysis of important and relevant aspects of the domain concerned. A conceptual model often serves as vehicle for reasoning and problem solving as well as for acquiring new knowledge about a domain. To be able for someone to use it, the conceptualisation should be expressed in a specific representation, such as a modelling language. The expression must be unambiguous and help users solve real world problems.

The proposed model combines concepts from the areas of cultural heritage, privacy, and trust. It can be used by software engineers when analysing or designing a cultural heritage information system. It enables them to capture information about the rights and obligations that agents have in relation to certain cultural heritage entities. It also enables them to capture privacy requirements related to obligations to allow the use or conserve a cultural heritage entity. Finally, it enables them to reason whether the agents assigned with privacy goals can be trusted to satisfy them. In cases where there is lack of trust, control mechanisms can be identified in order to fill in the gap and provide the necessary confidence in the fulfilment of the assigned privacy goals. Our combined model is depicted in Fig. 1. In the remaining section we describe its concepts, which are illustrated by using the following scenario.

An important aspect of cultural heritage are buildings that belong to a cultural heritage site. These buildings many times have an owner and a conservator who are different entities. The European Confederation of Conservator-Restorers' Organisations has issued a code of ethics. Article 3 states that the conservator-restorer works directly on cultural heritage and is personally responsible directly to the owner, to the heritage, and to the society. The conservator-restorer is entitled to practices without hindrance to her/his liberty and independence. Also, Article 18 states that the conservator-restorer is bound by professional confidentiality. In order to make a reference to an identifiable part of the cultural heritage she should obtain the consent of its owner or legal custodian. During the development of a conceptual model for such a scenario not only the cultural heritage aspects of the scenario have to be represented in the model, but also aspects that are related with the privacy of sensitive information and the trust relationships that affect the soundness of the model.

The following concepts have been adopted from CHARM:

An **Agent** is a primary entity corresponding to a person or group of people [11]. So, using the running example the owner of the building that constitutes cultural heritage is an agent and the conservator of the building is another agent.

An **Evaluable Entity** is an entity that has been, is or may be culturally evaluated [11]. The building that has a cultural heritage value is an evaluable entity in our running example.

A **Normative Situation** is an abstract entity corresponding to a right or obligation that one or more agents have, possibly in relation to a set of evaluable entities [11]. In the running example there are two normative situations that can be identified. First, the owner of the building has a right of ownership over it, and secondly, the conservator has the obligation to conserve the building in a good state.

A **Right** is a normative situation that provides its owners with specific liberties, guarantees or benefits, usually about certain evaluable entities [11]. In our conceptual model there are three types of rights, adopted from CHARM:

- A Right of Ownership is the right that provides its owner with the benefit of owning the associated evaluable entities.
- A Right of Use is the right that provides its owner with the benefit of being able to use the associated evaluable entities.
- A Right of Custody is the right that provides its owner with the benefit of keeping the associated evaluable entities in their possession.

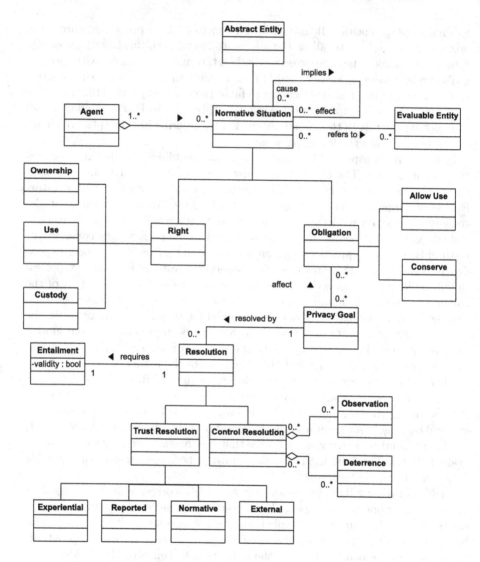

Fig. 1. Cultural heritage conceptual model with privacy and trust.

An **Obligation** is a normative situation that subjects its owners to specific obligations, usually in relation to certain evaluable entities [11]. In our conceptual model there are two types of obligation, adopted from CHARM:

- An Obligation to Conserve is the obligation that requires its owner to keep the associated evaluable entities in good condition.
- An Obligation to Allow Use is the obligation that requires its owner to allow the use of the associated evaluable entities to certain third parties.

A **Privacy Goal** expresses a privacy requirement which constraints the casual transformation of organisational goals into processes [6–8]. If a goal is assigned to an agent then this means that she has to make some adjustments in the processes that implement the organisational goals that are affected by the privacy goal. As mentioned in the previous section eight type of privacy goals are recognised: identification; authentication; authorisation; data protection; anonymity; pseudonymity; unlinkability; and unobservability. Privacy goals affect obligations and, therefore, in our running example the obligation of the conservator to conserve the cultural heritage building is affected by a data protection privacy goal as there are certain regulations that the conservator must comply with when handling private information. In particular, the conservator must not disclose any information that can be used to link related information about the owner. Also, the conservator must not disclose any identifiable information about the owner of the building. In order to make a reference to an identifiable part of the cultural heritage she should obtain the consent of its owner.

A **Resolution** is the way the uncertainty of the dependency on an agent is removed and confidence in the fulfilment of privacy goals is achieved [9]. In our running example, we assume that there is no control over the conservator company and we have confidence that it will handle the private data according to the relevant regulation because we trust it to do so. Therefore, there is trust resolution.

A **Trust Resolution** is the situation where confidence in the agent is achieved because of trust in the agent [9]. Four types of trust resolution are identified:

- Experiential trust is trust in the agent that originates from previous direct experience with the agent. If there was experiential trust resolution in our running example then this means that there is previous direct experience with the conservator and that is why we have confidence that it will fulfil its assigned privacy goal.
- Reported trust is trust in the agent that originates from a third party, the reporter. In a similar way, is a third party was reporting that the conservator will fulfil its privacy goal then we have confidence because of reported trust resolution.
- Normative trust is trust in the agent that originates from the system environment norms. If the conservator was a well established company in its field that everyone trusts it to respect and fulfil its privacy goal then we have confidence in the fulfilment of the goal because of normative trust resolution.
- External Trust is trust in the agent that originates from sources outside of the system environment. If there was an agent outside of the system environment that was suggesting us that the conservator will fulfil the privacy goal then we have confidence in the fulfilment of the goal because of normative trust resolution.

A **Control Resolution** is the situation where confidence in the agent is achieved because of the agent being controlled [9]. Control is the power that one agent has over another agent to influence its behaviour and consists of two mechanisms: observation and deterrence.

An **Observation** is the measure through which an agent's actions are monitored. Therefore, in the running example if we wanted the conservator to be controlled then we could have assigned another company to monitor and audit its processes and verify that it is complying with the relevant regulations concerning data protection.

A **Deterrence** is the measure through which a agent is prevented from accomplishing one of her own goals. Observation alone is not adequate in order control to be effective. Somehow, there has to be a way to prevent the controlled agent from accomplishing her own goals in order to have an incentive to show the desired behaviour. In the running example, a mechanism of deterrence could be the termination of the contract, in case we observe that the conservator does not comply with the relevant regulations. That will prevent the conservator from accomplishing one of its own goals, which is to get paid and provide the incentive to show the desired behaviour.

An **Entailment** is a condition of trust. It originates from a dependency through the identification of a dependency resolution. Entailments are required to be valid in order to have confidence in the dependencies from which they originated [9]. Every resolution can lead to an entailment, for example reported trust has an entailment that the reporter can be trusted for what is reporting. Such entailments have to be validated by collecting evidence, otherwise there is no confidence in the fulfilment of the dependency. In the running example, the dependency on the conservator is resolved through normative trust that has the entailment that the system norm can be trusted. Consequently, evidence has to be collected, perhaps through surveys, in order to prove that the entailment is valid.

4 Methodological Process

In this section, we propose a methodological process by which the conceptual model presented in the previous section can be applied. The process consist of five activities and is depicted in Fig. 2.

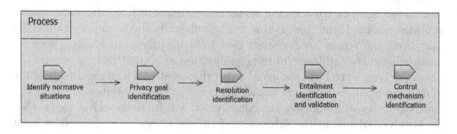

Fig. 2. Proposed process.

- **Identify normative situations between agents and evaluable entities.**
  The modeller identifies the relevant evaluable entities. Also, the agents that
  are related to them through with some kind of normative situation, as well
  as the type of normative situations themselves, have to be identified.
- **Privacy goal identification.** The modeller investigates the privacy issues
  that arise from the interconnected normative situations and models the privacy goals that affect the normative situations. Privacy goals can also be
  identified directly from respective legislation or directives.
- **Resolution identification.** Even though privacy goals have been defined
  and have been assigned to appropriate agents, this is still not sufficient,
  because there is uncertainty on whether these agents will behave as expected
  and fulfil their responsibilities. In order to remove the uncertainty, specific
  resolutions of dependencies on these agents have to be identified. The resolutions can be trust resolutions or control resolutions.
- **Entailment identification.** Having identified the resolutions, the next step
  is to identify the entailments, which essentially are trust assumptions. These
  have to be validated based on evidence that has to be collected. Evidence
  can be collected with the use of surveys, interviews with the stakeholders or
  investigation of historical data.
- **Control mechanism identification.** Not all entailments are valid and
  therefore, further actions are required. Control mechanisms need to be identified and put in place in order to build confidence that the assigned privacy
  goals will be fulfilled. The technical system or another agent need to act as
  the controllers who will drive the agents to show the expected behaviour. To
  this end, the modeller must identify the necessary observation and deterrence
  measures.

5   Case Study

In this section we describe a case study that was used to examine the applicability
of the proposed approach. The case study is based on an actual cultural heritage
place, the Iron Age settlement of Castrolandin, located in Galicia (North-West
Spain), where a series of research and public presentation projects have been
carried out in the last few years [12]. The site consists of a series of ramparts
and ditches on a hilltop, conforming a typical Iron Age hill fort, regionally know
as a 'castro'. It had been known and described since the mid 20th century by
archaeologists and was finally included in the official inventory of heritage sites
following the usual procedure. An archaeological consultancy was hired by the
regional government for the recording of heritage sites within the region. A record
log was assigned to the site as a heritage place and a series of land use regulation
were imposed to the area designated as its extent.

Moreover, another research project was developed on the site aimed at the
anthropological documentation of the local community's perceptions and feelings
about the site. This project allowed for the description and study of a traditional
feast, nowadays lost, that had occurred on the site at least between the late

19th and mid-20th centuries. Descriptions of the feast of San Xoan (St. John's) are known thanks both to some written records and the memories of local elderly people. Thanks to this project, the feast of San Xoan was brought back to life in 2003, and repeated since on an annual basis. As a result the regional government extended the area that was subject to heritage protection and land use restrictions, and also declared the feast of San Xoan as a protected intangible heritage element.

As a result of the generated archaeological, anthropological, and historical knowledge about Castrolandin, the regional government decided to intervene in order to apply the necessary protection schemes on both the site and the San Xoan celebration itself. The first scheme is called "Place of Cultural Interest" (BIC) and the second scheme "Celebration of Cultural Interest" (FIC), which is mainly applied to intangible entities. According to BIC, the owners of objects of cultural interest are obliged to facilitate their inspection by approved bodies, their study by researchers, and public entry at least four days a month and for movable objects to place them in a suitable position for viewing for a period of at least five months every two years [13].

In order all this information to be accessible to the public through an information system, it has to be organised and documented. However, such information contains private data that has to be kept confidential, such as the manifestation of the celebration every year that includes the private data of the individuals who have attended the San Xoan and the valorisation of the celebration that includes private data of the local elderly people. Therefore the private data has to remain confidential.

An information system that has to provide information about the cultural heritage of Castrolandin will be best designed at the conceptual level and will also facilitate better communication between the software engineers of the system and the stakeholders. This conceptual model has to consider not only the cultural heritage aspects of the information, but also the privacy and trust issues that are equally important for the stakeholders. The system development process will significantly benefit by being informed from such a conceptual model.

Next, the activities described in the previous section are applied to the case study of Castrolandin in order to demonstrate how to apply the proposed conceptual model and the developed model is depicted in Fig. 3.

Identify Normative Situations Between Agents and Evaluable Entities. In our case the evaluable entities, i.e. the entities that can have a cultural heritage value, are the Castrolandin hill fort and the celebration of San Xoan. On the other hand, the agents in the case study are the regional government, the local citizens of the area, the conservator of the Castrolandin hill fort, and the visitors that may desire to seek information about the site and the surrounding area. The visitors can be individuals who physically visit the site and the celebration, or visitors of a website who browse information about the site and the celebration. Having identified the evaluable entities and the agents involved, the following normative situations are identified through discussions with the agents and other stakeholders, and by inspecting the relevant laws.

(i) The regional government has the right of ownership of the San Xoan celebration.
(ii) The local citizens have the right of custody of the San Xoan celebration.
(iii) The visitors have the right to use the San Xoan celebration.
(iv) The regional government has the obligation to allow use of the San Xoan celebration.
(v) The regional government has the right of ownership of the Castrolandin hill fort.
(vi) The visitors have the right to use Castrolandin hill fort.
(vii) The regional government has the obligation to allow use of the Castrolandin hill fort.
(viii) The conservator has the obligation to conserve the Castrolandin hill fort.

Privacy Goal Identification. This activity aims at identifying the privacy goals that affect the normative situations identified in the previous activity. The first issue is with the organisation of the San Xoan celebration where the local citizens who are attending the celebration and want their private information to be kept anonymised. Furthermore, the conservator who has the obligation to conserve the Castrolandin hill fort is required to comply with the privacy regulations regarding the processing of personal data. Therefore, the respective privacy goals are incorporated into the conceptual model as shown in Fig. 3. There are two privacy goals. The fist one is to ensure the anonymity of the participants of the San Xoan celebration and it is assigned to the regional government. The second privacy goal is to ensure data protection when conserving the Castrolandin site and it is assigned to the conservator. In effect, the regional government and the conservator need to take appropriate actions in order to ensure the satisfaction of the identified privacy goals.

Resolution Identification. The dependencies though on the regional government and the conservator introduce an uncertainty on whether they will behave as expected, i.e. take actions in order to ensure the satisfaction of the privacy goals. To this end, resolutions of the two dependencies need to be identified that show the reasoning behind the removal of the uncertainty and the establishment of confidence in the fulfilment of the dependencies. The dependency on the regional government to hold the attendees anonymous is resolved with experiential trust. This means that the software engineer has previous direct experience with the regional government because of previous collaboration in other projects and believes that the regional government can be trusted to satisfy the privacy goal. The dependency on the conservator to comply with the relevant data protection laws is resolved with reported trust. The company of the software engineer has a business partner, who reports to her through discussions that the conservator will comply with the data protection regulations.

Entailment Identification. The identified resolutions of the previous activity can systematically reveal the explicit trust assumptions underlying the developed conceptual model. We call such assumption entailments of resolutions, which have to be valid otherwise the analysis made in order to construct the model is not justified. The experiential trust resolution of the dependency on the regional government requires an entailment that the software engineer can trust herself for that decision. The reported trust resolution of the dependency on the conservator requires and entailment that the business partner, who acts as a reporter, can be trusted for what it is reporting. After the identification of entailments, evidence is gathered in order to decide whether the entailments are valid. There is substantial evidence from previous direct experience with the regional government, such as documents, which show that the regional government was indeed carrying out actions in the past to satisfy the anonymity related privacy goal and therefore that it can be trusted to satisfy it in this case as well. On the contrary, there was no enough evidence that the business partner can be trusted for what it is reporting, i.e. the conservator will fulfil the data protection privacy goal assigned to her. Consequently, the uncertainty regarding the fulfilment of the data protection related privacy goal by the conservator still remains.

Control Mechanisms Identification. As long as there is no justification regarding the fulfilment of the second privacy goal then the developed model cannot be qualified as sound in terms of preserving the privacy of personal information. Further actions are required in order to gain confidence in the fulfilment of the privacy goal by the conservator. As a solution a new control resolution was added as shown in Fig. 3. It contains as an observation mechanism that the conservator will be audited periodically, and as a deterrence mechanism that the contract will terminate instantly in case she does not fulfil the privacy goal. This control resolution provides us the necessary confidence that the privacy goal will be fulfilled.

6   Related Work

The literature provides a number of approaches that support conceptual representation of cultural heritage. However, to the best of our knowledge, there is no work in the literature that incorporates privacy and trust modelling and analysis in such conceptual frameworks.

CIDOC CRM [14,15] is a core ontology to enable information integration for cultural heritage data and their correlation with library and archive information. It was developed empirically by an interdisciplinary team, based on real world cultural heritage information sources and may be used for analysing and designing cultural information systems. CIDOC CRM, ISO 21127:2006 [15,16] is a standard for knowledge sharing in cultural heritage. The FRBR model [17], which was initially intended as a conceptual framework for bibliographic data, but the report gives a detailed description of entities, relationships and attributes

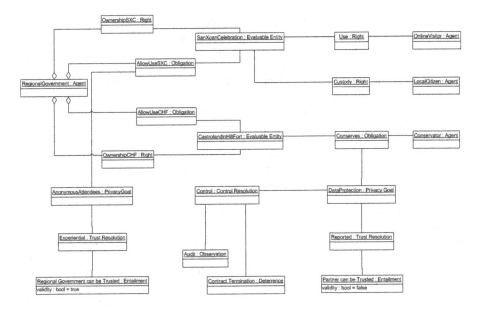

Fig. 3. Castrolandin site cultural heritage conceptual model.

that may be used to define type-vocabularies. The Dublin Core [18] is a flexible and usable metadata schema enabling information exchange and integration between digital sources. It is widely used by almost all digital libraries since it is simple, small and easily expandable, providing qualifiers enabling the semantic expression. The authors in [19] propose a Cultural Heritage application schema that enables the structured representation of natural sites that have been evaluated as cultural heritage.

7 Conclusion and Future Work

This paper has argued the need to incorporate privacy and trust into cultural heritage conceptual models, and it has presented the first conceptual model in the literature to include trust and privacy. Our work builds on approaches from cultural heritage, privacy, and trust conceptual modelling, and it combines them to develop a unified approach. A real cultural heritage case study from the area of Castrolandin in Spain, which has be characterised as cultural heritage site, has been employed in order to demonstrate the applicability of our work. We plan to apply our work to more case studies to enable us to increase the applicability of our approach.

References

1. Doerr, M.: Ontologies for cultural heritage. In: Staab, S., Studer, R. (eds.) Handbook on Ontologies. International Handbooks on Information Systems, pp. 463–486. Springer, Heidelberg (2009)

2. Garzotto, F., Salmon, T., Pigozzi, M.: Designing multi-channel web frameworks for cultural tourism applications: the muse case study (2003)
3. Ardissono, L., Kuflik, T., Petrelli, D.: Personalization in cultural heritage: the road travelled and the one ahead. User Model. User Adap. Inter. **22**(1–2), 73–99 (2012)
4. Gonzalez-Perez, C., Parcero-Oubiña, C.: A conceptual model for cultural heritage definition and motivation. In: Revive the Past: Proceeding of the 39th Conference on Computer Applications and Quantitative Methods in Archaeology, pp. 234–244. Amsterdam University Press. Beijing (2011)
5. Gonzalez-Perez, C.: Charm white paper, version 1.0.3. Technical report (2015)
6. Kalloniatis, C., Kavakli, E., Gritzalis, S.: Addressing privacy requirements in system design: the PriS method. Requirements Eng. **13**(3), 241–255 (2008)
7. Kalloniatis, C., Kavakli, E., Gritzalis, S.: PriS methodology: incorporating privacy requirements into the system design process. In: Proceedings of the SREIS 2005 13th IEEE International Requirements Engineering Conference-Symposium on Requirements Engineering for Information Security (2005)
8. Kalloniatis, C., Kavakli, E.: PriS tool: a case tool for privacy-oriented requirements engineering. In: Doukidis, G., et al. (eds.) Proceedings of the MCIS 2009 4th Mediterranean Conference on Information Systems, pp. 913–925 (2009)
9. Pavlidis, M., Islam, S., Mouratidis, H., Kearney, P.: Modeling trust relationships for developing trustworthy information systems. Int. J. Inf. Syst. Model. Des. (IJISMD) **5**(1), 25–48 (2014)
10. Pavlidis, M., Mouratidis, H., Islam, S., Kearney, P.: Dealing with trust and control: a meta-model for trustworthy information systems development. In: Sixth International Conference on Research Challenges in Information Science (RCIS), pp. 1–9, May 2012
11. Incipit: CHARM Online Reference, version 0.9.0.1. Accessed 3 Feb 2015
12. Ayán Vila, X., et al.: Pasado e futuro de castrolandín (cuntis): Unha proposta de recuperación e revaloración (2002)
13. Howard, P., Ashworth, G.: European Heritage, Planning and Management. Intellect Books, Exeter (1999)
14. Doerr, M.: The CIDOC conceptual reference module: an ontological approach to semantic interoperability of metadata. AI Mag. **24**(3), 75 (2003)
15. Doerr, M., Hunter, J., Lagoze, C.: Towards a core ontology for information integration. J. Digit. Inf. textbf4(1) (2006)
16. Doerr, M., Ore, C.E., Stead, S.: The CIDOC conceptual reference model: a new standard for knowledge sharing. In: Tutorials, Posters, Panels and Industrial Contributions at the 26th International Conference on Conceptual Modeling, vol. 83, pp. 51–56. Australian Computer Society Inc (2007)
17. Maxwell, R.L.: FRBR. ALA Editions (2007)
18. Weibel, S.L., Koch, T.: The Dublin core metadata initiative. D-lib Mag. **6**(12), 1082–9873 (2000)
19. Fernández Freire, C., Pérez Asensio, E., González, B.I.d., Uriarte González, A., Vicent García, J.M., Fraguas Bravo, A., Parcero-Oubiña, C., Fábrega-Álvarez, P., et al.: Proposal for a cultural heritage application schema within the INSPIRE directive (2012)

An Ontology Regulating Privacy Oriented Access Controls

Maherzia Belaazi$^{(\boxtimes)}$, Hanen Boussi Rahmouni, and Adel Bouhoula

Digital Security: Research Unit, Higher School of Communication of Tunis,
University of Carthage, Tunis, Tunisia
{maherzia.belaazi,hanen.boussi,adel.bouhoula}@supcom.tn

Abstract. Access Control is one of the essential and traditional security
weapons of data protection. In open and complex environments such as
the Internet or cloud computing, the decision to grant access to a resource
must ensure a secure management with a specific attention to privacy
and data protection regulations. In recent years, many access control
models and languages were proposed. Despite increasing legislative pres-
sure, few of these propositions take care of privacy requirements in their
specifications. In this paper we propose to enforce privacy compliance in
access control policies. Based on a semantic modeling approach, specifically formal ontology, we will try to incorporate data protection legislation requirements in policies specification and implementation. This
aims to abstract the complexity of legal requirements expression and to
facilitate their automation and enforcement at execution level. Indeed,
at run time, the interoperability of diverse information and the reference
to the text law are addressed in a novel manner.

Keywords: Security · Access control policies · Privacy policies ·
Legislation · Semantic web · Ontology

1 Introduction

Access control is defined as one of the most popular security tools ensuring that
every access to a system and its resources is controlled and only those access that
are authorized can take place. It is now evolving with the complex environments
that it supports. In recent years for different aims, many and different access
control models and languages have been proposed. In open and complex environments such as the Internet or cloud computing, the decision to grant access to
a resource must ensure a secure management with a specific attention to privacy
and secondary usage regulations [1]. Besides, in order to ensure an efficient data
access decision, the issue of interoperability between access policies related to
different usage scenarios must be addressed. For example, in the context of cloud
computing, we must ensure that the entity *requestor* and the entity *provider* of
an access control policy context share the same meaning or are equivalent [2].
In the scope of the previously mentioned requirement, we propose in this paper,

© Springer International Publishing Switzerland 2016
C. Lambrinoudakis and A. Gabillon (Eds.): CRiSIS 2015, LNCS 9572, pp. 17–35, 2016.
DOI: 10.1007/978-3-319-31811-0_2

to exploit technologies such as OWL (the ontology web semantic language), SWRL (Semantic Web Rule language) along with other languages forming the semantic web stack. The driver for our choice is the demonstrated powerful expressiveness capabilities in existing privacy protection related works [3,4].

In philosophy, the term ontology means a systematic account of existence [5]. The term has been widely adapted for formal use in the Artificial Intelligence domain and other computer science domains where knowledge representation is required. According to these domains, an entity can "exist" only if it can be represented. A formal ontology is a body of formally represented knowledge that is based on an explicit formal specification or conceptualization of concepts and the relationships that could exist between them [6]. Since open environments are creating a growing demand for sharing data as well as its semantics, ontologies are becoming increasingly essential for most computer applications. By sharing ontologies and knowledge bases, distributed environments can easily communicate to exchange data and thus make their transactions interoperate independently of their enabling technologies [7].

In order to ensure secure access to its resources, an organization defines a set of policies. A policy is a statement that defines and controls the behavior of a system. More specifically, an access control policy defines a set of conditions, which are evaluated to determine whether a set of actions may be performed on a resource. For example, an access control policy could state that only doctors (i.e. the condition) have the right to modify (i.e. the action) the patient's medical records (i.e. the resource). An access control policy acts as both, a declarative behaviour system (express in explicit and non ambiguous manner the requirements of control) and, a decision-support system (base of access control inference system). Semantic Web languages allow access policies to be described over heterogeneous data domain and promote common understanding among participants who might not use the same information model [2].

In our research, we focus on the requirements for sensitive data protection driven by legislation. We look on how to incorporate these requirements in an access control model for an open and dynamic environment such as the cloud. Our research is aiming to help enhancing privacy compliance when sharing private data across diverse states or countries where legislation could be different. Our approach (Fig. 1) is based first on bridging the gap between high level legislation on data protection and operational level controls by means of semantic modeling of important concepts. Second, this approach is also based on the use of inference systems on top of the modeled concepts in order to provide decision support on how to handle personal data.

In literature, and in order to deal with privacy compliance, traditional access controls (like role based access control or attribute based access control) [8,9] have been extended by introducing the purpose concept. We find also in literature, different proposed ontologies [3,4] (and associated semantic rule execution engines) that represent access control concepts in addition to other legal concepts (like the consent). In our perspective, these propositions lack the explicit expression of the law reference (the used text law and the authority location

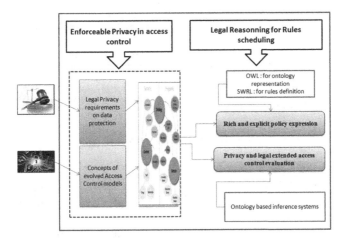

Fig. 1. Toward a secure and private access control requirements formalization

proposing this law). Certainly, using ontology helps to ensure interoperability between access control actors (access requestor, access provider and resource's owner) by providing the same shared conceptual semantic model. However, we need also to provide mechanisms for a privacy compliance access decision at runtime: which prior rule to apply? which law to apply if we deal with multi-authority (access requestor, access provider and resource's owner: when they belong to different jurisdiction areas)? So in our contribution, we will present and exploit knowledge about the regulation reference to conclude about which law to apply. Besides, we will formulate privacy requirements (purpose, consent, data privacy status, the authority obligation) (see Sect. 3.2) and use them as attributes to calculate the *legal strength* of an access rule in order to guide a *partial* scheduling of the access control rules (see Sect. 3.3). We believe that such legal reasoning will help to ensure a privacy compliant access decision in a distributed multi-authority environment. In order to achieve our goal, we proceed in parallel axes. The first axe is the abstraction level. In this level we formally define privacy and access control concepts and their relationships. We also formally define how rules and policies should be expressed in generic and fine-grained manner.

The remainder of this paper is organized as follows. Section 2 settles the methodology we follow in order to build and validate our ontology. In Sects. 3 and 4, we first define different concepts describing access controls and data protection requirements which we merge in a single extensible ontology. Secondly, we present formally how to express and evaluate an access control policy incorporating legal requirements extracted from data protection legislation. The formal presentation will be the base of rules and inference system definition on top of the proposed ontology. In Sect. 5, we experiment our model in a case study by instantiating the generic ontology in a specific domain (medical domain). Finally, we conclude by future work and perspectives.

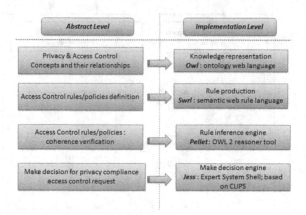

Fig. 2. Privacy requirement incorporation in access control: mapping between abstract and implementation levels

2   The Privacy Ontology Construction and Validation

Based on some literature lectures about ontology creation and maintenance [10–13], we define a methodology to follow in order to establish our ontology. The proposed methodology is divided in three principal phases: (Subsect. 2.1) ontology's purpose specification (Subsect. 2.2) ontology's construction (Subsect. 2.3) ontology's validation.

2.1   Ontology's Purpose Specification

Before starting the ontology's construction, we must explicitly answer the following questions [12] as follows.

– *What is the domain that the ontology will cover?* In this paper, we try to define a conceptual model of an access control scenarios. These scenarios invoke the policies definition, the request expression and the access decision assignment. The decision related to a request must be secure and privacy compliant too. In this spectrum, our ontology must cover, in a first stage, privacy requirements extracted from legislation and also from access control management frameworks applied to generic domains. In a second stage, some application domains could be introduced to experiment previous generic domains. We can experiment, as an example, the medical domain.
– *For what purpose we use the ontology?* Our ontology concepts will help us to establish closed real world reasoning. It will enable us (using clear rules and interference systems) to perform secure access control decisions while achieving: (i) complying with privacy requirements (ii) resolving the semantic interoperability issue on different concepts used by different actors across heterogeneous domains.

– *What type of questions should the ontology provide answers to?* This ontology could help the user to check an access request defined by a set of parameters (requester attributes, context specification,target attributes) allowed or prohibited? Is this privacy compliant? Is it a legal access request? In the case of positive permission for a resource access, does it require some obligations to be filled? In case of denial of the access request, because of privacy non compliance, what are the requirements to be reported to the access requestor?
– *Who will use and maintain the ontology?* The access control administrator should maintain this ontology. They need the help of law experts to understand emerging legislation requirements.

2.2   Ontology Construction

In order to construct our ontology [10–12], we propose to define in the following order. Firstly, we define a list of concepts (the Classes). Secondly, we specify the list of concept's properties. Thirdly, we define the possible hierarchical relations between defined concepts, as far as the list of conceptual relations between them. Finally, we instantiate the general concepts by defining the individuals.

2.3   Ontology Validation

In order to validate our ontology [13], we propose to proceed in this order. Firstly, we ensure that the structure and the conceptualization is valid. This encloses the fact to check that no redundancy is available and the logic coherence is respected. Secondly, we do the functional validation. This includes the validation of the ontology's purpose definition conformity. This will be achieved using specific questions (ontology interrogation using queries) and the evaluation of the ontology based system's answers.

Our approach uses a free, open source ontology editor framework named the Protg (version 4.3) [14]. We use the OWL-DL Ontology Language: (for knowledge representation) [15,16] and SWRL (Web rule language to express queries on top of the ontology) [17]. The OWL model we have built is used to represent privacy requirements extracted from the most internationally recognized privacy legislation in the context of secure and privacy oriented access control evaluation and decision making. OWL allowed us to model the conceptual domain of "access control policies" and "data processing" obligations for the usage of private personal information as a hierarchy of classes, subclasses and a hierarchy of data and object properties to represent the relationships between them. Classes and objects properties could easily be used to express privacy requirements. Additional class expressions including restrictions, Boolean expressions, enumerated classes and value partitions were also useful. SWRL allowed us to express privacy policies in order to ensure a privacy preserving access control decisions. In order to get clearer vision we will provide ontology graph (nodes and edges) following the OWL paradigm (Fig. 3).

In the next sections, we choose to work in stages. In a first stage, we build an ontology that models access control policies. In a second stage, we establish

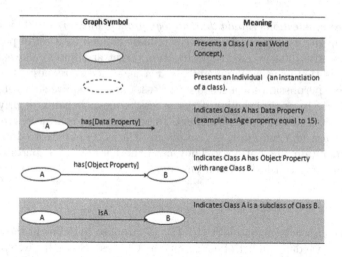

Fig. 3. Ontology graph symbols

an ontology that models Personal Data Privacy requirements for a legislation compliant access control. "Privacy Obligations" have been extracted from international privacy laws [18,19]. We have done a comparative study (some privacy's subject based thesis [20,21]) that concluded common mandatory legal concepts to express and check while dealing with privacy preservation.Finally, we will merge the two previous ontologies in order to incorporate privacy obligations while expressing an access control policy or while evaluating an access control request.

3   An Ontology-Based Description of Privacy Obligations in Access Control Policies

In this section, and following the previously defined methodology, we define an ontology that represents incorporating privacy obligations in access control policies. We start by defining an ontology for access control then we extend this ontology by privacy requirements. Indeed, we provide some formal definitions that will be the base for next stage which looks at access control reasoning operations.

3.1   Formalization of the Access Control Model

Security policies constitute the core of systems protection. They are made of a set of instructions specifying allowed and prohibited actions. Access control policies are examples of security policies defining which subject (requestor of a resource) could or not invoke an action (operation) on an object (resource). Access control is now evolving with complex environments that it supports. In recent years and for different aims, many access control models and languages have been proposed.

In order to build a knowledge base about access control policy specification and requirements, we study and analyze a set of novel and emerging models in the access control field to address the new needs of todays systems [8,9,22–24]. We studied also the OASIS standard access control language: the XACML [25]. In fact, XACML is a widely adopted policy language standard that has proven efficiency in the enforcement of policies at operational level [26]. Based on the previous studies and analysis we define our list of concepts and their relations. (Fig. 4)

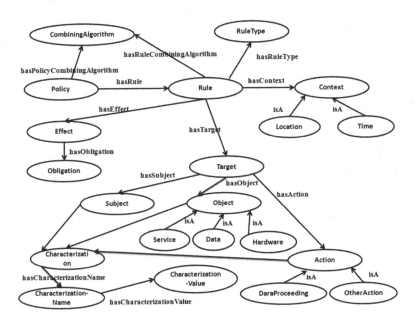

Fig. 4. Privacy oriented access control ontology: part 1

We define as relevant list of access control requirements related concepts the list below:

- *Policy:* Defines a set of rules expressing how an organization will manage, protect their resources.
- *CombiningAlgorithm:* Defines the way of merging the different rules of one policy. It defines also how to merge a set of policies and which rule to use.
- *Rule:* Defines the characteristic (including the identity and/or role) of a subject who is authorized to perform an action on a resource and under which conditions, the requested authorization is given or prohibited.
- *Rule Type:* Defines the type of a rule; it could be a user preference or organizational policy.
- *Effect:* Expresses the response to an access request: deny or allow or undetermined

– **Obligation:** Expresses the actions that a subject must perform following a positive access response. (example: duration of information retention) Or Express the missing requirements that a subject must perform following a negative access response. (Example: consent of data owner).
– **Target:** Defines the set of associated subject object and action. Optionally we can invoke a receiver if the action invoked needs them. (E.g. a doctor can share patients data with an-other doctor in order to get a second opinion, here the information about the other doctor could be relevant for access control decision). Each Target element is described by its **characterization** which is a couple of $< characterization_{name}, characterization_{value} >$. For instance, a Subject could have age as $characterization_{name}$.
– **Action:** Defines an operation (example: read, modify, collect, store, share, forward ....) required on some resources.
– **Object:** Defines a resource. It could be a service (for example the wifi access), a data (for example medical tests result) or hardware (for example a printer).
– **Subject:** Defines who requested an action on an object. A subject is identified by a set of his characteristics.
– **Context:** Defines some constraints on location and time.
– **Location:** Defines the location associated to an object.
– **Time:** Defines the time of the request (start time and end time implicitly the duration of the request)
– **Service:** For example: the use of a wifi connection.
– **Data:** Defines a kind of Resource, more precisely, the hosted information on the sys-tem/organisation
– **Hardware:** Defines a kind of Resource like the printer.
– **DataProcessing:** Defines a kind of action on data
– **OtherAction:** Defines any other kind of action on any other kind of resource different from data. (For example, configure the printer).

The main relations between previous detailed concepts are listed below. A relation is defined in the same manner as functions ($f : Domain \longrightarrow Range$). A semantic relation is defined between a "*domain* of concepts" and "*range* of other concepts":

– **hasRule:** Our domain is Policy and our range is Rule. So in simple words, a Policy is com-posed by a set of Rule.
– **hasPolicyCombinigAlgorithm:** Our domain is Policy and our range is CombiningAlgorithm. This property describes how to manage a set of policies (the order of execution? the combining manner?)
– **hasRuleCombinigAlgorithm:** Our domain is Rule and our range is CombiningAlgorithm. This property describes how a policy manages a set of rules. In which way it chooses a rule to apply if many rules respond to a request?
– **hasType:** Our domain is Rule and our range is Type. Each rule must be classified to a specific type. It could be a rule imposed by the organisation, or a rule imposed by the user. For example, in cloud computing the provider of the service has its secure policies and the customer could dictate some of its preferences.

- *has Target:* Our domain is Rule and our range is Target. Each defined rule has a Target.
- *has Context:* Our domain is Rule and our range is Context. Each defined rule may have contextual constraint.
- *has Effect:* Our domain is Rule and our range is Effect. Each defined rule has an effect.
- *has Obligation:* Our domain is Effect and our range is Obligation. Some effects are associated to some obligations that must be filled. (In case of "allow" effect, an obligation could be the fact to respect a duration of the retention.)
- *has Action:* Our domain is Target and our range is Action. A target is defined by an Action.
- *has Object:* Our domain is Target and our range is Object. A target is defined by an Object.
- *has Subject:* Our domain is Target and our range is Subject. A target is defined by a subject.

3.2   Formalization of Privacy Requirements

Privacy is the right of individuals to decide for themselves when, where what how and who can extent, disclose or use their personal information. Privacy principles (Fig. 5) have been developed thanks to many legislation. Internationally, the OECD (Organization of Economic Cooperation and Development) [18] provides the most commonly used privacy framework, they are reflected in existing and emerging privacy and data protection laws, and serve as the basis for the creation of leading practice privacy programs and additional principles. The XACML[1] OASIS Standard describes a profile for expressing privacy policies. This profile extracted Privacy requirements from the OECD guideline. Based on the OECD principles, the Privacy XACML profile and some other international legislation [19], we list the essential privacy obligations to respect in our ontology:

- *Collection Limitation Principle:* The collection of personal data requires the knowledge or the consent of data subject (the data owner). Such personal data should be obtained by lawful means.
- *Purpose Specification Principle:* The purposes for which personal data are collected should be explicit.
- *Use Limitation Principle:* Personal data should not be disclosed, made available or otherwise used for purposes other than those specified in accordance with previous paragraph except with the consent of the data subject; or by the authority of law.

According to the previously listed and explained privacy principles, we define below a list of our ontology concepts and their relationships. (Fig. 6) Starting by the list of concepts:

---

[1] XACML privacy profile is a new profile proposed by the last XACML version 3.0 (at the time of writing this paper).

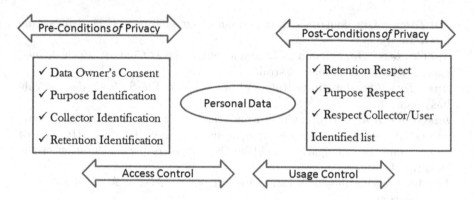

Fig. 5. Essential privacy conditions in access and usage control

- **data:** Defines a category of object that could be question of access request.
- **dataOwner:** Defines the owner of the data.
- **dataController:** Defines the controller of the data who is legally responsible to enforce the privacy. For example, in case of cloud computing the cloud provider who hosts the data.
- **dataRequestor:** Defines the requestor of the data. It is equivalent to the subject concept in the previous defined ontology.
- **dataCategory:** Defines the category of the data. We classify data in two main categories: non personal data and personal data.
- **NonPersonalData:** the non personal data category defines data that cannot be used to identify a person. Example, a person's hobbies.
- **PersonalData:** Personal data (as defined in EU directive or PII[2] in USA laws) is any information that can be used on its own or with other information to identify a person. For example, a card identification number (card-Id).
- **NonSensitivedata:** For example, age name ...
- **SensitiveData:** For example, religion medical information ...
- **Legislation:** Defines the legislation restricted to the location of the resource.
- **Purpose:** The reason for which something is done or created or for which something exists.
- **ProcessingType:** Equivalent to action type; data processing type
- **Collect:** It is a data processing type.
- **Share:** It is a data processing type.
- **Disclose:** It is a data processing type.
- **Modify:** It is a data processing type.
- **legalRequirement:** It is an optional requirement defined by "data" location and used for "data processing"
- **Consent:** It is a category of legal requirement.
- **Anonymity:** It is a category of legal requirement.
- **Notification:** It is a category of legal requirement.

---

[2] Personally identifiable information.

- *Legislation:* the associated legislation of one legal requirement.
- *legalStrength:* Defines the power of a law. In fact, all legal texts do not have the same value. For example, federal and state laws are not equivalents.
- *Reference:* the reference of a law. (For example, international convention)
- *textLaw:* Defines explicitly the referenced legal text law. (For example: constitution, laws, decrees, orders, proceedings ...)

The previous list of concepts has different relations (Fig. 6). These relations are used in the access control case expression. For example, the *data* concept has centric relations:

- *hasDataController:* Defines the controller of the data.
- *hasDataOwner:* Defines the owner of the data.
- *hasDataRequestor:* Defines the requestor of the data.
- *hasDataCategory:* Defines the category of the data.
- *hasProcessingType:* Defines the processing type on a data.

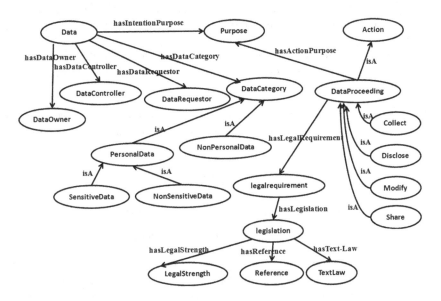

Fig. 6. Private access control ontology: part 2

3.3 Towards a Privacy Aware Decision Making Engine

In next paragraphs, we give some formal definitions of private secure rules. These definitions will be used in next stage for the reasoning engine construction. (Make decision engine explained in Fig. 2).

Formal definition (1): *Express a security policy based on a set of access control policies*

A security policy is a set of access control policies (P_i) and the manner to merge them (CA: combining algorithm). The utility of a CA is to manage some particular cases. The first case, if no rule is applicable, which decision to make? For example, if "deny-overrides" combining algorithm is set, the decision will be "no". The second case, if more than one rule is applicable, which rule to choose? For example, if "first-applicable" combining algorithm is set, the first rule is to be evaluated.

$$SP = (\{P_i, i \in IN\} \times CA)$$

$CA \in \{$deny-overrides, permit-overrides, first-applicable, only-one-applicable$\}$

- *Deny-overrides:* returns deny if any evaluation returns deny. Otherwise, permit is returned.
- *Permit-overrides:* If any rule evaluates to permit, then the result is permit. If any rule returns deny and all other rules evaluate to not applicable the result is deny. If all rules evaluate to not applicable, the result re-mains as not applicable.
- *First-applicable:* Returns the first result of a rule evaluation that is different from not applicable. If all rules return not applicable, this response is returned.
- *Only-one-applicable:* If only one policy is applicable its result is returned. If more than one applies the result is indeterminate. If no rule is applicable, the result is not applicable.

In this paper, we propose a general specification for one policy a set of rules evaluated according to a combining algorithm CA (the same list of CA defined previously):

$$P = (\{Rule_j, j \in IN\} \times CA)$$
$$Rule_j = Req_j \longrightarrow Resp_j \times [oblig_j]^*; j \in IN$$
$$Req = (s_j \times a_j \times o_j \times [c_j]^*); j \in IN$$
$$Resp \in \{yes, no, undetermined\}$$

In our scope, a rule $(Rule_j)$ is composed by two parts. The first part is the request (Req_j) (next definition explains the access request). The second part is the response $(Resp_j)$. A response values could be "yes", "no" or "undetermined". In our definition, the response could be optionally associated to a set of obligations $(Oblig_j)$.

In case of "yes" response, the obligation, could be for example, "the duration of retention".

In case of "no" response, the obligation, could be for example, "the consent of the data owner".

Formal definition (2): *Express an access request*

A request Req_i is defined by several fields: s is the "subject", o is the "object", a is the "action" and c is the "context". "s_j" field describes the subject who's the requestor of access. The subject is defined by a list of attributes and their values.

For example,

$doctor=\{(doctor\_speciality, doctor\_specility\_value)$,

$(doctor\_state, doctor\_state\_value), ...\}$

"o_j" field describes the object which's the resource, the question of the access request. The object is defined by a list of attributes and their values.

$medical\_test=\{(medical\_test\_type, medical\_test\_value)$,

$(medical\_test\_status, medical\_test\_status\_value), ...\}$

"a_i" field describes the action which is a specific requested operation on the object "o". The action is defined by a list of attributes and their values.

$share = \{(share\_receiver, share\_receiver\_value), ...\}$

Either for "s" or "o" or "a", the list of attributes gives a fine grained way for rules definition and expression. Finally, contextual constraints are useful to evaluate the context which a rule is applicable of a rule. We focus in temporal and special constraints.

$$Req_i(s_i \times a_i \times o_i \times [c_i]^*); i \in IN$$
$$s_i = \{(sa_j, sav_j); j \in IN\}$$
$$o_i = \{(oa_j, oav_j); j \in IN\}$$
$$a_i = \{(aa_j, aav_j); j \in IN\}$$
$$c_i = \{location, starttime, endtime\}$$

Formal definition (3): *Extend an access control policy to specify privacy requirements*

In order to enforce the privacy compliance while expressing access control policies and rules, we extend previous definitions with privacy requirements. As a new combining algorithm we add "legal-overrides"

$$SP = (\{P_i, i \in IN\} \times CA)$$

$CA \in$ {deny-overrides, permit-overrides, first-applicable, only-one-applicable, **legal-overrides**}

legal-overrides: In case of more than one rule that answers to a specific access request, we can override the legal rule in order to solve any issue about conflicts decisions. If more than one legal rule is applicable the first one of these legal rules will be chosen. If no rule at all is applicable, the deny response overrides as we are looking to avoid any risk about privacy preservation.

We extend definition (2) by adding a Rule type. Indeed, a policy is defined by its type ($type_i$) and the associated rule ($Rule_i$). The type of the rule will help us to classify rules. The classification could be helpful in order to set the priority of rules. In some cases, the priority is useful to resolve conflicts between rules. In our proposal, a rule could be "User Preference" rule or "Organization" rule or "legal" rule. In this case of a "legal rule", the rule much specify legal constraints $[l_i]$. Here constraints incorporate legislation specification such as the text law source location (the country, state, ...), the reference legislation (national law, international law, ...) and legal strength.

$$P = (\{type_j \times Rule_j, j \in IN\} \times CA)$$
$$type_j \in \{legal, userPreference, organisation\}$$
$$Rule_j = Req_j \longrightarrow Resp_j \times [oblig_j]^*; j \in IN$$
$$Req = (s_j \times a_j \times o_j \times [c_j]^* \times [l_j]^*); j \in IN$$
$$Resp \in \{yes, no, undetermined\}$$

In the same scope of privacy conformity, we improve the $\prec s_i, a_i, o_i \succ$ attributes by explicitly provide privacy profile-based characterization (Fig. 7).

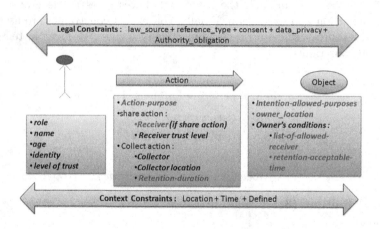

Fig. 7. Privacy characterizations in profile based access control

Then, in order to conclude about the privacy compliance of a request, we define some conditions to be respected. In the first condition, the "*action-purpose*" must belong to the set of "*intention-purpose-allowed*" allowed by the owner of the object. The second condition, if we deal with a disclose action with third party, the "*receiver*" must belong to the "*list-of-allowed-receiver*". The third condition, the "*collection-retention-duration*" must respect the "*retention-acceptable-time*" by the data's owner. The last condition is the "owner's consent".

3.4   Legal Constraints Reasoning

In this paragraph, some algorithms are proposed. The rule's scheduling algorithm is described in (Fig. 8). It aims for the resolution of rules priority conflicts

```
// Sorting i Rules associated to a policy Pi
// Resolution of Possible Priority conflicts : make legal rule prior ones
For each Pi :
    tri(Rulej, legal-override, legal-strength)
            // Sorting Rules (1) : Place Rules with type Legal in first rules
            // Legal strength calculation for legal rules
            // Sorting Rules (2) : Tri legal rules according to legal-strength values
```

Fig. 8. Scheduling rules according to legal power

```
Read(access-Request)
            // Extract access charcterisation
            // Extract privacy characterisation if possible
Rulej = Find-Suitable-Rule(access-Request)
            // Evaluate by one rule ; the first applicable rule is returned
Make-Decision(access-Request, Rulej)
            // Check access entities characterisation
            // Check privacy conditions
            // Return evaluation of one request
```

Fig. 9. Check privacy compliance algorithm

$$legal_{strength} = \frac{(c_1 \times consent + c_2}{dataPrivacy_{Status} + c_3\, Authority_{obligation})} \div 3$$

Fig. 10. Legal-strength calculation of one legal rule

by ordering security rules according to their type and their calculated power. So, "legal" rules type must be placed at the header of a rule. Then, this set of "legal" rules should be ordered based on their "legal strength" attribute. Another ongoing work (the associated paper is submitted), we proposed a formula calculating "legal-strength" of one "legal" rule based on legal conditions described in paragraph 3.3(Fig. 10). The "legal strength" calculation uses proportional coefficient defined by security administrator with the advice of a lawyer. The factors of evaluation are the number of legal conditions and their severity. For example, the authority obligation has the high severity. Another factor, the consent necessity, it depends on its conditions of specificity, format and destination criteria (see previous paragraph).

The decision making algorithm (Fig. 9) takes advantage of the previous Rules scheduling. It finds the first applicable rule, evaluates conditions with a special care for privacy conditions. So we get not only a security preserving access decision but also a privacy compliance decision.

4   Case Study

In order to provide the reader with a real situation of incorporating privacy in access control, we instantiate our generic model through the use of an example

---

Security policies: Access control policies

R1: The hospital save data patient tests results for a patient regular survey with a retention limited by 3 years.

R2: Only doctors could modify patient health state interpretation.

R3: If an information could threat national health security it should be "by force of law" disclosed to authority.

R4: A practitioner could share a patient sensitive test medical result (for example: mammogram) if patient has provided informed consent for a specific purpose of processing and the processing purpose is compatible with the purpose contented for.

R5: If UK medical data is to be processed by a medical professional for the purpose clinical research on breast cancer and the patient could be identified from the data. Then acquiring patient consent is necessary and consent must be an informed specific explicit consent.

R6: If Italy, the consent can be given in a single, one-off statement (general consent). No provision for the need for explicit consent.

R7: In France, express consent (written) is required for the processing of sensitive data.

Fig. 11. A set of informal access control policies in a hospital

Table 1. Scheduling rules according to a legal reasoning

Rule number	Rule type
R3	Legal
R4	Legal
R5	Legal
R6	Legal
R7	Legal
R1	Organization
R2	Organization

from the medical domain. We present the security policy of a hospital involved in a distributed search context. A context that involves multi-authority actors. The hospital in question is located in UK. It contributes to European breast cancer researches and shares medical results with some other European countries (Italy and France). They all work under the "Data Protection Directive" jurisdictions. In our case study, we imagine the hospital security policy and we describe it by a set of rules as specified in (Figs. 11 and 12). R1, R2 and R3 are organizational rules. R4, R5, R6 and R7 are legal based rules.

Based on previous algorithms for scheduling, the Table 1 shows the new ordered rules. Using our ontology we can make some inferences results on top of some requests of access. In this stage of work, we get limited inference possibilities regarding limits of owl in expressing rules. In a second stage of work, SWRL will be used to express rules in rich manner (Fig. 13).

Rule Number	Rule Type	Request fields			Response	Obligation
R1	Organization Rule	Subject	Role	Hospital administration		Retention limit is 3 years
		Object	Type	Patient data test	Permit	
		Action	Type	Save		
		General Constraints	Defined	Patient regular survey		
R2	Organization Rule	Subject	Role	Doctor		
		Object	Type	Patient data		
		Action	Type	Modify	Permit	
		General Constraints	Context	Health State interpretation		
R3	Legal Rule	Subject	Role	Law Authority		
		Object	Type	Patient data	Permit	
		Action	Type	Disclose		
		Legal Constraints	Law Source	Data Protection Directive		
			Reference Type	European Union Directive		
			Authority Obligation	yes		
		General Constraints	Defined	Threat national health security		
R4	Legal Rule	Subject	Role	User		
		Object	Type	Patient data		
			Intention Purpose	Same as Action purpose	Permit	
		Action	Type	Share		
			Action purpose	Some purpose		
		Legal Constraints	Law Source	Data Protection Directive		
			Reference Type	European Union Directive		
			Consent	Yes		
			Consent specific	Specific		

Fig. 12. Primary formalization of informal access control rules (R1-R4)

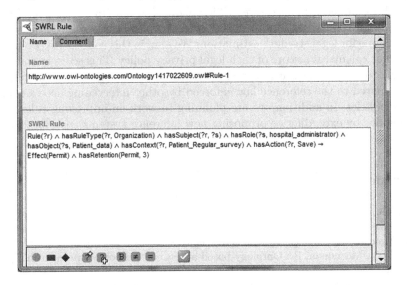

Fig. 13. Example of SWRL rule edition in Protg (R1)

5 Related Work and Conclusion

In literature, many works have employed ontology while expressing privacy requirements in access control. In fact, Ontology-based Information modeling is considered as a power tool for logic-based inference and reasoning. One category of proposed ontologies [3,4] have detailed in a clear semantic representation privacy rules. But it didn't deal with legislation that are the primary source of mentioned privacy requirements. Also it lacks answers on how to deal with ordering rules and possible conflicts resolution. Other category of proposed ontologies [2,27] focus on access control requirement representation.

These works demonstrate how ontology could be a useful tool for interoperability handling in open environments. However in this position, privacy preserving was not subject to checking while making access control decisions.

In this paper, we suggest a semantic formalization of access controls that ensures compliance with privacy requirements that are imposed by legislation. In order to achieve our goal, we take advantage of a semantic web standard for ontology representation this is because; ontologies could provide simple key tools to govern policy information heterogeneity over different domains in complex distributed environments. Moreover, we propose to incorporate references to text law and the legislative enforcement strength while expressing access control policies. Besides, it could be useful for some cases to resolve conflicts between access control rules at execution time.

For future work, we are working on extending the XACML standard architecture for access control. For this purpose we aim to build an ontology driven access control architecture. This could be presented as a distributed architecture with an added semantic layer which allows the integration of fine grained privacy requirements. Besides, we are looking to put together an ontology reasoning engine for legal strength estimation. We aim, in this context, to provide an engine that calculates a score of each legal privacy policy. This score is evaluated according to the law reference and an assessment of the weighting of the referred text compared to the reference law enforced by other intervening access control rules or policies. In addition, we are planning to work on improving rules inference engines by extending or proposing new inference systems ensuring conflict detection (e.g. duplication and contradiction) between rules.

References

1. Damiani, E., Samarati, S.: New paradigms for access control in open environments. In: Proceedings of the Fifth IEEE International Symposium Signal Processing and Information Technology, pp. 540–545 (2005)
2. Reul, Q., Meersman, R.: Ontology-based access control policy interoperability. In: STARLab (2013)
3. Zhang, N.J., Todd, C.: A privacy agent in context-aware ubiquitous computing environments. In: Leitold, H., Markatos, E.P. (eds.) CMS 2006. LNCS, vol. 4237, pp. 196–205. Springer, Heidelberg (2006)
4. Garcia, F.: Towards a base ontology for privacy protection in service-oriented architecture. In: IEEE International Conference on Service-Oriented Computing and Applications (SOCA) (2009)
5. Gruber, T.R.: A translation approach to portable ontology specifications. Knowl. Acquisition 5(2), 199–220 (1993)
6. Gruber, T.R.: Toward principles for the design of ontologies used for knowledge sharing. Int. J. Hum. Comput. Stud. 43(5–6), 907–928 (1995)

7. Spyns, P., Meersman, R.: An ontology engineering methodology for DOGMA. Appl. Ontology **3**(1–2), 13–39 (2008)
8. Byun, J., Li, N.: Purpose based access control of complex data for privacy protection. In: Proceedings of the Tenth ACM Symposium on Access Control Models and Technologies. ACM New York (2005)
9. Covington, M.J., Sastry, M.R.: A contextual attribute-based access control model. In: Meersman, R., Tari, Z., Herrero, P. (eds.) OTM 2006 Workshops. LNCS, vol. 4278, pp. 1996–2006. Springer, Heidelberg (2006)
10. Gilles, N., Kamel, M.: Ontology learning by analyzing XML document structure and content. In: Proceedings of the International Conference on Knowledge Engineering and Ontology Development KEOD Portugal (2009)
11. Kamel, M., Rothenburger, B.: Eliciting hierarchical structures from enumerative structures for ontology learning. In: Proceedings of the 6th International Conference on Knowledge Capture K-CAP (2011)
12. Noy, N.F., McGuiness, D.: An ontology development 101: a guide to creating your first ontology. Standford knowledge systems laboratory Technical report KSL-01-05 and standford medical informatics Technical report SMI-2001-0880 (2001)
13. Ben Abacha, A., Da Silveira, M., Pruski, C.: Medical ontology validation through question answering. In: Peek, N., Marín Morales, R., Peleg, M. (eds.) AIME 2013. LNCS, vol. 7885, pp. 196–205. Springer, Heidelberg (2013)
14. Noy, N.F., Musen, M.A.: The protégé OWL plugin: an open development environment for semantic web applications. In: McIlraith, S.A., Plexousakis, D., Harmelen, F. (eds.) ISWC 2004. LNCS, vol. 3298, pp. 229–243. Springer, Heidelberg (2004)
15. Protege. http://protege.stanford.edu
16. SWRL. http://www.w3.org/Submission/SWRL/
17. OWL. http://www.w3.org/TR/owl-guide/
18. OECD Privacy. http://www.ncbi.nlm.nih.gov
19. EC: Data Protection in the European Union. European Commission (2010)
20. Boussi, H.: Ontology based privacy compliance for health data disclosure in Europe. A thesis report (2010)
21. Caralt, N.: Modelling legal knowledge through ontologies. A thesis report (2008)
22. Horrocks, I.: OWL: a description logic based ontology language. In: van Beek, P. (ed.) CP 2005. LNCS, vol. 3709, pp. 5–8. Springer, Heidelberg (2005)
23. Zhu, J., Smari, W.W.: Attribute based access control and security for collaboration environments. In: Aerospace and Electronics Conference (2008)
24. Sandhu, R., Park, J.: Usage control: a vision for next generation access control. In: Gorodetsky, V., Popyack, L.J., Skormin, V.A. (eds.) MMM-ACNS 2003. LNCS, vol. 2776, pp. 17–31. Springer, Heidelberg (2003)
25. Oasis Web Site (2013). http://docs.oasis-open.org/xacml/3.0/xacml-3.0-core-spec-os-en.html
26. Anderson, A.H: A Comparison of Two Privacy Policy Languages: EPAL and XACML. GSun Microsystems Labs Technical report (2005)
27. Özgü, C.A.N., Bursa, O., Ünalir, M.O.: Personalizable ontology-based access control. Gazi Univ. J. Sci. **23**(4), 465–474 (2010)

A Literature Survey and Classifications on Data Deanonymisation

Dalal Al-Azizy[1,2](✉), David Millard[1], Iraklis Symeonidis[3], Kieron O'Hara[1], and Nigel Shadbolt[4]

[1] Web and Internet Science, School of Electronics and Computer Science, University of Southampton, Southampton, UK
{daaalg09, dem, kmo}@ecs.soton.ac.uk
[2] University of Tabuk, Tabuk, Saudi Arabia
[3] ESAT/COSIC, KU Leuven and iMinds, Leuven, Belgium
iraklis.symeonidis@esat.kuleuven.be
[4] Department of Computer Science, University of Oxford, Oxford, UK
nigel.shadbolt@cs.ox.ac.uk

Abstract. The problem of disclosing private anonymous data has become increasingly serious particularly with the possibility of carrying out deanonymisation attacks on publishing data. The related work available in the literature is inadequate in terms of the number of techniques analysed, and is limited to certain contexts such as Online Social Networks. We survey a large number of state-of-the-art techniques of deanonymisation achieved in various methods and on different types of data. Our aim is to build a comprehensive understanding about the problem. For this survey, we propose a framework to guide a thorough analysis and classifications. We are interested in classifying deanonymisation approaches based on type and source of auxiliary information and on the structure of target datasets. Moreover, potential attacks, threats and some suggested assistive techniques are identified. This can inform the research in gaining an understanding of the deanonymisation problem and assist in the advancement of privacy protection.

Keywords: Deanonymisation · Re-identification · Privacy

1 Introduction

Increasingly, the Web has become a world of interconnected information particularly in terms of social practices. People participate in different social platforms and post and publish their personal information and activities that are occasionally, and based on the context, set to be anonymous. They also consume other information from other platforms and applications such as government and commercial services through their social profiles. Governments and other institutional bodies are now releasing their data on the Web for transparency, accountability, economic, and service improvement purposes, among other reasons this extensive growth of the Web is continuously accompanied by increasing concerns about new threats to privacy, and this also applies to all other networking environments that depend on their private intranets or isolated

© Springer International Publishing Switzerland 2016
C. Lambrinoudakis and A. Gabillon (Eds.): CRiSIS 2015, LNCS 9572, pp. 36–51, 2016.
DOI: 10.1007/978-3-319-31811-0_3

databases. The key fact here about the threats to privacy is the enormous amounts of data that are increasingly available in different contextual forms.

Here, we study the problem of data re-identification resulting from the rich availability of data from heterogeneous resources. We conduct a survey of the state-of-the-art techniques of deanonymisation attacks. Our work extends similar work found in the literature; brief survey [1] on online social networks and another systematic review [2] of re-identification attacks on health data. In our survey, we include - on a large scale - recent techniques from various fields to provide a broad overview of the deanonymisation problem.

1.1 Research Motivation

This research is motivated by a number of issues. First, publishing data in the Web including personal data is becoming more advanced and growing immensely with a corresponding growth in publishable data links. Second, using online social networks, which include personal and private data. Third, mashup applications are also an issue in terms of collecting information from different platforms for third party interests. Fourth, the increasing concern about data leakage [3, 4]. Fifth, recent research has questioned the ability of anonymisation techniques to successfully preserve privacy [5–7]. Sixth, publishing open government data and the concern of jigsaw re-identification problem regarding private data (transparent government may lead to transparent citizens in terms of their private personal information) [8]. Finally, Political and commercial interests for advancing open data and linked open data with low interests in discussing privacy issues and challenges about publishing data that may affect their business.

Therefore, in considering all these issues that affect one context such as online social networks, it can be strongly inferred that the deanonymisation problem is more serious when considering all other different contexts.

1.2 Survey Purpose

The purpose of this research is to explore the deanonymisation problem and provide a broader conceptual view and understanding of how it - and all other issues related to this problem - occurs. In particular, it is important to understand how an adversary can exploit any data to use as background knowledge to achieve the deanonymisation attacks and what the possible threats are that result from that. This survey aims to provide analysis and classification for deanonymisation to include the broader audience of non-technical practitioners from legal and governmental fields. This is to help those interested to make sense of and understand the deanonymisation problem and how it might affect their decisions in terms of publishing data and protecting privacy rights.

This survey includes large scale of deanonymisation techniques to provide a broad overview of deanonymisation. We conduct the following steps: First, we design a deanonymisation framework for analysing several techniques in different environments. Second, we classify deanonymisation approaches based on the appropriate methodology that the adversary follows to enable them to exploit auxiliary information with target data structure.

1.3 Limitations

This research does not study the information gained as background knowledge by the adversary from real world information. For instance, information gathered from work environments such as colleagues' personal information, or neighborhood data regarding houses and population, any data that might be used and combined with other data to give meaningful information. That being the case, it is worth studying such scenarios. However, this is beyond of scope of our survey that focuses on published data.

The rest of this paper is organised as follows. In section two we review the related work. In section three, we explain our research methodology for this survey. In section four, we introduce our deanonymisation framework for analysis, followed by classification of approaches and other related issues with more details in section five. In section six, we discuss our insights and present arguments, and then the paper is concluded in section seven.

2 Related Work

In this section, we first briefly overview data anonymisation and data deanonymisation to provide an outlook on privacy solutions and their possible violations. Subsequently, we present the existing survey studies on deanonymisation that are similar to our work and then we state the features that distinguish this paper from existing work in the remarks section.

2.1 Data Anonymisation

This technique is the most common method used to preserve data privacy by removing personal identifiable information (PII). This ensures eliminating the risk of private data disclosure while these anonymous data are being processed or transferring between systems or networks [9]. A number of anonymisation models were developed for protecting privacy such as k-anonymity [10–12], l-diversity [13, 14] and t-closeness [15]. However, k-anonymity model is argued to ensure privacy [16].

2.2 Data Deanonymisation

Narayanan et al. [17] researched the problem of deanonymisation where disclosure of anonymous data succeeded. They could achieve structural and computational attacks exploiting auxiliary information from other data sources. A number of studies [18, 19] have investigated this problem and proved their theoretical and practical results about threats of re-identification and linkability. Deanonymisation becomes serious and practical when the structure of the target dataset is known and where large amounts of auxiliary data can be exploited.

2.3 Existing Surveys on Deanonymisation

There are two studies in the literature that systematically reviewed a number of deanonymisation techniques in detail. The first study is a brief survey [1] of five deanonymisation studies in online social networks. The purpose of surveying this problem is to technically show how it is both possible and practical to deanonymise released data in online social networks. In this brief survey, Ding et al. [1] unified the models of deanonymisation based on the feature matching between the data released in online social networks and the background knowledge acquired by the adversary. They also classified the five attacks of deanonymisation into two categories based on matching direction between released data D in online social networks and background knowledge K: mapping-based methods (match K against D) and guessing-based methods (match D against K).

The second study of related work [2] is a systematic review of re-identification attacks on health data and this was undertaken for slightly different purposes. It focused on re-identification attacks' representation among health data and compared these attacks with other deanonymisation attacks on other types of data. Furthermore, the review computed the total proportion of all successfully re-identified records in these attacks and assessed whether this highlights shortcomings in existing de-identification techniques. El Emam et al. [2] reviewed 14 articles of deanonymisation attacks for evaluation against health regulations and de-identification standards.

2.4 Remarks

Our research is more focused on the methodology by which deanonymisation can be achieved. In this paper, we proposed a framework to guide an in-depth analysis of the current deanonymisation techniques in the literature. Moreover, we classify the deanonymisation approaches and provide lists of attacks, threats and assistive techniques.

The major features that distinguish our work from existing surveys are as follows. We extends the brief survey [1] for a more systematic and thorough review in terms of number of deanonymisation techniques and various contexts to include, and this review also generates differently based classifications.

Our survey is more comprehensive in that it includes a large-scale number from the state-of-the-art investigation of the deanonymisation problem including their five attacks. Moreover, we cover not only online social networks, but we also include open data, databases, traces data and mobile sensors, and other heterogeneous networks and datasets. Pertaining to the classification method, our work is much broader and takes into account the deanonymisation methodology of exploiting the background knowledge of the structure of the target dataset with auxiliary information acquired by the adversary and then, based on that, following a certain approach to achieve the attack. We also provide details of types of attacks to commit deanonymisation and resultant threats. Regarding the second review study [2], only four studies are included in our survey as the remaining studies do not have the data needed for our research framework for analysis and or do not satisfy and technical level that we are looking for. For instance, Bender et al. [20] used cluster analysis for deanonymising register data of statistical agencies using survey data related to scientific purposes. Some few studies are reports relate to specific healthcare and legal bodies.

There are also more studies in the literature that researched deanonymisation [21–27] but these are not included in our survey as they are for analysis and evaluation purposes.

3 Research Methodology

Here, we explain our methodology in conducting this survey pertaining to selecting research papers of deanonymisation techniques and the way we analyse them.

3.1 Searching for Papers

We followed certain criteria to search for papers and articles to include in our survey. We searched for academic literature from several online conference and journal databases: IEEE, ACM, Springer and Google Scholar. Key words used for searching are: deanonymisation, re-identification, anonymisation and privacy risks. As our survey is focused on technical mechanisms in which deanonymisation is achieved, we only consider papers that report novel methods for successful deanonymisation attacks and that provide practical and theoretical results.

3.2 Methods of Analysis and Classifications

Our survey aims to achieve a comprehensive understanding and conceptualising of deanonymisation. To achieve this objective, we provide a systematic review for a large scale of various types of deanonymisation techniques in heterogeneous environments. Hence, we propose a deanonymisation framework to analyse the state-of-the-art techniques to understand all their related issues. The components of the framework will extract specific details from each technique to guide the analysis in reasoning how the deanonymisation is achieved in a specific way. Then we classify the deanonymisation approaches based on the analysis. We also provide classification for all possible attacks that practically perform the deanonymisation and assistive techniques that can help in achieving more effective deanonymisation.

4 Deanonymisation Framework

To survey the studies in the literature, a framework of all identified aspects of deanonymisation is designed for analysis and classifications. This framework is used as a guideline to understand the problem of deanonymisation and how it works in different contexts. The framework consists of major components as shown in Fig. 1; each of them reflects an essential stage of the deanonymisation process.

In this section, we present our classifications on deanonymisation. The major part of our research in this survey is to understand how the adversary can use type and

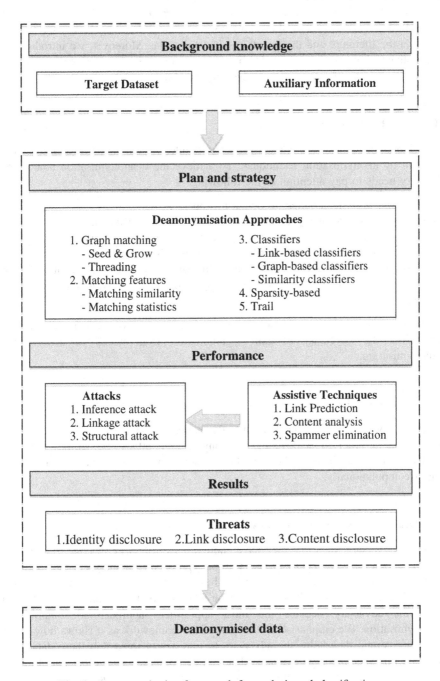

Fig. 1. Deanonymisation framework for analysis and classifications.

source of the auxiliary information with the structure of target dataset to form sufficient background knowledge, which in turn enables them to follow the most effective approach to achieve a successful deanonymisation attack. We also classify the type of attacks in the literature and the threats resulted from that. Moreover, we introduce all the assistive techniques that are used to boost the deanonymisation to be more effective. And we finally identify some of the adversary capabilities.

4.1 Target Dataset

This refers to the data source that the adversary is interested in attacking and is usually protected by anonymisation techniques. To achieve the deanonymisation attack, the adversary needs to pay attention to the following:

(a) *Anonymisation techniques:* to defeat it properly.
(b) *Anonymised data*: that they usually have interests to disclose it.
(c) *Dataset structure:* to configure the proper methodology and approaches of deanonymisation and what auxiliary information is needed for that.
(d) *Data sparsity:* which also has a relationship with data structure. Sparsity refers to the way in which data are populated through the Web and their relation with other data.

In some cases this target dataset can be used as a source of auxiliary information that assists the adversary to gain a foundation from which to achieve the deanonymisation.

4.2 Auxiliary Information

The adversary usually needs background information as a requirement to start from a strong base in order to achieve the deanonymisation attack. Sometimes auxiliary information is extracted from the same target datasets where the attacker can manipulate it computationally.

4.3 Deanonymisation Approaches

When the adversary finds that they have enough background knowledge to carry out the attack, then next stage is to choose a proper approach. We analyse a methodology that the adversary intend to find and follow based on the background knowledge that they could acquire from auxiliary information and the structure of target dataset. As a result, the adversary decides the most appropriate approach to commit the deanonymisation. We emphasise on this part of the framework as it shows how much publishing certain data helps the adversary to find a way to exploit these data. Furthermore, this specifies how available data can be combined with other data to form meaningful data that reveal many values that are not taken into account during publishing. A traditional approach of deanonymisation is matching data from different resources to disclose the anonymised parts in one of these resources. Some approaches can be combined for complex deanonymisation attacks. More details about these approaches are presented in the next section.

We classify deanonymisation approach as shown in Fig. 1 based on the way that the adversary uses to exploit the auxiliary information with the structure of target dataset to achieve the attack. The typical approach for deanonymisation is matching data in which auxiliary information is used for mapping with an anonymised target dataset. Therefore, any overlapping between information will act as a guide in revealing the hidden elements. The following approaches are taking unique form to perform the matching mission.

Now, we explain each approach separately providing definitions, examples and comparisons.

Graph Matching: this approach constitutes the common form among online social networks as these networks consist of nodes and edges. As a large number of deanonymisation studies were undertaken on online social networks, graph matching represents the most common approach introduced here in this research. This approach, in general, focuses on two graphs from the same target domain or perhaps from two different domains. Both graphs are used for mapping tests between the shared anonymised nodes and measuring overlaps. Zhang et al. [28] utilised this approach in heterogeneous networks.

Graph topology in [18] which built on [29], refers to the graph structure as a major information to achieve deanonymisation. The study argues that privacy can be breached once its structure is revealed, as a standard technique of re-identification can be developed based on that. Here, graph topology that makes use of structural properties of social graphs adopts the following steps:

(a) Find the largest common sub-graph between a pair of ego nets;
(b) Focus on common nodes of two graphs that are in distance of 1-hop from the centre; and
(c) Utilise the degree distribution of nodes of social networks and observe the 1-hop neighbourhood degree distribution of the common nodes, storing each node's degrees in a list as a signature if matching signatures are found between a pair of nodes from the two graphs, those nodes are considered to be the same. It does not work with graphs where their common nodes are at distance of 2-hop from the centre (one node in a pair, or both nodes in a pair) as in [30] which covers n-hop and therefore can deanonymise more data.

Other studies [31, 32] rely on aggregating networks from Twitter and Flickr to build up an auxiliary background and therefore can perform the graph matching.

Other studies [33, 34] also use graph matching for deanonymisation.

Seed & Grow: graph matching in some studies starts with a complex process called seeding to plant a node such as a user account in a social graph and then make it building up links with other nodes. This expansion process is called seed and grow in [35, 36]. Narayanan et al. [17] described their seeding method in two steps: seed and propagation. They combined that with link prediction to strengthen their approach and can manage the graph evolution. That could deliver high accuracy and coverage for their attack. They used graph matching by crawling Flickr with scrubbed user identities. The first step is seed identification where they deanonymise a small number of nodes. These nodes are used in the second step, which is called propagation, as anchors to breed the deanonymisation to a large number of nodes. This study used auxiliary information from the same target domain, crawling Flickr, but generating an evolved version. Also these studies [31, 32, 37–39] used seeding based deanonymisation techniques. Another study [39] presents a new graph matching algorithm that relies on smaller seeds than other methods.

Threading: is another starting point for complex graph matching. Ding et al. [40] utilised the threading method for correlating the sequential releases due to the rapid growth in dynamic social networks. Then they match these releases with eachother.

Matching Similarity: is an approach where attacks rely on similar features between the target dataset and auxiliary information to perform the matching. Gambs et al. [41] performed their attack on geolocated databases. They used mobility traces to find distance similarities and then match them with the help of statistical predictors. Likewise, Ji et al. [42] match similarity between social data and mobility traces data. Another study [43] used text similarity between resume and tweets. Moreover, some techniques use node similarity to match graphs in social networks [44].

Matching Statistics: in this approach attacks depend on using statistics to map datasets. In [45] the attack relies on the unique features of users' data to perform matching statistics. All these features in this approach led to users being identified.

Link-Based Classifiers: the second type of classifiers is link-based and group-based which use friendship and group membership to identify some private attributes as in [46].

Group-Based Classifiers: the second type of classifiers is group-based which use friendship and group membership to identify some private attributes as in [46]. Also the group-based classifier was combined with auxiliary information from the browsing history to identify users in social networks in [47].

Similarity Classifiers: The Classifiers approach depends on local features such as temporal activity, text, geographic, and social features to form similarity classifiers as in [48]. These classifiers predict whether or not two accounts from two different social platforms are belonging to the same individual by deciding on similarities between them.

Sparsity-Based: this technique is utilised to attack sparse data either high dimensional micro data or specified with certain relations such as location. Sparse data share comparatively few relationships. Lane et al. [49] used activity stream of the target within anonymised sets of streams gathered from other users. They designed a two-stage deanonymisation framework: the first stage follows activity relationship mining, which consist of rules that link various aspects of two captured activity types and can help to decide if two activities were probably achieved by the same individual or not. The second stage uses the SCORE algorithm: the adversary input the auxiliary info and a stream of one or more activity types of a single anonymised user. This attack focused on the risks of sharing data of inference-based representation. Another study [50] considers a hypothesis that deanonymisation improves due to database sparsity. It also considers another hypothesis that states if the auxiliary information consists of values matching with rare attributes of a target database, then the deanonymisation achieved is greater. Both hypotheses are observed and motivated by the heuristic deanonymisation of the study [19] that targets high-dimensional micro-data. Merener [50] suggests that to achieve a high level of deanonymisation in a less sparse database, using large auxiliary information is needed. Frankowski et al. [51] shows that re-identification is possible in sparse related spaces when matching data. They test data available in movie mentions with another data in movie rating. They found that data relate to a specific item in both datasets can lead to deanonymising users participating in such datasets.

Trail: The trail re-identification approach was developed for linking genomic data to their identified users whose records are publicly available in various databases. This method exploits the unique features of visited location and utilises visit pattern in distributed environment such as healthcare as in [52, 53]. Moreover, the concept of trail re-identification approach also includes deanonymising users by collecting network data and then mapping their anonymised traces with IP addresses [54]. Likewise, in [55] matching IP addresses with Tor hidden services using traffic analysis. Another technique of trail approach is tracking users by detecting their fingerprints in web browsers [56]. This method relies on visited web pages in the browser's history.

Table 1 summarises features that used to form each approach.

Table 1. Features utilised for exploitation in each approach.

Deanonymisation approach	Features to exploit	Reference
Graph matching	Network structure	[18, 28, 29, 30– 34]
Seed & grow	Growing links into the target graph	[17, 31, 32, 35–39]
Threading	Correlation between sequential release of dynamic OSN	[40]
Similarity matching	Similarity of specific features for mapping	[41–44]
Statistical matching	Statistics of unique features	[45]
Link-based classifiers	Friendship membership for classification	[46]
Graph-based classifiers	Group membership for classification	[47]
Similarity classifiers	Similarity of local features for classification	[48]
Sparcity-based	How data are sparse, high dimensional, microdata	[49–51]
Trail	Unique features of visited location	[52–56]

4.4 Deanonymisation Attacks

Deanonymisation attacks take different forms based on the method that the adversary finds is most effective to exploit background information. Attacks can be inference, linkage, structural, and predictive, active or passive. One attack can be described as more than one of these forms. Some attacks are supported with assistive techniques for more effective deanonymisation.

Deanonymisation attacks listed below are described in terms in the way it is committed. An attack may convey more than one description listed here.

Inference Attacks: is a major form of committing deanonymisation. In this attacks, the adversary tends to use some available information such as friendship or group relationship to infer sensitive properties that carry hidden values or behaviours [46, 41, 57]. Some techniques [58] use algorithms to infer about customers' transactions using auxiliary information about them with temporal changes of recommender systems. Danezis and Troncoso [59] use Bayesian inference to have knowledge about communication patterns and profiles information of users.

Linkage Attacks: is another common form of practical deanonymisation attacks. In this attack, adversary can link auxiliary information of certain users with their anonymised records in a dataset [22, 50].

Structural attacks: it is the typical method to deanonymise graph using its structure [24, 28, 60]. Structural based deanonymisation attacks are proved theoretically and empirically by quantification [61] that exploiting social network structures is enough and even more powerful than other attacks that use seeding knowledge. A novel technique called Grasshopper [38] shows also higher effectiveness of deanonymisation than other state-of-the-art algorithms of structural attacks using seeding knowledge.

4.5   Deanonymisation Threats

According to the survey study [1], there are two particular deanonymisation threats; identification and linkability. The first threat, identification, leads to re-identifying records, IDs, users, nodes, links and some private attributes. The second threat, linkability, leads to re-identifying some relationships between users or accounts from different networks belonging to a certain user that are meant to be anonymised. Sharma et al. [3] list the threats of privacy disclosure as identity, link and content disclosures.

The threats resulted from deanonymisation attacks are related to three major sets: identity, links and attributes. According to the survey study [1], there are two particular deanonymisation threats; identification and linkability. The first threat, identification, refers to any data disclosed to identify an identity of a user or any entity and also any attribute relates to them. Linkability refers to linking entities with links that meant to be anonymised or entities from different datasets. For instance, linking two accounts of a user from different resources with each other. There is another more specific classification [3] for privacy disclosure. We summarise this classification as follows.

Identity Disclosure: which refers to deanonymising a user identity that was anonymised by removing the PII or by assigning a pseudonym.

Link Disclosure: which refers to deanonymising relationships between users that meant to be hidden. This may be achieved by inference attack using observed links or users' attributes.

Content Disclosure: which refers to revealing any anonymised data related to the target user such as address, email, etc.

4.6 Assistive Techniques

This part is critical as it shows how much some techniques can contribute to boost the deanonymisation attacks for more effectiveness.

Link Predictions: is a method that the adversary uses to bridge the gaps between auxiliary information and target dataset if they are from different resources and have less in common for matching [1, 17].

Content Analysis: is a method suggested in [1] for analysing a user's content in online social networks. This content may display usefulness in terms of providing information about the structure or some attributes to advance the deanonymisation attacks.

Spammer Elimination: in online social networks there are users whom their accounts are created for spamming. Those accounts tend to make random links with other users. These developing edges may lower the effectiveness of deanonymisation attacks. Therefore, discovering and removing these spamming nodes may improve deanonymisation [1].

Adversary Capabilities: feature matching task is a major capability for an adversary to think of committing a deanonymisation attack [1]. Other technical capabilities include prediction and inference, which require computational, statistical or probabilistic skills to compute the feasibility of deanonymisation.

4.7 Deanonymised Data

There are no specific methods or standard metrics for measuring the disclosed data resulting from deanonymisation. Most of the studies we found in the literature report their results in statistics compared to the sample of data they tested with precision and recall. Therefore, it is hard to think about deanonymisation approaches in terms of their effectiveness in a comparable way. The surveys [1, 2], although following a systematic process, do not agree over a standard metric that can be used to measure the effectiveness of deanonymisation approaches.

5 Discussion

The aim of this research is to understand the problem of deanonymisation comprehensively in different contexts. We proposed a framework for analysis and classifications to survey a number of studies in order to understand the deanonymisation problem comprehensively. We classified the approaches in which the deanonymisation is committed based on the available background. This shows a significant fact about how might trivial data from a resource can contribute to form feasible approaches to attack another anonymised data in totally different resource. That is why we conduct this survey to extend similar work in the literature in different contexts such as the Semantic Web. Among different approaches found in the literature, matching methodology represents the traditional way in which deanonymisation is carried out. It exploits different features in order to achieve the mapping and overlapping process and that basically depends on the structure of the target dataset and the auxiliary information. What we found in the literature that is some published data can be combined with totally different contextual data from other resources. Therefore, this shows the risk behind that which we do not expect. And that must affect the way we think in terms of widening our thinking about possible scenarios of attacks and threats. Which in turns affect the decision making about publishing data and the privacy protection that must accompany such data.

It is appealing to compare deanonymisation methods in terms of effectiveness and reported results. However, this not reasonable as every study has its own measures and the whole deanonymisation process depends on chosen methodology, methods, and features used from the auxiliary domain into the target domain. Approaches are very specific to the situation where these attacks achieved. Additionally, it is expected to be high expensive computationally if we think to test different parameters in deanonymisation experiments.

Finally, we envisage the deanonymisation problem is more challenging with the evolution of the Web to include Linked Data, open data, and big data. This is due to the fact that the technologies advancing the Web to be more discoverable, linked and open is actually forming the requirements of deanonymisation attacks to be more possible and practical or even automated.

6   Conclusions and Future Work

We analysed the problem of deanonymisation and we classified its approaches, attacks and threats for a comprehensive understanding. The techniques in the literature show evidence that this problem may become more serious than we thought. This stimulated by advancement in technology from two angles. Firstly, the Web has become the environment for publishing, storing and sharing information from various resources covering and serving different fields. Secondly, recent researches argued that the challenge for preserving privacy is getting greater as the data leakage is highly possible in the Web. Therefore, matching data from heterogeneous resources is feasible and thus deanonymisation can be achieved successfully. Also, in isolated environments such as health care, which hold sensitive information, can be deanonymised using data from the Web such as open government data.

In future work, we aim to model the attack patterns of deanonymisation. Also understanding how the changing context is affecting the effectiveness of deanonymisation. And if there are dead ends where deanonymisation cannot be achieved. More importantly, how to balance between providing a value from publishing data while protecting privacy from possible threats. This will advance research in data disclosure control and policy support.

Acknowledgments. This research is funded by University of Tabuk in Saudi Arabia and supported by Saudi Arabian Cultural Bureau in London.

References

1. Ding, X., Zhang, L., Wan, Z., Gu, M.: A brief survey on de-anonymization attacks. In: Online Social Networks, in International Conference on Computational Aspects of Social Networks, pp. 611–615 (2010)
2. El Emam, K., Jonker, E., Arbuckle, L., Malin, B.: A systematic review of re-identification attacks on health data. PLoS ONE 6(12), e28071 (2011)
3. Sharma, S., Gupta, P., Bhatnagar, V.: Anonymisation in social network: a literature survey and classification. Int. J. Soc. Netw. 1(1), 51–66 (2012)
4. Toch, E., Wang, Y., Cranor, L.F.: Personalization and privacy: a survey of privacy risks and remedies in personalization-based systems. User Model. User-adapt. Interact. 22(1–2), 203–220 (2012)
5. Ohm, P.: Broken promises of privacy: responding to the surprising failure of anonymization. UCLA Law Rev. 57, 1701 (2010)
6. Alexin, Z.: Does fair anonymization exist? Int. Rev. Law, Comput. Technol. 28(1), 21–44 (2014)
7. Dwork, C., Naor, M.: On the difficulties of disclosure prevention in statistical databases or the case for differential privacy. J. Priv. Confidentiality 2(1), 93–107 (2008)
8. O'Hara, K.: Transparent Government, Not Transparent Citizens: A Report on Privacy and Transparency for the Cabinet Office (2011)
9. Sun, X., Wang, H., Zhang, Y.: On the identity anonymization of high-dimensional rating data, No. March (2011), pp. 1108–1122 (2012)
10. Sweeney, L.: k-anonymity: a model for protecting privacy. Int. J. Uncertainty, Fuzziness Knowl. Based Syst. 10(05), 557–570 (2002)
11. Bayardo, R.J., Agrawal, R.: Data privacy through optimal k-anonymization. In: 21st International Conference Data and Engineering, pp. 217–228 (2005)
12. Li, N.: Provably Private Data Anonymization: Or, k-Anonymity Meets Differential Privacy (2010)
13. Machanavajjhala, A., Kifer, D., Gehrke, J., Venkitasubramaniam, M.: L-diversity: privacy beyond k-anonymity. ACM Trans. Knowl. Discov. Data 1(1), 3–es (2007)
14. Zhou, B., Pei, J.: The k-anonymity and l-diversity approaches for privacy preservation in social networks against neighborhood attacks. Know. Inf. Syst. 28(1), 47–77 (2010)
15. Li, N.: t-closeness: privacy beyond k-anonymity and -diversity. ICDE 7, 106–115 (2007)
16. Domingo-Ferrer, J., Torra, V.: A critique of k-anonymity and some of its enhancements. In: Third International Conference Availability, Reliability and Security, pp. 990–993 (2008)
17. Narayanan, A., Shi, E., Rubinstein, B.I.P.: Link prediction by de-anonymization: how we won the Kaggle social network challenge. In: Neural Networks (IJCNN) (2011)
18. Sharad, K., Danezis, G.: De-anonymizing D4D datasets. In: Workshop on Hot Topics in Privacy Enhancing Technologies (2013)
19. Narayanan, A., Shmatikov, V.: Robust de-anonymization of large sparse datasets. In: IEEE Symposium on Security and Privacy, pp. 111–125 (2008)
20. Bender, S., Brand, R., Bacher, J.: Re-identifying register data by survey data: an empirical study. Stat. J. United Nations ECE 18(00311), 373–381 (2001)
21. Gulyás, G., Imre, S.: Analysis of identity separation against a passive clique-based de-anonymization attack. Infocomm. J. 3(4), 1–10 (2011)
22. Torra, V., Stokes, K.: A formalization of re-identification in terms of compatible probabilities. CoRR, abs/1301.5, pp. 1–20 (2013)
23. Datta, A., Sharma, D., Sinha, A.: Provable de-anonymization of large datasets with sparse dimensions. in principles of security and trust (2012)

24. Gulyas, G.G., Imre, S.: Measuring importance of seeding for structural de-anonymization attacks in social networks. In: The Sixth IEEE Workshop on SECurity and SOCial Networking, pp. 610–615 (2014)
25. Hay, M., Miklau, G., Jensen, D.: Resisting structural re-identification in anonymized social networks. Proceedings of the VLDB Endowment **1**(1), 102–114 (2008)
26. Dankar, F.K., El Emam, K., Neisa, A., Roffey, T.: Estimating the re-identification risk of clinical data sets. BMC Med. Inf. Decis. Making **12**(1), 66 (2012)
27. Cecaj, A., Mamei, M., Bicocchi, N.: Re-identification of anonymized CDR datasets using social network data. In: The Third IEEE International Workshop on the Impact of Human Mobility in Pervasive Systems and Applications, pp. 237–242 (2014)
28. Zhang, A., Xie, X., Chang, K.C.-C., Gunter, C.A., Han, J., Wang, X.F.: Privacy risk in anonymized heterogeneous information networks. In: EDBT (2014)
29. Pedarsani, P., Grossglauser, M.: On the privacy of anonymized networks. In: Proceedings of the 17th ACM SIGKDD International Conference on Knowledge Discovery and Data Mining - KDD 2011, p. 1235 (2011)
30. Zhu, T., Wang, S., Li, X., Zhou, Z., Zhang, R.: Structural attack to anonymous graph of social networks. Math. Probl. Eng. **2013**, 1–8 (2013)
31. Narayanan, A., Shmatikov, V.: De-anonymizing social networks. In: 30th IEEE Symposium on Security and Privacy, pp. 173–187 (2009)
32. Srivatsa, M., Hicks, M.: Deanonymizing mobility traces: using social networks as a side-channel. In: Proceedings of the 2012 ACM Conference on Computer and Communications Security. ACM (2012)
33. Sharad, K., Danezis, G.: An automated social graph de-anonymization technique. arXiv Prepr, arXiv:1408.1276 (2014)
34. Nilizadeh, S., Kapadia, A., Ahn, Y.-Y.: Community-enhanced de-anonymization of online social networks. In: CCS 2014 (2014)
35. Peng, W., Li, F., Zou, X., Wu, J.: A two-stage deanonymization attack against anonymized social networks. IEEE Trans. Comput. **63**(2), 290–303 (2014)
36. Backstrom, L., Dwork, C., Kleinberg, J.: Wherefore art thou R3579X? anonymized social networks, hidden patterns, and structural steganography. In: Proceedings of the 16th International Conference on World Wide Web. ACM (2007)
37. Bringmann, K., Friedrich, T., Krohmer, A.: De-anonymization of heterogeneous random graphs in quasilinear time. In: ESA, pp. 197–208 (2014)
38. Simon, B., Gulyás, G.G., Imre, S.: Analysis of grasshopper, a novel social network de-anonymization algorithm. Periodica Polytechnica Electr. Eng. Comput. Sci. **58**(4), 161–173 (2014)
39. Kazemi, E., Hassani, S.H., Grossglauser, M.: Growing a graph matching from a handful of seeds. In: 41st International Conference on Very Large Data Bases (2015)
40. Ding, X., Zhang, L., Wan, Z., Gu, M.: De-anonymizing dynamic social networks. In: IEEE Global Telecommunications Conference – GLOBECOM, pp. 1–6 (2011)
41. Gambs, S., Killijian, M.-O., Núñez del Prado Cortez, M.: De-anonymization attack on geolocated data. J. Comput. Syst. Sci. **80**(8), 1597–1614 (2014)
42. Ji, S., Li, W., Srivatsa, M., He, J.S., Beyah, R.: Structure based data de-anonymization of social networks and mobility traces (2014)
43. Okuno, T., Ichino, M., Kuboyama, T., Yoshiura, H.: Content-based de-anonymisation of tweets. In: The Seventh International Conference on Intelligent Information Hiding and Multimedia Signal Processing, pp. 53–56 (2011)
44. Fu, H., Zhang, A., Xie, X.: Effective social graph de-anonymization based on graph structure and descriptive information. ACM Trans. Intell. Syst. Technol. **6**(4), 1–29 (2008)

45. Unnikrishnan, J., Naini, F. M.: De-anonymizing private data by matching statistics. In: Allerton Conference on Communication, Control, and Computing, No. EPFL-CONF-196580 (2013)
46. Zheleva, E., Getoor, L.: To join or not to join: the illusion of privacy in social networks with mixed public and private user profiles, pp. 531–540 (2009)
47. Wondracek, G., Holz, T., Kirda, E., Kruegel, C.: A practical attack to de-anonymize social network users. In: IEEE Symposium on Security and Privacy, pp. 223–238 (2010)
48. Korayem, M., Crandall, D. J.: De-anonymizing users across heterogeneous social computing platforms. In: Proceedings of the Seventh International AAAI Conference on Weblogs and Social Media, pp. 1–4 (2013)
49. Lane, N.D., Xie, J., Moscibroda, T., Zhao, F.: On the feasibility of user de-anonymization from shared mobile sensor data. In: Proceedings of the Third International Workshop on Sensing Applications on Mobile Phones - PhoneSense 2012, pp. 1–5 (2012)
50. Merener, M.M.: Theoretical results on de-anonymization via linkage attacks. Trans. Data Priv. 5(2), 377–402 (2012)
51. Frankowski, D., Cosley, D., Sen, S., Terveen, L., Riedl, J.: You are what you say: privacy risks of public mentions. In: Proceedings of the 29th SIGIR 2006, pp. 565–572 (2006)
52. Malin, B., Sweeney, L.: How (not) to protect genomic data privacy in a distributed network: using trail re-identification to evaluate and design anonymity protection systems. J. Biomed. Inform. 37(3), 179–192 (2004)
53. Malin, B., Sweeney, L., Newton, E.: Trail re-identification: learning who you are from where you have been. In: Workshop on Privacy in Data (2003)
54. Foukarakis, M., Antoniades, D., Antonatos, S., Markatos, E.P.: On the anonymization and deanonymization of netflow traffic. In: Proceedings of FloCon (2008)
55. Biryukov, A., Pustogarov, I., Weinmann, R.-P.: Trawling for tor hidden services: detection, measurement, deanonymization. In: 2013 IEEE Symposium on Security and Privacy, pp. 80–94 (2013)
56. Pataky, M.: De-anonymization of an Internet user based on his web browser. In: CER Comparative European Research, pp. 125–128 (2014)
57. Danezis, G., Troncoso, C.: You cannot hide for long: de-anonymization of real-world dynamic behaviour. In: WPES 2013, pp. 49–59 (2013)
58. Calandrino, J.A., Kilzer, A., Narayanan, A., Felten, E.W., Shmatikov, V.: You might also like: privacy risks of collaborative filtering, privacy risks of collaborative filtering. In: IEEE Symposium on Security and Privacy. IEEE (2011)
59. Danezis, G., Troncoso, C.: Vida: how to use Bayesian inference to de-anonymize persistent communications. In: Privacy Enhancing Technologies (2009)
60. Ji, S., Li, W., Srivatsa, M., Beyah, R.: Structural data de-anonymization: quantification, practice, and implications. In: CCS 2014 (2014)
61. Ji, S., Li, W., Gong, N.Z., Mittal, P., Beyah, R.: On your social network de-anonymizablity: quantification and large scale evaluation with seed knowledge. In: The 2015 Network and Distributed System Security (NDSS) Symposium, San Diego, CA, US, pp. 8–11 (2015)

Privacy Policies and Policy Based Protocols

Improving Users' Trust Through Friendly Privacy Policies: An Empirical Study

Oluwa Lawani[1(✉)], Esma Aïmeur[1], and Kimiz Dalkir[2]

[1] Department of Computer Science and Operations Research,
University of Montreal, Montreal, Canada
{lawanio, aimeur}@iro.umontreal.ca
[2] School of Information Studies, McGill University, Montreal, Canada
kimiz.dalkir@mcgill.ca

Abstract. Trust is a crucial factor for the information sharing continuance on the Internet, such as on social networks and e-commerce websites. Various studies show that many users do not trust the websites with respect to the use of their private data. Similarly, they find it unfair that their data is used to generate revenue by online service without their knowledge or without their earning from this.

In this paper, we take as main assumptions that the control of their private data as well as caring about user interests would restore their trust. Based on an empirical model, we conducted a study of user trust by offering them the possibility to adhere to a new model of privacy policy. Conventional privacy policies confront the user with a dilemma of either fully accepting all the terms and losing control of their data, or rejecting the content of the policy and not being allowed access to the service. The privacy policy presented in this paper allows users to manage access and use of their data, and also to be rewarded.

The results indicate that caring about user interests is the main factor influencing trust. Private data Control, which is greatly influenced by the management of their data by users, also has a considerable effect on trust. Results also show that users are more willing to get control over their data rather than to be rewarded for disclosing them, when they really understand how these data will be used.

Keywords: Privacy policies · Trust · Economics of privacy · Incentives · Private data control

1 Introduction

Around three billion people use the Internet around the world, representing 42 % of the world's population. Among them, around two billion have a social network account, 890 million connect to Facebook every day, and more than 200 million Internet users shopped online in USA in 2015[1]. Yet many of them do not have trust in these services due to the use of their personal data by these same services. Indeed, only 10 % of users trust social networks to protect their data, 20 % of e-commerce sites and 22 % of

---

[1] http://www.statista.com, accessed on 12 May 2015.

© Springer International Publishing Switzerland 2016
C. Lambrinoudakis and A. Gabillon (Eds.): CRiSIS 2015, LNCS 9572, pp. 55–70, 2016.
DOI: 10.1007/978-3-319-31811-0_4

technology companies in general[2]. In addition, users are increasingly aware of the value of their data, and think it is unfair that companies generate revenue from their personal data.

Privacy policies are the channel through which Internet services communicate to their users the data they collect from them and the use that is made of it. Despite the concerns of users regarding their private data, few of them take the time to read the policies before making a purchase or using a service. This is due to the length of the privacy policies and the difficulty of reading and understanding them [1, 2]. Added to this are issues of translation for all languages, but also the fact that users are somewhat forced to fully accept the terms of the policy in order to use the service. Users are therefore facing a dilemma where they generally lose as they must select from two unappealing choices. Indeed, either they accept the terms of the policy at the risk of losing their privacy, or they refuse to adhere to the policy and then they do not have access to the service.

Two points have therefore to be addressed in order to establish a fair trade between users and online services: (i) are users willing to profit from the use of their private data by online services? And, (ii) how can we ensure that stakeholders abide by the terms of the contracts? The first point can lead to two fundamental questions: (a) If users are willing to profit from their data, how much do they consider their data to be worth?, (b) On the other hand, if they want greater protection of all or some of their private data, how can they stipulate this clearly to the online service? Although these problems have been studied in a number of research studies (discussed further in this paper), there are still many deficiencies.

This paper focuses on the question b: how to clearly stipulate user needs in a contract. A model that will allow users to manage their data is proposed. In addition, users can receive various rewards depending on the data they choose to disclose to the online service.

We also evaluate the impact of allowing users greater control over their data on their trust in online services with respect to the use of their private data. In fact, online services must regain the trust of users in order to preserve the development of trade on the Internet [1].

This paper is organized as follow. In Sect. 2, we explore the state of the art through a literature review. We then present our research and privacy policy model in Sects. 3 and 4. Section 5 focuses on data collection, testing and analysis followed by a discussion of the results. The end of the document covers the conclusions and future work.

2 Litterature Review

Privacy Policies. Privacy policies are the way through which websites inform their users how they collect and use their data. However, many studies show that these policies are often ignored by users.

---

[2] State of Privacy Report, Symantec, 2015.

More than 50 % of Canadians never read privacy policies [3]. Another study, in 2013, revealed that only 4 % of Internet users always read privacy policies while 55 % of respondents had never read the terms of the agreement and copyrights [4].

This is due to several factors, such as the length of the privacy policies [1, 5], their non-specific and vague content, and their non-standard formats [6].

One 2014 study collected data from an online survey and compared the results to a research study published by the Annenberg Public Policy Center in 2005. This study analysed the current attitudes of individuals towards privacy policies and changes in those attitudes in the last decade. Results show that peoples' attitudes have not changed over ten years. According to the respondents, privacy policies are still too long, too complex and serve mostly to protect organizations [7].

Reading privacy policies even has a cost to the user as it takes approximately 76 working days to read all the privacy policies of all websites visited in one year [5]. As a result, users do not really know what information is collected about them and shared with third parties [8].

One study [9] found that few companies were transparent with respect to their data retention times and they also failed to offer users the ability to consult the information collected about them. Self-regulation does not appear to provide for sufficient meaningful privacy policy choices to users.

A trust management mechanism has been proposed for monitoring data consumers' compliance with contractual agreements for data sharing. The objective was to monitor and penalize errant consumers who violated the terms of their agreement. This trust management mechanism receives users' complaints about suspected privacy violations and identifies the responsible parties [10]. This allows users to complain and identify online services abusing their data. However, it also seems important to allow users to clearly specify how their data should be used and shared.

In this context, PCAST suggested, in 2014, that people could sign up for one of a series of "privacy preference profiles"[3]. Users should also have the choice to opt out of certain specific uses of their data [8]. P3P (Platform for Privacy Preferences) is a W3C project enabling websites to express their privacy policies in a standard format. It allows users, through software agents, to automate decision making according to their preferences [11]. However, this platform does not allow users to have multiple choices on each term of the policy. The model proposed in this paper can be a part of this W3C platform.

Today, many tools are designed to help users manage their confidentiality. eTrust is one of them. Its symbol, when displayed at the bottom of a privacy policy, aims to reassure the user[4]. PrivacyFix is another one that allows the user to manage privacy settings of various services[5]. However, this does not guarantee real understanding by the user of issues related to the confidentiality of their data.

---

[3] PCAST President's Council of Advisors on Science and Technology, Report to the president big data and privacy a technological perspective, 2014.

[4] http://www.etrust.pro/p_intro.html, 2015.

[5] https://www.privacyfix.com/.

The ability for the user to choose which data to share is not, however, offered by current privacy policies. It is indeed a very important point that we consider in this paper.

Economics of Privacy. Privacy and economy are closely linked as disclosing or protecting personal information has significant economic benefits for both users and online services. We can talk about monetary benefits for users [12] and marketing spending reduction for online services [13].

A study on personal data markets [14] found that personal data is viewed as a new asset because of its potential to create added value for companies and consumers. It can help online services reduce search costs for their products, allow collaborative filtering, reduce transaction costs and increase advertising profits. However this personal data can also be a burden. According to them, companies face challenge with legal constraints which differ from one country to another. They also have to face cybercrime threats especially when personal data includes identifying and financial information.

Moreover, users are increasingly aware of the value of their personal information, and would like to earn as much profit as online services do [15]. It is therefore important to establish a trusted environment to enable continuity of information sharing, because the lack of sharing personal data could lead to fewer benefits for both parties [16].

This environment can include incentives for users. Indeed, financial incentives motivate users to share more personal information with online services [15, 17]. On the other hand, some users are willing to pay to protect their private data. However, there is a considerable gap between the number of people who want to be paid for their data and those who wish to pay for protection [18].

In this paper, we aim to establish a fair market by allowing users to choose which data they want to disclose, and, in exchange, be rewarded for the use of their data.

3　Research Model

In order to study the factors that affect users trust in the protection and use of their private data, we designed a model and defined various hypotheses, as illustrated in Fig. 1.

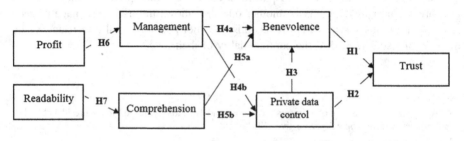

Fig. 1. Research model

Benevolence. Trust is a factor at the heart of business and trade on the Internet [19]. It is also the key to the success of social networks [20]. Trust includes three beliefs: ability, integrity and benevolence [21]. When the user finds these three factors sufficient, he grants confidence to the online service. According to the purpose of our study, we consider benevolence as a major factor influencing trust. Benevolence means the online service does not only care for his own interests, but also those of users. It refers to the intention of the trustee to do his best for the trustor, putting to one side his selfish profit motives, and generally always acting in the best interest of the trustor [22].

When the user also benefits from the use of his data, this can positively affect his trust in the online services because he does not feel they are behaving in an unacceptable manner. In this study, the user also benefits from the use of his data, so we suggest:

H1: Benevolence is positively related to trust.

Private Data Control. In 2012, the European Commission proposed changes to strengthen users' protection online. The new laws allow users take the control of their data. They state among other things that the user's permission has to be explicitly requested and all site settings have to be privacy-friendly. According to the law, users will trust companies who provide better information about how their data will be used and protected[6].

88 % of Europeans are interested primarily in the protection of their data before purchasing a product or subscribing to a service. Online services should then regain the trust of users by offering more transparency on their private data and enabling them to regain control over their data. This leads us to propose:

H2: Private data control is positively related to trust.

H3: Private data Control is positively related to benevolence.

Management. Management means the ability of each user to decide to disclose or hide an information. It also refers to a compromise between privacy and utility, allowing the user to make the right decision for himself. It is in a user's best interest to manage his private information. He then has absolute control over what and where his information flows [23]. Indeed, this gives him control by deciding who can have access to his data and how it would be used. This also influences benevolence because the user knows that his interests are at stake and vary according to his decisions. It is no longer only online service interests that matter. We therefore propose:

H4a: Management is positively related to benevolence.

H4b: Management is positively related to private data control.

Comprehension. Do people really understand the content of privacy policies, even though they are still the important source of information for users to know how companies collect, use and share their data? One study [24] investigated the difference in interpretation between experts and typical users. Their purpose was to analyse if people sufficiently understood privacy policies to make decisions about their confidentiality. To do this, they presented experts and non-experts users a set of privacy

---

[6] European Commission, Take Control of Your Personal Data, 2012.

policies and asked them a few questions about those policies. The results show that there were important discrepancies in the interpretation of privacy policy language, mostly with respect to data sharing. This indicates that privacy policies are sometimes unfair and may mislead people in making privacy decisions.

In fact, privacy policies sometimes use incomprehensible vocabulary and the way most of them are written serves to protect the organization from potential privacy lawsuits rather than address user privacy concerns [25]. Thus, the more a privacy policy is comprehensible, the more the user will be interested in reading it:

H5a: Comprehension is positively related to benevolence.

The control of user information is related to his right to know who's using his information and why. Good explanations have to be given to him before he gives permission to use his data (see footnote 6). In fact, it is important to understand something in order to have some control over it:

H5b: Comprehension is positively related to private data Control.

Profit. Profit motivates users to share more private data [15, 17]. Users are aware that their private data have a great value and are more engaged in the trade with an online service. Knowing that all data have not the same value for all users [15], we expect that each individual user will analyse the actual risks before deciding to disclose or protect a specific type of private information:

H6: Profit is positively related to management.

Readability. Users trust websites when they find their privacy policies readable, and therefore understandable [1].

Readability and comprehension are closely linked. Using a number of readability measures, one study [26] evaluated whether the representation of a privacy policy in terms of their format had an impact on its readability and comprehension. The study revealed that participants were not able to understand companies' privacy practices using any of the examined formats. They also found that around 20 % of privacy policies required an educational level approaching a post-graduate degree to support comprehension. We therefore propose:

H7: Readability is positively related to comprehension.

4 The Privacy Policy Model

The main purpose of this privacy policy model is to allow users to make a decision on each term of the policy.

As mentioned above, this model is not a substitute to other automated platform such as P3P, but a complement to existing platforms. The added value of this model is to provide multiple choices for each term of the policy. User can decide to share a specific type of data according to the options proposed to him, or incentives included in these options.

For example, a P3P user can specify that, for online shopping, he does not want to share his phone number. In the case where a website needs this user' phone number for an online purchase, the user will be informed by a pop-up window and can decide whether or not to continue the transaction.

In this research study, instead of simply allowing or not the transaction, the user can have multiple choices. These choices can include the use of the data, the retention period as proposed in a privacy policy framework [27], as well as incentives and functionalities of the service. This model then allows users to decide the level of personalization they want for the service according to how they allow the online service to use and share their data.

As shown in Fig. 2, this privacy policy model is designed by a policy creator (online service) and consists of a set of terms. Each term relates to a data or a data set. Added to this is an explicit explanation of the collection and use of data by the online service, and a set of proposals to the user. The user's choice is saved and will be taken into account when using the service.

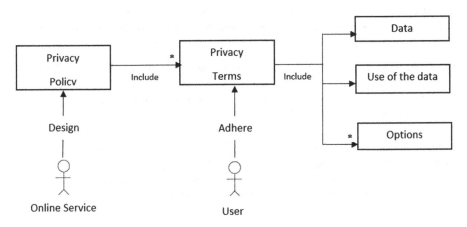

Fig. 2. Our privacy policy model

While other existing platforms struggle to be adopted because they need complementary tools and skills for users and online services, this model can be easily presented in a simple text format such as in this paper, or as an automated platform.

An example of an implementation of this model is presented in Appendix A. It was submitted to all participants of our study. The content of the terms of this policy was inspired from the Internet services Skype, Facebook and Google. We then adjusted them according to our model.

5   Methodology

In this section, we present the study design and data collection procedure.

Study Design. We developed a survey based on the trust factors identified above. Each factor was subdivided into questions, based on previous studies or their definition and main characteristics to improve content validity.

For instance, items of readability were adapted from [26]. The quick reading refers to the style of writing and the clarity of the policy. The easy of remembering refers to the length of the text. Items of comprehension were adapted from [26]. The text makes sense to the user when it is coherent and does not use many difficult words. Identification of important information refers to the structure of the policy. Understanding all the issues related to user's privacy refers to the difficulty of the language used in the policy. Items of trust were adapted from [28]. They allow us to measure online services' ability and integrity. Items of benevolence refer to the fact that the online service is on the side of customers, treats them as friends, and cares for them. They were adapted from [22].

The questions require a response to a five-item Likert scale ranging from "Strongly agree" to "Strongly Disagree". The questions were presented after participants read and adhered to a privacy policy according to the model shown in Fig. 2.

The survey was reviewed by some professors, with significant expertise in online privacy and surveys. The final version is presented in Appendix B.

Data Collection Procedure. The survey was conducted through Amazon's Mechanical Turk (MTurk) in March of 2015. Participants had to subscribe to a privacy policy of a fictional service, called Ikrani, and then answer questions about the experiment. A remuneration of $1.25 was offered to each participant.

363 responses were considered in the analysis. All participants were from USA and Canada. They were also required to have the following qualifications: Human Intelligence Task (HIT) approval rate ≥ 95 %, and number of approved HITs ≥ 100.

Self-reported demographic characteristics are illustrated in the following table (Table 1).

Study Limitations. We cannot neglect MTurk limitations such as the inability to control the experimental settings and the absence of a robust support for participant assignment. However, it can provide results as relevant as those from traditional survey methods [29].

6 Results

The first step of the analysis was to evaluate the measurement instruments to test reliability and validity. Then, we tested our research hypotheses and model fitness by evaluating the Structural Model (SM).

Reliability and Validity. We adopted AMOS 22.0.0 [30], a structural equation modelling software designed by IBM to conduct a Confirmatory Factor Analysis (CFA). We started by testing the validity and reliability of the model. Table 2 presents results with the standardized item loadings, the Average Variance Extracted (AVE), the Composite Reliability (CR) and the Cronbach Alpha values. All AVEs are greater than 0.5, all CRs greater than 0.7, indicating that the scale has a good convergence validity [31]. As suggested by Numaly [32], all Alpha values are greater than 0.7, indicating a good reliability.

Table 1. Demographic characteristics of the studied sample

Demographic	Category	Frequency
Gender	Female	44.8 %
	Male	54.9 %
	I prefer not to answer	0.3 %
Age	16–24	15.4 %
	25–34	51.6 %
	35–44	19.2 %
	45–54	9.3 %
	55+	4.4 %
	I prefer not to answer	0 %
Education	Junior High/Middle School	0.5 %
	High School	28 %
	Technical/trade school	15.4 %
	Bachelor's degree	46.2 %
	Master's degree	6.6 %
	Doctoral degree	1.6 %
	I prefer not to answer	0.5 %
	Other	1.1 %
Annual income	No income	1.6 %
	Under $ 10.000	15.4 %
	$10.001–25.000	23.1 %
	$25.001–35.000	19 %
	$35.000–45.000	11.5 %
	$45.000+	26.1 %
	I prefer not to answer	3.3 %

Accordingly, the study instruments are considered appropriate.

In Table 3, we can see that, for almost all factors, the square root of AVE is larger than its correlation coefficients with other factors, indicating a good discriminant validity [31, 33].

Model Evaluation. The second step, which consisted of measuring the overall goodness-of-fit for the research model, is presented in Table 4. The comparison of fit indices with the recommended values produced acceptable results. Chi^2/DF is the ratio between chi-square and the degrees of freedom. GFI (Goodness of Fit Index), AGFI (Adjusted Goodness of Fit Index), RMSEA (Root Mean Square Error of Approximation) allow us to evaluate the suitability of the search model. The fitness of the model was evaluated through NFI (Normed Fit Index) and CFI (Comparative Fit Index).

From these data, our model shows good fitness and validity [31].

Table 2. Reliability and validity analysis

Factor	Item	Standardized item loading	AVE	CR	Alpha value
Readability (REA)	REA1	1.00	0.70	0.81	0.767
	REA2	0.627			
Profit (PRO)	PRO1	0.567	0.66	0.78	0.715
	PRO2	1.00			
Comprehension (COM)	COM1	0.712	0.62	0.83	0.827
	COM2	0.838			
	COM3	0.809			
Management (MAN)	MAN1	0.850	0.70	0.83	0.824
	MAN2	0.827			
Private data Control (PDC)	PDC1	0.742	0.58	0.80	0.789
	PDC2	0.868			
	PDC3	0.652			
Benevolence (BEN)	BEN1	0.769	0.74	0.90	0.891
	BEN2	0.912			
	BEN3	0.899			
Trust (TRU)	TRU1	0.884	0.74	0.85	0.843
	TRU2	0.832			

Table 3. Square root of AVE and factor correlations coefficients

	PDC	COM	REA	PRO	MAN	BEN	TRU
PDC	**0.759**						
COM	0.446	**0.788**					
REA	0.323	0.745	**0.835**				
PRO	0.315	0.327	0.139	**0.813**			
MAN	0.787	0.557	0.359	0.454	**0.839**		
BEN	0.722	0.474	0.328	0.540	0.683	**0.862**	
TRU	0.790	0.444	0.326	0.493	0.646	0.843	**0.858**

Table 4. Measures of model fitness

	Chi^2/DF	GFI	AGFI	CFI	NFI	RMSEA
Recommended value	<3	>0.90	>0.80	>0.90	>0.90	<0.08
CFA	2.87	0.916	0.872	0.949	0.925	0.072
SM	3.07	0.906	0.860	0.942	0.918	0.075

7 Discussion

Of the nine hypotheses of this study, seven were found to be supported, as shown in Table 5 and Fig. 3.

Table 5. Hypothesis tests values

Attributes		Estimate	p	Hypothesis status	
BEN ➡ TRU		0.514	<0.001	H1	Supported
PDC ➡ TRU		0.497	<0.001	H2	Supported
PDC ➡ BEN		0.516	<0.001	H3	Supported
MAN ➡ BEN		0.092	0.298	H4a	Not supported
MAN ➡ PDC		0.756	<0.001	H4b	Supported
COM ➡ BEN		0.103	0.022	H5a	Supported
COM ➡ PDC		0.037	0.638	H5b	Not supported
PRO ➡ MAN		0.402	<0.001	H6	Supported
REA ➡ COM		0.714	<0.001	H7	Supported

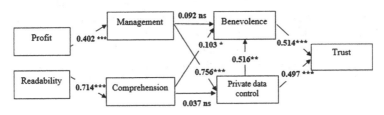

Fig. 3. Hypothesis tests values (Path significance: * < 0.05; ** < 0.01; *** < 0.001)

Unsurprisingly, readability positively affects comprehension (H7). This means that online services need to adopt an easily readable format to enable users to understand the issues related to their private data and then be more accessible to an average reader [1].

The H6 hypothesis stipulating that profit affects management was supported. The user is therefore able to manage access to his data when he is motivated by any interest. Management affects the private data control (H4b). To give control of their data to users, they must have opportunities to decide which data they want to share and for what purpose. This management is an important part of our privacy policy model.

To our surprise, benevolence was not much influenced by management (H4a not supported). Even analysing profit influences on benevolence and trust did not produce results that were significant. So incentives motivate users to manage the access and use of their private data but they do not affect their trust.

Comprehension influences the benevolence (H5a) without having an impact on the private data control (H5b). When the user is able to understand the content of a privacy policy and clearly identify the issues of privacy, this implies that the online service is concerned about his interests. This confirms a study done by the Office of the Privacy Commissioner of Canada. It reveals that many users find privacy policies content too vague and not specific regarding issues related to their confidentiality. It then recommends that companies should limit the amount of personal information they collect to what is necessary for the purposes of delivering a product or service, and they should make it clear to customers why they need such information, ideally through a privacy policy.

This was demonstrated in our study. Indeed, among the multiple options available to users on each term of the privacy policy, the majority chose to share their data only for the purpose of the service. For example, for Email address, 58.5 % of respondents did not want to share this information with third parties compared to 41.5 % who said they would in exchange for a reward. Regarding the analysis of the content of emails, only 15.9 % agreed that their email could be analysed to offer them advertisement against a reward. 67.6 % did not want any analysis of their email, and 16.5 % agreed to pay for the analysis to be made only for their service (malware and spam detection for example).

It is noticeable that most users want to protect their data rather than disclose them for rewards, when they really understand how their data will be used.

H3 Hypothesis stipulating that private data control influences benevolence is supported. Both benevolence and private data control influence the overall trust of users (H1 and H2). As shown in Fig. 3, benevolence has a greater effect than private data control. This indicates that although users wish to have control over their data, they feel more confident when the online services also care about their interests. Knowing that benevolence is mainly influenced by comprehension, it is therefore clear that users need to understand the use of their personal data in order to have trust in an online service.

8   Conclusion and Future Work

Conclusion. The main objective of our study was to determine the factors that influence the trust of users, with respect to the use of their personal data by online services. This study experimented with a new model of privacy policy that allowed users to choose which data to share with the online service as well as how the data will be used. In this model, users can receive incentives in exchange for their data.

The results indicate that benevolence positively influences the trust of users. The control of users over their personal data also has a positive impact on their trust. These factors are themselves determined by the level of comprehension of privacy policies, as well as the possibility of flexible management of user data. These are indeed the key points and the new contributions of our privacy policy model. Incentives motivate users to manage their data without significantly affecting their trust regarding their online service. Users are indeed more willing to control their data than to receive incentives.

For online services, these results show that they should give users more control over their data and provide more flexibility in adherence to privacy policies. Only then will users be freed from the dilemma of having to choose between two unappealing choices.

Future Work. This study is a starting point to establish a model of a simple privacy policy that is readable, understandable and that allows the user to manage their own private data. In this study, the same value was set for all user data. However, it appears that all data do not have the same value for online services, and also that users do not estimate their data value in the same way [15]. It would be useful to set up a virtual market in which the value of private data could fluctuate with demand and also with the importance placed upon each by users. It would also be interesting to take into account all the data that can be exchanged between users and online services.

Even if users are allowed to choose which data to share and how it would be used, the question of transparency still remains: how can the user be sure that his data will be used as he indicated in the privacy policy?

Appendix A

Your email address

Ikrani can compare your email address and those of your contacts provided to a website or a third party online service to see if you can benefit from the combined offering.

Mark only one oval.

- I agree (I earn 100 points)
- I do not agree (0 point)

Your Geolocation

We use services from other companies to help us derive a general geographic area based on your IP address in order to customize certain features or deals in your area.

Mark only one oval.

- I agree (I earn 100 points)
- I do not agree: I do not want any geolocation, even If it meant I would not benefit from a better quality of service (0 points)
- I do not agree: I wish my physical location to be collected only when I give my explicit agreement and only to be used for my service (I lose 100 points)

Demographics

We can obtain additional information about you, such as demographic data we purchase from other companies.

Mark only one oval.

- I agree (I earn 100 points)
- I do not agree (0 point)

Email content

Our automated systems analyse your content (including e-mail) to offer customized product features such as personalized search results, customized advertisements and spam detection and malware.

Mark only one oval.

- I agree (I earn 100 points)
- I do not agree: I do not want any analysis of my emails (0 point)
- I do not agree: I want the analysis of my emails to only be used to detect spam and malware (I lose 100 points)

Appendix B

Trust TRU (adapted from [28])
  TRU1: This online service is trustworthy.
  TRU2: This online service will keep their commitments.
  Benevolence (adapted from [22])
  BEN1: Through this privacy policy, I feel close to the online service.
  BEN2: Through this privacy policy, I think this online service cares about my concerns.
  BEN3: This online service keeps customers' interests in mind.
  Private data control
  PDC1: I know that my private data will not be disclosed to a third party without my permission.
  PDC2: I can decide who has access to my private data.
  PDC3: I can change my mind about my privacy settings whenever I want.
  Management (adapted from [23])
  MAN1: This online service allows me to choose which data I want to share.
  MAN2: This online service offers multiple choices on each of the terms of the privacy policy.
  Comprehension (adapted from [26])
  COM1: The content of this policy makes sense to me.
  COM2: Important information is easily identifiable.
  COM3: I understand all the issues related to my privacy.
  Profit
  PRO1: This privacy policy allows me to get benefits.
  PRO2: Incentives motivate me to deal with the online service.
  Readability (adapted from [26])
  REA1: Important points of this privacy policy are easily remembered.
  REA2: This privacy policy can be read quickly.

References

1. Ermakova, T., Baumann, A., Fabian, B., Krasnova, H.: Privacy policies and users' trust: does readability matter? In: Presented at the Twentieth Americas Conference on Information Systems (2014)

2. Furnell, S., Phippen, A.: Online privacy: a matter of policy? Comput. Fraud Secur. **2012**, 12–18 (2012)
3. Office of the Privacy Commissioner of Canada: Survey of Canadians on Privacy-Related Issues. https://www.priv.gc.ca/information/por-rop/2013/por_2013_01_e.asp
4. dos Santos Brito, K., Cardoso Garcia, K.V., Araujo Durao, F., Romero de Lemos Meira, S.: How people care about their personal data released on social media. In: Eleventh Annual International Conference on Privacy, Security and Trust (PST), pp. 111–118 (2013)
5. McDonald, A.M., Cranor, L.F.: The cost of reading privacy policies. J. Law Policy Inf. Soc. **4**, 543 (2008)
6. Schaub, F., Breaux, T.D., Sadeh, N.: Crowdsourcing the extraction of data practices from privacy policies. In: Second AAAI Conference on Human Computation and Crowdsourcing, pp. 56–57 (2014)
7. Williams, T.L., Agarwal, N., Wigand, R.T.: Protecting Private Information: Current Attitudes Concerning Privacy Policies (2015)
8. Richards, N.M., King, J.H.: Big data ethics, Wake Forest Law Review, p. 40 (2014)
9. Cranor, L.F., Hoke, C., Leon, P.G., Au, A.: Are they worth reading? An in-depth analysis of online advertising companies' privacy policies. In: TPRC Conference (2014)
10. Noorian, Z., Iyilade, J., Mohkami, M., Vassileva, J.: Trust mechanism for enforcing compliance to secondary data use contracts. In: IEEE 13th International Conference Trust, Security and Privacy in Computing and Communications (TrustCom), pp. 519–526 (2014)
11. W3C. P3P Specification. http://www.w3.org/TR/P3P11/. Accessed 28 May 2015
12. Acquisti, A.: The economics of personal data and the economics of privacy. In: Background Paper for OECD Joint WPISP-WPIE Roundtable, vol. 1, p. 50 (2010)
13. Linden, G., Smith, B., York, J.: Amazon.com recommendations: item-to-item collaborative filtering. IEEE Internet Comput. **7**, 76–80 (2003)
14. Spiekermann, S., Acquisti, A., Böhme, R., Hui, K.-L.: The challenges of personal data markets and privacy. Electron. Markets **25**, 161–167 (2015)
15. Acquisti, A., John, L.K., Loewenstein, G.: What is privacy worth? J. Legal Stud. **42**, 249–274 (2013)
16. Osothongs, A., Sonehara, N.: A proposal of personal information trading platform (PIT): a fair trading between personal information and incentives. In: Fourth International Conference on Digital Information and Communication Technology and its Applications (DICTAP), pp. 269–274 (2014)
17. Chorppath, A.K., Alpcan, T.: Trading privacy with incentives in mobile commerce: a game theoretic approach. Pervasive Mob. Comput. **9**, 598–612 (2013)
18. Grossklags, J., Acquisti, A.: When 25 cents is too much: an experiment on willingness-to-sell and willingness-to-protect personal information. In: Presented at the Workshop on the Economics of Information Security (2007)
19. Urban, G.L., Sultan, F., Qualls, W.J.: Placing trust at the center of your Internet strategy. Sloan Manag. Rev. **42**, 39–48 (2000)
20. Sherchan, W., Nepal, S., Paris, C.: A survey of trust in social networks. ACM Comput. Surv. **45**, 47 (2013)
21. Kim, D.J., Ferrin, D.L., Rao, H.R.: A trust-based consumer decision-making model in electronic commerce: the role of trust, perceived risk, and their antecedents. Decis. Support Syst. **44**, 544–564 (2008)
22. Raimondo, M.A.: The measurement of trust in marketing studies: a review of models and methodologies. In: 16th IMP-Conference, Bath, UK (2000)
23. Song, Y., Kunjithapatham, A., Messer, A.: Method and apparatus for user centric private data management. ed: Google Patents (2006)

24. Reidenberg, J.R., Breaux, T., Cranor, L.F., French, B., Grannis, A., Graves, J.T., et al.: Disagreeable Privacy Policies: Mismatches Between Meaning and Users' Understanding (2014)
25. Earp, J.B., Antón, A.I., Aiman-Smith, L., Stufflebeam, W.H.: Examining Internet privacy policies within the context of user privacy values. IEEE Trans. Eng. Manage. **52**, 227–237 (2005)
26. Sumeeth, M., Singh, R., Miller, J.: Are online privacy policies readable? In: Optimizing Information Security and Advancing Privacy Assurance: New Technologies, New Technologies, p. 91 (2012)
27. Iyilade, J., Vassileva, J.: A framework for privacy-aware user data trading. In: Carberry, S., Weibelzahl, S., Micarelli, A., Semeraro, G. (eds.) UMAP 2013. LNCS, vol. 7899, pp. 310–317. Springer, Heidelberg (2013)
28. Zhou, T.: An empirical examination of continuance intention of mobile payment services. Decis. Support Syst. **54**, 1085–1091 (2013)
29. Kittur, A., Chi, E.H., Suh, B.: Crowdsourcing user studies with mechanical turk. In: Proceedings of the SIGCHI Conference on Human Factors in Computing Systems, pp. 453–456 (2008)
30. Arbuckle, J.L.: IBM® SPSS® Amos™ 22 User's Guide. IBM, Chicago (2013)
31. Gefen, D., Straub, D., Boudreau, M.-C.: Structural equation modeling and regression: guidelines for research practice. Commun. Assoc. Inf. Syst. **4**, 7 (2000)
32. Nunally, J.C.: Psychometric Theory. McGraw-Hill, New York (1978)
33. Fornell, C., Larcker, D.F.: Evaluating structural equation models with unobservable variables and measurement error. J. Mark. Res. **18**(1), 39–50 (1981)

MPLS Policy Target Recognition Network

Abdulrahman Al-Mutairi[2]([⊠]) and Stephen Wolthusen[1,2]

[1] Norwegian Information Security Laboratory, Department of Computer Science,
Gjøvik University College, Gjøvik, Norway
[2] Information Security Group, Department of Mathematics, Royal Holloway,
University of London, Surrey, UK
{Abdulrahman.Almutairi.2009,stephen.wolthusen}@rhul.ac.uk

Abstract. Policy-based protocols such as Multi-Protocol Label Switching (MPLS) and Border Gateway Protocol (BGP) are deployed by service providers to increase the efficiency of their networks; particularly the MPLS protocol where traffic engineering is required for the guarantee of Quality of Service (QoS) that is crucial for real-time dependant systems such as financial services, government and public safety, critical infrastructures and smart grids. Network operators are cautious about revealing information of their network; mainly for security reasons. Whereas, sophisticated adversaries are known for launching reconnaissance attacks years in advance of more malicious attacks. Whilst, research in this area was limited to the BGP, this paper aims to analyse the ability to reveal MPLS policy states with limited knowledge using Bayesian Belief Network (BBN).

Keywords: Multi-Protocol Label Switching · Real-Time Networks · Bayesian Belief Network · Reconnaissance · Bayesian networks

1 Introduction

Internet Service Providers (ISPs) manage their networks according to the agreed services, business relationships or preferred operational aspects using the policy-based protocols. One of the widely deployed policy-based protocol in networks backbone is *Multi-Protocol Label Switching* (MPLS) protocol. MPLS is a connection oriented protocol that efficiently reduces the amount of packets processing on each router by a *label switching* approach. Instead of the explicit lookup at each router, in label switching a short fixed label which is assigned to a pre-identified optimum path is attached to each packet once in the network edge; therefore, the intermediate routers forward packets based on label entries rather than longest prefix matching. Consequently, MPLS allows network operators not only to reduce costs, network overhead or congestion, but also to provide *Quality of Services* (QoS) through processing traffic on per-flow basis where different flows sharing the same characteristics, e.g., the same destination are treated similarly, typically through a process of resource reservation. However, the process of offering a guaranteed QoS involves different techniques and policies in order to

© Springer International Publishing Switzerland 2016
C. Lambrinoudakis and A. Gabillon (Eds.): CRiSIS 2015, LNCS 9572, pp. 71–87, 2016.
DOI: 10.1007/978-3-319-31811-0_5

satisfy the different characteristics of critical applications through imposing tight bounds on time delays, delay variation or bandwidth, especially when processing real-time traffic flows those belong to a variety of time sensitive systems such as financial and security services, smart grids or military institutions that would conventionally have relied on dedicated point-to-point links.

At the same time, network operators wish not to reveal such functional information, e.g., routing policy mainly for security reasons. Where adversaries are known to conduct *footprinting* and *reconnaissance* attacks in order to analyse the network behaviour as a first step which is followed by more malicious attacks to disrupt service availability or re-direct traffic to advantageous paths to the adversary. Indeed, there is a few number of MPLS nodes in the backbone domain that are closely monitored and physically secured which would add some restriction on what the adversary might be able to do in order to interfere in the signalling process or the collection of the interesting information such as policy states. However, the adversary could make use of the probability models, e.g., Bayesian Belief Network (BBN) in constructing a belief about the MPLS policy states by having access to a limited information. This paper aims to study the ability of adversary to learn about the MPLS policy engine of network routers whilst having access to limited resources and data resources within the attacked network. An overview of BBNs and previous related work is introduced in Sect. 2. Then, the MPLS policy engine is introduced in Sect. 3. After that, we introduce our MPLS policy target recognition network in Sect. 4. An experiment to evaluate the ability of our MPLS target recognition network to reveal the MPLS policy engine is then introduced in Sect. 5. Finally, we conclude our work in Sect. 6.

2   Background

Bayesian Belief Network (BBN); also known as Causal Probabilistic Network, Causal Net, Belief Network, is a graphical representation of encoded probabilistic relationships among variables of interest. BBN is represented as a directed acyclic graph (DAG) of nodes which are connected by arcs unlike the Markov models which are represented as an undirected graph. Each node represents a variable of interest while arcs represent the causal relationships for these variables. Each node may take a set of possible states and the probability of each state is updated accordingly whenever the probability of any directly connected node changes. BBN does not require historical data set which is not the case with the other probability models such as Hidden Markov models (HMMs).

BBNs have been used to infer the uncertainty of model states in a variety of applications including battlefield strategy [1], fault diagnostics [2], sensor detection systems [3].

Alternatively, we use BBNs in our work for the sake of studying the ability of restricted adversary to reveal the MPLS policy engine with limited ability, e.g., restricted physical access and limited probing.

In our previous work [4] we have used a naive Bayesian Network and a limited probing algorithm in order to reveal the MPLS policy engine. Firstly, we identified the traces, i.e., evidence that are left by each state of MPLS policy engine, also we ensure the causal relationships between each MPLS policy state and the evidence left in the network with pure observation and experiments. The results have shown that we could reveal the MPLS policy machines of all MPLS cores that are directly attached to the compromised link and some of the MPLS cores that are non-directly attached to the compromised link.

However, in this work, we are going to use BBNs in our work to reveal MPLS policy machine states. BBNs offer a suitable solution for the target recognition problem where some attributes of a target such as identity, class and category need to be determined [5].

3   MPLS Policy Engine

Network operators and service providers implement policy-routing for the sake of efficiency, desirability, or other operational and political factors that are hard to consider in the classic shortest path routing. Unfortunately, there are many routing policies to be considered and hard to be defined in addition to the complexity of the policies implementation which is well known as an error prone process [6].

In addition, MPLS networks are associated with other mechanisms such as Differentiated Services (DiffServ) or Traffic Engineering (TE) in order to deliver QoS [7] which would result in more complicated policies other than those found in IP based routing networks. However, there is a certain number of policies in the pure implementation of MPLS which are included in the MPLS architecture design [8] as well as in Label Distribution Protocol (LDP) specification [9].

Mainly, MPLS networks treat packets based on common classes which are known as Flow Equivalent Classes (FECs) where each FEC presents a group of packets to be treated in the same manner. Furthermore, each FEC is bound to a unique label before each MPLS enabled router or what is known as Label Switch Routers (LSR) could treat them differently as configured. For that reason, there are certain policies used to govern the way of binding labels to FECs and exchanging of the binding among LSRs as well as the way of treating packets differently.

Policies in MPLS could be divided into two main classes. The first class which we refer to as *traffic policy* class which governs the operation carried by LSRs on traffic as per packet by packet. Generally, once each LSR receives a packet, it would carry one of the label operations (push, swap or pop) on it based on the configured policy.

The other type is related to the management of labels inside the MPLS domain which we refer to as the *labels management* class. The label bindings could be distributed to other LSRs that have not explicitly requested them when *Unsolicited Downstream* (UD) label distribution policy is configured. Alternatively, the upstream LSR has to explicitly request the label bindings from the next LSR when *Downstream on Demand* (DoD) label distribution policy is used. In addition, there are two policies govern label allocation in each LSR. The first

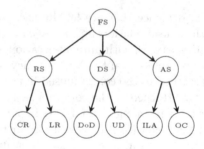

Fig. 1. MPLS label management policy states

label allocation policy is called *Independent Label Allocation* (ILA) where each LSR assigns a label to the recognised FEC whether or not it received the label assignment from the next hop. However, LSRs need to receive a label assignment for specific FEC in order to create and propagate their own label bindings in the *Ordered Control* (OC) label allocation policy. Also, there are two policies control labels retention strategy as LSRs may receive multiple labels but only use one of them. The *Liberal Retention* (LR) policy keeps the received labels even if they are unused. Alternatively, the *Conservative Retention* (CR) policy leads the LSR to only keep the labels those are used previously and discard the unused ones.

Labels management policies, i.e., label retention, label distribution and label allocation policies are concerned with the set-up of MPLS network environment rather than individual flows or nodes as the case with traffic policy. Therefore, we are going to focus on label management policies in this work. The traffic policies will be studied in future work. The MPLS label management policy state space is shown in Fig. 1 where FS represents MPLS policy and the nodes (RS, DS and AS) represent the three label management policies.

4   Probabilistic Model

In this part of the paper, we are going to construct the probabilistic model for MPLS model. Based on that model we are going to develop a suitable policy recognition network to measure the uncertainty about MPLS policy engine. First of all we are going to introduce two techniques that are useful in probabilistic model construction in Sects. 4.1 and 4.2, followed by a causation model for problem definition purposes in Sect. 4.3. Based on the above, we then introduce our finalised causal network.

4.1   Intervention

Learning by intervention is an important aspect of causal model which makes it different from probabilistic model, hence we are allowed to manipulate the values instead of just observing them [10]. This is important for our work because it gives the ability to manipulate the state of the evidence accordingly and observe the hypothesis nodes based on them. Interventions in causal relationships allow us to force the variable A to take the value a which can be expressed by the form $do(A := a)$, often abbreviated $do(A)$ where A in our study refers to the probe signal, e.g., label release signal. Consequently, the probability of the variable A with value a is set to be 1.

4.2   The Noisy-or-Gate and the Noisy-and-Gate

The noisy-or-gate and the noisy-and-gate is implemented as approximation techniques to model the relationships between binary variables [5]. The former technique is used when the likelihood of one of the parent values cause a certain value in the child. While, the later technique is used when the likelihood of two certain values of the parent nodes cause a certain value in the child. These techniques would help us to draw the correct causation relationship between the MPLS policies and their evidence as well as the correlation relationships among themselves.

4.3   Causation and Correlation

Each MPLS policy has at least one unique behaviour which we refer to as an evidence, i.e., label mappings or requests behaviour which could be observed passively or actively using LDP signals. Also, there are some evidence could be observed for specific combinations of some policy states which could be used with other pieces of evidence to reduce the uncertainty about MPLS policy engine state. According to Andersson et al. [9], when implementing DoD policy state with ILA policy state, a LSR would answer the requested label binding immediately without waiting for label binding from next hop. On the other hand, a LSR would advertise label bindings to its LSR peers whenever it is prepared to label switch those FECs when it is operating in ILA policy state with UD policy state. However, a LSR that is operating in OC policy state must only issue a label mapping after receiving a label mapping from the egress LSR.

The identification and confirmation process of MPLS policy engine evidence is documented by our previous work [4] using Network Simulator NS-2 [11]. Basically, we modelled a simulated MPLS network and configured each LSR of this network with one of the stated policies, i.e., label distribution and label allocation[1] and observed the evidence related to each policy. The study has shown that label release and withdraw signals propagated downstream and upstream respectively through the targeted LSRs causing each MPLS policy state to reply as expected at a time.

Furthermore, the possible evidence that are documented and testified for each MPLS policy state in our former work are extended and reformed here for analysis purposes. Each one of the concerned LDP messages is treated according

---

[1] Due to the limitation of the simulation tool, the simulation study was only conducted with the conservative label retention policy.

to it's implication in the reconnaissance of MPLS policy engine. For instance, we differentiate between request messages that has passed through a single hope and the other request messages that passed through multiple hops. By doing so, each one of the MPLS policy state would have a more defined and accurate chain of evidence as follows:

- **Ordered Control (OC):**
  1. Request message with a multi-entries TLV (Req_m): This is a strong evidence that any LSR issued this message, i.e., $TLV[1]$ is in OC policy state. Which means that the other LSRs forward this message are not necessarily has the same policy state.
- **Independent Label Allocation (ILA):**
  1. Mapping message with a multi-entries TLV (Map_m): This type of mapping messages could be caused by other policy states too, i.e., OC and UD. However, when this message is not generated by the FEC egress, it is considered as a strong evidence of ILA policy state for LSRs included in the message's TLV because LSRs in OC police state would not send a mapping message unless a label biding for the questioned FEC is received from its egress.
  2. Mapping message with a single-entry TLV (Map_s): This is a strong evidence that the LSR sent this message is in ILA policy state except the egress LSR of the questioned FEC.
- **Unsolicited Downstream (UD):**
  1. Upstream mapping message (Map_{um}): This is a weak evidence that all LSRs forward this message are in UD policy state. Even though, LSRs with DoD are not allowed to send an upstream label mapping, there is an exception specified in LDP specification [9] which allows such behaviour.
  2. Mapping message with a multi-entries TLV (Map_m): a mapping message with multi-hop count could be caused by other policy states too as mentioned previously. However, when this message is not a reply for a request $Req_{id} \notin Map_m$ it is considered as a weak evidence of UD policy for all LSRs included in the message's TLV. Eventhough each LSR reply to a label request message must include a label request's ID as a TLV optional parameter in the mapping message as stated in LDP specification [9], such messages could be sent by DoD policy state for the same reason specified for the former evidence.
- **Downstream on Demand (DoD):**
  1. Request message with a single-entry TLV (Req_s): This is a weak evidence that the LSR that sent this message is in DoD policy state because LSR with UD policy is allowed to send request messages by LDP specifications [9].
  2. Mapping message with a multi-entries TLV (Map_m): a mapping message with multi-hop count could be caused by other policy states too as mentioned previously. However, when this message is a reply for a request, i.e., $Req_{id} \in Map_m$, it is considered as a weak evidence of DoD policy for all LSRs included in the message's TLV because UD policy state could generate such a message when operating with OC policy state.

Indeed, the above identified evidence could be observed passively with no intervention needed. However, there are additional pieces of evidence arise interventions such as the usage of withdraw and release LDP signals which we refer to as P_{wr} as following:

- **ILA policy state with UD policy state:**
  1. Mapping message with single-entry TLV (Map_s) after a P_{wr} signal. However, the message must be independent and not a reply to a request message in order to be accepted as an evidence of ILA policy and UD policy state.
- **ILA policy state with DoD policy state:**
  1. Request message with single-hop count (Req_s) after a P_{wr} signal followed by a mapping message with single-entry TLV (Map_s).
- **OC policy state:** Request message with multi-hop count (Req_m) after a withdraw signal to the signal source.
- **CR policy state:** Unfortunately the LSR only discard the unused labels but not release them [12]. However, request or mapping message will be generated after a requirement for path changing, e.g., link failure ($Link_f$). P_{wr} signals might be sent if the the mapping is granted.

Moreover, there are some correlation relationships among these policy states. According to Andersson et al. [9] label retention and label distribution polices has some correlations because CR policy state typically is implemented with DoD policy state unlike the case with UD policy state which may implement one of the retention policies fairly [9]. Moreover, some configuration recommendation which is introduced by experts could be used as well in the probability domain.

For example, in case of policy conflicts such as live-lock situation [9]. When the upstream LSR is in UD policy state and the downstream LSR is in DoD policy state, the upstream LSR assumes the downstream LSR would distribute labels as needed, while downstream LSR assumes the upstream LSR would request for labels as needed which means there are no labels distributed. The solution for this problem is if the session is for a label-controlled ATM link or a label-controlled Frame Relay link which we refer to as $Link_{af}$ then DoD must be used, otherwise, UD must be used with other type of links which we refer to as $Link_o$.

In order to illustrate the causal relationships between each one of the MPLS policies and its evidence as well as the correlation relationships among those policies themselves, we consider the causal model as shown in Fig. 2. The variables in our network are classified as hypothesis, evidence, intervention or logic nodes. The hypothesis nodes are the root nodes which lie on a horizontal line in the network middle layer as shown in Fig. 2.

The hypothesis nodes represent the MPLS policy state in question, i.e., OC, UD, ILA, DoD and CR. The evidence nodes represent the variables caused by the hypothesis nodes, i.e., MPLS policy states as suggested by the evidence definition above. There are 9 evidence nodes in our causal model, i.e., Req_m, Map_m, $Link_o$, Map_{um}, Map_s, $Link_{af}$, Req_s. It should be noted that Map_f and Req_f are general evidence for every kind of mapping and request messages that

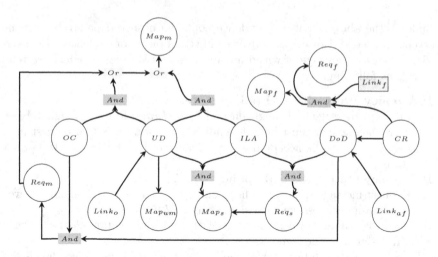

Fig. 2. MPLS causal network

are caused by link failure event which are introduced to simplify causal relationships in our model. Intervention node is represented by the block node to indicated the affect caused by Link failure event $Link_f$. On the other hand, the logic nodes express the the noisy-or-gate and the noisy-and-gate technique that was introduced in Sect. 4.2

4.4   MPLS Policy Recognition Network

Even though, the causal model that has been introduced in previous section might be complex to infer, it is suitable whenever detailed information is expected to update the causal network, for example, for network operators who wish to infer the policies in their networks to check for policy conflict or in cases where a certain policy implementation is restricted or to gain information about MPLS policy implemented by other competitive network operators based on a detailed information base. However, in case this kind of information was not available or some of the evidence was not observed, the uncertainty of the MPLS policy engine state is going to be high. Moreover, the strength of the evidence, i.e., weak or strong, could not be drawn as needed for each single LSRs. In addition, the inference of one of MPLS policy states is not fully presented which is LR policy state.

Therefore, we need a more suitable probabilistic model that updates the state of MPLS policy engine according to the received knowledge about each hypothesis or evidence node. The problem of finding the MPLS policy states of LSRs of a targeted MPLS network is likely to be a target recognition problem. Target recognition is improved by considering all available sources of data [13]. We refer the reader to [5] for more information about target recognition networks.

The target recognition network that we introduce here is extended to use the past knowledge, also, we assume more than one state that depends on the status of another. Unlike the causal probability model introduced in the later section,

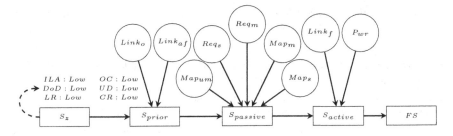

Fig. 3. MPLS policy recognition network

our MPLS policy recognition network updates the policy state of other LSRs depending on a limited information received from a specific LSR in case the observation point is limited, e.g., a single compromised link in the MPLS network. For example, if a Map_{um} message is received there's a higher probability that all of the LSRs included in the TLV header are running on UD policy.

In our MPLS policy recognition network, the MPLS policy engine has six variables which represent the MPLS policy states, i.e., ILA, OC, DoD, UD, LR and CR. Each variable could be set to one of three values, i.e., low, medium, high which represent the probability degree of that state. The MPLS policy engine state starts in the initial zero state S_z where every variable in S_z is set to low as shown in Fig. 3. The MPLS policy engine state is updated on three stages by testifying the current believe against the new received evidence. Each one of the evidence nodes has two values, i.e., true or false. In the first stage S_{prior}, the state S_z is fed with the prior knowledge about the evidence nodes of UD and DoD policy, i.e., $Link_o$ and $Link_{af}$. After that, the new state that was produced in the first stage is updated to state $S_{passive}$ after interpreting the evidence nodes ($Map_{um}, Req_s, Req_m, Map_m$ and Map_s) passively. The state S_{active} is then generated after sending probes $Link_f, P_{wr}$ in stage three. Finally, the final state FS is produced. The current possible state of each MPLS policy will be updated according to the received knowledge as stated in our updating law below.

Updating Law: Because there are different strengths of evidence for MPLS policy states as well as the exceptions in LDP specification that allow LSRs to implement two different policy states at the same time as mentioned previously in Sect. 4.3, we need an accurate updating law to govern policy state updating procedure whenever a recent evidence is revealed as follows:

- If the revealed evidence is a strong evidence, the related policy state is updated to probability degree $High$ by procedure $UpdateStrong$.
- If the revealed evidence is a weak evidence, the related policy state is increased by one degree by procedure $UpdateWeak$.
- The opposite state of the same policy that is related to the revealed evidence is only updated if the current state is set to probability degree $High$ by procedure $UpdateOpposite$. Hence, any single weak evidence that could be

caused by LDP exception behaviour has no implication on probability belief of the opposite policy state, unless it was supported by another weak evidence.

Policy Target Recognition Algorithm: In order to use the introduced policy recognition network for LSRs policy state inference effectively, we use the following inference algorithm. Our algorithm takes the LDP messages as an input and returns the MPLS policy engine state of the LSRs. It starts with the initialisation stage followed by the three phases of the MPLS policy target recognition network and finally ends with the finalisation part before returning the final state of MPLS policy engine for the LSRs. The overall complexity of this algorithm is $\mathcal{O}(n^2)$, mainly because each LSR entry is checked in some LDP messages.

Algorithm Policy Reveal Algorithm

Require: LDP messages LDP_m on the compromised link(s) and/or some static information
Ensure: The policy state of LSRs $FS[n][6]$ ▷ n=number of LSRs in network, 6= number of MPLS policies

---

Initialisation
1: Declare integer variables n, i, x
2: Declare a string array $FS[n][6]$
3: Declare updating procedures
4: Set all $i \in FS[n][6]$ to Low

Phase 1 - Prior Information
5: Declare integer variables a, b
6: **for each** $Link_{a,b} \in network$ **do**   ▷ a,b = any two connected LSRs
7:   **if** $Link_{a,b} = Link_{af}$ **then**
8:     $FS[a, b][3] = Medium$
9:     $FS[a, b][6] = Medium$
10:   **else if** $Link_{a,b} = Link_o$ **then**
11:     $FS[a, b][4] = Medium$
12:   **end if**
13: **end for**

Phase 2 - Passive Reconnaissance
14: **for all** LDP_m **do**
15:   **if** $LDP_m = Req_m$ **then**
16:     $i = TLV_{[1]}, x = 2$
17:     UPDATESTRONG(i, x)
18:     UPDATEOPPOSITE(i, x)
19:   **else if** $LDP_m = Map_m$ **then**
20:     **if** $e \notin Map_m$ **then**   ▷ e = the FEC egress
21:       $x = 1$
22:       **for all** $i \in TLV$ **do**
23:         UPDATESTRONG(i, x)
24:         UPDATEOPPOSITE(i, x)
25:       **end for**
26:     **end if**
27:     **if** $Req_{id} \notin Map_m$ **then**
28:       **for all** $i \in TLV$ **do**
29:         $x = 4$
30:         UPDATEWEAK(i, x)
31:         UPDATEOPPOSITE(i, x)
32:       **end for**
33:     **else**
34:       **for all** $i \in TLV$ **do**
35:         $x = 3$
36:         UPDATEWEAK(i, x)
37:         UPDATEOPPOSITE(i, x)
38:       **end for**
39:     **end if**

```
40:    else if LDP_m = Map_s then
41:        i = TLV_{[1]}
42:        x = 1
43:        if i ≠ e then
44:            UpdateStrong(i, x)
45:            UpdateOpposite(i, x)
46:            if Req_id ∈ Map_s then
47:                x = 3
48:                UpdateWeak(i, x)
49:                UpdateOpposite(i, x)
50:            else if Req_id ∉ Map_s then
51:                x = 4
52:                UpdateWeak(i, x)
53:                UpdateOpposite(i, x)
54:            end if
55:        end if
56:    else if LDP_m = Map_{um} then
57:        if e ∉ Map_{um} then
58:            for all i ∈ TLV do
59:                x = 1
60:                UpdateStrong(i, x)
61:                UpdateOpposite(i, x)
62:                x = 4
63:                UpdateWeak(i, x)
64:                UpdateOpposite(i, x)
65:            end for
66:        end if
67:    else if LDP_m = Req_s then
68:        i = TLV_{[1]}
69:        if F[i][4] = Low then
70:            x = 3
71:            UpdateWeak(i, x)
72:            UpdateOpposite(i, x)
73:        end if
74:    end if
75: end for
```

Phase 3 - Active Reconnaissance

```
76: do(Link_f := True)                                    ▷ Send Link_f probe
77: x = 6
78: for all Map do
79:     if 0s ≤ Map_{time} − Link_{f_{time}} ≤ 10s then
80:         if Req_id ∉ Map then
81:             for all i ∈ TLV do
82:                 UpdateWeak(i, x)
83:                 UpdateOpposite(i, x)
84:             end for
85:         end if
86:     end if
87: end for
88: for all Req do
89:     if 0s ≤ Req_{time} − Link_{f_{time}} ≤ 10s then
90:         x = 6
91:         for all i ∈ TLV do
92:             UpdateWeak(i, x)
93:             UpdateOpposite(i, x)
94:         end for
95:     end if
96: end for
97: do(P_{wr} := True)                                    ▷ Send P_{wr} probes
98: for all Req do
99:     if P_{wr_{fec}} = Req_{fec} then       ▷ If the request message is for the same effected FEC
100:        if 0s ≤ Req_{time} − P_{wr_{time}} ≤ 10s then
101:            if Req = Req_m then
102:                Execute lines 16 to 18
103:            else if Req = Req_s then
104:                Execute lines 68 to 73
```

```
105:            end if
106:          end if
107:        end if
108:  end for
109:  for all Map do
110:      if P_wr_fec = Map_fec then
111:          if 0s ≤ Map_time − P_wr_time ≤ 10s then
112:              if Map = Map_m then
113:                  Execute lines 20 to 39
114:              else if Map = Map_s then
115:                  Execute lines 41 to 55
116:              else if Map = Map_um then
117:                  Execute lines 57 to 66
118:              end if
119:          end if
120:      end if
121:  end for
```

Phase 4 - Finalisation

```
122:  for all i ∈ n do
123:      if (FS[i][3] = High ∨ medium) ∧ (FS[i][4] = Low) then
124:          x = 6
125:          UPDATEWEAK(i, x)
126:      end if
127:  end for
128:  return FS
```

In the initialisation part of the algorithm, variables n, i, x are initialised where variable n refers to the number of LSRs in MPLS network, i refers to the sequential number for the current LSR which we assume here is identical to the current LSR's ID and x refers to the sequential number of the current MPLS policy in question. Also, the final state array $FS[n][6]$ is initialised where 6 is the number of MPLS policy engine states. It should be noted that each state of MPLS policy engine is assigned to a sequential number as following: $ILA = 1$, $OC = 2$, $DoD = 3$, $UD = 4$, $LR = 5$ and $CR = 6$. Also, the updating procedures are declared according to our updating law. There are three updating procedures. Procedures UpdateStrong and UpdateWeak update FS array according to the received strong or weak evidence respectively. On the other hand, procedure UpdateOpposite updates the opposite policy state of the current policy according to our updating law. In phase 1 of the algorithm, the available prior knowledge about MPLS network links is processed and so the FS array is updated accordingly. Then, the algorithm shifts to phase 2 where the LDP messages are checked and the FS array is updated again according to the type and the strength of the received evidence. In phase 3, the probes are sent on the compromised link or links and the related LDP messages are checked again, then the FS array is updated accordingly. Firstly, the link failure probe $Link_f$ is sent and every map message is checked if it was sent due to the $Link_f$ probe by using a time estimation equation in line 79 of the algorithm. Consequently, any LSR sent or forwarded a map message independently, i.e., not upon a request, is probably has CR policy state. Also, the same thing applies to request messages. Then, probes P_{wr} are sent and the same former procedure is used here to identify the correct map and request messages. Consequently, the related functions are recalled depending on which type is the generated LDP message. After that, the correlation relationship between MPLS policy state DoD and CR is drawn in line 123 of the algorithm and the FS array is updated accordingly. Finally, the MPLS policy final state FS of all LSRs is returned.

5   Experiment

In this section, we are going to run an experiment using a network simulation tools to testify the ability of our policy recognition algorithm to gain information about the LSRs current policy state. We use NS-2 [11] network simulator to simulate MPLS networks. Firstly, the simulation network model and scenarios are introduced in Sects. 5.1 and 5.3 respectively. In Sect. 5.2, an adversary model is introduced for experimental purposes. Finally, the results are shown in Sect. 5.4.

5.1   Network Model

We consider a typical MPLS network. The network topology is structured as a map for Darkstrand network that was chosen only for clarity purposes from Topology Zoo project for data network topologies collection [14] as shown in Fig. 4. Also, we consider the MPLS network to be stable. There is no addition or removal of LSRs or changing of LSRs location according to FECs during the adversarial event. Each LSR is trusted to treat LDP messages as expected and act upon them. There is at most one link connecting each peer LSRs and all Links are bidirectional. The network is assumed to working properly at the adversarial event. So, there is no channel errors or packet loss. There are 28 LSRs where LSR-1 and LSR-28 are the edges of the network. There are one source of data traffic as well as one destination connected to each one of the network edges. Therefore, we assume that each edge is configured as a network ingress and egress at the same time according to MPLS flows.

5.2   Adversary Model

We are going to extract a restricted adversary model which we refer to as $\mathcal{A}$ by following the same method that was introduced by Al-Mutairi, and Wolthusen [15] to extract MPLS adversary models as following:

- **Adversary knowledge:** $\mathcal{A}$ has knowledge about the physical and logical topology information. Specifically, $\mathcal{A}$ knows the ingress and egress LSRs for the MPLS network which is considered as physical topology information. Also, we assume $\mathcal{A}$ to know the logical ingress and egress as well as the logical upstream and downstream LSRs for FEC where the next hop to a LSR is not necessarily the next hop for a packet. Additionally, $\mathcal{A}$ is assumed to know at least one of FECs that passes through the compromised links.
- **Intervention Type:** $\mathcal{A}$ has access to the link between LSR-8 and LSR-9.
- **Intervention Operation:** $\mathcal{A}$ has a Read/write operation on the compromised link.

- **Multi-intervention:** $\mathcal{A}$ coordinates with an observer who has a read operation to the link between LSR-14 and LSR-15 as well as the link between LSR-24 and LSR-25.
- **Capabilities:** $\mathcal{A}$ can fabricate and send P_{wr} signals as well as link failure notification messages to the upstream/downstream LSRs.

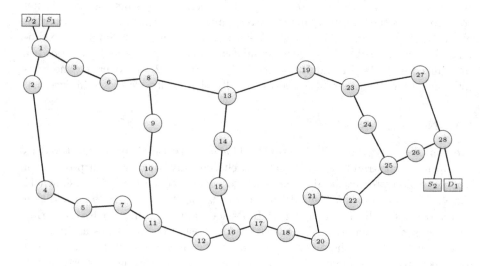

Fig. 4. MPLS network topology

5.3   Simulation Scenarios:

Unfortunately, our simulation tool does not support OC policy with UD policy, also the simulation tool does not support LR policy. Therefore, we configured all LSRs with the three states of policies in three different scenarios. In the first scenario, MPLS policy engine has the following policy states: OC, DoD and CR. In the second scenario, ILA, UD and CR policy states. And in the third scenario, ILA, DoD and CR policy states.

There are four flows (1a, 1b, 2a, 2b) in all of the previous three scenarios. Each two flows following the same path but in different directions. Flows 1a and 1b traverse the path on LSRs 1-3-6-8-9-10-11-12-16-15-14-13-19-23-24-25-26-28 from source S_1 to destination D_1 and from source S_2 to destination D_2 respectively. While, flows 2b and 2b traverse the path on 1-2-4-5-7-11-10-9-8-13-14-15-16-17-18-20-21-22-25-24-23-27 from source S_1 to destination D_1 and from source S_2 to destination D_2 respectively. In each of the previously mentioned scenarios, Adversary $\mathcal{A}$ runs the target recognition algorithm and analyses the collected information.

5.4 Results

The results of using the policy recognition network on the simulated network have shown the ability of our method to reveal MPLS policy engine states. The results of the experiment is listed according to the scenario case as follows:

- **In the first scenario:** Adversary $\mathcal{A}$ revealed 64.29 % of the LSRs policy states as shown in Table 1a.
- **In the second scenario:** Adversary $\mathcal{A}$ revealed 66.67 % of the LSRs policy states as shown in Table 1b.
- **In the third scenario:** Adversary $\mathcal{A}$ revealed 21.43 % of the LSRs policy states as shown in Table 1c.

Table 1. LSRs final states

LSR ID	Policy States					
	ILA	OC	DoD	UD	LR	CR
LSR-1	Low	High	Low	Low	Low	Low
LSR-2	Low	Low	Medium	Low	Low	Medium
LSR-3	Low	Low	Medium	Low	Low	Medium
LSR-4	Low	Low	Medium	Low	Low	Medium
LSR-5	Low	Low	Medium	Low	Low	Medium
LSR-6	Low	Low	Medium	Low	Low	Medium
LSR-7	Low	Low	Medium	Low	Low	Medium
LSR-8	Low	Low	High	Low	Low	Medium
LSR-8	Low	Low	High	Low	Low	Medium
LSR-9	Low	Low	High	Low	Low	Medium
LSR-10	Low	Low	High	Low	Low	Medium
LSR-11	Low	Low	High	Low	Low	Medium
LSR-12	Low	Low	High	Low	Low	Medium
LSR-13	Low	Low	High	Low	Low	Medium
LSR-14	Low	Low	High	Low	Low	Medium
LSR-15	Low	Low	High	Low	Low	Medium
LSR-16	Low	Low	High	Low	Low	Medium
LSR-17	Low	Low	High	Low	Low	Medium
LSR-18	Low	Low	High	Low	Low	Medium
LSR-19	Low	Low	High	Low	Low	Medium
LSR-20	Low	Low	High	Low	Low	Medium
LSR-21	Low	Low	High	Low	Low	Medium
LSR-22	Low	Low	High	Low	Low	Medium
LSR-23	Low	Low	High	Low	Low	Medium
LSR-24	Low	Low	High	Low	Low	Medium
LSR-25	Low	Low	High	Low	Low	Medium
LSR-26	Low	Low	Medium	Low	Low	Medium
LSR-27	Low	Low	Medium	Low	Low	Medium
LSR-28	Low	High	Low	Low	Low	Low

(a) First Scenario

LSR ID	Policy States					
	ILA	OC	DoD	UD	LR	CR
LSR-1	High	Low	Low	High	Low	Low
LSR-2	High	Low	Low	High	Low	Low
LSR-3	High	Low	Low	High	Low	Low
LSR-4	High	Low	Low	High	Low	Low
LSR-5	High	Low	Low	High	Low	Low
LSR-6	High	Low	Low	High	Low	Low
LSR-7	High	Low	Low	High	Low	Low
LSR-8	High	Low	Low	High	Low	Low
LSR-9	High	Low	Low	High	Low	Low
LSR-10	High	Low	Low	High	Low	Low
LSR-11	High	Low	Low	High	Low	Low
LSR-12	High	Low	Low	High	Low	Low
LSR-13	High	Low	Low	High	Low	Low
LSR14	High	Low	Low	High	Low	Low
LSR-15	High	Low	Low	High	Low	Low
LSR-16	High	Low	Low	High	Low	Low
LSR-17	High	Low	Low	High	Low	Low
LSR-18	High	Low	Low	High	Low	Low
LSR-19	High	Low	Low	High	Low	Low
LSR-20	High	Low	Low	High	Low	Low
LSR-21	High	Low	Low	High	Low	Low
LSR-22	High	Low	Low	High	Low	Low
LSR-23	High	Low	Low	High	Low	Low
LSR-24	High	Low	Low	High	Low	Low
LSR-25	High	Low	Low	High	Low	Low
LSR-26	High	Low	Low	High	Low	Low
LSR-27	High	Low	Low	High	Low	Low
LSR-28	High	Low	Low	High	Low	Low

(b) Second Scenario

LSR ID	Policy States					
	ILA	OC	DoD	UD	LR	CR
LSR-8	High	Low	High	Low	Low	Medium
LSR-9	High	Low	High	Low	Low	Medium
LSR-14	High	Low	High	Low	Low	Medium
LSR-15	High	Low	High	Low	Low	Medium
LSR-24	High	Low	High	Low	Low	Medium
LSR-25	High	Low	High	Low	Low	Medium

(c) Third Scenario

It should be noted that the location of the accessed link has no significant implication on the simulation outcome unlike the number of accessed links which would obviously increase the exposed area for the adversary. Indeed, these results were produced with a tight limitation on the adversary model and the available information that the adversary could capture is less than it would be in such environment were LSRs are more likely assumed to communicate for traffic services needs as well as the liveness of LSRs purpose. Also, there was no prior information assumed in our simulation which would make additional source of knowledge which changes the uncertainty about LSRs MPLS states. Consequently, the introduced policy target recognition network is supposed to be more accurate and efficient if one of the assumed models was relaxed, e.g., adversary model.

6 Conclusions

In this paper we introduced a policy recognition policy algorithm to reveal MPLS policy engine states. Firstly, we introduced a causal network for MPLS policy state and their possible evidence. A policy recognition network associated with an inference algorithm based on the introduced causal network was designed. Finally, an experiment was implemented using the MPLS policy recognition network to reveal the MPLS policy engine states of a simulated network. The MPLS policy recognition network was clearly accurate and capable of revealing the policy states of all LSRs in the simulated MPLS network. Future work will be to misuse the knowledge about MPLS policy engine state in more malicious attacks.

References

1. Sanzotta, M.A., Sherrill, E.T.: Approximation probability of detection in the Janus model. Technical report, DTIC Document (1997)
2. Lampis, M.: Application of Bayesian Belief Networks to system fault diagnostics. Ph.D. thesis, Mariapia Lampis (2010)
3. Dawsey, W.J., Minsker, B.S., VanBlaricum, V.L.: Bayesian belief networks to integrate monitoring evidence of water distribution system contamination. J. Water Resour. Plan. Manag. **132**(4), 234–241 (2006)
4. Al-Mutairi, A., Wolthusen, S.: Malicious MPLS policy engine reconnaissance. In: De Decker, C.M.S., Zúquete, A. (eds.) CMS 2014. LNCS, vol. 8735, pp. 3–18. Springer, Heidelberg (2014)
5. Krieg, M.L.: A tutorial on Bayesian belief networks. Technical report, Defence Science and Technology Organisation (2001)
6. Caesar, M., Rexford, J.: BGP routing policies in ISP networks. IEEE Netw. **19**(6), 5–11 (2005)
7. Awduchea, D.O., Jabbarib, B.: Internet traffic engineering using multi-protocol label switching (MPLS). Comput. Netw. **40**(1), 111–129 (2002)
8. Rosen, E., Viswanathan, A., Callon, R.: Multiprotocol label switching architecture. IETF, RFC 3031 (2001)
9. Andersson, L., Doolan, P., Feldman, N., Fredette, A., Thomas, B.: LDP specification, October 2007

10. Koller, D., Friedman, N.: Probabilistic Graphical Models: Principles and Techniques. MIT Press, Cambridge (2009)
11. NS-2. http://www.isi.edu/nsnam/ns/
12. Davie, B.S., Farrel, A.: MPLS: Next Steps. Morgan Kaufmann Publishers Inc., San Francisco (2008)
13. Stewart, L., McCarty Jr., P.: Use of bayesian belief networks to fuse continuous and discrete information for target recognition, tracking, and situation assessment. In: Aerospace Sensing, International Society for Optics and Photonics, pp. 177–185 (1992)
14. Zoo, T.I.T. http://www.topology-zoo.org
15. Al-Mutairi, A., Wolthusen, S.D.: A security analysis of mpls service degradation attacks based on restricted adversary models. In: Kayem, A. (ed.) Information Security in Diverse Computing Environments. IGI Global, Hershey (2014)

Risk Management

Context Aware Intrusion Response
Based on Argumentation Logic

Tarek Bouyahia[✉], Fabien Autrel, Nora Cuppens-Boulahia,
and Frédéric Cuppens

Télécom-Bretagne, 35576 Cesson-Sévigné, France
{tarek.bouyahia,fabien.autrel,nora.cuppens,
frederic.cuppens}@telecom-bretagne.eu

Abstract. Automatic response in an intrusion detection process is a difficult problem. Indeed activating an inappropriate countermeasure for a given attack can have deleterious effects on the system which must be protected. In some cases the countermeasure can be more harmful than the attack it is targeted against. Moreover, given an attack against a specific system, the best countermeasure to apply depends on the context in which the system is operating. For example in the case of an automotive system, the fact that the vehicle is operating downtown or on a freeway changes the impact an attack may have on the system. This paper introduces a novel approach which uses an argumentative logic framework to reason and select the most appropriate countermeasure given an attack and its context.

Keywords: Intrusion detection · Context aware reaction · Argumentative logic · Security policy

1 Introduction

Designing a secure system has always been a complex exercise, because the challenge of modern security systems is not only to maintain system in safety conditions, but also to ensure the best possible level of performance and quality of service. We believe that the security process must be based on a smart reasoning which allows the system, according to a detected attack, to apply the suitable decision and to preview the potential related actions that may occur. For instance, we consider a single physical server hosting a set of services such as an HTTP server, an SSH server and a database server. An attacker can detect those services by scanning the open ports for example, then try to fingerprint those services to check if a known vulnerable version is running. From the detection point of view, detecting the port scanning and fingerprinting can be used to formulate hypotheses on the future attacks the attacker may perform on those services and select appropriate countermeasures against the inferred attack scenario. However the attacker may decide to modify his/her intrusion objectives, because he/she does not have the tools to attack the detected services

© Springer International Publishing Switzerland 2016
C. Lambrinoudakis and A. Gabillon (Eds.): CRiSIS 2015, LNCS 9572, pp. 91–106, 2016.
DOI: 10.1007/978-3-319-31811-0_6

for instance. In such case the attacker may execute new attacks corresponding to a new intrusion objective. From the detection point of view, this means that the reaction plan inferred from the first attack is no longer valid and must be revised in the light of the newly detected attacks. For mobile systems, such as those which are present in vehicles, the environment in which they operate can evolve as they move and impact the reasoning process.

In this paper, we present an approach for monitoring systems that allows the system user to choose the best intrusion response among all appropriate intrusion responses possibilities and which considers the current context on which the system is operating. This approach is driven by argumentative logic (AL) [1]. The purpose of this approach is to give a dynamic aspect to the intrusion response process of attacked systems that may operate while different contexts are active. The security system will be able to take the suitable decision, against any scenario of attack, and which ensure the system safety while satisfying the prioritized system requirements. The paper is organized as follows: Sect. 2 explains how we model the intrusion process. Section 3 introduces existing argumentation frameworks. Section 4 explains our approach to construct the set of arguments set corresponding to an attack scenario, and defines our new framework which is an extension of the value based argumentation framework. We present deployment scenarios highlighting how our approach is applied in the use case of automotive system in Sect. 5. Section 6 presents related works. Section 7 concludes the paper and outlines future work.

2   Modeling the Intrusion Processes

The attacker is modeled as an agent which can choose from a set of actions a subset to execute in order to reach one or several intrusion objectives. The set of actions executed by an attacker can be organized in a scenario of correlated actions. Informally, by correlated actions we mean that in an intrusion scenario, some action effects makes other actions possible. From the attacked system point of view, given a set of observed actions organized into an attack scenario, reacting against an ongoing attack consists in selecting a set of countermeasures which modifies the system state to stop the attack progression or mitigate its effects.

2.1   Modeling the Attacker

We use the Lambda formalism [2, 3] to model the intrusion process. In our context, we consider that several probes are distributed in the monitored system to generate events which corresponds to actions executed by the agents acting on the system. Those agents can be legitimate users as well as malicious agents. The probes can be intrusion detection users [4] or programs monitoring system logs for interesting events.

Actions. We generalize the notion of Lambda attack to the notion of Lambda action as some of the actions an attacker execute do not have malicious effects on the attacked system, i.e. their effects do not violate the security policy of the system. A Lambda action description is composed of the following elements:

Definition 1. *Lambda action*
name: the action name
pre-condition: *defines the state of the system required for the execution of the action.*
post-condition: *defines the state of the system after the successful execution of the action.*
detection: *is a description of the expected alert corresponding to the detection of the attack.*

The detection attribute may be empty as some actions cannot be detected by probes. For example the modification of a file in the file system may not be logged. Although it is technically possible, for example on Linux systems using the audit infrastructure, logging such events for every components of a system may result in generating too many events and flood the process responsible for reasoning on possible intrusions on the system.

The pre-condition and post-condition are written using conjunctions of literals, a literal being defined as follows:

- a constant is a string starting with a lower case character or a number
- a variable is a string starting with an upper case letter
- a term is either a constant, a variable or a functional symbol over a list of terms
- a literal is a predicate symbol over a list of terms expressing a boolean property.

The detection attribute is written as a list of affectations of values to a subset of the free variables in the pre-condition. An action model is instantiated, i.e. values are assigned to the list of free variables in the pre-condition, when a new alert is generated. Predefined function symbols corresponding to alert attributes are used to specify the detection field. The alert contains the name of the Lambda model to instantiate if such model exists.

Literals with specific semantics are defined. The literal *not*, of arity one, models the negation. The literal *knows* of arity two models the fact that an agent has some knowledge: $knows(a, b)$ means that agent a knows that b is true. The set of Lambda action models is called $\mathcal{A}$.

Correlation Between Actions. An attacker may executes several actions to modify the system state in order to reach a state where the security policy is violated. Some actions are executed in order to make the execution of other actions possible. When the effects of an action are a subset of the pre-conditions of another action, we say that the two actions are correlated. More formally, the notion of correlation between two Lambda actions is defined as follows:

Definition 2. *Let a and b be two Lambda descriptions of actions, post(a) is the set of literals of the post-condition of a and pre(b) is the set of literals of pre-condition of b.*
Correlation: *a and b are correlated if the following condition is satisfied:*
$\exists E_a$ *and* E_b *such that*

- *($E_a \in post(a) \land E_b \in pre(b))or(not(E_a) \in post(a) \land not(E_b) \in pre(b)$)*
- E_a *and* E_b *are unifiable through a most general unifier u.*

Given a set of Lambda action models, searching for such correlation links between action models results in a set of correlation rules. A correlation rule is a triple $\{A, B, u\}$, which represents the fact that model A is correlated with model B through the most general unifier u.

Correlation Between Instantiated Actions. An action model is instantiated by assigning values to the free variables in the pre-condition. This is done by evaluating the detection field but this may not be sufficient to assign values to all variables. The rest of the free variables are instantiated through unification with the system state, the system state being represented by a conjunction of literals with no free variables. More formally, an action model instance is a couple composed of the instantiated model and a finite substitution σ. The instance number i of action model A, denoted A_i, is $A_i = \{A, \sigma\}$. An instantiated action A_1 instance of model A and an instantiated action B_1 instance of model B are correlated iff A and B are correlated and if the corresponding unifier is satisfied. Correlated actions, models or instances, can be represented as graphs [5]. The set of action instances if denoted $\mathcal{A}_i$.

Intrusion Objectives. An intrusion objective represents a state in which the system security policy is violated. An intrusion objective model description is composed of the following elements:

Definition 3. *Lambda intrusion objective*
name: *the objective name*
condition: *defines the state of the system in which the system security policy is violated.*

The condition is a conjunction of literals representing a violation of the security policy. Actions can be correlated with intrusion objectives using the same principle as in Definition 2 by replacing the $pre(b)$ set of literals by the intrusion objective condition.

2.2 Anticipating the Attacker Intentions

Anticipating the intentions of the attacker consists in generating sequences of virtual action instances, i.e. actions not instantiated from alerts, so that the set of action instances created from alerts unified with the set of virtual action instances is correlated with an intrusion objective. The generation of such virtual actions is described in [5].

2.3   Intrusion Scenario

An intrusion scenario is defined as a set of correlated action instances correlated with an intrusion objective as defined in [5]. The set of scenarios constructed from the set of action instances is denoted $\mathcal{S}$. We define the $hyp : \mathcal{S} \rightarrow \mathcal{A}_i$ function which returns the set of hypotheses in a scenario.

2.4   Modeling Countermeasures

Countermeasures are actions which are executed to mitigate the effects of an attack or prevent the execution of other attacks. More generally, they are actions which have a negative effect on the execution of other actions. More formally, we model a countermeasure the same way an action is modeled except that its detection field is empty. A countermeasure is not instantiated from an alert, values are assigned to its free variables by examining the effects it must have on the system state in order to mitigate the effects of an attack or prevent the execution of other attacks. The notion of anti-correlation formalizes the notion of negative effect.

Anti-correlation Between Actions. The notion of anti-correlation between two Lambda actions is defined as follows:

Definition 4. *Let a and b be two Lambda descriptions of actions, post(a) is the set of literals of the post-condition of a and pre(b) is the set of literals of pre-condition of b.*
***Anti-correlation:** a and b are anti-correlated if the following condition is satisfied:*
$\exists E_a$ *and* E_b *such that*

- $(E_a \in post(a) \wedge not(E_b) \in pre(b))or(not(E_a) \in post(a) \wedge E_b \in pre(b))$
- E_a *and* E_b *are unifiable through a most general unifier u.*

Given a set of Lambda action models, searching for such anti-correlation links between action models results in a set of anti-correlation rules. An anti-correlation rule is a triple $\{A, B, u\}$, which represents the fact that model A is anti-correlated with model B through the most general unifier u.

We also define the notion of anti-correlation between an action and an intrusion objective by replacing the $pre(b)$ set of literals by the intrusion objective condition in Definition 4. We introduce the $anticor$ binary relationship to express that two action models or action instances are anti-correlated. If A and B are anti-correlated, then $(A, B) \in anticor$, which can also be represented by the fact that $anticor(A, B)$ is true.

Instantiating Countermeasures. Given a scenario of instantiated actions correlated to an intrusion objective, we can create a set of countermeasures instances anti-correlated with either virtual actions or virtual intrusion objectives. Since a countermeasure is not instantiated from an alert, the free variables in its precondition and postcondition are instantiated using the unifier in the anti-correlation rule used to select the countermeasure.

3 Argumentation Frameworks

Argumentation frameworks [1,6] (AF) have been applied successfully to formalize non monotonic reasoning among other forms of reasoning. In the context of intrusion detection, the process of reacting against attacks can be seen as a form of non monotonic reasoning. Actually, given a set of detected attacks, it is possible to reason on the state of the system, described as in Sect. 2.1, to choose countermeasures to apply among a set of possible reactions [3,7]. As shown in the attack example presented in Sect. 1, the set of countermeasures selected for an attack can evolve as new attacks are observed or if the system state evolves.

An argumentation framework such as defined by Dung [1] is a pair $\langle AR, attacks \rangle$ where AR is a set of arguments and $attacks$ a relationship over $AR \times AR$. For two arguments A_1 and A_2, $attacks(A_1, A_2)$ means that A_1 represents an attack on A_2. In this approach, arguments are abstracted into entities whose role is solely determined by their relation to other arguments. In such frameworks, attacking arguments have the same force. When two arguments attack each other, it is not possible to decide which one should be preferred. This fact has been addressed in [8] where the author extends ARs to define Value-based Argumentation Frameworks ($VAFs$). The author argues that in many contexts the soundness of an argument is not the only consideration and that arguments have also a force.

A VAF is a 5-tuple $\langle AR, attacks, V, val, valpref \rangle$ where AR and $attacks$ have the same definition as in a standard AF, V is a non-empty set of values, val is a function which maps elements from AR to elements of V and $valpref$ is a transitive, irreflexive and asymmetric preference relation. $valpref$ defines the order relationship over the forces of the arguments. The purpose of this extension of standard AFs is to distinguish between two arguments attacking each other and that one argument defeats another one. The attacked argument is then said to be defeated. More formally, an argument $A_1 \in AR$ defeats an argument $A_2 \in AR$ iff $attacks(A_1, A_2) \wedge \neg valpref(val(A_2), val(A_1))$.

The next section shows how $VAFs$ can be used and extended in the context of reaction against attacks on an information system.

4 Argumented Intrusion Response Against Attacks

In the context of intrusion detection, we believe that the process of reasoning on the observed attacks against a system to select the most adapted countermeasure for a given attack can be modeled as an argumentation process using a VAF.

We think that modeling the attack and reaction processes using the semi-explicit correlation approach can be seen as two agents arguing against each other. On one side the attacker chooses his arguments, a set of actions, to try to reach an intrusion objective, and on the other side the agent defending the target chooses his arguments, a set of countermeasures, to block the attacker progress or mitigate the attack effects. We argue that the anti-correlation relationship between two Lambda model instances can be seen as an attack relationship over arguments.

Since we model the argumentation process using a VAF, a force, called here rationale, is associated with every action model. We add an extra element to an action model, the *rationale* attribute. This attribute models the reason motivating the execution of an action. From the attacker point of view, this reason is related to the success of the attack. For example the reason associated with the action of fingerprinting an operating system is to find vulnerabilities. From the point of view of the agent defending the system, the reason associated with the execution of a countermeasure is related to restoring some properties of the system. For example adding a filtering rule to a firewall to block a host which connected to a server containing sensible information is associated with the *confidentiality* reason.

4.1   Constructing the Set of Arguments

The set of Lambda models Λ is the union of the Lambda action models set, $\mathcal{A}$ and the Lambda intrusion objective models set, $\mathcal{O}$, i.e. $\Lambda = \mathcal{A} \cup \mathcal{O}$. We denote by $\mathcal{A}_i$ and $\mathcal{O}_i$ respectively the sets of action instances and intrusion objective instances. Then $\Lambda_i = \mathcal{A}_i \cup \mathcal{O}_i$ is the set of all Lambda model instances. We denote by $\mathcal{L}$ the logic of predicates which is used to express the pre-condition, post-condition and system state condition of the action, reaction and intrusion objective models. The function $model : \Lambda_i \rightarrow \Lambda$ returns the Lambda model corresponding to a Lambda model instance. For an intrusion objective, the function $cond : \Lambda \rightarrow \mathcal{L}$ returns its system state condition.

Given an intrusion scenario S, constructed as specified in Sect. 2.3, and the set of countermeasures C computed for S, we build the set of arguments used to reason as the union of the two sets:

Definition 5. *Argument set: the set $\mathcal{AR}(S)$ of arguments corresponding to an intrusion scenario S contains all the Lambda model instances of S plus all the Lambda countermeasures instances anti-correlated with the hypotheses of S: $\mathcal{AR}(S) = S \cup \{cm \mid \forall h \in hyp(S), (anticor(post(cm), pre(h)) \lor anticor(post(cm), cond(h))) \land model(cm) \in (\mathcal{A} \cup \mathcal{O})\}$.*

Now that we know how to build the set of arguments corresponding to an intrusion scenario, we define the attack relationship *attacks* between arguments:

Definition 6. *Attack relationship: let S be an intrusion scenario and $\mathcal{AR}(S)$ the corresponding set of arguments. Let $a_1 \in \mathcal{AR}(S)$, $a_2 \in \mathcal{AR}(S)$ be two arguments. $attacks(a_1, a_2)$ is true iff $anticor(post(a_1), pre(a_2)) \lor anticor(post(a_1), cond(a_2))$.*

The notions of acceptability, conflict free set, admissible set, preferred extension and stable extension defined by Dung in [1] apply here. However we think that a force should be associated with each argument to correctly model the reaction process against an attack. Actually in our model the effects of a countermeasure are characterized by its effects on the system through the specification of its post-condition but it does not represent the reason why a countermeasure should be chosen. For instance some countermeasures may enhance the performance of an attacked system to the detriment of the availability of some services. If for some reason the performance of the system should be favored over the availability of the services it provides, then we can choose the countermeasure associated to the favorite reason.

According to this modeling, we think that $VAFs$ are well-suited for our problematic since they allow to associate a value to each argument. In a VAF, acceptability, conflict-free set and admissible set [8] using the notion of defeat presented in Sect. 3 are defined as follows:

Definition 7. *Argument $A \in AR$ is acceptable with respect to a set of argument S, acceptable(A, S), if: $(\forall x \in AR \mid defeats(x, A)) \rightarrow (\exists y \in S \mid defeats(y, x))$.*

Definition 8. *A set S of arguments is conflict-free if:*
$\forall x \in S, \forall y \in S, \neg attacks(x, y) \vee valpref(val(y), val(x))$.

Definition 9. *A conflict-free set S of arguments is admissible if:*
$\forall x \in S, acceptable(x, S)$.

The notions of admissible set, preferred extension and stable extension have the same definition as in a AR. However in our case, the order relationship over the rationales associated with each argument is highly dependent on the context in which an attack is detected. For instance if we consider a database server in the intranet of a company, then the availability property may be favored during work time when employees are using it but the performance property shall be preferred outside of working hours when database backups are created.

In the next section we extend $VAFs$ to take into account the contextual aspect of our reasoning.

4.2   Extending Value-Based Argumentation Frameworks

Due to the dynamic nature of information systems, we argue that using a static preference relation $valpref$ is not adapted. We extend the definition of VAF to that of a contextual VAF.

Definition 10. *A contextual value-based argumentation framework, denoted $CVAF$, is a 6-tuple $\langle AR, attacks, V, val, C, ContPref \rangle$ where:*

- *AR, $attacks$, V and val have the same definition as in $VAFs$*
- *C is a set of contexts. A context is either active or inactive. At a given time multiple contexts can be active*

– *ContPref is a transitive, irreflexive and asymmetric preference relation on $V \times V$ which depends on the set of active contexts in C.*

In this model we do not explicit the activation condition for each context in C, we consider that this set is extracted from a contextual security policy specification, such as an OrBAC [9] policy for example. The *ContPref* relation is not defined for every possible combination of active contexts. A default order relation is defined and other definitions are specified for some active context combinations. If no definition is given for some combination of active contexts, then the default order relation applies. *ContPref* has the same definition as the *valpref* used in VAF except that it allows to generate the preference between the arguments forces depending on the current contexts configuration. To define exceptions in priority order for a subject s when a combination of n contexts is active, the system user defines the necessary updated preferences as following:

$$\bigwedge_{j=1}^{n} holds(s, c_j) \rightarrow ContPref(v_1, v_2) \wedge \ldots \wedge ContPref(v_{m-1}, v_m)$$

Where $c_j \in C$ and $v_1, v_2 \ldots v_{m-1}, v_m \in V$. We consider in this paper that the elements of V are rationales that describe the application effect of the countermeasure on the system state. In the next section, we present how the system can take into account the context change during the reaction process.

4.3 Argumented and Context Aware Reaction Mechanism

Given an intrusion scenario, from the point of view of the agent defending the system under attack by another malicious agent, the reaction process consists in choosing among the possible countermeasures the best subset according to his/her preferences, those preferences being encoded in the *ContPref* relation. According to our approach, this consists in using the attack relationship we have defined to build admissible sets of arguments, each set representing a coherent set of candidate countermeasures. Note that we only consider the argumentation process from the defending agent point of view, we do not try to construct extensions corresponding to actions the attacker could make. Taking into account a context change, the system recomputes the admissible extensions according to the updated *ContPref* relation. Building admissible extensions ensures us that they do not contain conflictual countermeasures, which would make the execution of the corresponding set of countermeasure impossible. The system operator manages the detected attacks and chooses the reaction that suits the best the current security state. The operator can choose the reaction among the stable extension of the arguments set $\mathcal{AR}(S)$ corresponding to the considered scenario S which offers the set of countermeasure that mitigate all the possible attacks that may occur on the system. Preferred extensions are maximal sets of arguments (with respect to set inclusion) that defend themselves against all attacks. The preferred extension of $\mathcal{AR}(S)$ is the maximal admissible set of arguments.

The process of countermeasures selection depends on the type of reasoning used by the system operator: The credulous reasoning consists in the selection of countermeasures (arguments) appearing in at least one preferred extension, this offers the system more intrusion response possibilities that may be defeated by other countermeasures. Whereas the skeptic reasoning consists in selecting countermeasures from the grounded extension which present the least (with respect to set inclusion) complete extension. In this kind of reasoning, the selected countermeasure will not be defeated by any other reaction model. We summarize our approach in Algorithms 1 and 2 where we show how the security system generates the arguments set corresponding to a detected attack, and how it constructs the preferred extension.

Algorithm 1. GenerateArgumentsSet(detected_action)

$current\_action \leftarrow detected\_action$
$S \leftarrow current\_action$; $intrusion\_objective\_found \leftarrow false$
do
for all $model \in \mathcal{A} \cup '\mathcal{O}$ **do**
  if $correlated(current\_action, model) == true$ **then**
    if $model \in \mathcal{O}$ **then**
      $S \leftarrow S \cup \{model\}$; $intrusion\_objective\_found \leftarrow true$
    else
      $S \leftarrow S \cup \{model\}$; $current\_action \leftarrow model$
    end if
  end if
end for
while$(intrusion\_objective\_found == false)$
for all $action \in S$ **do**
  for all $reaction \in \mathcal{A}$ **do**
    if $anticorrelated(action, reaction) == true$ **then**
      $\mathcal{C} \leftarrow \mathcal{C} \cup \{reaction\}$
    end if
  end for
end for
$\mathcal{AR} \leftarrow \mathcal{C} \cup S$
$GenerateArgumentsSet(detected\_action) \leftarrow \mathcal{AR}$

In the next section, we show the deployment of our approach in an automotive system using the credulous reasoning.

5   Reaction Process in an Automotive Context

We apply our approach on an automotive system as an example of a case study to explore the issues that can meet complex systems during the reaction process. This use case illustrates the potential need for dynamic enforcement of security requirements to control the various security activities. Modern automotive system consists on one hundred of micro-controllers, called electronic control units (ECU) arranged in the architecture specific areas and connected by bridges as

Algorithm 2. ConstructPreferredExtension(AR,attacks)

---

do
  for all $argument1 \in \mathcal{AR}$ **do**
    for all $argument2 \in \mathcal{AR}$ **do**
      if $\neg defeats(argument2, argument1)$ **then**
        $PreferredExt \leftarrow argument1$
      end if
    end for
  end for
  for all $argument1 \in \mathcal{AR}$ **do**
    for all $argument2 \in PreferredExt$ **do**
      if $defeats(argument2, argument1)$ **then**
        $\mathcal{R} \leftarrow argument1$
      end if
    end for
  end for
  $\mathcal{AR}' \leftarrow \mathcal{AR}/(PreferredExt \cup \mathcal{R})$
  $attacks' \leftarrow attacks/((PreferredExt \times \mathcal{R}) \cup (\mathcal{R} \times \mathcal{AR}) \cup (\mathcal{AR} \times \mathcal{R}))$
  return $PreferredExt \cup ConstructPreferredExtension(\mathcal{AR}', attacks')$
while$(PreferredExt! = \emptyset)$

---

shown in Fig. 1. Most attacks, in automotive system, occur by bypassing the filtering performed between domains or by brute-forcing ECU cryptography-based protection mechanisms [11]. The attacks are mainly originating from the Internet and the Bluetooth connection pairing of a compromised mobile phone situated inside the vehicle.

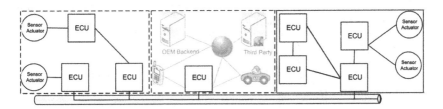

Fig. 1. Automotive on-board network architecture [10]

5.1 Attack Modeling

We consider in this section, that the automotive system detects a malicious action (a1) consisting in cracking the wifi passkey modeled as following:

$name : wifi\_passkey\_crack(A, T)$
$pre :\quad knows(A, role(T, wifi\_gateway)) \wedge knows(A, is\_on(T))$
$post :\quad network\_access(A, T, wifi)$

The system generates the attacks that may be performed by correlation to reach a potential intrusion objective. In the following, we consider the "manipulation of relayed message" as a potential intrusion objective (io1) that the attacker can achieve through the "Message saturation" attack. This intrusion objective is modeled as followed:

> $name$: $manipulation\_relayed\_messages$
> $condition$: $manipulate(A, T)$

Thus the system considers the "message saturation" as an attack hypothesis (h1) which consists in overflowing the ITS server with messages (Denial of service attack). We consider several implementations of this attack: through wifi connection, bluetooth connection or direct connection to the system bus. This attack is modeled as followed:

> $name$: $message\_saturation(A, T, M)$
> pre : $network\_access(A, T, M) \wedge knows(A, role(T, its\_server)) \wedge$
> $knows(A, is\_on(T))$
> $post$: $dos(T)$

Where the access type is held by the M variable. The $role(T, its\_server)$ means that the entity T acts as an ITS server, the meta-predicate $knows(A, role(T, its\_server))$ shows that the attacker A knows this information.

5.2 Response Model

Once the attack scenario is generated, the system selects anti-correlated models that remedy the detected attack, the intrusion objective and all the attack hypothesis. For instance, the system has two intrusion responses against the passkey crack attack in the network: $disable\_wifi$ and $filter\_host$. We model these two countermeasures as the following:

> $name$: $disable\_wifi(A, T)$
> pre : $is\_on(T) \wedge network\_access(A, T, wifi) \wedge is\_on(wifi)$
> $post$: $not(network\_access(A, T, wifi)) \wedge not(is\_on(wifi))$
> $rationale$: $precaution$

The $disable\_wifi$ countermeasure is usually used when critical contexts are active and when we cannot predict the level and the current impact of the detected attack.

> $name$: $filter\_host(A, T)$
> pre : $is\_on(T) \wedge network\_access(A, T, wifi) \wedge is\_on(wifi)$
> $post$: $not(network\_access(A, T, wifi))$
> $rationale$: $availability$

Once the $filter\_host$ countermeasure is applied, the attacker identified by his/her IP address, cannot access the service. Here, we can identify a relation of anti-correlation between these countermeasures ($filter\_host$ requires, in its preconditions, that wifi must be on whereas $disable\_wifi$ turns the wifi off).

5.3   Rationales

We consider three main contexts in the automotive system:

- in_car: context defined to activate or deactivate specific activity in the vehicle
- V2V: context defined to manage communication within vehicles
- V2I: context defined to manage communication between vehicle and infrastructure.

The rationales order is initially defined for the three main contexts. For instance, the rationales order in the *in_car* context is defined as followed:
1. *confidentiality*, 2. *performance*, 3. *availability*, 4. *integrity*, 5. *precaution*.
This rationales order depends on the context on which we reason. For instance, when communicating with external entities like vehicle to infrastructure (*V2I*), it is preferable to apply the traffic filtering rules to limit the computational load which ensure precaution for the system. However, applying such kind of countermeasures in the *in_car* context reduce the performance of the vehicle. When reasoning in a specific main context, extra contexts can become active which may change the rationales order. For instance, in the *in_car* context and the vehicle (a) is in *highway* context the "precaution" rationale becomes more prioritized than "availability" and "integrity", because we become reasoning in a critical context. In a formal way, this exception is defined as following:
$holds(a, highway) \land holds(a, in\_car) \rightarrow$
$ContPref(precaution, availability) \land ContPref(availability, integrity)$.

5.4   Intrusion Response Selection

In this section, we consider the scenario of attack described in Sect. 5.2 we denote it $s1$. Once the system generates the attack scenario $s1$, it selects the appropriate intrusion response for $a1$ and also for potential attacks that may be triggered in coordination [7] with it. The system generates the set of admissible arguments (countermeasures) for the detected and potential attacks. Here, the arguments set $AR(s1)$ content is $AR(s1) = \{a1, h1, io1, r1, r2, r3, r4, r5, r6, r7, r8\}$. Where $r1$: *filter host*, $r2$: *disable wifi*, $r3$: *reduce frequency*, $r4$: *add source identification*, $r5$: *limit message traffic*, $r6$: *digitally sign each message*, $r7$: *include a non_cryptoghraphic checksum*, $r8$: *remove requirements for message relay*. The intrusion response $(r1, r2)$ and $(r2, r8)$ are attacking each other according to the anti-correlation definition ($r1$ and $r8$ need that the wifi connection must be on in their preconditions). $r1$ and $r8$ defeat $r2$ when the system is reasoning in *in_car* context defined by default as shown in Fig. 2a. Defeated countermeasures are presented in gray in Fig. 2. The system generates the preferred extension $Exp=\{r1, r3, r4, r5, r6, r7, r8\}$ which presents the maximal (with respect to set inclusion) admissible set of $AR(s1)$. The generation of the preferred extension depends on the current active contexts. For instance, when reasoning in the *highway* context, the system updates the rationale order as described in the previous section. Thus, the *disable_wifi* countermeasure defeats *filter_host* and *no_cryp_cheksum* since the rationale of $r2$

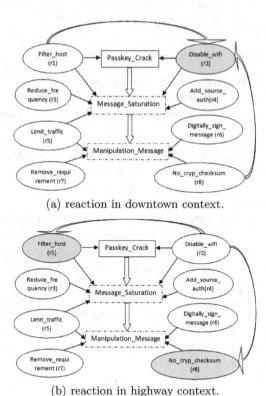

(a) reaction in downtown context.

(b) reaction in highway context.

Fig. 2. Reaction process against crack passkey attack in *in_car* context

which is "precaution" becomes more prioritized than "performance" (the rationale behind $r1$ and $r8$) as shown in the Fig. 2b. The updated preferred extension becomes $Ex_p=\{r2, r3, r4, r5, r6, r7\}$.

6   Related Work

Dung introduces the basics of argumentative logic by defining algebraically the abstract argumentation framework [1]. Argumentation is used in the security field mainly in conflict resolution of the firewall rules. The work done in [12] is based on the general idea of the Dung framework [1], to support the generation of the low-level rules from high-level policies. The argumentation is used in [13] to determine the order of rules which is crucial in the firewall configuration. Because of the big number of firewall rules, the new rules added by firewall administrator are often situated in a bad order which induce certain anomalies. To deal with anomalies that may occur, Kakas used the argumentative logic to prioritize the rules that are shadowed or generalized by other rules. The authors used the Logic Programming with Priorities (LPP) framework which allows preferences to be encoded. Applebaum [14] used a new approach for firewall rules configuration. This approach is based on the definition of rationales for each firewall rule, these rationales will then be sorted in order of priority to resolve any conflicts that may exist. In [14] Applebaum defines a static order of priorities for the rationales behind the firewall rules. However, administrators can decide in specific cases to change the order of rationales priority. In this case, firewall administrators are obliged to update the firewall configuration for each required change in order priorities. In our previous work [15], we provide a general approach for security system and we give a dynamic aspect to the approach of Appleabaum; the order of rationales depends on the context on which we reason. In this paper, we extend the value-based framework introduced by Bench-Capon in [16] to a contextual value-based framework that take into account the contexts change. More related to our work, the authors in [17] propose to use the Abstract Argumentation Frameworks (AAFs) and to associate the system decision and decision manipulation with a score that enables solution optimization. In [18] the authors suggest the use of argumentation to provide automated support for security decisions and in reconfiguration problem, to diagnose the root cause of security attack, and to set policies.

7 Conclusion and Future Works

In order to protect a system from modern attacks, it is necessary to have a dynamic and intelligent enforcement of security policies. We consider the argumentative logic driven system the most appropriate to achieve this objective. We have proposed an approach based on the argumentative logic and modeled via Lambda models which ensures the automatic reaction for security system. This approach considers the different active contexts on which the system is operating. In this work we showed how to improve the existing argumentation framework. We proposed a new approach that allows us to take the suitable and dynamic decisions that maintain the system in safe conditions while satisfying the prioritized system requirements. In our future works, an approach that reasons on the cost of each countermeasure can be considered by defining the cost and the impact of different reaction possibilities as well as the restore time of each countermeasure applied.

References

1. Dung, P.M.: On the acceptability of arguments and its fundamental role in non-monotonic reasoning, logic programming and n-person games. Artif. Intell. **77**(2), 321–357 (1995)
2. Cuppens, F., Ortalo, R.: LAMBDA: a language to model a database for detection of attacks. In: Debar, H., Mé, L., Wu, S.F. (eds.) RAID 2000. LNCS, vol. 1907, pp. 197–216. Springer, Heidelberg (2000)
3. Cuppens, F., Autrel, F., Bouzida, Y., García, J., Gombault, S., Sans, T.: Anti-correlation as a criterion to select appropriate counter-measures in an intrusion detection framework. Annales des Télécommunications **61**(1–2), 197–217 (2006)

4. Axelsson, S.: Intrusion detection systems: a survey and taxonomy. Technical report (2000)
5. Benferhat, S., Autrel, F., Cuppens, F.: Enhanced correlation in an intrusion detection process. In: Gorodetsky, V., Popyack, L.J., Skormin, V.A. (eds.) MMM-ACNS 2003. LNCS, vol. 2776, pp. 157–170. Springer, Heidelberg (2003)
6. Dimopoulos, Y., Kakas, A.C.: Logic programming without negation as failure. In: Lloyd, J.W. (ed.) ILPS, pp. 369–383. MIT Press (1995)
7. Samarji, L., Cuppens, F., Cuppens-Boulahia, N., Kanoun, W., Dubus, S.: Situation calculus and graph based defensive modeling of simultaneous attacks. In: Wang, G., Ray, I., Feng, D., Rajarajan, M. (eds.) CSS 2013. LNCS, vol. 8300, pp. 132–150. Springer, Heidelberg (2013)
8. Bench-Capon, T.J.M.: Value-based argumentation frameworks. In: 9th International Workshop on Non-monotonic Reasoning (NMR 2002), Proceedings, Toulouse, France, 19–21 April 2002, pp. 443–454 (2002)
9. Cuppens, F., Cuppens-Boulahia, N.: Modeling contextual security policies. Int. J. Inf. Sec. 7(4), 285–305 (2008)
10. EVITA Project: E-safety Vehicle InTrusion protected Applications. http://www.evita-project.org
11. Koscher, K., Czeskis, A., Roesner, F., Patel, S., Kohno, T., Checkoway, S., McCoy, D., Kantor, B., Anderson, D., Shacham, H., Savage, S.: Experimental security analysis of a modern automobile. In: 2010 IEEE Symposium on Security and Privacy (SP), pp. 447–462, May 2010
12. Bandara, A.K., Kakas, A.C., Lupu, E.C., Russo, A.: Using argumentation logic for firewall configuration management. In: Integrated Network Management, pp. 180–187. IEEE (2009)
13. Bandara, A.K., Kakas, A.C., Lupu, E.C., Russo, A.: Using argumentation logic for firewall policy specification and analysis. In: State, R., van der Meer, S., O'Sullivan, D., Pfeifer, T. (eds.) DSOM 2006. LNCS, vol. 4269, pp. 185–196. Springer, Heidelberg (2006)
14. Applebaum, A., Levitt, K.N., Rowe, J., Parsons, S.: Arguing about firewall policy. In: Verheij, B., Szeider, S., Woltran, S. (eds.) COMMA. Frontiers in Artificial Intelligence and Applications, vol. 245, pp. 91–102. IOS Press (2012)
15. Bouyahia, T., Idrees, M.S., Cuppens-Boulahia, N., Cuppens, F., Autrel, F.: Metric for security activities assisted by argumentative logic. In: Garcia-Alfaro, J., Herrera-Joancomartí, J., Lupu, E., Posegga, J., Aldini, A., Martinelli, F., Suri, N. (eds.) DPM/SETOP/QASA 2014. LNCS, vol. 8872, pp. 183–197. Springer, Heidelberg (2015)
16. Bench-Capon, T.J.M.: Persuasion in practical argument using value-based argumentation frameworks. J. Log. Comput. 13(3), 429–448 (2003)
17. Martinelli, F., Santini, F.: Debating cybersecurity or securing a debate? In: Cuppens, F., Garcia-Alfaro, J., Zincir Heywood, N., Fong, P.W.L. (eds.) FPS 2014. LNCS, vol. 8930, pp. 239–246. Springer, Heidelberg (2015)
18. Rowe, J., Levitt, K., Parsons, S., Sklar, E., Applebaum, A., Jalal, S.: Argumentation logic to assist in security administration. In: Proceedings of the 2012 Workshop on New Security Paradigms, NSPW 2012, pp. 43–52. ACM, New York (2012)

Countermeasure Selection Based on the Attack and Service Dependency Graphs for Security Incident Management

Elena Doynikova$^{(\boxtimes)}$ and Igor Kotenko

Laboratory of Computer Security Problems,
St. Petersburg Institute for Informatics and Automation (SPIIRAS),
39, 14 Liniya, St. Petersburg, Russia
{doynikova, ivkote}@comsec.spb.ru

Abstract. The paper suggests an approach to countermeasure selection that is based on the application of quantitative risk metrics. The approach incorporates several techniques. These techniques differ for the static and dynamic modes of operation of the security analysis and countermeasure selection component. The techniques consider available input data on the network security state. The approach is based on the application of open standards for unified specification of security data, application of attack graphs and service dependency graphs to calculate different security metrics, and takes into account events and information from security information and events management (SIEM) systems.

Keywords: Security metrics · Attack graphs · Service dependency graphs · Security events · Countermeasure selection

1 Introduction

Currently when computer networks spread into all areas of modern life, computer attacks targeted to impact end users, corporations and organizations are developed as well. According to the [1] there are two main approaches to security assessment and selection of safeguards: basic and detailed assessments. There is multitude of standards and techniques that use basic security measures. For example, it is Facilitated Risk Analysis and Assessment Process FRAAP [2], Operationally Critical Threat, Asset, and Vulnerability Evaluation (OCTAVE) [3], process of the self-dependent risk analysis COBRA [4] and may others. When recommend safeguards, these techniques are focus on the risk assessment on the base of expert knowledge and use databases of basic safeguards. Advantages of these techniques are their simplicity and opportunity of operative countermeasure selection. Disadvantage consists in absence of consideration of possible attack sequences, service dependencies and (or) whole complex of different quantitative security metrics.

Basic approach is not always sufficient for the organizations with high security requirements. Besides, modern systems are complex enough. Their distribution, requirements to the openness, continuous modifications of hosts configurations, growth of power and intelligence of modern attacks require automatized approaches to risk

© Springer International Publishing Switzerland 2016
C. Lambrinoudakis and A. Gabillon (Eds.): CRiSIS 2015, LNCS 9572, pp. 107–124, 2016.
DOI: 10.1007/978-3-319-31811-0_7

assessment and countermeasure selection. In these cases detailed risk assessment is used. Its advantages consist in orientation on a specific system and enhanced accuracy in countermeasure selection. But this process is usually complex, and cost and time consuming. Such techniques as RiskWatch [5] and CRAMM [6] use detailed risk assessment considering annual losses (it is their advantage) but threats and vulnerabilities are defined by experts in these techniques. Disadvantages of these techniques consist in time consuming and volume of manual work.

Despite of a number of research works in the area of risk assessment and security analysis that are based among others on different models of attacks and countermeasures there is flagrant necessity in techniques for automatized countermeasure selection on the base of adequate quantitative metrics. These metrics should describe different aspects of security incident management.

To resolve this problem the paper suggests an approach based on a integrated system of security metrics. These metrics were suggested by the authors and distinguish the suggested approach from existent solutions. The approach is partially based on the models that were defined in [7]. Distinctive features of the approach and main contribution of the paper consist in application of the original integrated security metrics [8], application of the suggested model of countermeasure selection and definition of the techniques of different levels for countermeasure selection (static and dynamic). In this paper we are focused on the approach to the countermeasures selection. The approach is based on the quantitative risk assessment technique that was described by the authors in [7]. The paper is organized as follows. Section 2 reviews main related work in the area of security metrics and countermeasure selection. Section 3 suggests the countermeasure selection approach. Section 4 specifies the techniques of static and dynamic countermeasure selection. In Sect. 5 an example of the approach application is shown. In conclusion main results and future research are outlined.

2   Related Work

To date there is a number of researches on automatization of security analysis process and countermeasure selection.

They suggest techniques on the base of game theory [9, 10, etc.], techniques of the decision support on the base of logical inference on the attack graphs [11, 12, etc.], techniques of the countermeasure selection in the dynamic mode of system operation that are based on Bayes attack graphs [13, 14], etc.

In [12] methods of security assessment and defense in depth that use attack graphs are presented. Defense in depth use different levels of firewalls to protect critical assets of the corporative networks. Authors suggest a tool that analyzes firewall rules and vulnerabilities to generate attack graph. Then it is automatically analyzed to generate reasonable set of the prioritized recommendations that allow to restore defense in depth. In [9] analysis of the network security on the base of game theory is reviewed. The notions of cost and benefit are introduced. It allows to consider financial aspect in network security analysis (costs of attack implementation, impact from attack and costs of its prevention). Outcome of approach operation includes optimal strategy, i.e. the best sequence of actions for the administrator or attacker to achieve their goals (for example, the most efficient strategy of patches implementation in terms of time and cost). One of the advantages of the suggested methods on the base of game theory is possibility to consider temporal aspect. In [11] an approach to reduction of costs for the improvement network security level on the base of exploit dependency graphs is presented. Authors transform a path to a goal on the attack graph into an expression. This expression includes initial attack prerequisites in conjunctive normal form. Further for countermeasures implementation the disjunctions, that include maximum number of variables corresponding to the initial attack prerequisites, are selected. In [10] a technique of the risk assessment on the base of the game theory is described. Authors introduce two models: GTADM (Game Theoretical Attack-Defense Model) and HRCM (Hierarchical Risk Computing Model). GTADM is defined as non-cooperative non-zero-sum static game with complete information. Players are attacker and defender. The utilities for them are defined as $Benefit_{ij} - Cost_{ij}$. Authors outline entities for the specification of risk assessment process (e.g. network, asset, threat etc.) and components (activities) that are defined as transformation of input data into output data. Three-level structure of risk assessment is suggested. On the data gathering level data on network status is generated. On the data processing level system vulnerabilities are defined on the base of data on network status and all possible attacks on the network are defined on the base of knowledge on relations between vulnerabilities and threats and physical and logical connections between nodes. On risk calculation level GTADM model is constructed to define threat probabilities and expected losses in case of success of every threat.

Some papers suggest a common security level metric. It allows to define if the security level is sufficient and compare network security before and after countermeasures implementation [15, 16].

In other works metrics to assess possible losses and countermeasure effectiveness are used [17–20, 27]. For example, in [20] countermeasures are evaluated by three parameters that are used to define a common benefit from implementation of the k-th countermeasure: benefit from the countermeasure implementation; costs of the countermeasure; additional profit from the countermeasure implementation. In [21] metric for countermeasure selection for attack response on the base of service dependency graphs is suggested – *Return-On-Response-Investment* (*RORI*), which takes into account response effectiveness, collateral damage in case of response, countermeasure costs. Countermeasure with maximum *RORI* is selected for the implementation.

In [22] modified *RORI* is presented. It considers absence of countermeasures and size of system infrastructure. Main parameters considered are: annual loss expectancy (consequences of security incident in case of absence of countermeasures), depend on attack criticality and probability; risk mitigation in case of countermeasure implementation; expected annual costs on countermeasure implementation; annual costs on infrastructure (equipment and support) in case of countermeasure implementation.

In our paper it is suggested to automatize the risk assessment and countermeasure selection. We suggest the approach that includes a hierarchical metrics system and algorithms of their calculation considering different input data. In general this approach contains: gathering of data about the network, calculation of security metrics on this base and calculation of the most efficient countermeasures based on the metrics.

The approach is based on the related works above. Main difference of our approach consists in application of the original complex of metrics for automatized countermeasure selection in static and dynamic modes of system operation.

3   Countermeasure Selection Approach

In development of the suggested approach the next main requirements were considered: (1) taking into account last research in the security metrics area; (2) modeling of the attacker steps as attack graphs; (3) specification of network services as service dependency graphs; (4) application of the Security Content Automation Protocol (SCAP) and incorporated standards for the specification of input data; (5) consideration of requirements and opportunities of the SIEM systems.

The second requirement is a result of a fact that suggested approach is based on the attack models that were suggested in [16, 23]. Attach graphs allow to define possible steps of attacker in a system on the base of existing vulnerabilities, network configuration and attacker possibilities. So attack graphs are powerful tool for analysis of security situation. The third requirement is defined by the necessity to consider information on interconnections of network services for the countermeasure selection. This includes consideration of possible negative impact of the countermeasures on the objective functions of the system under protection. The fourth requirement is connected with necessity to automatize the security analysis process and countermeasure selection. It is especially important for countermeasures selection in the dynamic mode of system operation because manual processing of different security related data is complex task. The last requirement is connected with active expansion of SIEM systems. That is connected with increasing size and complexity of modern information networks of organizations and volume of information and security events for processing. In general suggested approach is based on the procedures of gathering of data on network and security events, calculation of security metrics on the base of this data and selection of the most efficient countermeasures on the base of calculated metrics. Distinctive feature of the approach is implementation of the set of techniques for security assessment and countermeasure selection of different levels including static and dynamic techniques. These techniques are divided on the base of the available input data and used security metrics on techniques of the topological level, attack graph level, attacker level and events level. Topological level, attack graph level and attacker level are related to the static level. And events level is related to the dynamic level. This division is caused by difference of requirements to the decision support in static and dynamic modes. Static mode is usually implemented on design and setup stages, dynamic mode – on operation stage. In static mode countermeasures for enhancement of common security level are selected. Temporal aspect is usually not critical in this mode. In dynamic mode temporal aspect is critical. Also in this mode information on specific attack appears.

To disclose the approach at first we describe input data. The next information is used as input data for metrics calculation: (1) Network topology and configuration (hosts and network tools, connections between them, software and hardware, dependencies and trust relationships between services, assets and their value); (2) Model of dependencies between network services; (3) Data on vulnerabilities and weak places of the software and hardware including their criticality and risks; (4) Model of attack actions in the form of attack graph (it is generated on the base of network configuration and information about network vulnerabilities); (5) Attacker profile (model that include information on attacker location, attacker skills and goals); (6) Security events; (7) Countermeasure models (including information about countermeasure and its influence on security).

To specify input data in the developed models of security information and events management systems [23] standards of SCAP [24] are applied. That is why Common Remediation Enumeration (CRE) standard [25] that provides scheme for counter-measures definition and specification in XML format, and Extended Remediation Information (ERI) standard [26] that includes additional to the CRE information for countermeasure representation, were selected for the countermeasure specification.

Figure 1 outlines connections between input data (blocks of the top level), models and components of the security analysis and countermeasure selection system (blocks of the second level), SCAP protocol (italic text outside of blocks) and levels of metrics. Solid arrows define mandatory data and dashed arrows define additional data.

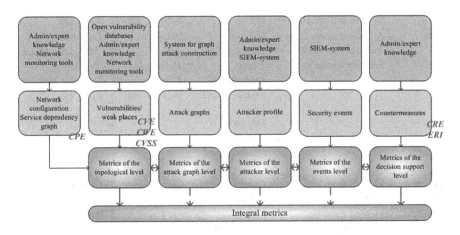

Fig. 1. Security metrics and input data for their calculation

Main classes (levels) of metrics, input data and examples of the main metrics of complex system of security metrics are given in Table 1 [7, 8, 27].

To select countermeasures risk assessments are used (in the form of expected losses). To include countermeasures in the suggested approach to the risk assessment [27] connections between possible countermeasures and attack graph were defined. Their influence on the risk metrics and common security state of a system is defined on the base of the additional metrics of the decision support level (see Table 1) [7, 8, 27].

In [27] authors suggested countermeasure model on the base of CRE and ERI standards. Model includes: definition of the characteristics for the application of the model in countermeasure selection technique; possible values of the characteristics; and connections of the characteristics with technique of the countermeasure selection.

Table 1. Security metrics

Level	Input data	Security metrics		
		Main	0-day	Cost
Topological	- System model (including service dependencies); - Information about system vulnerabilities/weak places (including indexes of CVSS [34])	- *Host Vulnerability;* - *Host Weakness;* - *Intrinsic Criticality;* - *Propagated Criticality; etc.*	- *Host Vulnerability to 0-Day attacks; etc.*	- *Business Value;* etc.
Attack graph	- All information from the previous level; - Attack graphs	- *Attack Potentiality;* - *Attack Impact; etc.*	- *Attack Potentiality Considering 0-Days; etc.*	- *Monetary Attack Impact;* - *Response Cost;* etc.
Attacker	- All information from the previous level; - Attacker profile (skills, location in the system, level of the privileges)	- *Attacker Skill Level;* - *Profiled Attack Potentiality;* etc.	- *Profiled Attack Potentiality Considering 0-Days; etc.*	- *Profiled Monetary Attack Impact;* - *Profiled Response Cost; etc.*
Events	- All information from the previous level; - Security incidents	- *Dynamic Attacker Skill Level;* - *Probabilistic Attacker Skill Level;* - *Dynamic Attack Potentiality;* etc.	- *Dynamic Attack Potentiality Considering 0-Days; etc.*	- *Dynamic Monetary Attack Impact;* - *Dynamic Response Cost; etc.*
Decision support	- Metrics from the previous levels	- *Countermeasure Effectiveness;* - *Collateral Damage*		- *Countermeasure Cost*
Integral (system)	- Metrics from the previous levels	- *Risk Level;- Security Level;* - *Attack Surface;* - *Countermeasure Selection Index*		- *Annual Loss Expectancy*

Features of the static and dynamic modes of decision support resulted in necessity to redefine this model with additional fields: "system operation mode" (can take values "static"/"dynamic"/"both"); "implementation tool" (tool for the countermeasure implementation); "scope" (can take values "attack graph element"/"host"/"subnet"/ "network").

Fields of the countermeasure model and examples of their values are presented in Table 2.

In static mode possible countermeasures include various tools that generally allow to reduce risks beforehand. In dynamic mode these tools are used for the realization of actions that can prevent ongoing attack actions. This division is fair in case when in

Table 2. Fields of the countermeasure model and examples of values

Field	Group of fields	Description	Example
Name	Countermeasure description	Text value	Deny or redirect requests
Description	Countermeasure description	Text value	Deny or redirect url-requests from the suspicious accounts
Vulnerability for which countermeasure can be used	Connection with attack graph	CVE [28]	CVE-2010-1870
Platform or configuration where countermeasure can be used	Connection with attack graph	CPE [29] or CCE [30]	cpe:/a:apache: struts:2.0.0
Implementation tool	Connection with technique of the countermeasure selection	Text value, defined by expert	Firewall
System operation mode	Connection with technique of the countermeasure selection	Static /dynamic /both	Dynamic
Scope	Connection with technique of the countermeasure selection	Attack graph element /host /subnet / network	Attack graph element
Influence on the attack graph	Connection with attack graph	Remove link /add link /remove node /add node /modify node	Remove node
Influence on operation (*Collateral Damage*, CD)	Metric	It is calculated on the base of the service dependency graph	$CD = [0\ 0\ 0,5]$
Effectiveness or risk mitigation (*Countermeasure Effectiveness*, CE)	Metric	Defined by expert	$CE = [0,5\ 0,5\ 0,5]$
Cost (*Countermeasure Cost*, CC)	Metric	Defined by expert	€500

dynamic mode there is no time for the additional deployment of safeguards. On example of [1] for the different threats different variants of safeguards can be provided for confidentiality, integrity and availability assurance (Table 3). The next notations are used in the table: S - applicable in static mode, D - applicable in dynamic mode, SD - applicable in both modes; C - confidentiality, I - integrity, A - availability.

Table 3. Examples of threats, security properties and safeguards

Examples of threats	Security property	Examples of safeguards							
		Protection against malicious code	Identification and authentication	Logical access control and audit	Network management	Cryptography	Incident processing	Backup copies	Personnel management
Malicious code	C	SD					D		
	I	SD					D	SD	
	A	SD					D		
Masquerading of user identity	C	SD	S	SD	SD	S			
	I	SD	S	SD	SD	S		SD	
	A	SD	S	SD	SD	S		SD	
Misrouting/re-routing of messages	C				SD	S			
	I				SD	S			
	A				SD	S			
Unauthorized access to computers, data, services and applications	C		S	SD	SD	S			
	I		S	SD	SD	S		SD	
	A		S	SD	SD	S			
Destructive attack	C								
	I								
	A		S	SD				SD	S
Misuse of resources	C								
	I								
	A		S	SD	SD				S
Traffic overloading	C								
	I								
	A				SD			SD	

In dynamic mode countermeasures are directed to prevent ongoing attack. On the base of [1, 14, 22, 32] the next countermeasures of the active (dynamic) response can be outlined: deny full/selective access to file, restrict user activity, disable user account, shutdown compromised service/host, restart suspicious process, terminate suspicious process, abort suspicious system calls, delay suspicious system calls, enable/disable additional firewall rules, restart targeted system, block suspicious incoming/outgoing network connection, block ports/IP addresses, etc. These lists, measures of counter-measures effectiveness, tools of countermeasures implementation and cost of the countermeasures are usually defined by experts. E.g., identification and authentication can be implemented by tools of multifactor authentication, cost of deployment and support of this countermeasure per year can be for example € 3000, risk mitigation can be - 0,55 [31].

4 Techniques for Countermeasure Selection

4.1 Countermeasure Selection in the Static Mode

On the *first stage* risk assessment is performed (it is described in [27]). According to the threats classification risks of confidentiality, integrity, and availability violation, and illegitimate privileges on host are outlined. To consider monetary aspect of the possible impact formula for the risk calculation contains multiplication on the annual frequency of every type of threat (it is defined by the experts).

Risk for each host is defined by two values: maximum risk value among all host threats and cumulative risk for all threats. Risk for the network is also defined with two values: cumulative risk for all nodes and maximum risk among all nodes. Two values are provided because from the one hand there are shouldn't be risks that exceed threshold value and from another hand risk for system should be minimal.

For the attack graph level and the attacker level, an *additional stage* is performed that is based on the approach from [15].

It includes calculation of the deviation of attack probability and selection of the vulnerabilities that give maximum deviation value. Deviation value is calculated for the attacks where the risk exceeds threshold:

$$C_k = P(TE = 1) - P(TE = 1 | \pi(v_k) = 0.0)(1 \leq k \leq n),$$

where v_k – system vulnerability, $v_k \in V$; $V = \{v_1, v_2, ..., v_n\}$ – set of all system vulnerabilities; $\pi(v_k)$ – probability of the successful exploitation of vulnerability v_k; TE – probability of successful attack on the node with risk that exceeds threshold.

This deviation value allows to define the most critical nodes (vulnerabilities) of the attack graph on the base of deviation between actual probability of attack access and probability of attack access if appropriate vulnerability will be absent in system.

Vulnerability v_k is considered as the most critical if there is no other vulnerability $v_j(1 \leq j < n, j \neq k)$ that $C_j > C_k$.

On the *second stage* assessment of effectiveness of patches implementation is provided. For their implementation the most critical vulnerabilities according to the CVSS scores are selected (for the topological level) or according to the deviation value from the additional stage (for the attack graph and attacker levels) are selected. For each patch *Countermeasure Selection Index* is calculated considering its cost:

$$CI = \sum_i G\_Risk_{b_i} - G\_Risk_{a_i} + CC, \tag{1}$$

where i – number of the node vulnerability; $G\_Risk_{b_i}$ – risk before the countermeasure implementation [27]; $G\_Risk_{a_i}$ – risk after the countermeasure implementation; CC – cost of patch implementation (normalized with maximum losses).

On the *third stage* information about high risk nodes of system, and appropriate threats and weak places, is provided to the experts to generate lists of the counter-measures and their costs. Further for each critical node the most effective countermeasure is selected according to the *Countermeasure Selection Index* (taking into account values of index for patches), i.e. countermeasure with minimal index.

4.2 Countermeasure Selection in Dynamic Mode

Difference of a purpose of countermeasure selection technique in dynamic mode from the static mode consists in direction on prevention of specific ongoing attack instead of the common security level enhancement. The technique is as follows.

1. Definition of the attacker location on the attack graph on the base of the security events from the SIEM-system: (a) definition of the list of vulnerabilities for the host from the security event; (b) selection of the vulnerabilities that give privileges and \or lead to the impact from the security event (the next steps of the technique are executed for the nodes that correspond to the exploitation of the selected vulnerabilities; if there is no such vulnerability than security event is defined as exploitation of 0-day vulnerability).
2. Definition of the attacker skills level on the base of the security event: (a) definition of the most probable attack path to the node that corresponds to the current attacker location (on the base of the Bayes theorem); (b) selection of nodes with maximum CVSS index *Access Complexity* on the most probable attack path; (c) definition of the attacker level as maximum value of the index from the previous step on scale "High"/"Medium"/"Low" (appropriate quantitative values are 0.7, 0.5 and 0.3 accordingly); (d) definition of accuracy of assessment of the attacker skill level as (number of path nodes with selected *Access Complexity* level)/(total number of nodes in path).
3. Calculation of the probabilities of attack paths that go through the attacker location considering attacker skill level and the fact that event of successful attack on this node is true.
4. Calculation of risks for the attack paths that go through the compromised node on the base of the criticality of the target node, attack impact and path probability.
5. Selection of path with maximum risk as the most probable attack path and definition of its end node as attack goal.

Depending on the supposed attack goal, classification of attacks and countermeasures from the previous section, and depth of the attack graph to the goal, the decision on the countermeasures implementation is made in two steps: (1) Nodes on the path to the attack goal and appropriate countermeasures to prevent attack are selected; (2) For each countermeasure *Countermeasure Selection Index* is calculated and countermeasure with minimal index is selected.

5 Experiments and Analysis

Below application of the suggested approach is reviewed for the test network in Fig. 2. Software of the test network and its vulnerabilities are depicted in Table 4.

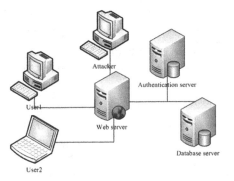

Fig. 2. Network for experiments

5.1 Static Mode

Results of the experiments for the technique of the countermeasure selection on the topological level and attack graph level are presented below.

Topological Level. First we define criticality of the assets (in our example it is information on the web-server) on the scale from 0 to 1 as damaging: $Criticality(c) = 0,8$, $Criticality(i) = 0,8$ and $Criticality(a) = 0,8$. Loss of confidentiality, integrity or availability of this information will result in the losses €3000.

Further on the base of the service dependencies criticality of all network services is defined (Fig. 3) with technique that was presented in [27] based on the technique from [21]. Risks from the specific threats (vulnerability exploitation) are defined on the base of formulas from [27] as CVSS environmental score:

$$Risk = round\_to\_1\_decimal(AdjustedBase), \qquad (2)$$

Where $AdjustedBase = BaseScore$, and $BaseScore\ Impact$ is replaced with $AdjustedImpact$;

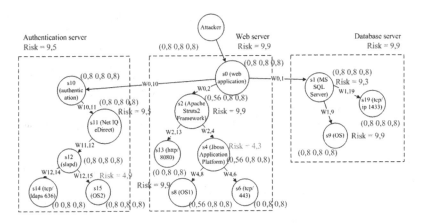

Fig. 3. Service dependency graph with criticality and risk values

Table 4. Description of the software and its vulnerabilities

Host	Software	Vulnerabilities (the most critical)
Web server	Windows Server 2008 R2 (64 bits);	Threat of confidentiality/integrity/availability violation and illegitimated privileges
		CVE-2010-0020 (BaseScore: 9.0 H; AV:N/AC:L/Au:S/C:C/I:C/A:C); give admin access.
		Data on vulnerability is from the open base NVD [33], metrics are provided according common vulnerability scoring system (CVSS) [34]:
		BaseScore – base score on scale 1 to 10 that have appropriate qualitative values (H – high, M – medium, L – low);
		AV – access vector for the vulnerability (L – local, A – adjusted network, N – network);
		AC – access complexity for the vulnerability (H – high, M – medium, L – low);
		Au – index if additional authentication is needed (M – multiple authentication is needed, S – single authentication is needed, N – no);
		C, I and A – impact for confidentiality, integrity and availability in case of the successful vulnerability exploitation (N – no, P – partial, C – complete).
	JBoss AS 5.0.1;	Threat of confidentiality (network access)
		CVE-2012-4529 (BaseScore: 4,3 M; AV:N/AC:M/Au:N/C:P/I:N/A:N)
	ApacheStruts2 framework (cpe:/ a: apache: struts:2.0.0);	Threat of confidentiality/integrity/availability violation (network access)
		CVE-2013-4316 (BaseScore: 10,0 H; AV:N/AC:L/Au:N/C:C/I:C/A:C)
Database server	Windows Server 2008 R2 (64 bits);	Threat of confidentiality/integrity/availability

(Continued)

Table 4. (*Continued*)

Host	Software	Vulnerabilities (the most critical)
		violation and illegitimated privileges
		CVE-2010-0020 (BaseScore: 9.0 H; AV:N/AC:L/Au:S/C:C/I:C/A:C); give admin access
	MS SQL Server 2008 R2 cpe:/a: microsoft:sql_server:2008:r2: x64	Threat of confidentiality/integrity/availability violation (network access)
		CVE-2012-1856 (BaseScore: 9.3 H; AV:N/AC:M/Au:N/C:C/I:C/A:C)
Authentication server	SUSE Enterprise Linux 11 SP1 (32 bits) (cpe:/o: novell:suse_linux:11:sp1: server)	Threat of confidentiality violation (network access)
		CVE-2010-3110 (BaseScore: 4,3 M; AV:N/AC:M/Au:N/C:N/I:P/A:N)
	NetIQ eDirect server 8.8.7.1 (cpe:/a:netiq: edirectory:8.8.7.1)	Threat of confidentiality/integrity/availability violation (network access)
		CVE-2012-0432 (BaseScore: 10,0 H; AV:N/AC:L/Au:N/C:C/I:C/A:C)

$$AdjustedBase = round\_to\_1\_dicimal(((0.6) \times AdjustedImpact)$$
$$+ (0.4 \times Exploitability) - 1.5) \times f(AdjustedImpact));$$

$$AdjustedImpact = min(10, 10.41 \times (1 - (1 - ConfImpact \times ConfReq) \times (1 - IntegImpact$$
$$\times IntegReq) \times (1 - AvailImpact \times AvailReq)));$$

ConfImpact, IntegImpact, AvailImpact - impacts on the confidentiality, integrity and availability; *ConfReq, IntegReq, AvailReq* - criticality of asset confidentiality, integrity and availability.

$$Exploitability = 20 \times AccessVector \times AccessComplexity \times Authentication,$$

where *AccessVector* - access vector; *AccessComplexity* - access complexity; *Authentication* - authentication;

$$f(AdjustedImpact) = \begin{cases} 0, & if\ AdjustedImpact = 0 \\ 1.176, & if\ AdjustedImpact \neq 0 \end{cases}.$$

Risks are defined: (1) For each service; (2) For each host - maximum risk (*Risk_max*) that is defined as maximum risk of the host threats and cumulative risk (*Risk_sum*) that is defined as sum of risks from each threat (Table 5); (3) For network -

Table 5. Risks on the topological level

Network object\level	Topological level
Authentication server	$Risk\_max = 9,5$; $Risk\_sum = 14,4$
Web-server	$Risk\_max = 9,9$; $Risk\_sum = 24,1$
Database server	$Risk\_max = 9,9$; $Risk\_sum = 19,2$
Network	$Risk\_max = 9,9$; $Risk\_sum = 57,7$

maximum risk of network hosts (network shouldn't contain high risks) and cumulative risk (for calculation of *Countermeasure Selection Index*).

We define the next security measures (just example) to mitigate impacts of the confidentiality/integrity and availability threats: Multifactor Authentication (*Cost* – €3000 per year (after normalization according to the maximum losses in network – 1); *Risk mitigation* – 0,55; *scope* – host); Network Monitoring that allows to add rules for the user actions (*Cost* – €2650 per year (after normalization according to the maximum losses in network – 0,9); *Risk mitigation* – 0,56; *scope* – host); Firewall that allows to deactivate user accounts (*Cost* – €2500 per year (after normalization according to the maximum losses – 0,8); *Risk mitigation* – 0,35; *scope* – subnet).

Countermeasure selection process is as follows.

Bypass topology from the available from external network hosts.

Step 1 – select safeguard for the Web-server. Begin from the safeguard with maximum scope – Firewall, and calculate risks reduction after safeguard implementation. Risk before safeguard implementation is calculated with formula 2, risk after safeguard implementation is calculated by multiplication of the risk before on *Risk mitigation* value: $Risk\_max = 9,9 - 9,9 \cdot 0,35 = 6,435$; $Risk\_sum = 24,1 - 24,1 \cdot 0,35 = 24,1 - 8,435 = 15.755$. $CI = 15,755 + 0,8 = 16,555$ (according to the formula (1)). For the node Authentication server $Risk\_max = 9,5 - 9,5 \cdot 0,35 = 6,175$; $Risk\_sum = 14,4 - 14,4 \cdot 0,35 = 9,36$. For the node Database server $Risk\_max = 9,9 - 9,9 \cdot 0,35 = 6,435$; $Risk\_sum = 19,2 - 19,2 \cdot 0,35 = 12,48$. So common metric for the network is $CI = 15,755 + 12,48 + 9,36 + 0,8 = 38,395$ (because Firewall on this host influence on all nodes that are connected with it).

Step 2 – review other countermeasures for the Web-server. In case of measure Multifactor Authentication: $Risk\_max = 9,9 - 9,9 \cdot 0,55 = 9,9 - 5,445 = 4,455$; $Risk\_sum = 24,1 - 24,1 \cdot 0,55 = 24,1 - 13,255 = 10,845$; $CI = 10,845 + 1 = 11,845$. In case of measure Network Monitoring $Risk\_max = 9,9 - 9,9 \cdot 0,56 = 9,9 - 5,544 = 4,356$; $Risk\_sum = 24,1 - 24,1 \cdot 0,56 = 10,604$; $CI = 10,604 + 0,9 = 11,504$. So for this node on step 2 measure Network Monitoring is selected. For the node Authentication server select Firewall firstly (because its scope includes two hosts): $Risk\_max = 9,5 - 9,5 \cdot 0,35 = 6,175$; $Risk\_sum = 14,4 - 14,4 \cdot 0,35 = 9,36$. $CI = 9,36 + 0,8 = 10,16$. Common metric for the step 2 $CI = 11,504 + 10,16 + 12,48 = 34,144$.

Step 3 – review other countermeasures for the Authentication server. In case of measure Multifactor Authentication $Risk\_sum = 14,4 - 14,4 \cdot 0,55 = 6,48$; $CI = 6,48 + 3000 \cdot 10/30000 = 7,48$. In case of measure Network Monitoring $Risk\_sum = 14,4 - 14,4 \cdot 0,56 = 6,336$; $CI = 6.336 + 0,9 = 7,236$. So on step 3 Network Monitoring is selected. For the Database server: in case of measure Multifactor Authentication: $Risk\_sum = 19,2 - 19,2 \cdot 0,55 = 8,64$; $CI = 8,64 + 1 = 9,64$. In case of measure Network Monitoring $Risk\_sum = 19,2 - 19,2 \cdot 0,56 = 8,448$; $CI = 8.448 + 0,9 = 9,348$. On this step Network Monitoring is selected. Common metric for the step 3 $CI = 11,504 + 7,236 + 9,348 = 28,088$.

Step 4 – select minimum *Countermeasure Selection Index*. It is metric on step 3 where Network Monitoring measure for all hosts was selected.

Attack Graph Level. In Fig. 4 attack graph for the test network with calculated probabilities (*P*) and risks (*Risk*) is represented. On the first stage we define that the most critical vulnerability that is used in the most number of attack paths is CVE-2010-0020. Appropriate node is "web server". So countermeasures should be implemented on this node. Countermeasure that minimize *Countermeasure Selection Index* on this level is – "Network Monitoring" (as calculated on the previous level). Thus consideration of the attack graph allows to minimize cost of the countermeasures.

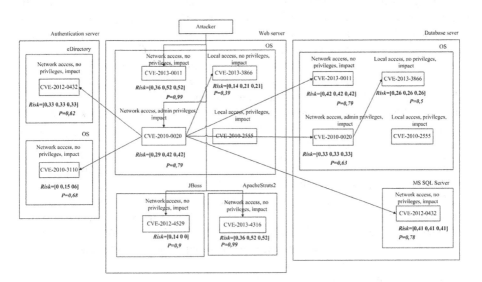

Fig. 4. Attack graph

5.2   Dynamic Mode

Below experiments for the countermeasure selection technique on the events level are presented. To model input data we used additionally developed tool – attack generator. This tool allows to generate attack sequences on the base of attack patterns from Common Attack Pattern Enumeration and Classification (CAPEC) database [35].

We consider the next attack sequence that was generated with attack generator and that results in compromise of the web server (admin privileges on the web server): (1) Scanning of the web server for the vulnerable software: CAPEC-170 (Web Application Fingerprinting). Event 1: a large amount of HTTP requests from the same host; (2) Attempt of the attack on the ApacheStruts2: CAPEC-250 (XML Injection). Event 2: Too many exceptions generated by the application as a result of malformed queries; (3) Successful exploitation of vulnerability of operation system CVE-2010-0020 that results in confidentiality, integrity and availability violation, and illegitimate admin access on the host.

Countermeasure selection process includes three following steps.

Step 1 – message about security event on the web server arrives. This node is critical, so the system decides to response immediately.

Step 2 – calculation of the *Countermeasure Selection Index* for the possible counter-measures. For example we consider the next countermeasures: shutdown compromised service/host ($CC = 0$, $CE = 1$ (i.e. *Risk* become 0), $CD = 0,8$, because host availability for the legitimate users will be lost); enable/disable additional firewall rules ($CC = 0$, $CE = 1$ (i.e. *Risk* become 0), $CD = 0$); block suspicious incoming/outgoing network connection ($CC = 0$, $CE = 1$ (i.e. *Risk* become 0), $CD = 0,2$, because it is possible that connection was legitimate), block ports/IP addresses ($CC = 0$, $CE = 1$ (i.e. *Risk* become 0), $CD = 0,8$, because host availability for the legitimate users will be lost).

According to the formula for the dynamic case ($CI = Risk + CD + CC$) values of the *CI* are as follows: *CI*(shutdown compromised service/host) = 0 + 0 + 0,8 = 0,8; *CI* (enable/disable additional firewall rules) = 0 + 0 + 0 = 0; *CI*(block suspicious incoming/outgoing network connection) = 0 + 0 + 0,2 = 0,2, *CI* (block ports/IP addresses) = 0 + 0 + 0,8 = 0,8.

Step 3 – selection of the countermeasure with minimal *CI*. For the example case it is: enable/disable additional firewall rules.

Thus, in case of the absence of countermeasures the losses would be €30 000 (example value of violation for the web-server). In case of the static countermeasures the losses would stay €30 000. In case of static and dynamic measures the losses would decrease to 0. The set of experiments with different sequences from the attack generator shown that in general the combined application of static and dynamic process allows to avoid or decrease the losses from attacks.

Nevertheless, there is a number of disadvantages: the experiments were made for the generated attack sequences instead of the real attacks; the attacker model is abstract and limited with three types of attackers; mapping between security events and attack graph need additional research; in cases of the small number of security events and short attack sequences the countermeasure selection effectiveness reduces.

Despite of these disadvantages the approach allow to represent current security situation in static mode and for ongoing attacks, and select effective countermeasures.

6   Conclusion

In the paper the countermeasure selection approach based on the application of quantitative risk metrics is proposed. Approach incorporates several techniques that differ for the static and dynamic modes of operation of the security analysis and countermeasure selection component. Work of the approach is shown on the examples. Experiments on the attack sequences that were generated by the additionally developed tool – attack generator – shown that in general approach allows to decrease losses from computer attacks. This technique still has some disadvantages for short sequences of attacks and low number of events. It will be investigated in the future work. We planning to provide experiments on real studies with long sequences of attacks.

Acknowledgements. This research is being supported by the Ministry of Education and Science of The Russian Federation (contract # 14.604.21.0137, unique contract identifier RFMEFI604 14X0137).

References

1. ISO/IEC TR 13335-4:2000. Information technology — Guidelines for the management of IT Security — Part 4: Selection of safeguards
2. Peltier, T.R.: Information Security Risk Analysis, 3rd edn. CRC Press, Boca Raton (2010)
3. Caralli, R., Stevens, J.F., Young, L.R., Wilson, W.R.: Introducing OCTAVE Allegro: improving the information security risk assessment process. Technical report (2007)
4. Visintine, V.: Global Information Assurance Certification Paper. SANS Institute (2003). http://www.giac.org/paper/gsec/3156/introduction-information-risk-assessment/105258
5. RiskWatch. http://www.riskwatch.com/
6. CRAMM. www.cramm.com
7. Kotenko, I., Doynikova, E.: Evaluation of computer network security based on attack graphs and security event processing. J. Wirel. Mob. Netw. Ubiquit. Comput. Dependable Appl. (JoWUA) 5(3), 14–29 (2014)
8. Kotenko, I., Chechulin, A.: Attack modeling and security evaluation in SIEM systems. Int. Trans. Syst. Sci. Appl. 8, 129–147 (2012)
9. Bursztein, E., Mitchell, J.C.: Using strategy objectives for network security analysis. In: Bao, F., Yung, M., Lin, D., Jing, J. (eds.) Inscrypt 2009. LNCS, vol. 6151, pp. 337–349. Springer, Heidelberg (2010)
10. He, W., Xia, C., Zhang, C., Ji, Y., Ma, X.: A network security risk assessment framework based on game theory. In: Proceedings of the Second International Conference on Future Generation Communication and Networking, vol. 2, pp. 249–253. IEEE (2008)
11. Noel, S., Jajodia, S., O'Berry, B., Jacobs, M.: Efficient minimum-cost network hardening via exploit dependency graphs. In: Proceedings of the 19th Annual Computer Security Applications Conference, pp. 86–95. IEEE (2003)
12. Ingols, K., Lippmann, R., Piwowarski, K.: Pratical Attack Graph Generation for Network Defense. Computer Security Applications Conference. Miami Beach, Florida (2006)
13. Poolsappasit, N., Dewri, R., Ray, I.: Dynamic security risk management using Bayesian attack graphs. IEEE Trans. Dependable Secur. Comput. 9(1), 61–74 (2012)

14. Dantu, R., Kolan, P., Cangussu, J.: Network risk management using attacker profiling. Secur. Commun. Netw. **2**(1), 83–96 (2009)
15. Chunlu, W., Yancheng, W., Yingfei, D., Tianle, Z.: A novel comprehensive network security assessment approach. In: IEEE International Conference on Communications, pp. 1–6. IEEE, Kyoto (2011)
16. Kotenko, I., Stepashkin, M.: Attack graph based evaluation of network security. In: Leitold, H., Markatos, E.P. (eds.) CMS 2006. LNCS, vol. 4237, pp. 216–227. Springer, Heidelberg (2006)
17. Cremonini, M., Martini, P.: Evaluating information security investments from attackers perspective: the Return-On-Attack (ROA). In: Workshop on the Economics of Information Security (2005)
18. Kanoun, W., Cuppens-Boulahia, N., Cuppens, F.: Automated reaction based on risk analysis and attackers skills in intrusion detection systems. In: Proceedings of the CRiSIS 2008, pp. 117–124. IEEE, Tozeur (2008)
19. Wu, Y.-S., Foo, B., Mao, Y.-C., Bagchi, S., Spafford, E.: Automated adaptive intrusion containment in systems of interacting services. Comput. Netw. Int. J. Comput. Telecommun. Netw. **51**(5), 1334–1360 (2007). Elsevier North-Holland, Inc. New York, NY, USA
20. Hoo, K.J.S.: How much is enough? a risk-management approach to computer security. Ph.D. thesis, Stanford University (2000)
21. Kheir, N.: Response policies and counter-measures: management of service dependencies and intrusion and reaction impacts. Ph.D. thesis (2010)
22. Gonzalez Granadillo, G., Débar, H., Jacob, G., Gaber, C., Achemlal, M.: Individual countermeasure selection based on the return on response investment index. In: Kotenko, I., Skormin, V. (eds.) MMM-ACNS 2012. LNCS, vol. 7531, pp. 156–170. Springer, Heidelberg (2012)
23. Kotenko, I., Chechulin, A.: A cyber attack modeling and impact assessment framework. In: CyCon 2013, pp. 119–142. IEEE and NATO COE Publications (2013)
24. Waltermire, D., Quinn, S., Scarfone, K., Halbardier, A.: The Technical Specification for the Security Content Automation Protocol (SCAP): SCAP Version 1.2 (2011)
25. McGuire, G.T., Waltermire, D., Baker, J.O.: Common Remediation Enumeration (CRE) Version 1.0 (Draft). NIST Interagency Report 7831 (Draft) (2011)
26. Johnson, C.: Enterprise remediation automation. In: NIST, Proceedings of the IT Security Automation Conference (2010)
27. Kotenko, I., Doynikova, E.: Countermeasure selection in SIEM systems based on the integrated complex of security metrics. In: 23rd Euromicro International Conference on Parallel, Distributed and Network-Based Processing (PDP 2015), pp. 567–574. IEEE (2015)
28. Common Vulnerabilities and Exposures (CVE). http://cve.mitre.org/
29. Common Platform Enumeration (CPE). http://cpe.mitre.org/
30. Common Configuration Enumeration (CCE). https://cce.mitre.org/
31. MASSIF FP7 Project. MAnagement of Security information and events in Service Infrastructures. http://www.massif-project.eu
32. Strasburg, C., Stakhanova, N., Basu, S., Wong, J.: Intrusion response cost assessment methodology. In: Proceedings of the 4th International Symposium on Information, Computer, and Communications Security, New York, NY, USA, pp. 388–391 (2009)
33. National Vulnerability Database. https://nvd.nist.gov/
34. Mell, P., Scarfone, K.: A Complete Guide to the Common Vulnerability Scoring System Version 2.0 (2007)
35. Common Attack Pattern Enumeration and Classification (CAPEC) [Internet resource]. https://capec.mitre.org

Risk Analysis and Vulnerability Assessment

Quantitative Risk, Statistical Methods and the Four Quadrants for Information Security

Gaute Wangen[(✉)] and Andrii Shalaginov

NISlab, Norwegian Information Security Laboratory,
Center for Cyber and Information Security,
Gjøvik University College, Gjøvik, Norway
{Gaute.Wangen2,Andrii.Shalaginov2}@hig.no

Abstract. Achieving the quantitative risk assessment has long been an elusive problem in information security, where the subjective and qualitative assessments dominate. This paper discusses the appropriateness of statistical and quantitative methods for information security risk management. Through case studies, we discuss different types of risks in terms of quantitative risk assessment, grappling with how to obtain distributions of both probability and consequence for the risks. N.N. Taleb's concepts of the Black Swan and the Four Quadrants provides the foundation for our approach and classification. We apply these concepts to determine where it is appropriate to apply quantitative methods, and where we should exert caution in our predictions. Our primary contribution is a treatise on different types of risk calculations, and a classification of information security threats within the Four Quadrants.

Keywords: Risk assessment · Information security · Statistical methods · Probability · Four quadrants · Black swan

1 Introduction

Being able to predict events and outcomes provide a great benefit for decision-making in both life and business environments. For information security risk management (ISRM), the aim is to find the appropriate balance in risk-taking relative to the organization's risk appetite and tolerance. Too many security controls will inhibit business functionality, and the opposite will lead to unacceptable exposure. The inherent complexity of information community technology (ICT) makes it challenging to gather enough relevant data on information risks for building statistical models and making quantitative risks calculations [2]. It is therefore generally perceived as being too much work, complex and time-consuming [14]. However, we argue that the cause for the lack of prevalence of statistical methods is just as much lack of maturity in the field as the reasons stated above. Prediction of information security risks has therefore been reliant on the intuition and heuristics of the subject matter experts [2,14]. Although qualitative methods are the predominant approach to forecasting information

© Springer International Publishing Switzerland 2016
C. Lambrinoudakis and A. Gabillon (Eds.): CRiSIS 2015, LNCS 9572, pp. 127–143, 2016.
DOI: 10.1007/978-3-319-31811-0_8

risks, there is ample evidence from psychological experiments suggesting that qualitative risk predictions are unreliable [9,13,14]. Moreover, the qualitative risk analysis is not suitable when dealing with expected monetary losses such that Annualized Loss Expectancy. Quantitative and statistical methods should provide better results than guesswork and improve decisions in the long run. However, there are many types of information risks, and it is not likely that we can predict all equally well. Information security risks are more often than not products of complex systems and active adversaries. The main topics in Black Swan [13] is risk unpredictability caused by lack of data and knowledge about the complexity and the limitations of statistical methods in predicting risks in such systems. Lack of understanding and overconfidence in models often leads to the costly mistake of underestimating risk. The Four Quadrants [12] is a risk classification system developed primarily for economics for determining where the risk analyst safely can apply statistical methods, where he should show caution, and where to discard traditional statistical approaches. In this article, Taleb's Four Quadrants are adapted to address the feasibility of applying statistical methods to predict information risks. To the extent of our knowledge, there has not been published any previous work on this particular issue.

To provide a clear view on the problem, we did a feasibility study of applying statistical methods to several major information risk case studies that can affect any businesses or even countries. This work addresses the following research questions and finds answers with relevant support from the case studies: (i) *Can we apply statistical methods to deal with Information Security Risks? Sketch the applicability domains and possible failures to predict extreme events* and (ii) *In which information security domains can statistical methods be applied to improve the decision-making process in risk management even if the methods do not seem reliable and accurate?*. The implication from answering these research questions are both theoretical, corresponding knowledge and historical data was collected, simulated and analyzed in this study. For practical implications, a family of various statistical approaches was analyzed with scientifically sound proof for specific methods and applications for ISRM even if the prediction results are not entirely reliable. Furthermore, we discuss factors that contribute to our lack of knowledge about the quantitative ISRM using statistical methods as the most promising approach to numerical characterization of the ICT risks. Additionally, a classification of risks within the Four Quadrants is proposed.

The remainder of this article is as follows: First; we present the state of the art in ISRM in the Sect. 2, define the terminology and describe the Four Quadrants classification scheme. In the Sect. 3 we describe the applied method. We present three case studies and their relation to quantitative risk assessment and their relation to the Four Quadrants in Sect. 4. Section 5 discusses our findings, factors that reduce predictability, and classification of information risks within the Four Quadrants. The conclusion is found in Sect. 6.

2   Information Security and Risk Assessment

ISO/IEC 27005:2008 defines information or ICT risk in as *the potential that a given threat will exploit vulnerabilities of an asset or group of assets and thereby cause harm to the organization.* Probabilistic risk analysis (PRA) is the preferred approach to risk in information security. Where impact to the organization (e.g. loss if a risk occurred) and probability calculations of occurrence express risk. There are no standardized statistical approaches to information risks. To calculate risks (R) we, therefore, apply the definitions provided by Aven in [3] (p. 229) for discussion and risk calculation. Where risk is described by events (A), consequences (C), associated uncertainties (U) and probabilities (P). U and P calculations rely on background knowledge (K). Also, model sensitivities (S) are included to show how dependencies on the variation of the assumptions and conditions. Thus, $R = f(A, C, U, P, S, K)$. A quantitative risk assessment in this sense derives from applying statistical tools and formal methods, mainly based on historical data (e.g. law of large numbers), obtained distributions and simulations. So, based on the definition of risk by Aven, we will consider applications of relevant methods for quantitative risk evaluation in terms of R. A risk assessment is very seldom purely quantitative as there are assumptions K underlying the forecast. Exposure is a crucial concept in risk management that we define as how susceptible an organization is to a particular risk.

2.1   The Black Swan and the Four Quadrants

N.N. Taleb [13] developed Black Swan theory to describe rare, extreme and unpredictable events of enormous consequence. These events, known as Black Swans, are so rare that they are impossible to predict, and they go beyond the realm of reasonable expectations. A Black Swan has three properties; (i) It is an outlier. (ii) It carries an extreme impact. (iii) Moreover, despite its outlier status, human nature makes us formulate explanations for its occurrence after the fact, rendering it explainable and predictable. The Four Quadrants risk classification concept of comes from the core concepts of the Black Swan, which links risk management to decision theory. *The classification system allows us to isolate situations in which forecasting needs to be suspended – or a revision of the decision or exposure may be necessary* [12], and to determine where it is safe to apply statistical risk models. The classification consists of two types of randomness and decisions [12,13]:

Mediocristan randomness is predictable; the Gaussian bell curve applies and applying statistical methods is safe. Examples of Mediocristan are human height, weight and age probability distributions, where no single outcome can dramatically change the mean. We can accurately predict events in Mediocristan with a little uncertainty, e.g. hardware lifetimes are from Mediocristan. Mediocristan randomness represents risks in Quadrants 1 and 3 in the classification.

In *Extremistan* randomness is Black Swan domain where small probabilities and rare extreme events rule. Since samples of events are so rare, the probability models will be sensitive to minor calculations changes and prone to error.

In Extremistan, events scale and are subject to *fat-tails*[1], and can appear as power law or Pareto distributions. An example of such an event is the development of the amount of malware in the wild, with a growth trend that follows a Pareto distribution, where the theoretical malware amount is close to infinity. Extremistan randomness represents risks in Quadrants 2 and 4 of the classification.

The two types of payoffs from decision making are; (1) Simple Payoffs and (2) Complex Payoffs. In the former, decisions are binary form, e.g. either true or false, infected or not infected, which is where mainly probabilities play. Decisions are more complex for the latter, where the decision-maker must also consider the impact or a function of the impact, and weight benefits against disadvantages. Type 1 is thin-tailed and non-scalable while type 2 decisions can be fat-tailed.

This accumulates into Taleb's risk classification system of four quadrants; where risks in the First Quadrant has Mediocristan randomness and low exposure to extreme events. The payoffs are simple and statistical models works. Exposure to events in the Second Quadrant comes with Mediocristan randomness with complex payoffs, where it is generally safe to apply statistical models, factoring in awareness of possible incomplete models. Exposure to Third Quadrant risks comes with Extremistan randomness and low exposure to extreme events. The Fourth Quadrant is *"the area in which both the magnitude of forecast errors is large, and the sensitivity to those errors is consequential"* [12].

The Black Swan and Four Quadrants in ICT Risk. For explicitly information security risk, the Black Swan concept has been treated by Hole and Netland [8], who treats the subject of risk assessing large-impact and rare events in ICT. Where the authors provide a basic discussion of what black and gray swans are in information systems and discuss events that may qualify as Swans. They define cascading risks and single points of failure as sources for swans, viruses, and other malware are sources for cascading risks. Additionally, Hole [7] addresses how to manage hidden risks, and how to recover quickly from Black Swan ICT incidents. Audestad (pp. 28–37) [2] discusses the limitations of statistics from an information security perspective. Audestad does not apply the term Black Swans, but he briefly discusses extreme events and limitations of statistics.

3   Methodology for Statistical Risk Analysis and Classification of Events

The primary approach for the feasibility study in this paper is theoretical and statistical analysis of several types of information risks by considering a set of related cases that accompanied by historical data. The main classification scheme that we follow in the case study is the Four Quadrants as described by Taleb [12,13]. The work to classify risks within the Four Quadrants consisted

---

[1] In comparison to the Normal distribution a Fat-tailed distribution exhibits large skewness or kurtosis.

of gathering data and analyzing information security risks to determine their properties, and if statistical data is available if it would be appropriate to run calculations. The motivation is to use conventional statistical methods with a hope to extract particular characteristics that are suitable for quantitative risk analysis and further Threat Intelligence and Threat Forecasts. Additionally, we make a hypothesis about the applicability of a particular method. The information risks we have addressed where chosen from ISO/IEC 27005:2011, and we consider risks towards entities and not persons. This work focuses on risks from the compromise of information, technical failures, and unauthorized actions and does not address risks posed by natural events or similar. The calculations in this article are based on acquired data published by others. Furthermore, we perform specific statistical tests of whether such models are applicable for historical data or not, and extract corresponding quantitative measures. Our approach focuses on usefulness and limitations of statistical methods for information security risks analysis and predictability. In particular, we have analyzed risks to determine their properties with respect to the Four Quadrants (randomness and payoff). The following subsection describes the statistical methods and probabilistic models applied in this paper.

3.1 Supplementary Statistical Methods for Historical Data Analytic

One makes a decision about information security risks mostly based on the previously collected data within the company or based on the publically available historical data about causes and results [10]. We introduce several community-accepted methods to deal with historical data and be able of making quantitative risk assessment possible since qualitative risk assessment has precision limitations when it is necessary to make predictions in numbers.

Probabilistic Modeling. This type of analysis is applied when it is a need for probability estimation of a particular event x occurrence in a given historical dataset. Initially, the model $p(x)$ is built, and an estimation of the corresponding set of parameters from the data [6]. Then, this model can be used to estimate the probability of similar events in this very period or later on. We can state that there exist many obstacles related to the probabilistic modeling. First, very few data points from history may cause a wrong decision. Second, very rare events, like in the case of Fourth Quadrant, have negligibly small probabilities. However, this does not mean that this event are not going to happen.

Numerical Analysis. Numerical analysis is a broad field of data modeling, in particular, time series. The function $f(x)$ is build using previous period of time $x_0, \cdots, x_t$. To construct a proper model, available historical data have to be decomposed into trends, seasonal components, and noise in order to build a precise prediction model. At this point, the recent data should possess the biggest degree of trust rather than data from a long time before [1]. For the defined earlier research questions that statistical models can be applied to support risk assessment within the four quadrants, yet under some limitations, we consider the following supplementary statistical approaches [1] from the previous Section:

1. **Logistics function** describes the process when the initial impact causes exponential increase until some moment of time. After this moment, the growth will be decreasing until it is saturated to some ceiling value [5].
2. **Conditional Probability** and **Bayes Theorem** are the probability methods used to calculate the likelihood of occurrence of some event when another dependent or independent event already happen.
3. **Gamma distribution** represents a family of continuous probability distributions that can describe data with quite various characteristics. The main parameters are shaped k and scale of the distribution θ.
4. **Exponential growth** characterize an event that does not have an upper boundary, and the observed outcome will grow more during the next period in comparison to previous.
5. **Log-normal probabilistic model** defines the distribution of some historical data under the condition that the logarithm of the data follows the Gaussian distribution.

So, these methods are the most promising from our point of view for estimation of possible event outcomes based on the previously analyzed information.

Statistical Hypothesis Testing. Further for each case study we will justify the usage of specific statistical methods and make a hypothesis about their applicability in that particular case. At this point, we need to use statistical tests to verify suggested hypothesis[2]. The two following approaches can be applied with probability distributions: QQ-PLOT, a Quantile-Quantile plot represents a probability plot by depicting expected theoretical quantiles E and observed practical quantiles O against each other and STATISTICAL TESTS that estimates the quantitative metrics of how well the data fit hypothesized distributions.

Confidence Intervals or CI relates to the probabilistic estimation of whether a particular data or data sample is being placed within a hypothesized distribution. It also means that the defined in CI % of data will be in the hypothesized distribution. To be precise, the tests evaluates the actual observed data O with the expected data E from the hypothesized distribution.

4   Case Studies

In this Section, we answer RQ 1 and show the application of models for ISRA with corresponding failures and Confidence Intervals (CI). This study is a comprehensive overview since a particular Case may require several methods to give a broader model. Our approach discusses specific types of risk for information security and where risks can be computed using statistical methods. We characterize information risks by the following predicate:

$$Malicious\ Intentions \xrightarrow{Action} Observable\ Outcomes \qquad (1)$$

---

[2] http://www.ats.ucla.edu/stat/stata/whatstat/whatstat.htm.

Since the original *Malicious Intentions* may not be known, the quantitative risk analysis relies on the historical data about *Observable Outcomes* that can be either published by the information security labs or available within an organization. Each risk calculation in the following case studies are made for the purpose of illustrating and discussing the risks properties, and all risks are considered from the viewpoint of an organization. Based on the publicly available sources of information we made tentative calculations to give our answers on the research questions. Although not present in this paper, we have also explicitly treated risks of Insider attacks and phishing for the classification.

4.1 Advanced Persistent Threats (APT) and Cyber Industrial Espionage

APT are professional, resourceful and global actors often supported by Nation-States. These threats conduct targeted attacks over extended periods, aiming to compromise institutions for through cyber espionage and sabotage.

There are several problems when risk assessing APT attacks; tailored malware and techniques, making signature based scanners obsolete, and detection extremely resource intensive. APTs are generally very low probability (few incidents), although some companies daily deal with this threat. Modus operandi for APTs is stealth and extract data unnoticed, and even with a large ongoing compromise, the target's operations will be business as usual, making losses hard to visualize. Observing the severity of an APT breach is only possible after an extended period, which makes consequences both hard to predict and communicate. There are several different potential outcomes ranging from benign to malicious, all associated with a considerable amount of uncertainty. The discovery of an incident will have consequences, the "Initial Shock", where the harm comes from the loss of resources from general incident handling to before returning to normal. From there, the future of the incident has a large amount of variables affecting the outcome, all with their associated uncertainties. For example if the stolen data was production information, we must consider the probability of product replication, and what harm this would bring to the company in the future. Meaning that without extensive knowledge about the attacker and historical data, we cannot assign probabilities to these variables. Thus, there is a significant amount of uncertainty related to APT attacks.

We propose the following answer to the RQ1 for APTs:

- *Data source.* Targeted organizations generally do not reveal much information about APT. Therefore, the statistics for the particular events and actions are not shown to the public, and most data are available in vague numbers after the damage done. Therefore, the only data we can rely on to deduce the exact flow of the attack can be the analysis reports published by the security labs.
- *Discussion of statistical approach.* Since the exact data in most cases are unavailable or not computable, we can rely on the potential outcomes of the APT attacks. At this point as independent variable *Time* comes after the initial shock. The dependent variable, *Consequence*, therefore follow the

numerical analysis model (1) LOGISTIC FUNCTION since at the beginning the range of probable outcomes growth exponentially until it reaches some point, where the attack approaches maximum damage. Ideally, it will grow as an (2) EXPONENTIAL FUNCTION, yet in real life there are logical boundaries unless cascading happens. In Fig. 1 we have modeled an APT incident; after the initial shock, the system returns to normal, and the uncertainty of the damage is growing until the consequences become evident. Therefore, we conclude that the best way to describe this process is to use Logistic Function, where dependent on the type of business the harm (Y-axis) must reach a maximum amount after some time.

- *Results - Uncertainty/Confidence intervals.* The second problem when estimating the risks of APT is the Confidence Interval (CI) estimation of the risk management decision. The uncertainty of the attacks against organization increases after the evidence of the initial attack, which makes the confidence interval of the predicted risk value too low to rely on it:

$$R|_{CI} \approx \frac{1}{uncertainty} \tag{2}$$

Bigger uncertainty causes less confidence in the predicted outcomes of the damage done. The larger range, the harder to estimate final risk and make an appropriate risk management decisions.

- *Results - Applicability of statistical methods and possible failures for each risk.* Since no data available, it is hard to derive any meaningful decision from the unreliable model that follows EXPONENTIAL FUNCTION. At this point, we do not have any other sources to rely on, so this model helps to understand the way of damage developing. Also, we may derive the qualitative prediction using monotonicity of the process development. This model can be used (1) to show the importance of finding the attack evidences and cause in the initial phase, and (2) impossibility to say the exact cause in the final stage until it is obvious.

- *Classification of Risk* - Without knowledge about attacker intentions and capabilities, a victim of an APT attack, particularly industrial espionage, can only make risk predictions based on knowledge about internal processes and the value of the stolen information. Even if the Logistic function corresponds to the nature of the APT harm, it is still rather a random prediction than reliable results for risk analysis. No outcomes of an APT attack will be identical, and outcomes are complex in nature, prone to cumulative effects. There is also a lack of both data and knowledge about attacks with corresponding consequences, which makes it a *Fourth Quadrant* risk.

4.2   Malware and Botnet Distributions

Successful malware distributions such as different versions of botnets, e.g. Zeus, Conficker[3] and others, have shown considerable resilience towards eradication.

---

[3] Conficker was initially a computer worm, but when the payload was uploaded post-infection, it turned out as a Botnet.

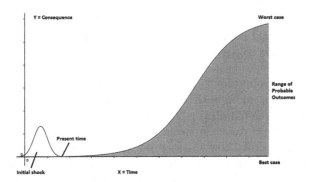

Fig. 1. Example of potential outcomes from an APT/Espionage attack, Y = Consequence X = Time. The initial shock comes from detecting and responding to the breach. The long-term C is represented as a Logistic function, where P of all A are bound with a close to unsolvable U.

Epidemic models have proven useful for estimating propagation rates [2,15], however, historical data is more useful for obtaining probability distributions. We propose the following answer to the RQ1 for Malware and Botnet distributions:

- *Data source.* For our calculations, we obtained data from the Shadowserver Foundation[4], which has monitored the infection rates of the Gameover Zeus botnet and Conficker with respect to time. Gameover Zeus is a Peer 2 Peer botnet built by cyber criminals by sending emails with embedded malicious links or attachments, or enticing the victim to visit an infected website where a Trojan infected the victim. In comparison to the APT statistics, the information about botnet distribution relatively easy to gather from publicly available sources like Shadowserver, cause the anti-virus companies construct corresponding signatures shortly after the first discovery of botnet and starts logging occurrences.
- *Discussion of statistical approach.* Based on the available statistics collected over the months by Shadowserver, we ran a fitting test as described in Sect. 3. The results concluded that the most promising hypothesis about the probabilistic model is that data follow the (1) LOGNORMAL distribution. Therefore, it can be possible to predict the exact percentage of probability of the distribution of the botnet in some period in the future. From the other side, numerical methods for time series analysis can estimate the number of malware species in the wild after a defined period. The value of the last two methods is that the trends of the malware distributions can be predicted with better accuracy that just random guessing, cause human expert may fail to do it accurately.
- *Results - Applicability of statistical methods and possible failures for each risk.* We can state that (1) the available data follows LOGNORMAL distribution, so we can use these methods to say about future conditions. (2) That is not possible to fully rely on these methods since the uncertainty in the predictions is

---

[4] Gameover Zeus. https://goz.shadowserver.org/stats/.

quite significant due to versatility in the data and tail sensitivity in the graph. However, the derived information can be used in qualitative ISRM since it is rather a set of fuzzy metrics.

We ran the data points for Gameover Zeus in QQ plot and got the best fit with a Log-Normal curve with a tendency towards a thick tail, Fig. 2. Our results show that the Gameover Zeus botnet distribution is left-skewed (positive). The initial propagation speed is high (see Fig. 4(b)), until saturation or patch released slows down the propagation, from which point the existing population deteriorates. In addition to adhering to epidemic propagation theory, there are several aspects that will influence the thickness of the tail. For example new versions of the malware being released, either exploiting a new vulnerability for increased propagation or changing behavior/coding to avoid scanners. In addition, we know that Conficker followed similar propagation and deterioration patterns, although Conficker[5] was self-replicating [15]. According to our model: if the entity is vulnerable, the general probability of infection is 30 % from the initial dissemination until the first month has passed. With a Mean population = 134,527, Standard Deviation = 64,797, and $\delta = 0.491$. The graph is sensitive to changes in the tails; this is also visible in the Q-Q plot results. The right tail of the graph in Fig. 2 would likely have been thicker if the data came from Conficker A+B, which remains active and deteriorating after six years.

– *Classification of Risk* - Single non-zeroday malware infections are generally detected and removed by antivirus software, and generally pose very little risk. However, dependent on the target infected and type of malware, the payoff can be complex. Self-propagating malware is usually more severe as they pose a threat to larger parts of the infected system. With some computer worms, the payoff can be considered simple, as the computer is infected (meaning non-operational) or not infected. Effectively having only two states of being. It is partially possible to predict exposure from such generic attacks, e.g. amount of vulnerable systems, but there is exposure to multi-vectored and other random effects which puts this risk in the *Third Quadrant*.

4.3   Distributed Denial of Service (DDoS) Attacks

One of the most feared information attacks is the DDoS attacks, as they have the potential to break servers and deny access to a service to customers over an extended period causing massive revenue losses. By monitoring activity, we can obtain reliable numbers on how large the average DDoS attack is, and generate distributions of attack magnitudes. The answer to the RQ1 for DDoS:

– *Data source.* There is available open access statistics on DDOS attacks. So, we can use available statistics, yet it can not be fully relied on due to misleading detections or hardware malfunctions. Using numbers gathered from

---

[5] See also http://www.shadowserver.org/wiki/pmwiki.php/Stats/Conficker.

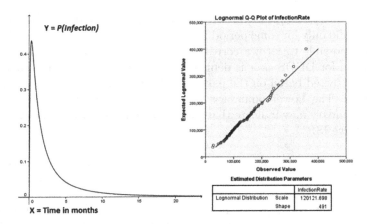

Fig. 2. Gameover Zeus infection probability distribution and timeline. Right shows results of Q-Q plot of LogNormal distribution. Data source: The Shadowserver Foundation.

open access, we generated an example of possible distribution of DDOS occurrences for different bandwidth, shown in the Fig. 3. Available threat intelligence indicated that the commonly observed DDoS magnitude at the time was between 0–90 Gbps, with distributions as seen in Table 1. Our test dataset corresponded to the numbers provided open access sources, having an arithmetic mean = 7.31, and Std. Dev = 13.55. The so-far largest reported DDoS attack was 500 Gbps, we can guesstimate that the generic probability of such an attack occurring annually is large; while the probability of such a large-scale directed attack at a single organization is negligible. There was no observed attack magnitudes over 90 Gbps in the surveys. However, we add such scenario A5 in Table 1.

- *Discussion of statistical approach.* There are several possible ways of approaching the statistical analysis of DDOS attacks. At first the probability of the DDOS attack can be calculated as simple (1) CONDITIONAL PROBABILITY, which gives an exact risk of being targeted for a DDOS attack out of possible attacks. Table 2 shows the results of calculations made for an organization that expects $P(B) = 50\%$ annual chance of DDoS attack. At second, we can say something about the number of attacks and maximal used bandwidth by considering the historical information. However, the number of maximum reported DDOS attacks follow the (2) EXPONENTIAL FUNCTION and can not be predicted for the next years: $N = N_0 \cdot e^{t'}$ since some covert parameters are not taken into consideration like breakthrough network controller speed. At third, the particular scenario can be considered when discretion intervals of DDOS bandwidth are considered like $P(DDOS > 90\,\text{Gbps}) = P(DDOS) \cdot P(> 90\,\text{Gbps}|DDOS)$. Also the (3) γ-DISTR. is the most applicable way of modeling such variety in scenarios.

– *Results - Uncertainty/Confidence intervals.* The data and estimated parameters are valid only for some period until new attack methods emerge. However, it is still possible to form a corresponding γ-distribution to characterize the bandwidth for DDOS as it is depicted in the Fig. 3(a). So, corresponding CI can be extracted based on the parameters of the distribution to estimate the DDOS [4]. The Lower boundary can be neglected, however, exceeding the upper boundary may indicate that the parameters need to be re-evaluated for quantitative ISRM.

Though the data distribution can vary and, therefore, change the form depending on newly emerged technologies in network adapters industry, we can still use CI to estimate the boundary of the desired mitigation frame. It can be stated that the company wants to eliminate some % of the DDOS attacks and estimates the threshold of the attacks based on the previously collected information. The Table 2 presents an exact range of the bandwidth at which a particular % of the attacks can be mitigated. Our particular interest is the upper boundary of the CI since the lower boundary can be ignored at this point. For example, to withstand 95 % of the DDOS attacks according to modeled γ-DIST. in the Fig. 3(b) a company has to place a DDOS protection not lower than 62.82 Gpbs.

– *Results - Applicability of statistical methods and possible failures for each risk.* We can estimate and put a threshold for an intrusion detection system to be capable of handling such attacks. Since it might be significant when guesstimating the risk that the organization takes when ignoring a particularly intensive attacks. For example, the network adapters increase capacity from 100 Mbps up to 1 Gbps over previous years. Therefore, the statistical models can be used for (1) DDOS bandwidth, and probability prediction and estimation, though constant failures of these models may indicate a need for re-evaluation of the maximal DDOS bandwidth. Furthermore, using the estimated probability, we can built also a qualitative risk estimators as more general linguistic characterization of the risk.

– *Classification of Risk* - As we have shown, it is possible to obtain distributions of DDoS attack magnitudes with associated probabilities. However, our observations can be offset by a single massive attack, such as Russia's DDoS attack on Estonia in 2007. This area is also subject to Moore's law, which means that historical observations of attack magnitudes will quickly become obsolete. We consider the payoff from DDoS attacks as simple; it either succeeds in denying service, or it does not while the duration of the attack determines the consequence. Our analysis, therefore, places risks of DDoS attacks in the *Third Quadrant*.

5   Discussion

Before presenting the Four Quadrant classification, we discuss issues that make information risks less predictable, which we have factored into our classification.

Table 1. Example of DDoS attack magnitude distributions and probabilities, with conditional probabilities of semi-annual occurrence.

Scenario	Gbps	% of attacks	P(A|B)
A1	<1	55.00 %	27.50 %
A2	1–5	15.00 %	7.50 %
A3	5–10	10.00 %	5.00 %
A4	10–90	20.00 %	10.00 %
A5	90+	Not observed (0.1 %)	0.05 %

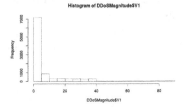

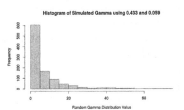

(a) Histogram of DDOS magnitude up to 90GBps

(b) Simulated γ-distribution of DDOS from collected data

Fig. 3. Comparison of the original DDOS data and modeled distribution

5.1 Factors Leading into the Fourth Quadrant

– *The Complexity-Knowledge Gap* - Knowledge about system security quickly diminishes through the increase of *complexity* and *interconnectivity*, and the larger the system, the more uncertainty. Research on complex networks has demonstrated that the number of hosts on a network follows the power law [15], and our knowledge of risks in such systems and environments diminishes quickly. Audestad [2] calls this development the Complexity-Knowledge gap Fig. 4(a).

– *Interconnection and Single Points of Failure (SPOF)* – While there is extensive knowledge of SPOF problems in the ICT domain, the risk posed by interconnectivity are easily overlooked and underestimated. For example in a Banking incident from 2001 reported in [8], a human error triggered a SPOF at an operations company delivering ICT services to banks. This mistake caused a DoS for 114 banks and roughly one-fourth of the Norwegian population at the time. Such consequences would not have been possible without a

Table 2. Confidence Intervals for defined % of the DDOS attacks to be eliminated

To eliminate	50 %	90 %	95 %	99 %
Limit_lower, Gbps	0.531143	0.012634	0.002547	0.000061
Limit_upper, Gbps	9.411601	29.566104	39.241385	62.822911

large interconnected operations company representing a SPOF for much of the transactions in Norway. A centralization of operations and processes, which allows for the creation of one large strongly interconnected hub, in which the consequences of failure can become catastrophic for the system as a whole. The society and ICT have never been as interconnected at any period in the past, which quickly outdates most risk predictions based on historical data, as systems will find new ways to fail. The Complexity-Knowledge gap will also come into play, and we are likely to miss or overlook severe risks and potential consequences.

- *The Unpredictable Active Adversary* - In most cases, the activities that lead to a targeted attack are not visible, or they are negligible. The complexity of the extreme events such as cyberwarfare or cyberterrorism in the information security domain is so high that we can hardly notice it unless the damage is done, and the outcomes are obvious [11]. Since these activities are well-planned and rather exceptional cases, there is a need for enormous data analytic and reconsideration of the Internet Crime like in the case with Stuxnet. For rare events, sophisticated classification/regression models have to be applied to conventional statistical methods to understand the nature of the event. It is sometimes necessary to get expert knowledge on the underlying adversary process rather than just rely on numbers for risk analysis. There is also the problem that the past will not reflect the future when it comes to resourceful and adaptable attackers. Advanced attackers will seek novel ways of achieving their objectives, which makes over-reliance on historical data dangerous.
- *Vulnerabilities to Cascading and Systemic risk in ICT* - Cascading and systemic risks are two types of high-level risks that are known to be large impact and low probability events. A cascading risk is when several components of a network fail in a cascade due to a crucial node going down, which subsequently causes an overload on the remaining nodes. Or when one component causes failure in interconnected components [8]. Whereas a systemic risk affects the global system and not just a particular entity. We define cascading risks as having the ability to cause localized harm, and systemic risks as having the capacity to cause global harm to a system. Of the latter, the Morris worm is probably the only known instance to have posed a systemic risk to all systems connected to the internet. The malware forced a segregation of the internet regions to prevent contamination and recontamination.

The consequences of a cascade can be devastating: In 2009, a Conficker infection within the Norwegian Police ICT systems reportedly caused damage ranging 30–50 million NOK and a downtime of 10 days. The Police computer system was largely homogenous, running older and vulnerable versions of Microsoft Windows, and Conficker was reported to have saturated at about 16 000 infections. Figure 4(b) shows general dissemination patterns of self-propagating malware; the stapled line indicates propagation in homogeneous networks. The distribution in the homogenous network follows exponential growth while the propagation in heterogeneous networks produces a model rather close to joint logistic function. Consequences from self-replicating mal-

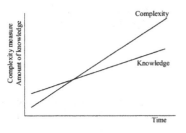

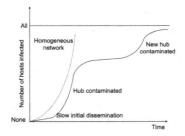

(a) The Complexity-Knowledge gap

(b) Dissemination of malware, showing Pareto curve distribution in homogenous network towards saturation.

Fig. 4. Factors leading into the Fourth Quadrant. *Pictures reprinted with permission, from Audestad, 2009* [2]

	1 Simple Payoff	2 Complex Payoff
A Mediocristan 	*First Quadrant, Extremely safe* 1. Hardware and component failure risks 2. Simple user errors	*Second Quadrant, Safe* 1. Hardware system failure risks 2. Single Malware infections 3. Generic Phishing campaigns (4. Insider attacks)
E Extremistan	*Third Quadrant, Safe* 1. DDoS Attacks 2. Self-propagating automated alware	*Fourth Quadrant, Black Swan Domain* 1. Cascading risks 2. Systemic risks 3. APT / Targeted attacks 4. Terrorist attacks 5. Cyberterror/war 6. Insider attacks 7. Complex User Errors

Fig. 5. The Four Quadrants with risk classifications. *Based on Taleb* [12]

ware and cascading risks are subject to fat tails, which requires caution when dealing with such phenomena.

The Four Quadrants Classification of Information Security Risk. Based on the case studies and the factors provided in the previous section, the non-exhaustive classification of information risks is presented in Fig. 5. This classification can help risk analyst in deciding whether to apply quantitative or qualitative risk analysis methods based on risk properties and where he can safely rely on statistical methods. The classification should not be used as an argument to not do risk assessments of Fourth Quadrant risks. However, we recommend avoiding long-term quantitative predictions with these risks due to their uncertain properties caused by a considerable complexity-knowledge gap. It is also possible that with more information and understanding, statistical risk analysis can move several of these risks out of the Fourth Quadrant.

6   Conclusion and Future Work

In this paper we investigated quantitative risk calculations based on the available data. We provided a classification of where it is safe to apply statistical methods and where to expect a reasonable return on investment in improved decision making within the Four Quadrants. This work studied whether the statistical approaches are feasible to deal with Information Security Risks at all and what are the advantages of using such methods considering fact that they are purely reliable for the prediction. One can state that conventional statistical methods provides reliable accuracy only in case of significant amount of historical data and when the event in question is located within the tolerance interval from the past data. This article has presented several major cases within the Information Security area, with a corresponding applicability study of statistical methods. We can conclude that there is a trade-off between the complexity of supplementary analytic and the risk's harm. It implies that trivial statistical methods are not suitable to deal with threat Intelligence in dangerous risks, yet general knowledge derived from such methods are reliable to make predictions better than random. Moreover, the statistical methods can not only be useful in quantitative analysis, yet also give a basis for qualitative measures. The observable outcomes may not always find a justification from the history since it might be some coincidence of logical triggers and human errors. Also, the implications of the study have discovered severe limitations of quantitative forecasts when it comes to targeted attacks, namely malicious individuals, and sophisticated threat agents. The increase in both complexity and interconnectivity limits our ability to forecast. It means that future advanced models such as Soft Computing should be considered to be able to expand the understanding of the covert malicious actions and make a better quantitative risk assessment.

Acknowledgments. The authors acknowledge Professors Jan Arild Audestad, Einar Snekkenes and Katrin Franke, and the data contributions made by the Shadowserver Foundation. The authors also recognize the sponsorship from COINS Research School for information security.

References

1. Armstrong, J.S.: Long-Range Forecasting: From Crystal Ball to Computer. Wiley, New York (1978)
2. Audestad, J.: E-Bombs and E-Grenades: The Vulnerability of the Computerized Society. Gjovik University College (2009)
3. Aven, T.: Misconceptions of Risk. Wiley, New York (2011)
4. Geyer, C.J.: Stat 5102 notes: More on confidence intervals. http://www.stat.umn.edu/geyer/old03/5102/notes/ci.pdf. Accessed 07 April 2015

5. Dey, A.K., Kundu, D.: Discriminating between the log-normal and log-logistic distributions. Commun. Stat. Theory Meth. **39**(2), 280–292 (2009)
6. Ghahramani, Z.: Probabilistic modelling, machine learning, and the information revolution. In: Presentation at MIT CSAIL (2012)
7. Hole, K.J.: Management of hidden risks. Computer **46**(1), 65–70 (2013)
8. Hole, K.J., Netland, L.-H.: Toward risk assessment of large-impact and rare events. IEEE Secur. Priv. **8**(3), 21–27 (2010)
9. Kahneman, D.: Thinking, Fast and Slow. Macmillan, New York (2011)
10. Milkman, K.L., Chugh, D., Bazerman, M.H.: How can decision making be improved? Perspect. Psychol. Sci. **4**(4), 379–383 (2009)
11. Lewis, J.A.: Assessing the risks of cyber terrorism, cyber war and other cyber threats. Technical report, Center for strategic & internation studies (2002)
12. Taleb, N.N.: Errors, robustness, and the fourth quadrant. Int. J. Forecast. **25**(4), 744–759 (2009)
13. Taleb, N.N.: The Black Swan: The Impact of the Highly Improbable, 2nd edn. Random House LLC, New York (2010)
14. Wangen, G., Snekkenes, E.: A taxonomy of challenges in information security risk management. In: Proceeding of Norwegian Information Security Conference/Norsk informasjonssikkerhetskonferanse - NISK - Stavanger, vol. 2013. Akademika forlag (2013)
15. Shui, Y., Guofei, G., Barnawi, A., Guo, S., Stojmenovic, I.: Malware propagation in large-scale networks. IEEE Trans. Knowl. Data Eng. **1**, 170–179 (2015)

Exploring a Controls-Based Assessment of Infrastructure Vulnerability

Oliver J. Farnan[(✉)] and Jason R.C. Nurse

Cyber Security Centre, University of Oxford, Oxford, UK
{oliver.farnan,jason.nurse}@cs.ox.ac.uk

Abstract. Assessing the vulnerability of an enterprise's infrastructure is an important step in judging the security of its network and the trustworthiness and quality of the information that flows through it. Currently, low-level infrastructure vulnerability is often judged in an ad hoc manner, based on the criteria and experience of the assessors. While methodological approaches to assessing an organisation's vulnerability exist, they are often targeted at higher-level threats, and can fail to accurately represent risk. Our aim in this paper therefore, is to explore a novel, structured approach to assessing low-level infrastructure vulnerability. We do this by placing the emphasis on a controls-based evaluation over a vulnerability-based evaluation. This work aims to investigate a framework for the pragmatic approach that organisations currently use for assessing low-level vulnerability. Instead of attempting to find vulnerabilities in infrastructure, we instead assume the network is insecure, and measure its vulnerability based on the controls that have (and have not) been put in place. We consider different control schemes for addressing vulnerability, and show how one of them, namely the Council on Cyber Security's Top 20 Critical Security Controls, can be applied.

1 Introduction

Finding vulnerabilities is a difficult and arduous task [39]. Nevertheless, assessing the vulnerability of computer systems and networks to attacks is a critical enterprise security activity. This includes two major types of vulnerability assessment: low-level (e.g. penetration tests or automated vulnerability scans looking for vulnerabilities such as MS08-067[1]) and high-level (e.g. ISO 27001 [20] audits looking for the existence of appropriate cryptographic storage). Both are required for various types of security risk assessments, and assist in making critical business decisions, demonstrating an organisation's security credentials, and determining the risk of compromise of its information assets. In the language of risk assessment, vulnerabilities are identified and then mitigated by controls. These are taken into consideration (sometimes with additional factors such as specific threats or threat actors) when used to assess the security of the scoped infrastructure.

---

[1] MS08-067 is a low-level vulnerability in the Windows Server Service that allows remote code execution when sent a specially crafted RPC request.

© Springer International Publishing Switzerland 2016
C. Lambrinoudakis and A. Gabillon (Eds.): CRiSIS 2015, LNCS 9572, pp. 144–159, 2016.
DOI: 10.1007/978-3-319-31811-0_9

This paper aims to explore the possibility of a more structured and rigorous approach to assessing the overall vulnerability of infrastructure against low-level vulnerabilities (e.g. whether its OpenSSL implementation is vulnerable to Heartbleed [17]). Our approach attempts to provide an unbiased assessment of infrastructure vulnerability, based on external controls from well-researched sources. We scope our work away from high-level risk analysis, where there are already several approaches in use (e.g. ISO 27001) and instead intentionally focus on the low-level technical vulnerability of an infrastructure. Moreover, at this stage we avoid higher-level factors (e.g. security procedure and policy) and do not attempt to judge the overall risk to the infrastructure.

Basing our approach on the presence or absence of controls is a different approach to previous technical assessment methodologies. Most proposed academic methods base their judgement on attempting to count the low-level vulnerabilities present, and using this as the basis for their assessment of the security of the network, infrastructure or system [1,18,21]. Similarly, within businesses, assessment of low-level vulnerability is performed by vulnerability scanning or penetration testing to discover and enumerate existing vulnerabilities on the network. Instead, our low-level evaluation takes inspiration from higher-level risk assessment methodologies, whose assessments are based on the existence (or lack thereof) of controls that an organisation has in place. An example of these is the ISO 27001:2013 standard, where auditors check to see whether a series of controls have been implemented. These controls exist at a higher-level than the vulnerabilities discovered by penetration testing or vulnerability scanning, and include checks such as whether an access control policy is in place or whether staff have been appropriately vetted.

With our approach, instead of basing the assessment on vulnerability lists and the vulnerabilities present, we base the assessment on whether certain low-level controls are in place. This is more in line with the higher-level risk assessments such as ISO 27001. Whereas typical low-level vulnerability assessments assume the network is secure unless found otherwise, we argue that the network should be considered insecure until the necessary controls (relevant to that infrastructure) have been implemented. Unknown vulnerabilities will always exist and will be impossible to defend against. Controls defending against a wide variety of attacks (such as a whitelist-based firewall, or the use of a No Execute bit against memory injection attacks) provide a greater guarantee than firefighting individual vulnerabilities. This is in line with a growing belief that networks and systems should be considered insecure by default [7,8,26].

Despite the need to assess low-level vulnerability, there is not a generally accepted way of doing so. Different methods exist for measuring the higher-level risks to an infrastructure (e.g. ISO 27001), but there is no established way of providing the low level equivalent. On the one hand there exists technical testing such as vulnerability scanning tools (e.g. Nessus [38]) and penetration testing techniques, which are widely employed but often unstructured and unsystematic. On the other hand there are several highly-structured proposed academic methods, which have not been successfully adopted into widespread use.

In the remainder of this paper, we present related work that is relevant to this discussion (Sect. 2), describe our approach (Sect. 3) and discuss an example (Sect. 4). We then critically reflect on our proposal (Sect. 5) and draw conclusions and discuss areas for future research (Sect. 6).

2   Related Work

Currently, there are several accepted methods for organisations to assess infrastructure vulnerability. Typically these involve some type of audit or risk assessment being carried out. These can range from comparing the infrastructure to standard procedural checklists (e.g. ISO 27000), to hands on technical audits (e.g. penetration tests). Each type of assessment takes into account different factors, considerations and controls, to give feedback on the strengths and weaknesses of the system.

One problem assessors face when evaluating network security is that the assessment may be biased towards their own knowledge and previous experiences. Left to their own devices, assessors may be prone to letting the systems they have previously worked with affect the assessment of that which they are currently assessing. To combat this, strict high-level information security assessment methodologies have been created such as ISO 27001 [20] and COBIT [19]. These aim to provide an explicit framework for assessors, to ensure that a structured process is maintained, while also reducing the risk of bias affecting the results of the assessment. Assessors are then trained to follow these frameworks and be objective in their assessment.

One of the criticisms of these approaches is that they are simplistic, and can be performed as checklists of controls. Recent research aims to address this. Bhattacharjee et al. [5] proposed a formal method of risk assessment that aims to take other factors into account, such as asset and vulnerability dependency. Szwed and Skrzynski [37] also consider this, with a proposal based on Fuzzy Cognitive Maps. They argue their lightweight risk assessment methodology is easy to apply, and more appropriately takes into consideration the value of assets.

While widely accepted assessment methodologies are in place for the procedural side of information security, there is nothing analogous when it comes to assessing technical vulnerabilities. Technical assessors and penetration testers frequently rely on the experience of their previous assessments to judge the overall vulnerability of the network that they are testing. Technical assessments of this kind focus on specific low-level vulnerabilities (e.g. MS08-067 present on a specific host) and do not have a structured way of building on these to provide an overall assessment of the vulnerability of an infrastructure. Executive summaries are often included to provide this bigger-picture assessment, but as there is no accepted process it is often tainted by the testers' prior experience [41].

Modern penetration testing arguably began with Karger and Schell's evaluation of Multics for the US Air Force [22,23]. They performed a thorough evaluation of Multics, and found several ways to bypass its multi-level user control system. Penetration testing is at times a controversial approach, and Valli *et al.* [41] recently assessed some of the weaknesses of relying on penetration testing. They argue that penetration testing is often not the best process to base security decisions on, and can be driven by ulterior motives. In contrast, Shah and Mehtre [33] provide an overview of current penetration testing techniques, and describe how they can be beneficial for an organisation.

Ken Thompson's 'Reflections on Trusting Trust' [39] is the classic paper on the difficulty of detecting vulnerabilities. He demonstrates the possibility of a vulnerability invisible even to thorough source code review, and gives a clever example of a vulnerability that would be difficult to detect via automated means. Nevertheless, vulnerability scanners are a common tool used for the detection of low-level vulnerabilities in systems and networks. Examples of scanners include Nessus [38], OpenVAS [29] and Core Impact [9], which are used in many proposed academic methods for assessing infrastructure vulnerability [18,21].

In practice, both vulnerability scanning and penetration testing work by targeting specific systems and devices, and sequentially testing for the existence of vulnerabilities, generally by attempting to exploit them with non-malicious payloads. Details of these vulnerabilities can be found in comprehensive databases such as CVE Details [14] or NIST NVD [28], where there is also information available on their impact (via CVSS scores). Vulnerability scanning involves scanning the infrastructure with automated tools which are designed to find and fingerprint vulnerabilities, while penetration testing involves performing the process manually, resulting in a more thorough analysis. If the infrastructure proves vulnerable to an attack it is recorded and presented in a report. A report is then produced listing the vulnerabilities that were discovered on the host.

There has also been a noteworthy amount of academic research on assessing infrastructure vulnerability. These primarily aim to judge the vulnerability of infrastructure based on the low-level vulnerabilities detected. Jajodia and Noel [21] have proposed a method for assessing the vulnerability of network topologies based on the accumulative vulnerabilities of paths into and out of the network. These vulnerabilities are detected using scanners such as Nessus [38], and can be used with the network intrusion detection system Snort [34] to correlate received alerts. Ahmed *et al.* [1] describe a method for assessing the vulnerability of a network based partly on the vulnerabilities that have historically been present. They find that if a service has a history of vulnerabilities, there is a higher probability that the service will be vulnerable in the future.

Holm *et al.* [18] analyse the effectiveness of different rubrics for judging systems vulnerabilities through CVSS scores. They base their work on the time taken to compromise systems in the cyber-defence exercise Baltic Shield [16], an exercise which pitched a red team of attackers against blue teams of defenders trying to prevent the compromise of a network. The known vulnerabilities of the systems had their CVSS scores combined using several methodologies proposed by other researchers, and the assessment of these methodologies was compared to the actual time taken to compromise the systems. The study found that simple methodologies only looking at the most serious vulnerabilities present in each system or service (based on the security belief of 'weakest link in the chain') were not as effective at estimating the difficulty to compromise the network as those that took more information into account. Teodor *et al.* [35] followed on from this by presenting a modelling language for analysing the security of enterprise system architectures. They found that analyses using their model can be as accurate as assessments performed by security professionals. In a similar vein, Feng *et al.* [15] recently proposed a method to consider the relationship between risks. Their approach uses Bayesian networks to consider not just the vulnerability, but its context within an infrastructure.

To summarise, most of the research into proposed methods of low-level vulnerability analysis are based on the presence of vulnerabilities. Despite these proposals, none of these methodologies appear have gone on to widespread use on live systems. This is in contrast to the higher-level vulnerability assessment methodologies (e.g. ISO 27001), which are primarily controls-based. While there are many possible reasons for this, one major factor may be the difficulty in determining which low-level vulnerabilities are present. While processes that rely on knowing which low-level vulnerabilities exist may work in controlled tests, they are likely to be more difficult to implement when analysing live systems.

Not content with the frequently ad hoc nature of low-level information security defences, there have been several attempts to produce standardised lists of controls. Two examples relevant to this discussion are the Council on Cyber Security's Top 20 Critical Security Controls [10,12] and Australian Signals Directorate (ASD) 35 Cyber Security Mitigation Strategies [3].

The Council on Cyber Security's Top 20 Critical Security Controls (CSC 20) is a set of 20 security controls based on an observed need for a standardised controls list of this type. It was drawn up by an array of 'companies, government agencies, institutions, and individuals from every part of the [security] ecosystem' [10], based on an 'offence informs defence' approach. They have been widely adopted by other organisations [30], including SANS [31] and the UK Centre for the Protection of National Infrastructure (CPNI) [13]. The CSC 20 is regularly updated, and is on version 5.1 since its inception in 2012. An example of a CSC 20 control is: Limitation and control of network ports, protocols and services.

The ASD's 35 Cyber Security Mitigation Strategies is a series of 35 controls ranked in order of overall effectiveness at network protection. It places particular emphasis on their top 4 mitigation strategies, which they argue stop 85 % of targeted cyber intrusions [3]. It is written at a slightly lower-level of abstraction than the CSC 20, and largely include similar and overlapping controls [11]. An example of an ASD control is: Restrict access to Server Message Block (SMB) and NetBIOS services (this example would be covered by the slightly-higher level CSC 20 control mentioned above – i.e. Limitation and control of network ports, protocols and services).

3   A Controls-Based Approach

Our approach to vulnerability assessment is based on the thesis that all infrastructures are vulnerable, and that this vulnerability can only be mitigated with the implementation of certain controls. This is similar to higher-level risk assessment methodologies (e.g. ISO 27001). Using control schemes such as the CSC 20, we are instead exploring the possibility of basing low-level vulnerability assessments on the controls present. A system that correctly and securely implements all controls is considered as secure as it can be under the scheme, while a system that implements no controls is assessed as being insecure. This view is supported by the growing belief that we cannot take the trustworthiness of network infrastructure for granted [7,8]. Unfortunately devices are still often not built with security in mind, and contain numerous undiscovered vulnerabilities [32]. Instead of assuming technology is secure until proven otherwise, it is prudent to consider it insecure until proven secure.

Instead of attempting to create an exhaustive list of vulnerabilities or controls that affect infrastructure vulnerability, our approach relies on lists of controls compiled from other sources. We see two primary advantages in doing so. Firstly, the method itself can be static and not constantly changing. This makes the process more robust, not dependent on specific vulnerabilities, and not impacted by the changing vulnerability landscape. Secondly, there is already a large amount of research into the most effective controls to address vulnerability. Instead of replicating this work, we can build on it. Moreover, determining the vulnerabilities or controls which have the most effect on infrastructure vulnerability is a large and complex task, and far beyond the scope of this current paper.

Our approach follows a multi-step process. We envisage that the steps can be repeated using different control schemes, without losing the overall structure of the assessment. The approach is defined as follows:

Step 1 – Scope the infrastructure to be evaluated. When performing any security assessment it is important to determine exactly which assets are to be covered. This will allow the assessors focus on the area where risk has been identified, and not spend time assessing assets not considered vital to the organisation. This can be a complex process, and must consider the interdependencies within and across the organisation.

Step 2 – Select the control list to be applied. Compliance with different control lists will offer different levels of assurance to the infrastructure. Two control lists that currently meet these requirements are the CSC 20 and ASDs 35 Cyber Security Mitigation Strategies. Control schemes should be chosen with consideration of the following criteria:

- *It is appropriate for the infrastructure* – e.g. the controls it contains are relevant and provide relevant defences to the infrastructure being assessed.
- *It is held in high regard with the stakeholders and industry* – e.g. the control list should be an accepted national or international standard.
- *It is relatively up-to-date such that it addresses current vulnerabilities* – e.g. the control list addresses the current threats to infrastructure security.

Step 3 – Determine whether all controls are appropriate, and how to deal with conflicts against the control set and the infrastructure. Not all controls will apply to all infrastructures. For example, an external firewall is not necessary if the network is airgapped. If a control is not relevant this will normally mean that the infrastructure is secure against the attacks that the control is used to defend against. Continuing the example, the airgapped network is not vulnerable to attacks from external networks.

Step 4 – Assess whether each identified control has been implemented, and whether the level of implementation is appropriate and adequate. This is checked against each control in the list, one at a time. For control lists that give multiple sub-controls (as with the CSC 20, discussed in Sect. 4), it may be desirable to further detail the assessment of the infrastructure's compliance with the control. For example, using logging:

- No Logging: No logging takes place.
- Local Logging: Logging exists but it is basic and localised (e.g. occurring in Windows Event Viewer rather than a dedicated application).
- Centralised Logging: Logging occurs in a standardised output and is centralised (e.g. syslog format is stored in rsyslog).

Step 5 – Combine individual control assessments to give an overall assessment of the infrastructure. Once the status of the relevant controls has been determined, they can be combined to give an overall vulnerability score, a simplified heuristic. If the controls were broken down into sub-controls, the assessment can take this into account using the coverage of the sub-controls to give a finer granularity of vulnerability score. There are certainly more intelligent ways of calculating the network vulnerability score, in a similar way that there are more intelligent ways of assessing the vulnerability of a network than adding up the scores of its vulnerabilities [18]. Determining how to best consider controls to produce an overall and meaningful network vulnerability score is a critical area for future research if controls-based approaches are to be adopted.

4   Applying the Approach to a Scenario Using CSC 20

To demonstrate and discuss how our method can be applied in practice, we have applied it to an example network below.

Step 1 – Scope the infrastructure to be evaluated. The example network that we are going to be analysing is a small network for 20 IT professionals. It is primarily a Windows network, with two Windows 2008 Domain Controllers (DC) and 20 Windows 7 laptops which can either connect directly to the network (if they are in the office), or connect to the network via a VPN (if they are outside of the office). As well as these, there are several internal servers offering services to the staff, including file storage and bespoke applications for help with report writing, issue tracking and code repositories. The network is connected to the Internet which is protected by a firewall, and within the office there is a physical Ethernet connection.

Step 2 – Select the control list to be applied. The control set that we will be applying to this network is the CSC 20 [12]. The CSC 20 offers a comprehensive list of low-level controls that are sub-divided into further sub-controls. These controls are up-to-date at the time of the assessment, and are appropriate to the infrastructure that we are assessing.

Step 3 – Determine whether all controls are appropriate, and how to deal with conflicts against the control set and the infrastructure. While most of the controls from the CSC 20 are valid and can be applied to our network, CSC 7: Wireless Access Control is not applicable as the network does not have wireless access. As this control is aimed at preventing unauthorised access from wireless connections it is assessed that the network does not require this control, and can be assumed secure against associated attack vectors.

Step 4 – Assess whether each identified control has been implemented, and whether the level of implementation is appropriate and adequate. While it is not possible to fully assess all CSC 20 controls within this paper, we assess the implementation of one control to demonstrate how the assessment is performed.

Within the CSC 20, each control can be further divided into sub-controls. For example, CSC 1 - Inventory of Authorised and Unauthorised Devices, is divided into 7 sub-controls. These range from having an automated asset discovery tool (CSC 1-1) to using client certificates to validate and authenticate systems prior to their connection to the network (CSC 1-7). Each of these sub-controls has a property relating to their difficulty to implement. Sub-controls are listed as 'quick wins', visibility and attribution, configuration and hygiene, or advanced.

There are many ways these sub-controls can be combined to give the overall effectiveness of the defence against the vulnerabilities they are mitigating. While there are several attempts at accumulating vulnerabilities' risk to give an overall assessment [6,25,27,40], no equivalent has been proposed for controls.

The method we will use for this example is simply to divide the sub-controls in place by the total sub-controls for that control. For example, if there are seven sub-controls for a control, and four of them are in place, that control will receive a score of 0.57 (4/7). If there are nine sub-controls and eight of them are in place, that control will receive a score of 0.89 (8/9). Using this method, an individual score for all of the CSC 20 controls can be quickly calculated.

To assess the 19 remaining CSC security controls we must go through each of them in turn. To give an example of the system, we will cover the controls in CSC 5: Malware Defence.

CSC 5: Malware Defence looks at the different defences that are in place to defend against malware. It has 11 sub-controls. A full listing of CSC 5 can be found online [10].

The example network has thorough anti-malware practices in place. On their workstations, DCs and other servers they have an enterprise malware solution that is automatically updated and has receives new signatures periodically. This software automatically scans email attachments and the contents of removable media before they can be opened. In addition to this, they have both a behavioural and signature-based Intrusion Detection System (IDS). See Table 1 for the completed CSC 5: Malware Defence assessment sheet.

Step 5 – Combine individual control assessments to give an overall assessment of the infrastructure. Once the analysis is complete, the scores of each control

Table 1. CSC 5: Malware Defence

5-1	Yes	The network meets this requirement as they have the necessary antivirus and host-based functionality deployed
5-2	Yes	Antivirus signatures are pushed out from a centralised repository
5-3	Yes	The systems have been configured to not auto-run content from removable media
5-4	Yes	The antivirus software has been configured to automatically scan removable media
5-5	Yes	Emails going into the organisation are scanned for malicious content before the user receives them
5-6	Yes	Address Space Layout Randomisation (ASLR) and Data Execution Prevention (DEP) are enabled by default on Windows 7 and Server 2008
5-7	No	There is no system in place for monitoring the use of external devices, so this requirement is not met
5-8	Yes	Both signature-based and behavioural IDS are running on the network
5-9	No	Although there are IDS in place, they only generate alerts when malware is detected, and do not actively prevent its delivery
5-10	No	There is no incident response process in place for unrecognised malware
5-11	Yes	DNS query logging is part of their IDS solution

CSC 5: Malware Defence Score: 0.727 (Yes - 8 / No - 11)

are combined to give the overall vulnerability score of the example network. The overall vulnerability score for the entire example network is 0.639. See Table 2 for the completed CSC assessment sheet, with values for each CSC control.

This is a simplified example, but demonstrates how control lists can be used to provide a potentially useful metric of vulnerability. This could easily be converted into a Low, Medium and High rating (as is often used for penetration testing and vulnerability scanning) or Fail, Partial and Pass rating (as is often used for high level assessments) depending on how the organisation prefers the information to be presented and how it is going to be used.

5   Reflection on the Approach, Its Utility, and Acceptance

The aim of this paper is to explore the use and value in adopting a controls-based approach to assessing infrastructure vulnerability, as opposed to the traditional methods based on detecting and counting low-level vulnerabilities. Below, we reflect on the advantages and limitations of our approach, and compare it against traditional analyses of low-level vulnerability. While this comparison is not exhaustive, it provides a critical reflection on the approach, including its benefits and limitations, and situations where it may be most applicable.

Table 2. Control score

CSC 1: 0.8	Inventory of Authorised and Unauthorised Devices
CSC 2: 0.74	Inventory of Authorised and Unauthorised Software
CSC 3: 0.545	Secure Configurations for Hardware and Software on Mobile Devices, Laptops, Workstations, and Servers
CSC 4: 0.777	Continuous Vulnerability Assessment and Remediation
CSC 5: 0.727	Malware Defences
CSC 6: 0.5	Application Software Security
CSC 7: N/A (1)	Wireless Access Control
CSC 8: 0.666	Data Recovery Capability
CSC 9: 0.75	Security Skills Assessment and Appropriate Training to Fill Gaps
CSC 10: 0.5	Secure Configurations for Network Devices such as Firewalls, Routers, and Switches
CSC 11: 0.5	Limitation and Control of Network Ports, Protocols, and Servers
CSC 12: 0.545	Controlled Use of Administrative Privileges
CSC 13: 0.75	Boundary Defence
CSC 14: 0.925	Maintenance, Monitoring, and Analysis of Audit Logs
CSC 15: 0.667	Controlled Access Based on the Need to Know
CSC 16: 0.235	Account Monitoring and Control
CSC 17: 0.4	Data Protection
CSC 18: 0.333	Incident Response and Management
CSC 19: 0.688	Secure Network Engineering
CSC 20: 1	Penetration Tests and Red Team Exercises

Final CSC 20 Vulnerability Score: 0.653

5.1 Potential Advantages of Controls-Based Approach

(1) More vulnerabilities exist than controls – While there many known vulnerabilities [14], the majority of these can be mitigated with a competitively small number of controls. Indeed, the ASD strongly argue that 85 % of targeted cyber intrusions can be stopped with 4 controls [4]. This is because controls have a one-to-many relationship with vulnerabilities, with one control mitigating or removing many different vulnerabilities. For example, a 'No Execute' bit will prevent many memory injection vulnerabilities.

(2) It is quicker and more efficient to determine the presence of controls than vulnerabilities – Finding the vulnerabilities present in a system is a time consuming and subsequently, often time-limited process. This is because of the large number of vulnerabilities that could exist over an infrastructure. Regardless of the infrastructure being tested, there will often be more potential vulnerabilities than it is possible to check for [24].

In penetration testing, the time limitation is expressed in the time scoped for the test. Whoever is scoping the assessment will judge how long the test will need, and then the testers attack the network until that time is up. Penetration testing gives diminishing returns over time. Given a five day test, many vulnerabilities will likely be found over the first one or two days, and fewer will be discovered towards the end of the week. While many vulnerabilities are easy to test for (in part because of vulnerability scanners, which are themselves part of a penetration tester's tool kit) the more esoteric vulnerabilities can take longer to manually test for, and the majority of any in-depth penetration test will be spent testing for these. With vulnerability scanning, the time is limited by the signatures available to the scanner. When vulnerabilities are discovered, signatures testing that vulnerability are written. These are generally a non-malicious payload sent to the service to observe its response. These signatures take time to write, and there are no vulnerability scanners that claim to find all vulnerabilities.

(3) It is less risky to measure the presence of controls than vulnerabilities – While vulnerability scanners can scan for the existence of many vulnerabilities, there are exploits that it is either not possible, or not desirable, to test for (e.g. denial of service vulnerabilities on live systems). This is in contrast to controls, which have all been deliberately implemented by administration staff, ensuring that someone is always aware of their presence. Related to that is the issue that scanning or testing for vulnerabilities can have side effects. Performing scans of devices, even relatively benign scans such as port scanning, can cause device issues and crashes. More advanced tests (e.g. testing vulnerability payloads) can cause increasingly complex problems, such as data corruption or putting a system into an unknown state. Malware, in particular, can result in unwanted side effects, and is a tool not often used in penetration tests (especially against live systems) for this reason. Although this risk can be addressed by taking a virtual image of the infrastructure to test against rather than the live system, this can be a complex and costly process. As a result, such virtualisation is not performed routinely for vulnerability scanning or penetration testing.

(4) Vulnerability-based risk assessment does not consider unknown vulnerabilities – Zero day exploits will not be found by vulnerability scanners, and are unlikely to be detected during penetration tests (depending on the nature of the vulnerability, and the skill, detection and time of the testers). In contrast, controls can and do protect against zero day attacks. For example, Address Space Layout Randomisation will protect against a buffer overflow attack whether the vulnerability it is exploiting is known or not. As a result, the vulnerability of a system to zero day attacks is better measured by the controls it has in place, than its vulnerability to other exploits.

5.2   Potential Limitations of Controls-Based Approach

(1) The vulnerability landscape is constantly changing – New attacks (or even whole classes of attacks) can be discovered, and an assessment methodology should be flexible and able to take this into account. Most methodologies used in practice attempt to do this by manually reassigning their assessment criteria (or

controls) periodically. With ISO 27001 this happened in 2013, with the update from ISO 27001:2005 to ISO 27001:2013 making changes to the controls (as well as the broader assessment methodology) that were included in the assessment. While the control schemes we have discussed aim to take this into account, there still needs to be a manual update and new version of the control list in order to do so.

(2) Current methods of assessment already have traction and assessment within industry – Penetration tests, vulnerability scans, and high-level information security audits are already established within industry. There already exist trained auditors and organisations who can perform these assessments, and there is a demand and an acceptance of them within business. Compared to low-level vulnerability-based risk assessments, using controls at this level is a relatively unexplored idea. Low-level controls-based risk assessment needs a large amount of development to give it the same maturity as the existing approaches.

While a lack of precedent may be fatal in other areas of organisational decision making, it is an even greater problem within the security industry. Security status is often proven via certification or accreditation, and performing a new approach that does not offer this greatly reduces the benefit of performing the security evaluation in the first place.

(3) Vulnerabilities with no known controls are not taken into account, regardless of their presence – New attack vectors with no known controls are not taken into consideration during a controls-based assessment. A good recent example of that is BadUSB [36], which opened up an entirely new line of attacks that had previously not been considered. As a result of this, there are few (if any) controls in place to mitigate against it. This is in contrast with traditional penetration testing and vulnerability scanning, which can consider new vulnerabilities immediately upon their discovery. We saw this with Heartbleed [17], where vulnerability scanners were available to check for its presence the same day that the vulnerability became public knowledge.

Control lists have to be manually updated with a new version produced before a vulnerability is taken into consideration. Generally speaking, this is a bigger weakness against new attack vectors (e.g. BadUSB [36]) than against new vulnerabilities (e.g. Hearthbleed [17]), as new vulnerabilities are often mitigated by existing controls (due to the nature of the one control to many vulnerability relationship). The control lists mentioned in this paper are attempting to stay up-to-date with currently vulnerabilities, but this process is not always easy, and will never be immediate.

(4) More research is needed to find suitable methods for determining overall vulnerability – Simply adding the number of scores together to give a value is not as thoroughly researched as many of the referenced vulnerability-based approaches. This is inevitable given the amount of work already in this area. Ideally, to take our work forward, some research and experimentation of that depth should be repeated based on a controls-based approach.

5.3 Approach Acceptance

Ultimately, assessments of infrastructure vulnerability are often driven by business interests. While an organisation may be able to 'sell' a new evaluation methodology, this is not achievable or desirable from an academic perspective. In order for any method of evaluating security to be successful, organisations must see benefit in adopting it. In reality, the vulnerability and risk assessment market is dominated by established vendors, who have little incentive to change their methodology.

One possible motivator for change is that the standard ways of assessing low-level vulnerability (penetration testing and vulnerability scanning) are expensive. As the majority of the proposed academic approaches [1,18,21] that we have found are based on having pre-existing knowledge of the low-level vulnerabilities in place, this cost exists with them as well. This expense is due to the high-level of assessor skill required to correctly find and identify the vulnerabilities. Even with vulnerability scanners, while they are easy to operate, they often report false positives which require verification to be certain of their existence [42]. This high skill requirement is expensive, and one reason why penetration testing is performed so sparingly.

The expense of finding low-level vulnerabilities contrasts with performing assessments based on control lists. As seen with higher-level assessment (such as ISO 27001) it is possible for assessors to ensure that controls are in place without being highly skilled in the technology they are assessing. It takes a comparatively small amount of training for assessors to be able to correctly identify that controls are in place, and ensure that they are configured correctly. This difference in required knowledge could result in controls-based assessments being more cost effective to perform, and therefore make good business sense, and could help the approach be applied to small and medium sized enterprises (which often have difficulty justifying the resources required to perform security assessments [2]).

6 Conclusion and Future Work

A repeatable and accepted method of judging the low-level vulnerability of an infrastructure would be a useful tool in ensuring system and network security. We argue that one achievable way to do this is transitioning from vulnerability-based risk assessment to controls-based risk assessment. To this end, we proposed an approach based on controls to assess the vulnerability of a computer infrastructure. We then illustrated with an example, how our approach could be applied using a control set, namely the CSC 20, to assess an infrastructure's vulnerability. This presents a simple but effective method of using the sum of all offered (sub-)controls to measure the overall control coverage.

The main difference between our method and earlier approaches is that prior methods attempt to rate overall vulnerability based on the number of low-level vulnerabilities found. We have discussed in depth why we believe this may not be the ideal approach to the situation. While the method that we propose does have drawbacks, we believe these are outweighed by the benefits. Detecting all vulnerabilities is simply not possible, therefore measuring the controls is more likely to give an accurate and achievable indication of true vulnerability.

In terms of future work, there are many avenues to pursue, particularly around demonstrating the validity of this process. As seen with vulnerability-based assessments, there are many different ways that the measured data can be combined to give an overall evaluation of the risk to the network. A first step would be to apply our approach to real networks, and see how well the results correlate against other risk assessment methodologies. This approach could be taken further by performing a similar assessment to Holm *et al.* [18], comparing different methodologies against the time-to-compromise of a known system. This methodology could also be used to analyse how to best determine the vulnerability scores that our final assessment is based on. At this stage, our research is primarily exploring the advantages to using a controls-based measurement over a vulnerability-based one; repeating their work considering controls-based assessments against vulnerability-based assessments, and comparing those to time-to-compromise would be a key indicator of the validity of this approach.

Similarly, work should be conducted on the optimal way to combine compliance over multiple controls to calculate a realistic vulnerability assessment. An example of this would be looking at whether certain controls should be weighted differently, or how a single major control failure should impact the overall assessment of the infrastructure (i.e. the validity of the weakest link security model in this context). In the example network (Sect. 4) we merely give a mean of the number of controls that have been complied with. This is clearly a simplistic approach, and is unlikely to give the strongest indicator of the vulnerability of the network. This is similar to other work which has been performed on assessing overall vulnerability by the presence of low-level vulnerabilities [6,25,27,40]. One potentially viable way to do this would be to combine it with control lists that have different levels of controls, e.g. the CSC 20 with 'quick win' controls versus 'advanced' controls. It would be interesting to see which of these give a better indication of the vulnerability of the network, and how this correlates to the cost (both in time and resources) in implementing them.

There should also be further research into different control sets and their efficacy. While the CSC 20 and ASD 35 were discussed in this paper, research should analyse other control sets and how they are generated, to determine what actually makes an effective set of controls. We should study which controls are the most effective at increasing time-to-compromise, and how controls can be combined to offer the most security.

Although this work is mainly intended to be an exploration into the utility of controls-based, low-level risk assessment, we believe there could be genuine benefit to exploring it further. Given the amount of work that has gone into vulnerability-based risk assessment there is still a long way to go to reach that level of maturity.

References

1. Ahmed, M.S., Al-Shaer, E., Khan, L.: A novel quantitative approachfor measuring network security. In: INFOCOM 27th Conference onComputer Communications. IEEE (2008)
2. Allan, C., Annear, J., Beck, E., Van Beveren, J.: A framework for the adoption of ICT and security technologies by SMEs. In: 16th Annual Conference of Small Enterprise Association of Australia and New Zealand, vol. 28, pp. 65–81 (2003)
3. Austrailian Signals Directorate - Strategies to Mitigate TargettedCyber Intrusions (2014). www.asd.gov.au/infosec/top35mitigatestrategies.htm
4. Austrailian Signals Directorate - Top 4 Strategies to MitigateTargetted Cyber-Intrusions (2014). www.asd.gov.au/infosec/top-mitigations/top-4-strategies-explained.htm
5. Bhattacharjee, J., Sengupta, A., Mazumdar, C.: A formal methodology for enterprise information security risk assessment. In: International Conference on Risks and Security of Internet and Systems (CRiSIS), pp. 1–9. IEEE (2013)
6. Boyer, W., McQueen, M.: Ideal based cyber security technical metrics for control systems. In: Lopez, J., Hämmerli, B.M. (eds.) CRITIS 2007. LNCS, vol. 5141, pp. 246–260. Springer, Heidelberg (2008)
7. Chakrabarti, A., Manimaran, G.: Internet infrastructure security: a taxonomy. IEEE Netw. 16(6), 13–21 (2002)
8. Chen, H., Chen, Y., Summerville, D.H.: A survey on the application of FPGAs for network infrastructure security. IEEE Commun. Surv. Tutorials 13(4), 541–561 (2011)
9. Penetration Testing with Core Impact Pro (2014). http://www.coresecurity.com/core-impact-pro
10. Council on Cybersecurity (2014). www.counciloncybersecurity.org
11. Council on Cybersecurity: The ASD 35 and the Council on CyberSecurity Critical Security Controls (2014). http://www.counciloncybersecurity.org/bcms-media/Files/Download?id=a681a325-e26c-40f4-ad6e-a34200f79084
12. Council on Cybersecurity: The Critical Security Controls for Effective Cyber Defence, version 5.1 (2015). http://www.counciloncybersecurity.org/bcms-media/Files/Download?id=a52977d7-a0e7-462e-a4c0-a3bd01512144
13. CPNI: Critical Security Controls Guidance (2014). www.cpni.gov.uk/advice/cyber/Critical-controls
14. CVE Details The ultimate security vulnerability datasource (2014). www.cvedetails.com
15. Feng, N., Wang, H.J., Li, M.: A security risk analysis model for information systems: causal relationships of risk factors and vulnerability propagation analysis. Inf. Sci. 256, 57–73 (2014)
16. Geers, K.: Live fire exercise: preparing for cyber war. J. Homel. Secur. Emerg. Manage. 7(1), 1–6 (2010)
17. The Heartbleed Bug (2014). http://heartbleed.com
18. Holm, H., Ekstedt, M., Andersson, D.: Empirical analysis of system-level vulnerability metrics through actual attacks. IEEE Trans. Dependable Secure Comput. 9(6), 825–837 (2012)
19. COBIT 4.1: Framework for IT Governance and Control (2014). www.isaca.org/Knowledge-Center/COBIT/Pages/Overview.aspx
20. ISO/IEC 27001 Information security management (2014). www.iso.org/iso/home/standards/management-standards/iso27001.htm

21. Jajodia, S., Noel, S.: Topological vulnerability analysis. In: Jajodia, S., Liu, P., Swarup, V., Wang, C. (eds.) Cyber Situational Awareness, pp. 139–154. Springer, New York (2010)
22. Karger, P.A., Schell, R.R.: Multics Security Evaluation Volume II. Vulnerability Analysis. Technical report, DTIC Document (1974)
23. Karger, P.A., Schell, R.R.: Multics security evaluation: vulnerability analysis. In: 18th Annual Computer Security Applications Conference, pp. 127–146. IEEE (2002)
24. Will vulnerabiliy assessments and penetration testing find all the security vulnerabilities in your systems? (2014). http://www.krypsys.com/news/will-vulnerability-assessments-and-penetration-testing-find-all-the-security-vulnerabilities-in-your-systems
25. Lai, Y.P., Hsia, P.L.: Using the vulnerability information of computer systems to improve the network security. Comput. Commun. **30**(9), 2032–2047 (2007)
26. Liu, S., Kuhn, R., Rossman, H.: Surviving insecure IT: effective patch management. IT Prof. **11**(2), 49–51 (2009)
27. McQueen, M.A., Boyer, W.F., Flynn, M.A., Beitel, G.A.: Time-to-compromise model for cyber risk reduction estimation. Quality of Protection, pp. 49–64. Springer, New York (2006)
28. NIST: National vulnerability database (2014). http://nvd.nist.gov
29. OpenVAS Open Vulnerability Assessment System (2014). http://www.openvas.org
30. SANS: 90% of SANS Survey Respondents Are Adopting, or Plan toAdopt, the Critical Security Controls (2014). http://www.counciloncybersecurity.org/articles/90-of-sans-survey-respondents-are-adopting-or-plan-to-adopt-the-critical-security-controls-2
31. SANS Critical Security Controls for Effective Cyber Defence (2014). http://www.sans.org/critical-security-controls
32. Schneier, B.: Schneier on Security: The Internet of Things is Wildly Insecure and Often Unpatchable (2014). http://www.schneier.com/essays/archives/2014/01/the_internet_of_thin.html
33. Shah, S., Mehtre, B.: An overview of vulnerability assessment and penetration testing techniques. J. Comput. Virol. Hacking Tech. **11**, 1–23 (2014)
34. Snort (2014). http://www.snort.org
35. Sommestad, T., Ekstedt, M., Holm, H.: The cyber security modeling language: a tool for assessing the vulnerability of enterprise system architectures. IEEE Syst. J. **7**(3), 363–373 (2013)
36. Bad USB (2014). http://srlabs.de/badusb/
37. Szwed, P., Skrzyński, P.: A new lightweight method for security risk assessment based on fuzzy cognitive maps. Int. J. Appl. Math. Comput. Sci. **24**(1), 213–225 (2014)
38. Tenable Network Security Nessus (2014). http://www.tenable.com
39. Thompson, K.: Reflections on trusting trust. Commun. ACM **27**(8), 761–763 (1984)
40. Tupper, M., Zincir-Heywood, A.N.: VEA-bility security metric: A network security analysis tool. In: Third International Conference on Availability, Reliability and Security (ARES), pp. 950–957. IEEE (2008)
41. Valli, C., Woodward, A., Hannay, P., Johnstone, M.: Why penetration testing is a limited use choice for sound cyber security practice. In: Proceedings of the Conference on Digital Forensics, Security and Law, pp. 35–40 (2014)
42. Vieira, M., Antunes, N., Madeira, H.: Using web security scanners to detect vulnerabilities in web services. In: International Conference on Dependable Systems & Networks (DSN), IEEE/IFIP, pp. 566–571. IEEE (2009)

Quantifying Security in Web ETL Processes

Salma Dammak$^{(\boxtimes)}$, Faiza Ghozzi Jedidi, and Faiez Gargouri

MIR@CL Laboratory, University of Sfax, BP 242, 3021 Sfax, Tunisia
damak.salma@gmail.com, jedidi.faiza@gmail.com
faiez.gargouri@isimsf.rnu.tn

Abstract. Nowadays, security represents the new attention of current world. It is the key issue for assuring the quality of software development. Since, security is one of the non-functional requirements; it is recurrently ignored in the requirements phase. And within limited financial statement, security managers have to patch up the increasing number of WeBhouse vulnerabilities. It is possible to reduce software development cost and time to identify user security requirement in the early stage of the software development process.

To develop a secure system, security managers need to assess vulnerabilities in order to prioritize them. In this paper, we discuss security in the WEB ETL processes taking into account business needs and vulnerabilities assessments. To this end, our work evaluates vulnerabilities according to two metrics: severity impact and remediation cost. We adopt the Common Vulnerability Scoring System (CVSS) to quantify the severity impact and extend the Cosmic used for security measuring purposes to estimate the effort needed for remediation.

Keywords: Web ETL · Vulnerabilities · Measure · Severity · Remediation cost · CVSS

1 Introduction

Security is an important issue that must be considered as a fundamental requirement in information systems development, and particularly in software development. With the recent popularity of Internet and new ways of communication, the opportunity for logging and analyzing the user's navigation path grows. Though, a new architecture in decisional systems has emerged, named WeBhouse.

WeBhouse [9] collects huge amount of heterogeneous data. These data are complex and concern different types of information, coming from different sources, and presented on different supports. A great variety of different vulnerabilities exist for WeBhouse. Each one has different impact on the quality and security attributes of the WeBhouse such as confidentiality, integrity and availability. Therefore security must be tackled at all stages of the development. The use of quantitative security vulnerability assessment methods enables efficient prioritization of security efforts and investments to mitigate the discovered vulnerabilities and thus an opportunity to lower expected losses. Lord Kelvin said, "If you cannot measure it, you cannot improve it. When you can measure what you are speaking about, and express it in numbers, you know something about it; but when you cannot measure it, when you cannot express it

© Springer International Publishing Switzerland 2016
C. Lambrinoudakis and A. Gabillon (Eds.): CRiSIS 2015, LNCS 9572, pp. 160–173, 2016.
DOI: 10.1007/978-3-319-31811-0_10

in numbers, your knowledge is of a meager and service quality, and to improve a process. However, measuring security is hard because the discipline itself is still in the early stage of development.

In a WeBHouse architecture, Extraction-transformation-loading (ETL) processes play an important role because they are responsible of integrating data from heterogeneous data sources into the WeBhouse repository. Although this importance, security are not taken into account in the ETL development. Noting that, ETL processes represent the most complex task in a WeBhouse project. They are continuously reported to be vulnerable to attacks and compromises. Securing these processes is highly important and helps in mitigating security defects in decisional system.

In this paper, we discuss this problem taking into account unsatisfactory kind" [19]. Metrics provides a universal way to measure the product or business requirements and vulnerabilities assessments. To this end, our work evaluates vulnerabilities according to two metrics: severity impact and remediation cost. We adopt the Common Vulnerability Scoring System (CVSS) to quantify the severity impact and extend the Cosmic used for security measuring purposes to estimate the remediation effort. We define a rule to prioritize vulnerabilities according to computed metrics values. The main contributions of this paper are, first, to early quantify the anticipated vulnerability in the project, and second, to apply adapted remediation to detected vulnerabilities.

This paper is organized as follows: Sect. 2 surveys security measurement related works. Section 3 describes our proposed metrics for securing ETL process. In Sect. 4, we present our secure Web-ETL Meta-model integrating vulnerabilities specification. Section 5 depicts our secure web-ETL case study instantiating our Meta model and applying the proposed metrics. The last section concludes the paper with some pointers to future directions.

2 Related Works

The growing of the vulnerabilities and potential attacks requires the ETL designers to consider security needs during the ETL design process. In this section, we introduce works evaluating security in information systems and those that exploit CVSS metrics. Finally, we survey security approaches for ETL design.

2.1 Measuring Security

Such focus on quantitative assessment of security has become more popular in recent years. A thorough survey has been published in 2009 [16], covering quantitative representation and analysis of operational security since 1981, and addressing the question whether "security can correctly be represented with quantitative information?" The major finding of this study was that "there exists significant work for quantified security, but there is little solid evidence that the methods represent security in operational settings." This brings us to the question "Is security measurable?" Before that, it would be even more important to answer a more fundamental question: "Why do we measure?"

To secure a system, we must identify and assess vulnerabilities. So we need to prioritize these vulnerabilities and remediate those that pose the greatest risk. Several research papers addressing topics of measuring information security have been written in the last few years. National Institute of Standards and Technology have published Special Publications dealing with topics of Risk Management and Information Security Metrics [13–15]. [16] proposes an approach to quantitatively measure different aspects of information security. The proposed schema leverages many of the features of current Risk, IT Management and Audit frameworks, Security Guidelines and Standards. It is composed of three elements: A security control matrix (SCM), which is a comprehensive list of security controls collected from a number of NIST guidelines. A selection of security performance metrics (SPM) considered as the high priority security controls selected from the SCM. SPM are quantitatively measurable controls which can be directly mapped with security goals and intended to be periodically reported to senior management. The last element is the measurement model. It takes into consideration the priorities for each aspect of security to deliver levels of security from different perspectives: Organizational, Operational and Technical and for each information criteria.

2.2 CVSS Researches

Several studies are based on the CVSS which is an adopted standard that enables security analysts to assign numerical scores to vulnerabilities according to their severity [2]. In [17], authors propose the novel approaches of handling dependency relationships at the base metric level, and aggregate CVSS metrics from different aspects. A CVSS risk estimation model is presented in [18]. The proposed model estimates a security risk level from vulnerabilities information as a combination of frequency and impact estimates derived from the CVSS.

In [5], authors targets the quantitative understanding of vulnerability severity taking into account contextual information within the vulnerability assessment process, especially the economic aspects reflecting vulnerability response costs, and potential economic damage if the vulnerability is exploited. The proposed approach is based on the Multiple Criteria Decision Analysis (MCDA) methods to perform a prioritization of the existing vulnerabilities within the target system.

In [4], authors propose to apply the temporal and environmental CVSS metric groups in the scoring process with the base metric. They argue that the use of the two optional metrics improves the scores quality because they better reflect the actual vulnerability impact. In the presented method, authors compare the NVD's CVSSBase-scores with context-enriched scores that apply CVSS's additional Temporal- and Environmental-Metric. The founded results exemplify the potential improvements in an organization. The presented methodology enables security managers to make informed decisions on whether investing in improved vulnerability prioritization in their organization.

[7] proposes an approach bridging formal risk theory with industrial approaches. Authors define a stochastic risk evaluation approach which considers the vulnerability

lifecycle. A conditional risk measure and assessment approach are also presented when only known vulnerabilities are considered.

2.3 ETL and Security

The complexity of the ETL system arises as the sources use different data formats, which has to be cleaned, transformed, aggregated and loaded into the data warehouse as homogeneous data. With the emergence of the web, different security problems are triggered and a security approach for the ETL process becomes an urgent need.

[11] extends the UML use case and sequence diagrams and proposes a simulation model for the extraction of secure data during ETL processes. An algorithm is proposed based on the user's authentication, the encryption of the extracted data, the verification of data corruption. This work is extended in [12] where authors analyze the ETL process under two security metrics: vulnerability index and security index. A framework for securing any phase in the ETL process has been suggested together with a methodology for assessing the system security in the early stages. An object-oriented approach to model the ETL process embedding privacy preservation is proposed in [10]. The researchers present a class diagram for ETL embedding Privacy Preservation. The main component is PPA. Its task includes cleaning and transforming data followed by privacy preserving attributes.

There are few research papers on ETL security. These researches do not take into account non-functional security needs of ETL processes in the Web business level and they do not address the vulnerabilities between processes of Web ETL.

3 Quantify Vulnerability in the Web ETL Process

The use of quantitative vulnerability assessment methods enables efficient prioritization of security efforts and investments to mitigate the discovered vulnerabilities and thus constitutes an opportunity to lower expected losses.

In this context, we define a quantified approach offering a pair of score noted **(S, R)** where **S** the severity impact (measured by the CVSS base score) and R the remediation cost (measured by the COSMICFFP) for each anticipated vulnerability. The advantage of our proposal is the establishment of two scores: severity impact and remediation cost, allowing us to define a rule facilitating the sequencing of corrections handling anticipated vulnerabilities.

In the next subsections, we present the component of scoring pair S and R and we present our defined rule for sequencing remediation steps.

3.1 Measuring the Severity Impact

The Common Vulnerability Scoring System (CVSS) is an adopted standard that enables security analysts to assign numerical scores to vulnerabilities according to severity. We adopt this standard to calculate the vulnerability score using attributes grouped into three metric groups: (1) the "Base Metric", which describes the general characteristics of vulnerabilities (2) the optional "Temporal Metric", which represents changes in the severity over time and (3) the optional "Environmental Metric", which introduces context information that is unique to a particular user, organization or business environment [4]. A CVSS score is a decimal number in the range [0.0, 10.0], where the value 0.0 has no rating (there is no possibility to exploit vulnerability) and the value 10.0 has full score (vulnerability easy to exploit). The base metric group quantifies the intrinsic characteristics of vulnerability in terms of two sub-scores: (i) exploitability_subscore (Exp); composed of access vector (AV), access complexity (AC) and authentication instances (Au), and (ii) impact_subscore (Imp) to confidentiality (C), integrity (I) and availability (A) [16]. (see Subsect. 5.2 for more details).

$$BaseScore = ((0.6*Imp)+(0.4*Exp)1.5)*f(Imp)$$

$$Imp = 10.41*(1-(1-C)*(1-I)*(1-A))$$

$$Exp= 20* AV*AC*Au$$

$$f(imp) \begin{cases} = 0 \text{ if impact } =0 \\ = 1.176 \text{ otherwise} \end{cases}$$

3.2 Measuring the Remediation Cost

A functional size measurement method, COSMIC-FFP, which was adopted in 2003 as the ISO/IEC 19761 standard [6], measures software functionality in terms of the data movements across and within the software boundary. It focuses on the functional user requirements of the software and is applicable throughout the development life cycle, from the requirements phase up and including to the implementation and maintenance phases [1].

[8] extends the COSMICFFP, developed by the Common Software Measurement International Consortium (COSMIC) and now adopted as an international standard (ISO/IEC 19761 [6]), for Non Functional Requirements (NFR) testing purposes. Authors mention that it is an essential step for improving NFR development and testing effort estimates, and consequently for managing the scope of NFRs. In COSMIC-FFP, the unit of measurement is the data movement, which is a base functional component that moves one or more data attributes belonging to a single data group. It is denoted by the symbol Cfsu (Cosmic Functional Size Unit). Data movements (DMT) can be of four types: Entry, Exit, Read or Write.

We adopt this extension to quantify the remediation cost. Our proposal defines the necessary movement to correct an anticipated vulnerability and calculate the corresponding Cosmic Functional Priority (CFP). Based on the four types of data movements, we will describe the remediation activities of each vulnerability and next sum the CFP total. (see Subsect. 5.2 for more details).

3.3 Proposed Rule for Sequencing

Threshold Definition. Most work dealing with the security metrics, define qualitative scale to classify the base score factor. In [5], authors define a scale from 0 to 10, where [0–3.9] interval indicates Low severity vulnerability,]4.0–6.9] indicates Medium severity vulnerability, and]7.0–10.0] indicates High severity vulnerability. These propositions classify a vulnerability V1 having a base score 6.9 as medium when another vulnerability V2 having a base score 7 as a high. Although the difference is quite fine (0.1) but each one is placed in a different class. Belonging to the High class, V2 will be corrected first. Nevertheless, this solution is not efficient becauseV1can be most severe.

As a solution to this problem, we propose an empirical study to define a severity threshold. This threshold enables us to facilitate the security manager decisions. Our empirical study comprises 21 (V1, V21) vulnerabilities extracted from ETL WeBhouse processes. The analysis of the vulnerability scores demonstrates that the difference between scores of two neighbours don't exceed 1 in almost cases. So, we adopt an assumption that the threshold value should not exceed 1. In our study, we calculate the difference between all anticipated vulnerabilities in the Web ETL processes. We find that there are 54 results in]0,1[with 32 results in]0,0.5] corresponding to 70,2 %.

Proposed Rule. We consider two vulnerabilities Vi and Vj having the correspondent pair score (Si, Ri) and (Sj, Rj). Then, we calculate the difference between the two severity score. If the result is low or equal to the proposed threshold, vulnerability having the lowest remediation cost is chosen to be remediated first. Else vulnerability having the largest severity impact is chosen Our proposition intend that correcting the vulnerability requiring less time is more objective and increase the system protection.

4 The Proposed Meta Model for Secure ETL Web

Based on the activity diagram Meta model UML OMG (2007), [3] proposes a Web ETL meta-model. The proposed Meta model is composed of two packages: the Web ETL Meta model and the security Meta model.

In the secure package, we represent the Environmental Metric Group in a Meta Class while the Temporal Metric Group factors are represented in the vulnerability catalog. Some of the Base Metric Group factors are presented as Meta class like Access, Security Aspect, others are presented as Meta class association like the Authentication, the Access Complexity.

Web ETL Meta Model. The Web ETL Meta model is represented in Fig. 1 and described as follow:

- Steps inherit from "ActivityGroup" class. It models the extraction, transformation and loading processes. Each "Step" is composed of "Activities".
- Sons and Parents inherit respectively from the "inputPin" and the "outputPin"classes.

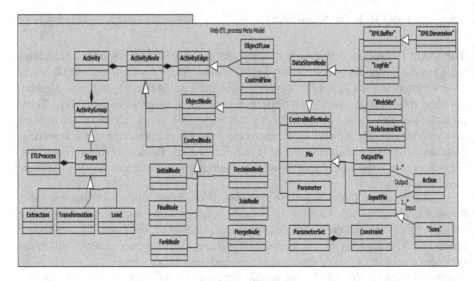

Fig. 1. Web ETL Meta model

- Xml Buffer, Log file, Website and Relational DB inherit from the DataStoreNode class are used as storage means.
- XML Dimensional is an XMLBuffer class. It represents a dimensional structure (fact, dimension, attributes …)

Secure Meta Model. The security Meta Model is presented with blue color in (Fig. 2) and composed by the following elements:

- Security Need represent user requirements that must be satisfied in our security approach
- Risk is security problems preventing the achievement of security goals.
- Vulnerability Catalog is the anticipated vulnerability having as attribute the three factors of the temporal Metric Group: confirmation of the technical details of vulnerability, the remediation status of vulnerability, and the availability of exploiting code or techniques. Since temporal metrics are optional, they include a metric value that has no effect on the score. This value is used when the user feels that the particular metric does not apply and wishes to "skip over" it.
- Vulnerability inherits from the Vulnerability Catalog Meta class.
- Access present the type of access to the data (local, adjacent network, …)
- Security Aspect are Confidentiality, Integrity, Availability.
- Environmental Metric Group captures the characteristics of vulnerability that are associated with a user's IT environment.
- Impact is an association class between the Security Aspect and the Vulnerability and measures the impact value.
- Affect is an association class between the Access and the Vulnerability and measures the Access Complexity.

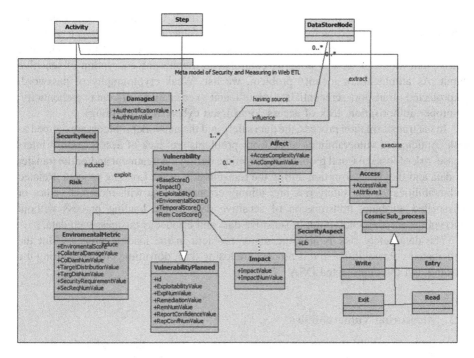

Fig. 2. Meta model Secure Web ETL

- Damage is an association class between the Steps and the Vulnerability and presents the authentication metric.
- COSMIC sub process which is composed by four data movements (Entry, Exit, Read, and Write).

5 Case Study

To apply our proposal and determine the results of the theoretical analysis, we present a case study for the Web ETL processes of an online banking system, due of the risk that may come across this system and the sensitivity of the data that they process. This section is composed by three parts: First, anticipated vulnerabilities are categorizes. Then, our task is to measure the severity impact and the remediation cost of each defined vulnerabilities. Finally, vulnerabilities are prioritized based on the defined rule.

5.1 Categorization Vulnerabilities

The variety, the increasing number and the sensibility of data augment security problems detected in ETL processes. In this section, we categories for each process the vulnerabilities that can affect the development and the data quality [3].

For the Extraction process, two risks are defined: the improper input and the administrator identity problem. As improper input vulnerabilities, we detect: violation of Customer Private information, Erroneous and entrusted URL data, unsafe data (virus, malware, …), lack of integrity controls and the missing encryption of sensitive input. As administrator identity problem, we list: Weak cryptography of password, unprotected transport credentials, inssufficient verification of data authenticity, improper authorisation, lack of access control and cybercrime (phishing).

In the transformation process, the data safety and the network problems are defined as risk. Anticipated vulnerabilities of network problems are: lack of access control inters phase, risk of loss data, and problem of downtime during the treatment and/or the transfer of data and the data corruption during the transmission to the Loading process. Related vulnerabilities to data safety risk are: joining erroneous data with incorrect values or misspelled attribute, transmission of sensitive data to the loading process without encryption, missing encryption of sensitive data and erroneous business web data.

The data safety risk is also the major problem in the loading process. But the anticipated vulnerabilities in this process are losing data, downtime problem during the loading and the unprotected DSA.

5.2   Measuring Vulnerabilities

After the vulnerabilities categorization, it is time to evaluate them and define the pair score of each one and instantiate the proposed Meta model. In this paper, we will treat some vulnerability.

Unprotected Transport of Credentials. Figure 3 presents "LogFileStructure" activity describing the log files structuring process enriched by the security problem that can decrease the process quality. To measure the vulnerability "Unprotected transport of credentials", we set values for each factor of the three metric groups of CVSS and define the data movement's needed to remediate it. This vulnerability affects greatly (AC: 0,35) the access by an AdjacentNetwork (AT: 0,646). It affects widely Confidentiality (C: 0,660), and has no impact on Integrity (I: 0) and availability (A: 0). It does not damage the authenticity (Au: 0). Computing the Base score equation, the score is equal to 4,58.

$$Impact = 10.41*(1-(1-0,660)*(1-0)*(1-0))$$
$$= 6.9$$
$$f(impact)= 1$$
$$Exploitability = 20* 0.35*0.646*0.704$$
$$= 3.2$$
$$BaseScore= ((0.6*6.9) + (0.4*3.2)-1.5)*1$$
$$= 4.58$$

The data movements' identification needed to remediate this vulnerability are presented in Table 1. The CFP is 3 defined as follow: check the credential (Read

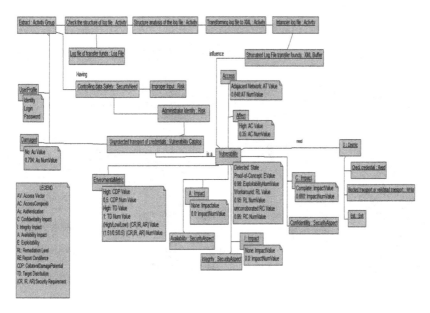

Fig. 3. Unprotected transport of credentials' security factors in the "Log File Structure" activity diagram

movement), Blocked transport if invalid check else validated transport (Write movement) and finally an Exit movement.

Table 1. Data movement's to remediate Unprotected transport of credentials

Vulnerability description	Triggering event	Data movement identification	DMT	CFP
Unprotected transport of credentials	Sente credentials	Check credentials	R	1
		Blocked transport or validated transport	W	1
		Exit	X	1
CFP				3

Violation of Customer Private Information. In Fig. 4, we present the same activity but we treat the protection of the authentication parameters. We attribute the corresponding CVSS factors value and define the needed data movements to correct this vulnerability. The pair metric to this vulnerability is (5.2, 3). Beginning by the severity metric value of the 'Violation of customer private information', equals to 5.89, defined by the application of the base score equation. We note that this vulnerability affects a lot (AC: 0.35) the Network (AV: 1). It requires multiple instances of authentication (AU: 0.45). It has no impact in Confidentiality (C: 0), but affects completely Integrity (I: 0.660) and partially Availability (A: 0.275). The base score is calculated as follow:

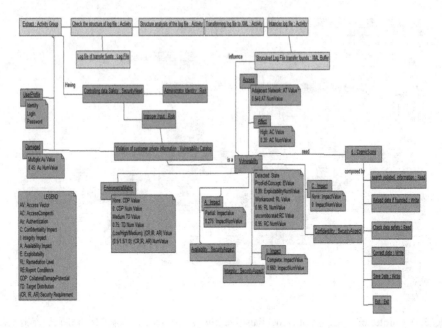

Fig. 4. Violation of customer private information' security factors in the "Log File Structure" activity diagram

$$Impact = 10.41*(1-(1-0)*(1-0.660)*(1-0.275))$$
$$= 7.8$$
$$f(impact) = 1$$
$$Exploitability = 20* 0.35*1*0.45$$
$$= 3.2$$
$$BaseScore = ((0.6*7.8) + (0.4*3.2)-1.5)*1$$
$$= 5.2$$

The data movements' identification needed to remediate this vulnerability are presented in Table 2. Six data movement are defined: Search violated information (Read movement), Reload data if founded (Write movement), Check data safety (Read movement), Correct data if problem founded (Write movement), Save data (Write movement) and Exit.

5.3 Prioritizing Vulnerabilities

In this subsection, we present the severity impact and the remediation cost for 9 vulnerabilities extracted from a set of 23 vulnerabilities detected in our banking system case study. Then, we apply the proposed rule to prioritize them:

a. Unprotected transport of credentials (4.58, 3)
b. Violation of customer private information (5.2, 6)

Table 2. Data movement's to remediate Violation of customer private information

Vulnerability description	Triggering event	Data movement identification	DMT	CFP
Violation of customer private information	Data loosed	search violated information	R	1
		Reload data if founded	W	1
		Check data safety	R	1
		Correct data	W	1
		Save data	W	1
		Exit	X	1
CEP				6

c. Joining erroneous data with incorrect values (7.3, 4)
d. Transmission of sensitive data to the loading process without encryption (8.8, 3)
e. Problem of downtime during the treatment and/or the transfer of data (8.8, 3)
f. Entrusted Website (8.8, 4)
g. Erroneous and incorrect URL data (9, 4)
h. Erroneous business web data (6.3, 4)
i. Missing encryption of sensitive data (6.2, 3)

If prioritizing is based only on the Base score, vulnerabilities are treated in this order: first, *Erroneous and incorrect URL data (g)* with the base score of 9, then *d*, *e* and *f* vulnerabilities having the same base score value 8.8 and finally, *c, h, I, b* and *a* vulnerabilities.

Applying our rule, first we calculate difference between vulnerabilities base score values. Only differences lower than the fixed threshold (0.5) change the order of priority.

For example, the difference between base score values between *d, (eq e)* and *g* vulnerabilities having different remediation cost is $|8.8-9| = 0.2$ which is lower than the fixed threshold 0.5. In this case, following our rule, the remediation cost (CFP) will be considered in the prioritization. So, the first vulnerability to treat is *d(eq e)*. We note that when we have the same CFP, the same order is kept.

Treating another case, we apply our rule between vulnerabilities *h* and *i*. The base scores difference is 0.1 lower than 0.5. Comparing the CFP, vulnerability *i* has the higher value despite it has the lower base score value. So, this vulnerability will be remediated first.

Finally and after analyzing all vulnerabilities scores, the new priority order is:

d *Transmission of sensitive data to the loading process without encryption (8.8, 3)*
e. *Problem of downtime during the treatment and/or the transfer of data (8.8, 3)*
g. *Erroneous and incorrect URL data (9, 4)*
f. *Entrusted Website (8.8, 4)*
c. *Joining erroneous data with incorrect values (7.3, 4)*
i. *Missing encryption of sensitive data (6.2, 3)*
h. *Erroneous business web data (6.3, 4)*

b. *Violation of customer private information (5.2, 6)*
a. *Unprotected transport of credentials (4.58, 3)*

6 Conclusion

The Extraction-transformation-loading (ETL) processes play an important role in WeBhouse architecture because they are responsible for integrating data from heterogeneous data sources. It is therefore widely recognized that the appropriate design and security of the ETL processes are key factors in the success of WeBhouse projects.

In this paper, we propose a quantitative approach to evaluate vulnerabilities anticipated during the Web ETL processes development life cycle. Our approach evaluates vulnerabilities according to two metrics: severity impact and remediation cost. We adopt the Common Vulnerability Scoring System (CVSS) to quantify the severity impact and extend the Cosmic used for security measuring purposes to estimate the effort needed for remediation. To evaluate the security and safety level in WeBhouse, we define a secure Meta model for the Web ETL process. Our Meta enriches the Meta-model of UML activity diagram defined by OMG (2007) by adding security classes. In summary, this work investigated the impact of adding remediation cost to the scoring process software vulnerabilities based on the CVSS. We found that the addition of remediation cost improves the vulnerabilities prioritization. Security manager is not notified only by the severity of vulnerability but also knows the data movements needed to remediate it.

Our future work is to validate our approach the extension of Talend Open source by defining new components. These last ensure Web ETL safety by evaluating vulnerabilities and defining the security policy needed to protect system and to correct detected security's problem.

References

1. Talib, M.A., Abran, A., Buglione, L.: Scenario based black-box testing in COSMIC-FFP: a case study. ASQ Softw. Qual. Prof. J. **8**(3), 23–33 (2006)
2. Cheng, P., Wang, L., Jajodia, S., Singhal, A.: Aggregating CVSS base scores for semantics rich network security metrics. In: SRDS, pp. 31–40 (2012)
3. Dammak, S., Ghozzi Jedidi, F., Gargouri, F.: Security measures for Web ETL processes. In: IEEE/ACIS 14th ICIS (2015, to appear)
4. Frühwirth, C., Mannisto, T.: Improving CVSS-based vulnerability prioritization and response with context information. In: Proceedings of the 3rd International Symposium on Empirical Software Engineering and Measurement, ESEM 2009 Proceeding, pp. 535–544 (2009)
5. Ghani, H., Luna, J., Suri, N.,: Quantitative assessment of software vulnerabilities based on economic-driven security metrics. In: CRiSIS 2013, pp. 1–8 (2013)
6. ISO/IEC19761: Software Engineering – COSMIC: A Functional Size Measurement Method. International Organization for Standardization (ISO), Geneva (2011)

7. Joh, H., Malaiya, Y.K.: Defining and assessing quantitative security risk measures using vulnerability lifecycle and CVSS metrics. In: SAM 2011, International Conference on Security and Management, pp. 10–16 (2011)
8. Kassab, M., Daneva, M., Ormandjieva, O.: Early quantitative assessment of non-functional requirements. Technical report TR-CTIT-07-35, Centre for Telematics and Information Technology, University of Twente, Enschede (2006). ISSN 1381-3625
9. Kimbal, R., Merz, R.: Le DATA WEBHOUSE: Analyser les comportements client sur le Web. Eyrolles Edition, Paris (2000)
10. Kiran, P., Kumar, S.S., Kavya, N.P.: Modelling extraction transformation load embedding privacy preservation using UML. Int. J. Comput. Appl. (2012)
11. Muralini, M., Kumar, T.V.S.; Kanth, K.R.: Simulating secure data extraction in extraction transformation loading (ETL) processes. In: Third UKSim European Symposium on Computer Modeling and Simulation, pp. 142–147 (2009)
12. Muralini, M., Kumar, T.V.S.; Kanth, K.R.: Secure ETL process model: an assessmentof security in different phases of ETL. In: Software Engineering Competence Center (2013)
13. National Institute of Standards and Technology Special Publication 800-30: Risk Management Guide for Information Technology Systems, June 2001
14. National Institute of Standards and Technology Special Publication 800-53: Recommended Security Controls for Federal Information Systems, December 2007
15. National Institute of Standards and Technology Special Publication 800-55: Performance Measurement Guide for Information Security, July 2008
16. Leon, P.G., Saxena, A.: An approach to quantitatively measure information security. In: Proceedings of the 3rd India Software Engineering Conference, ISEC 2010
17. Pengsu, C., Lingyu, W., Sushil, J., Anoop, S.: Aggregating CVSS base scores for semantics-rich network security metrics. In: SRDS, pp. 31–40. IEEE (2012)
18. Houmb, S.H., Franqueira, V.N., Engum, E.A.: Quantifying security risk level from CVSS estimates of frequency and impact. J. Syst. Softw. **83**(9), 1622–1634 (2010). ISSN 0164-1212
19. Thompson, W.: Electrical units of measurement. Popular Lect. Addresses **1**, 73–136 (1889). Lecture at the Institution of Civil Engineers, London, 3 May 1883

Cloud Systems and Cryptography

A Meta-model for Assisting a Cloud Forensics Process

Stavros Simou[1](✉), Christos Kalloniatis[1], Haralambos Mouratidis[2],
and Stefanos Gritzalis[3]

[1] Cultural Informatics Laboratory, Department of Cultural Technology
and Communication, University of the Aegean,
University Hill, 81100 Mytilene, Greece
{SSimou, chkallon}@aegean.gr
[2] School of Computing, Engineering and Mathematics,
University of Brighton, Watts Building, Lewes Road, Brighton BN2 4GJ, UK
H.Mouratidis@brighton.ac.uk
[3] Information and Communication Systems Security Laboratory,
Department of Information and Communications Systems Engineering,
University of the Aegean, 83200 Samos, Greece
sgritz@aegean.gr

Abstract. Cloud forensics introduce processes for resolving incidents occurring in cloud computing environments. However, designing cloud services capable to assist a cloud investigation process is of vital importance and recent research efforts concentrate on these directions. In addition, digital forensics methods cannot support a cloud investigation since cloud environments introduce many differences compared to traditional IT environments. This paper moves current research one step further by identifying the major concepts, actors and their relationships that participating in a cloud forensics process through the introduction of a new meta-model. The paper presents a running example as well for better understanding the suggested concepts.

Keywords: Cloud forensics meta-model · Cloud forensics process · Cloud forensics case study · Conceptual model

1 Introduction

Cloud computing market has raised the past few years since an increased number of people, companies, organizations etc. make use of cloud services on a daily basis for professional or recreational reasons. Cloud computing gained much attention due to numerous advantages that offer especially flexibility and elasticity to customers through the existence of pay-as-you-use services. However, many drawbacks do exist that make cloud environments vulnerable to various threats depending on the service model used [1–3]. Based on these vulnerabilities specific tasks that were solved in traditional environments need to be dealt with a different way due to the challenges that cloud environments introduce. One of these issues is the conduction of forensic investigation over the cloud. To deal with cyber-crime in the new field, investigators forced to mutate

© Springer International Publishing Switzerland 2016
C. Lambrinoudakis and A. Gabillon (Eds.): CRiSIS 2015, LNCS 9572, pp. 177–187, 2016.
DOI: 10.1007/978-3-319-31811-0_11

digital forensics to cloud forensics. The definition of the term was first introduced by Ruan [4], to designate the need for digital investigation in cloud environments, based on forensic principles and procedures.

The extensive use of cloud by malicious users brought forth all the weaknesses of the new technology. The investigation of an incident based on the same concept for digital forensics. The two forensic techniques (digital and cloud), although they are very close to each other, they do have fundamental differences. The most important difference is the access to devices and evidence. In a traditional investigation to seize the hardware containing the data and have access to hard drives and evidence is a "simple" process. In cloud environments where data is stored in unknown locations around the world due to systems' distribution, seizing (physically) the devices is an issue and also a painful process with unpredictable results. As NIST indicates the challenges associated with data replication, transparency and multi-tenancy are unique to cloud forensics [5].

Over the past years a number of researchers introduced various frameworks and models concerning cloud forensics (i.e. Integrated Conceptual Digital Forensic Framework [6], Advanced Data Acquisition Model [7]). A detailed review at the respective methods has been also conducted and presented in [8, 9]. This particular review revealed the main challenges related to cloud forensics, the possible solutions and the need to create a well-structured and defined framework to support cloud forensics based on a clear set of cloud investigation concepts and entities and the relations between them.

This paper advances the state of the art by proposing the first effort, to the best of our knowledge, to present a meta-model for assisting the cloud forensics process. The paper is organized as follows. Section 2 summarizes related work and lists a number of challenges related to the development of a meta-model for cloud forensics, while Sect. 3 introduces the steps that need to be followed during a cloud forensic investigation based on the respective literature and research conducted so far. Also in Sect. 3 the new meta-model is presented based on the review analysis and the concepts identified before. In Sect. 4, the applicability of the meta-model model is demonstrated with the aid of a running example related to a cloud forensic investigation scenario. Finally, Sect. 5, concludes the paper by raising future research on this innovative research field.

2 Related Work

The related work presented here is derived from a systematic literature review where the most cited papers presented in respective scientific journals, conferences and industrial reports where examined (e.g. "Digital Investigation", "Advances in Digital Forensics", "International Journal of Digital Evidence", "Digital Forensic Research Workshop", "Cyber Security, and Cyber Warfare and Digital Forensic" etc.). After that, a research including industrial related publications from the field of security in information systems took place.

The review research identified initially the work of Ruan [4], who was one of the first researchers who dealt with cloud forensics and revealed the differences between cloud and digital forensics. Unfortunately, and despite the existing effort in the literature, there are still plenty of open issues concerning acquisition, analysis and presentation of digital evidence [10–14]. Our analysis [8, 9] revealed the challenges and the open issues in cloud forensics, together with the proposed solutions of these challenges. It has also highlighted that there is an urgent need for designing new methodologies and frameworks on cloud forensics. To the best of our knowledge, the literature fails to provide evidence of a methodology, concerning cloud forensics, which covers every aspect and every phase in a cloud forensic investigation [6, 15–18]. In particular, two issues are important: (i) there are some processes such as preservation and documentation that should be running concurrently with all the other processes. They should be carried out throughout the cloud investigation process and (ii) most authors dealing with cloud forensic solutions have focused on specific challenges such as access to evidence in logs, privacy and SLAs. There is a lack of solutions for the rest of the challenges; there are still open issues to be explored. Unless there is a proper solution on these matters cloud forensics could not cope with cyber-crime.

3 Cloud Forensics Process

According to the related work there is still no concrete work dealing with the cloud forensic process in a holistic and methodological way. In order to develop a new methodology on cloud forensics our primary scope is to identify the process that should be followed for fulfilling all necessary tasks. Thus, all possible aspects and elements must be identified. When an incident occurs the process of forensic investigation is initiated and different stages and concepts should be clearly stated. Each one of the stages and concepts should be described in detail in order to understand how they work and how it contributes to the cloud forensics process.

To identify the main concepts for building a meta-model for cloud forensics, a literature review has been conducted [19–23]. Based on this review analysis the most important components of a cloud forensic investigation model are as follows.

3.1 Cloud Forensic Stages

The investigation process in cloud forensics occurs whenever an incident takes place. Without it, no investigation exists. The incident is produced by a person who wants to proceed in illegal or malicious actions. It is identified either by the company's personnel involved in or by special agents working on similar cases (or even by citizens). When the incident is identified a special team is formed in order to identify and resolve it. The team is formed by experienced and trained personnel, in the fields of digital security, protection and law enforcement. The team is often referred as Law Enforcement Agents (LEA) and its scope is to protect users from the acts of malicious defenders.

LEA's first priority is to identify the type of the incident, resolve it and prosecute the perpetrator to justice. Due to the cloud-distributed environment it is very difficult to identify the potential evidence stored in data centers, geographically spanned in various locations. On the other hand Cloud Service Providers (CSPs) are hosting the illegal content in their storages. This means, that LEA need to co-operate with the CSPs to give them access to the data, so they can identify the source of the problem. During the identification process all personnel involved in (both LEAs and CSPs) should be capable to handle with special care the potential evidence in order to preserve its integrity and validity and maintain the chain of custody. Data may reside in different jurisdictions; this is a problem that LEAs need to cope with and a warrant should be obtained in order to get the evidence.

After identifying the source of the incident, experienced technician should find the proper way to collect the data and preserve the integrity of it. In most cases the personnel involved in this process is one of the CSP's employees, due to the fact that CSPs either do not allow the investigators to take control of their infrastructures or they are operating in different countries. Collecting the potential evidence is not always an easy task, especially in cloud environments. The different types of media where the data may reside need different types of tools. Investigators should collect the assets such as software, hardware and data related to the investigation and examine them to produce evidence. The process of the collection of potential evidence is carried out in accordance with forensic principles. The tenants sharing the same data centers with the perpetrator should not be affected by the investigation and they should maintain their confidentiality, and preserve their privacy. Data to be collected should be focus on the specific tenant and no other. Assets and resources should be documented and a full report should be produced.

Next step in the cloud forensic process is the analysis and examination of the potential evidence. It involves the extraction of data from the collection process and their inspection with proper forensic tools. The data found should be analyzed using different resources and techniques for revealing any useful information in order to use them as evidence in the court of law. From the analysis process also, the technicians might find that the data is encrypted using complex algorithms. Revealing the decoded keys is a hard task that involves experienced and well-trained personnel. Data reconstruction should be also implemented using the different timestamps and metadata from the analysis. Methods and procedures should be clearly defined and documented proposing the best available solution according to the incident.

To conclude with the investigation, reports and presentations need to be implemented. With the term report the study mostly focuses on the case preparation and presentation in a court of law or corporate management. All the information gathered from the analysis of the evidence should be transformed into reports. In most of the times the outcome of a case depends on the presentation of the report. Therefore experts should be chosen with personal knowledge of the procedures that generated the records, having participated in or observed the event [24]. Experts should be prepared to confront the jury who lacks knowledge of cloud computing and try to present the information in a language that anyone can understand. The reports concerning the legal aspect of the presentation should be presented by people with great knowledge of the law issues and not only from people with a good technical background.

3.2   Meta-model

Taking under consideration the previous section concerning cloud forensic stages we proceed on identifying a number of concepts in order to compose the proposed meta-model. Figure 1, summarizes the critical components of the model. The main concepts have been identified concerning an incident in cloud forensics are actors, assets, resources, evidence and documentation.

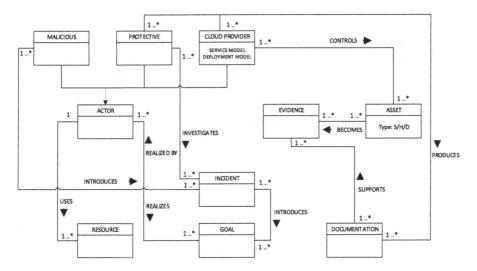

Fig. 1. Meta-model for assisting a cloud forensics process

As mentioned in the previous paragraphs a forensic investigation always starts with an incident. Malicious actors are the ones introducing an incident and protective actors are people investigating it and trying to find a solution. On the other hand whenever there is an attack there is always a target (victim). In cloud forensics, targets are usually individuals, organizations, companies, etc. Malicious actors use Cloud Service Providers' services to launch their attacks hidden behind anonymity. CSPs major concern is to rent as many services to clients. So far we distinguished four different actors involved in a cloud forensic investigation: malicious actors, protective actors, cloud provider and the victim.

An incident most of the times affects one target and in parallel introduces goals. There is an interaction between the victim and the rest of the actors. All actors use resources (personnel, tools, plans, methods, trainings, etc.) either to create the incident or to resolve it. The resources that can be used related to personnel are the technicians (provider, protective or victim), the law persons and anyone who will work on the case. Planning and organizing the steps an actor will make in case of an incident, is very productive when the time comes. An actor can be relief to see that personnel, operations and infrastructures are able to support an investigation in case of an incident [18]. A well-organized preparation can improve the quality and availability of digital evidence collected and preserved, while minimizing cost and workload [25]. Developing an incident response plan, ensures that it was taken under consideration all possible calculated risks [25]. Policies and procedures should be clearly defined and as many likely scenarios should be considered and tested. To support the plans, actors need to have skilled and experienced personnel. The personnel should be trained to the new technologies and follow the latest market trends and methods. Training plays a vital role to all investigations, by minimizing risks and mistakes.

According to Liu "Cloud provider is a person, organization, or entity responsible for making a service available to interested parties" [26]. CSPs should be responsible to assist and help practitioners and consumers with all the information and evidence found in their infrastructures. They should be willing to provide the right access to potential evidence shortly after a request has been placed, without compromising the privacy and security of their tenants. In other words CSP is the one who controls all the assets during a forensic investigation. There are three types of assets; hardware, software and data. After collecting the assets with the appropriate resources, they might become useful evidence. Analyzing the assets with the use of software tools investigators can find evidence to build a case in the court of law. The types of assets that can be transformed to evidence include the following:

Remote computers, hard discs, USB drives, memory cards, CD/DVD, files and folders, deleted files, times and dates associated with modifications, computer names and IP addresses, usernames and passwords, web server logs, windows event logs, application logs, registry entries and running processes, temporary files and recent documents, network shortcuts and mapped drives, browser history, temporary internet files and cache memory, emails, notes and address books. Assets related to cellular phones could be SIM cards, call logs, contacts, SMS and MMS, calendar, GPS locations and routes.

The last concept is documentation. The main objective of this is to keep the investigation proper documented in order to increase the probabilities of winning a case in a court of law or in an internal investigation. When the actors start to investigate an incident there is the need to produce proper documentation and detailed reports. Documentation at the early stages of the incident also helps to keep track of all the actions have been taken and to proceed with different techniques. Any risk analysis or assessment tests performed during the training and preparation should be documented in order to assist the team. All tools, processes, methods and principles performed should be documented properly in order to maintain the chain of custody. Any changes made to the evidence should be also recorded. According to Grispos et al. "A properly maintained chain of custody provides the documentary history for the entire lifetime of evidence discovered during an investigation" [27]. To present the evidence in a court as admissible, all the parties (staff, CSPs, third parties) conducted the investigation should record their actions through logs and notes e.g. who handled the evidence, how was it done, did the integrity of the evidence maintained, how was it stored, etc.

4   Running Example

In this section, a running example is presented to demonstrate all the activities that might occur in an investigation in relation to the proposed meta-model. The running example deals with trafficking illegal digital material in cloud environment. The scenario is similar to [28].

John, a malicious actor who is living in Greece, opens an account with Microsoft Azure Cloud Service Provider (CSP). He registers to use IaaS services. He creates a Virtual Machine (VM) and a webserver where he uploads illegal content of photographs, videos, etc. using the storage (hard disks), Azure is providing. All data is encrypted using cryptographic function and anyone can download the material anonymously as long as is a registered user. Once a day the VM is switched off resulting in the loss of data, leaving it to restart from a clean state. Most of the times John pays the provider with a pay-safe or a pre-paid card, thus his ID remains unknown. Protective actors', such as Law Enforcement Agents (LEA), primary purpose is to find malicious actor and prosecute him.

Malicious actor's action is responsible for the initiation of an incident, resulting in the beginning of the cloud forensic investigation process.

Protective actors, who are responsible for conducting the investigation and solving the incident need to locate the malicious actor in order to seize the webserver with the illegal content. The preliminary investigation only reveals cloud provider's id. Protective actors' first concern is to identify malicious actor's id and terminate the service, through procedures which do not drive a suspicion, affecting the disappearance of malicious actor. To do this, protective actors contact the CSP, inform him that a warrant is on the way aiming for the preservation of data and evidence. The identification of the malicious actor's IP address is unsuccessful, due to the third countries proxy servers, is using. At the same time protective actors try to find more evidence such as card payment information, cloud providers' subscriber id's, access logs, Net-Flow records, webserver virtual machine and cloud storage data [28]. All the above mentioned items are assets concerning the incident that protective actors are trying to identify and analyze according to the data preservations procedures and principles. In a different case the assets are not reliable as evidence and the malicious actor cannot be prosecuted. In parallel, a research is conducted by protective actors to identify the source of the evidence and the remaining assets, such as computers, laptops, mobiles, etc. The procedures followed for both obtaining authorization of the warrant and identifying assets need to be documented in a proper way with detailed reports on every step.

The ability to create an image of the VM is not possible without the involvement of the provider. It also depends on the state of the VM (in case of a termination or restart is very likely that the image cannot be saved). A proper forensic image contains metadata, such as, hashes and timestamps and it compresses all empty blocks. A new warrant is obtained and sent it to CSP in order to give to protective actors access to data and information (assets) related to the malicious actor. Once the provider is operating in another country and the data are stored in data centers geographically spanned in various locations, proper procedures need to be followed to cope with the different jurisdictions. A trained personnel of the protective actor, specialized on legal issues, must be hired in order to overcome the existing bureaucratic hurdle and also to get approval for asset collection from the various locations. Usually this process is time-consuming something that contradicts with LEA's goals of resolving the incident rapidly (the malicious actor at any time can close the account and opens a new one in a different cloud provider).

Once the remaining issues relating to jurisdiction have been resolved, the CSP assigns an experienced and skilled technician to produce an exact copy of all data of the original media (hard disk) that is under the supervision of the provider, using appropriate software such as the EnCase or FTK. The tools are the resources being used to investigate the incident. Then, the technician verifies the image for integrity and authenticity of data by creating MD5 hash values. These tests reveal any alteration of the evidence, in order to use the evidence in a court of law, through forensically acceptable procedures. The problem identified in this process is whether the hired technical staff of the cloud provider has the necessary knowledge and training to properly manage forensic evidence collected from the malicious actor's assets and how trustworthy the whole process is mainly against intentional or accidental data alteration. The technician can be challenged in a court of law for lacking specialized knowledge, required, on dealing with these kinds of issues. The chain of custody can be considered to have been violated with negative results. The entire process of creating the image should be documented in detail, presenting the exact methods and tools (resources) that have been used, the produced outputs and the results, the technical knowledge of the personnel responsible for the creation, the supervisor's position and any other relevant detail that will help in a lawsuit.

A parameter to be considered is that there are multiple users storing their data in the same data centers' storage media where the malicious actor stores his data. The protective actor together with the CSP must ensure the privacy and the functionality of the users' services and information. With the completion of the controls, the provider sends the image and all the data collected to protective actors in order to carry on with the investigation. The assets should be ensured that they will reach the recipients on the same condition as they were before. It should be also ensured that no alteration concerning data integrity and authenticity occurred during the transportation and that all respective procedures according to a crime scene investigation were followed. The resources used, the path with all the intermediate steps followed and the personnel involved in should be documented in detail.

Once protective actors receive the VM image and respective data new checks and controls are taking place to ensure the integrity and validity of the assets. Using appropriate resources (software tools), data is being analyzed for any useful information such as files containing photos, videos and sounds, event logs, IP addresses etc. At this point, protective actors realize that data is encrypted and a search for finding and identifying decode keys is starting. With Azure, where the location of applications and data is abstracted, storing a public key in cloud makes it very difficult to find and retrieve it. File system and windows registry is also analyzed. Time is valuable and crucial during an investigation and it is directly related to the amount of data to be analyzed. Let us assume that the CSP managed to produce 20 MB of event logs, 150 MB from NetFlow records, 50 GB of VM snapshot and 1 TB of data. It is clear that analyzing all the produced data will last for many hours and a number of people to work with. Additionally, protective actors load the VM snapshot to be able to get more information regarding the structure of the web site and the encryption methods used. The personnel responsible for analyzing the data follows an action plan drawn up with methodologies, procedures and results of previous cases. The trained personnel also enriches the action plan with new information for future uses and creates a report containing the findings of every stage.

After a thorough investigation protective actors manage to locate and retrieve the decoding keys and the analysis of 1 TB data is starting in order to reveal any evidence. Due to the fact that data is stored and distributed in different data centers around the world, timestamps and dates should be examined in detail in order to produce a precise timeline with evidence related to the investigation. From the examination of the evidence, protective actors manage to trace malicious actor's IP address.

Protective actors inform the investigator in charge, about the research findings. Reports are being produced and handled with all the evidence and techniques followed, to make a concrete case in the court of law. The reports contain information about the CSP, the persons involved in the investigation, evidence analysis, methods and techniques followed, respective findings and all technical terms used. A final report is produced by the head of the investigation and presented to the legal authorities.

All the stages followed during the above mentioned investigation should be well documented in accordance with forensic principles and procedures, with clear steps and methodologies in order to ensure the integrity and the validity of the evidence and to preserve the chain of custody (who did what, what software has been used, what procedure has been followed, etc.). The chain of custody should be kept robust so no third parties can challenge its quality.

In Table 1 an identification of the concepts related to the running example is produced to understand the different meanings in the cloud forensic investigation.

Table 1. Running example concepts

Concepts	Example
Malicious actor	John
Protective actor	Law enforcement agents
Cloud provider	Microsoft azure
Incident	Traffic illegal digital material
Goals	Resolve the case – Prosecute John
Resources	EnCase, FTK, LEA's and CSP's trained personnel, analyzing tools, action plans
Assets	Card payment information, CSP's subscriber id, access logs, NetFlow records, webserver virtual machine and cloud storage data, files and folders, deleted files, times and dates associated with modifications, usernames and passwords, web server logs, windows event logs, application logs, registry entries and running processes, temporary files and recent documents, browser history, temporary internet files and cache memory
Evidence	IP address, username and password, web server logs, windows event logs, application logs, registry entries, photos and videos
Documentation	Action plan report, methodology report, resource report, assets report, evidence report, presentation report

5 Conclusion

Within this work a new meta-model for cloud forensics was presented. It was designed taking under consideration a list of challenges related to the development of meta-model and the steps that need to be followed during a cloud forensic investigation. In order to do so, there was a detailed study on the challenges and methodologies based on the respective literature and research, proposed by the researchers on this area. The new meta-model was designed based on the review analysis and the concepts identified in cloud forensics stages. Finally, the applicability of the meta-model was demonstrated using a running example related to cloud forensic investigation scenario.

References

1. Kalloniatis, C., Mouratidis, H., Manousakis, V., Islam, S., Gritzalis, S., Kavakli, E.: Towards the design of secure and privacy-oriented information systems in the cloud: identifying the major concepts. Comput. Stand. Interfaces **36**(4), 759–775 (2014). Elsevier
2. Manousakis, V., Kalloniatis, C., Kavakli, E., Gritzalis, S.: Privacy in the cloud: bridging the gap between design and implementation. In: Franch, X., Soffer, P. (eds.) CAiSE Workshops 2013. LNBIP, vol. 148, pp. 455–465. Springer, Heidelberg (2013)
3. Kalloniatis, C., Manousakis, V., Mouratidis, H., Gritzalis, S.: Migrating into the cloud: identifying the major security and privacy concerns. In: Douligeris, C., Polemi, N., Karantjias, A., Lamersdorf, W. (eds.) Collaborative, Trusted and Privacy-Aware e/m-Services. IFIP AICT, vol. 399, pp. 73–87. Springer, Heidelberg (2013)
4. Ruan, K., Carthy, J., Kechadi, T., Crosbie, M.: Cloud forensics: an overview. In: Peterson, G., Shenoi, S. (eds.) Advances in Digital Forensics VII. IFIP AICT, vol. 361, pp. 35–46. Springer, Heidelberg (2011)
5. NIST. In: Group CFSW. NIST Cloud Computing Forensic Science Challenges (Draft NISTIR 8006). NIST Publication (2014)
6. Martini, B., Choo, K.-K.R.: An integrated conceptual digital forensic framework for cloud computing. Digital Invest. **9**(2), 71–80 (2012)
7. Adams, R.: The emergence of cloud storage and the need for a new digital forensic process model. In: Ruan, K. (ed.) Cybercrime and Cloud Forensics: Applications for Investigation Processes, pp. 79–104. IGI Global, Hershey (2013)
8. Simou, S., Kalloniatis, C., Kavakli, E., Gritzalis, S.: Cloud forensics: identifying the major issues and challenges. In: Jarke, M., Mylopoulos, J., Quix, C., Rolland, C., Manolopoulos, Y., Mouratidis, H., Horkoff, J. (eds.) CAiSE 2014. LNCS, vol. 8484, pp. 271–284. Springer, Heidelberg (2014)
9. Simou, S., Kalloniatis, C., Kavakli, E., Gritzalis, S.: Cloud forensics solutions: a review. In: Iliadis, L., Papazoglou, M., Pohl, K. (eds.) CAiSE 2014. LNCS, vol. 8484, pp. 299–309. Springer, Heidelberg (2014)
10. Zawoad, S., Hasan, R.: Cloud Forensics: A Meta-Study of Challenges, Approaches, and Open Problems. arXiv preprint, arXiv:1302.6312 (2013)
11. Birk, D., Wegener, C.: Technical issues of forensic investigations in cloud computing environments. In: 2011 IEEE Sixth International Workshop on Systematic Approaches to Digital Forensic Engineering (SADFE), May 2011, pp. 1–10. IEEE (2011)

12. Mishra, A.K., Matta, P., Pilli, E.S., Joshi, R.C.: Cloud forensics: state-of-the-art and research challenges. In: 2012 International Symposium on Cloud and Services Computing (ISCOS), December 2012, pp. 164–170. IEEE (2012)
13. Aydin, M., Jacob, J.: A comparison of major issues for the development of forensics in cloud computing. In: 2013 8th International Conference on Information Science and Technology (ICIST), pp. 77–82. IEEE (2013)
14. Zargari, S., Benford, D.: Cloud forensics: concepts, issues, and challenges. In: 2012 Third International Conference on Emerging Intelligent Data and Web Technologies (EIDWT), September 2012, pp. 236–243. IEEE (2012)
15. Palmer, G.: A road map for digital forensic research - report from the first Digital Forensics Research Workshop (DFRWS). Paper presented at the First Digital Forensic Research Workshop, Utica, NY, USA, pp. 1–48 (2001)
16. Reith, M., Carr, C., Gunsch, C.: An examination of digital forensic models. Int. J. Digital Evid. 1(3), 1–12 (2002). Fall
17. Ciardhuáin, S.Ó.: An extended model of cybercrime investigations. Int. J. Digital Evid. 3(1), 1–22 (2004). Summer
18. Carrier, B., Spafford, E.H.: Getting physical with the digital investigation process. Int. J. Digital Evid. 2(2), 1–20 (2003). Fall
19. Pooe, A., Labuschagne, L.: A conceptual model for digital forensic readiness. In: Information Security for South Africa (ISSA), pp. 1–8. IEEE (2012)
20. Al-Fedaghi, S., Al-Babtain, B.: Modeling the forensics process. Int. J. Secur. Appl. 6(4), 97–108 (2012)
21. Ruan, K., Carthy, J.: Cloud computing reference architecture and its forensic implications: a preliminary analysis. In: Rogers, M., Seigfried-Spellar, K.C. (eds.) ICDF2C 2012. LNICST, vol. 114, pp. 1–21. Springer, Heidelberg (2013)
22. von Solms, S., Louwrens, C., Reekie, C., Grobler, T.: A control framework for digital forensics. In: Olivier, M.S., Shenoi, S. (eds.) Advances in Digital Forensics II. IFIP AICT, vol. 222, pp. 343–355. Springer, New York (2006)
23. Selamat, S.R., Yusof, R., Sahib, S.: Mapping process of digital forensic investigation framework. Int. J. Comput. Sci. Netw. Secur. 8(10), 163–169 (2008)
24. Orton, I., Alva, A., Endicott-Popovsky, B.: Legal process and requirements for cloud forensic investigations. In: Ruan, K. (ed.) Cybercrime and Cloud Forensics: Applications for Investigation Processes, pp. 186–229. IGI Global, Hershey (2012)
25. Beebe, N.L., Clark, J.G.: A hierarchical, objectives-based framework for the digital investigations process. Digital Invest. Int. J. Digital Forensics Incident Response 2(2), 147–167 (2005)
26. Liu, F., Tong, J., Mao, J., Bohn, R., Messina, J., Badger, L., Leaf, D.: NIST cloud computing reference architecture. NIST Special Publication-500, p. 292 (2011)
27. Grispos, G., Storer, T., Glisson, W.B.: Calm before the storm: the challenges of cloud. In: Li, C.T. (ed.) Emerging Digital Forensics Applications for Crime Detection, Prevention, and Security, pp. 211–233. IGI Global, Hershey (2013)
28. Dykstra, J., Sherman, A.T.: Understanding issues in cloud forensics: two hypothetical case studies. In: Proceedings of the Conference on Digital Forensics, Security and Law, Richmond, Virginia, USA, pp. 45–54 (2011)

POR-2P: Network Coding-Based POR for Data Provision-Payment System

Kazumasa Omote and Tran Phuong Thao[✉]

Japan Advanced Institute of Science and Technology (JAIST),
1-1 Asahidai, Nomi, Ishikawa 923-1292, Japan
{omote,tpthao}@jaist.ac.jp

Abstract. Proof Of Retrievability (POR) is a protocol that supports a data owner to check whether the data stored in cloud servers is available, intact and retrievable. Based on the POR, network coding technique has been applied to increase efficiency and throughput in data transmission and data repair. Although many network coding-based PORs have been proposed, most of them have not considered a practical scenario in which not only the data owner can check and can retrieve the data stored in the untrusted servers, but also an untrusted user can check and can retrieve the data stored in the servers without learning the secret keys of the data owner. This scenario occurs commonly in reality. For instance, in a *data provision-payment system*, the user must pay money to get data stored in the servers. In this paper, we propose a new network coding-based POR, named POR-2P (a network coding-based POR for data Provision-Payment system), to deal with this scenario. Furthermore, the complexity analysis and the performance evaluation show that the POR-2P is very efficient and applicable for a real cloud system.

Keywords: Cloud storage · Proof of retrievability · Network coding · Homomorphic MAC

1 Introduction

Since the amount of data is increasing exponentially, storage remote providers called clouds have been proposed to support data owners to reduce the burdens of data storage and data management. However, a cloud provider could be untrusted. Thus, it introduces three data security challenges in data security: availability, integrity and confidentiality. Confidentiality consists of two research approaches: cryptographic approach and information-theoretic approach. In this paper, we focus on availability, integrity and information-theoretic confidentiality.

Proof of Retrievability (POR). POR [1–3] has been proposed to support a data owner to check whether his/her data stored in the servers is available,

This study is partly supported by Grant-in-Aid for Young Scientists (B) (25730083).

C. Lambrinoudakis and A. Gabillon (Eds.): CRiSIS 2015, LNCS 9572, pp. 188–206, 2016.
DOI: 10.1007/978-3-319-31811-0_12

intact and retrievable. POR is a challenge-response protocol between a data owner and a server, and consists of five functions: keygen, encode, check, repair, and retrieve. Based on the POR, the following techniques are commonly used.

- *Replication.* Replication, proposed in [4,5], is a technique that allows the data owner to store a file replica in each server. The data owner can perform periodic server checks. When a corrupted server is detected, the data owner can use one of the healthy replicas to repair the data in the corrupted server. The drawback of this technique, however, is high storage cost because the data owner must store a whole file in each server.
- *Erasure Coding.* Erasure coding was applied [6,7] for optimal data redundancy. Instead of storing a file replica in each server like replication, the data owner stores file blocks in each server. Thus, the storage cost can be reduced. However, the drawback of this technique is that: in order to repair a corrupted server, the data owner must reconstruct the original file before repairing. Hence, the computation cost is increased during data repair.
- *Obvious RAM (ORAM).* Recently, the ORAM has been applied to the POR [8,9]. Basically, this technique was proposed for privacy-preserving data access pattern. By using ORAM structure, the servers cannot obtain the access patterns when the data owner performs data checks. For data repair, ORAM-based POR embeds the erasure coding to repair the corruption. The ORAM structure leads to high storage cost because of its hierarchical storage layout. The ORAM structure also leads to high computation cost because of its shuffling procedure every a number of read/write operations.
- *Network Coding.* To address the drawback of erasure coding, network coding has been applied [10–12] to improve efficiency and throughput in data transmission and data repair. Unlike erasure coding, the data owner does not need to reconstruct the entire file before generating new coded blocks. Instead, the coded blocks which are collected from healthy servers can be used to generate new coded blocks. Compare with the ORAM, the structure of network coding is much simpler. It has no hierarchical storage, no shuffling procedure like ORAM, and no the drawback of the erasure coding. Therefore, this paper focuses on network coding.

MAC vs. Signature. The data stored in the servers cannot be checked without additional authentication information, i.e., Message Authentication Code (MAC) or signature. A MAC is also called a *tag*. The traditional MAC and signature are not suitable for network coding. Thus, new techniques called homomorphic MAC [14–16] and homomorphic signature [17,18] have been proposed. Furthermore, a MAC is used in a symmetric key setting while a signature is used in an asymmetric key setting. Because this paper focuses on a symmetric key setting for efficiency, we thus use homomorphic MAC in our scheme.

Contribution. In this paper, we propose a network coding-based POR (named POR-2P) which has the following contributions:

1. POR-2P can deal with *data provision-payment system* in which not only data owner and servers but also user can participate in the system. The user pays money to get data stored in the servers. This system exists two security problems:

   - *The user may not pay enough money*: POR-2P can address this problem by only allowing the user to retrieve a partial data (called data piece), not whole data each time. After getting a data piece, the user must pay money before getting the next data piece. The user can retrieve the whole data if he gathers enough data pieces. In other words, if the number of retrieved data pieces is larger than or equal to a threshold, the whole data can be fully recovered. That is the reason why we choose information-theoretic confidentiality in this paper.
   - *The servers may not provide the valid data*: POR-2P can address this problem by requiring the user to check each data piece provided from the servers. Herein introduces the following challenge. The data is encoded by the data owner before being stored in the untrusted servers. Furthermore, the user is also untrusted. Thus, the data owner cannot give his/her secret keys, which are used to compute the MACs, to the user. Therefore, how can the user check whether the data piece provided from the servers is valid without having any information about the secret keys of the data owner? POR-2P can address this challenge by using a technique called orthogonal keygen.

2. POR-2P is constructed based on a symmetric key setting which is well-known to be more efficient than asymmetric key setting. The user can check the data piece sent by the untrusted servers without any public key.

3. POR-2P can deal with access control during retrieve process by using our key management. Concretely, data owner can control which data that the user is allowed to retrieve and which data that the user is not allowed to retrieve.

4. The complexity analysis of POR-2P show that its communication and computation costs are lower than these costs in some comparable previous schemes. The performance evaluation shows that POR-2P is very applicable to a real system.

Roadmap. The related work is introduced in Sect. 2. The preliminaries are described in Sect. 3. The system model and adversarial model are presented in Sects. 4 and 5. The POR-2P scheme is proposed in Sect. 6. The security and efficiency analyses, and the performance evaluation are discussed in Sects. 7 and 8. Finally, the conclusion and future work are drawn in Sect. 9.

2   Related Work

There are a few notable network coding-based PORs. Dimakis et al. [12] are the first to apply network coding for distributed storage systems. Their work achieved a remarkable reduction in the communication overhead of the repair component. Acedanski et al. [13] demonstrated that when the random linear coding is applied to distributed storage system, it performs as well without suffering additional storage space required at the centralized server before distribution among multiple locations. Further, with a probability close to one, the minimum number of storage location a downloader needs to connect to (for reconstructing the entire file), can be very close to the case where there is complete coordination between the storage locations and the downloader. Li et al. [19] proposed a tree-structure data regeneration with the linear network coding to achieve an efficient regeneration traffic and bandwidth capacity by using an undirected-weighted maximum spanning tree and the Prim algorithm. Chen et al. then proposed RDC-NC [20] (Remote Data Checking for Network Coding-based distributed storage systems) which provides a decent solution for efficient data repair by recoding encoded blocks in the healthy servers. Chen et al. proposed NC-Cloud [21] (a Network-Coding-based storage system in a Cloud-of-Clouds) to improve cost-effective repair using the functional minimum-storage regenerating (FMSR) code and to relax the encoding requirement of storage nodes during repair. NC-Audit [22] (Auditing for Network Coding storage) was proposed also for efficient data check and repair and data leakage using a combination of a homomorphic MAC (called SpaceMac) and a chosen-plaintext attack (CPA)-secure encryption (called NCrypt).

In most of these previous schemes, the system model consists of two entities: (i) a data owner who outsources, encodes and checks his/her data, and (ii) servers which store the data and provide proofs to the data owner. Some papers deal with multiple data owners [23,24]. However, none of previous schemes considers the very practical scenario that: besides data owner(s) and servers, the system model should consist of one more entity which is user. This user can retrieve the data stored in the servers. For instance, in a *data provision-payment system*, the user pays money to get data stored in the servers.

3   Preliminaries

3.1   Proof of Retrievability (POR)

The POR [1–3], which is a challenge-response protocol between a data owner (verifier) and a server (prover), was proposed to help the verifier to check whether his/her data stored in the server is available, intact and retrievable. The POR has the following functions:

- keygen(1^λ): The data owner executes this function which inputs a security parameter (λ) and outputs a secret key (sk) along with a public key (pk). For a symmetric key system, pk is set to be null.
- encode(sk, F): This function allows the data owner to encode a raw file (F) to an encoded file (F'). F' is then stored in the server.
- check(sk): This function conducts the challenge-response protocol between the data owner and the server during which the data owner uses sk to generate a challenge (c) and sends the c to the server. The server computes a corresponding response (r) and sends the r back to the data owner. The data owner then verifies the server based on c and r.

- retrieve($c_0, \cdots, c_{m-1}$): This function is performed when the data owner wants to retrieve F based on a set of coded blocks of some servers. This function selects some healthy servers and requests those selected servers to send their coded blocks (c).
- repair(): When a corrupted data from a server is detected in the check function, this function is executed by the data owner to repair the corrupted data. The repair function is depended on the used techniques, e.g., replication, erasure coding, or network coding.

3.2   Network Coding

The network coding [10–12] was proposed for cost-efficiency in data transmission. Suppose that a data owner owns a file F and wants to store the redundant coded blocks in the servers in a way that the data owner can reconstruct F and can repair the coded blocks in a corrupted server. The data owner firstly divides F into m blocks: $F = v_1 || \cdots || v_m \in \mathbb{F}_q^z$. $v_k \in \mathbb{F}_q^z$ where $k \in \{1, \cdots, m\}$ and $\mathbb{F}_q^z$ denotes a z-dimensional finite field of a prime order q. The data owner then augments v_k with a vector of length m which contains a single '1' in the position k and $(m-1)$ single '0's elsewhere. The resulting block is called *augmented block* (says, w_k). w_k has the following form:

$$w_k = (v_k, \overbrace{\underbrace{0, \cdots, 0, 1, 0, \cdots, 0}_{k}}^{m}) \in \mathbb{F}_q^{z+m} \qquad (1)$$

Thereafter, the data owner randomly chooses m coefficients $\alpha_1, \cdots, \alpha_m \in \mathbb{F}_q$ to compute coded blocks using the linear combination:

$$c = \sum_{k=1}^{m} \alpha_k \cdot w_k \in \mathbb{F}_q^{z+m} \qquad (2)$$

The data owner stores these coded blocks in the servers. To reconstruct F, any m coded blocks are required to solve m augmented blocks $w_1, \cdots, w_m$ using the accumulated coefficients contained in the last m coordinates of each coded block. After the m augmented blocks are solved, m file blocks $v_1, \cdots, v_m$ are obtained from the first coordinate of each augmented block. Finally, F is reconstructed by concatenating the file blocks. Note that the matrix consisting of the coefficients used to construct any m coded blocks should have full rank. Koetter et al. [25] proved that if the prime q is chosen large enough and the coefficients are chosen randomly, the matrix has full rank with high probability. When a server is corrupted, the data owner repairs it by retrieving the coded blocks from the healthy servers and linearly combining them to regenerate the new coded blocks. An example of the data repair is given in Fig. 1.

3.3   Homomorphic MAC

Inner-Product MAC. This MAC is the simplest homomorphic MAC which consists of the following algorithms:

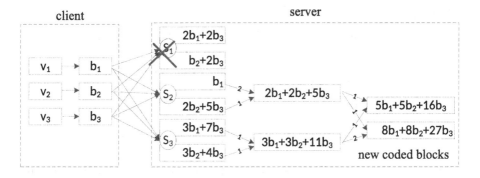

Fig. 1. An example of data repair in network coding

- Gen(1^λ) → k: the algorithm inputs a security parameter λ and outputs a secret key k.
- Tag$_k(M)$ → t: the algorithm inputs k and a message M; and outputs a tag t such that:

$$t = M \cdot k \qquad\qquad (3)$$

- Ver$_k(M, t)$ → $\{0, 1\}$: the algorithm inputs M, t and k; and outputs 1 if t is a valid tag. Otherwise, it outputs 0.

Wegman-Carten MAC. The inner-product MAC nay not be secured from the response replay attack (see Sect. 5.2) when it is combined with the network coding. The Wegman-Carten MAC was then introduced as follows:

- Gen(1^λ) → $\{k, k'\}$: the algorithm inputs a security parameter λ and outputs secret keys $\{k, k'\}$. k is used for tagging the message M. k' is used for permuting the tag.
- Tag$_{\{k,k'\}}(M)$ → t: the algorithm inputs $\{k, k'\}$ and a message M; and outputs a tag t such that:

$$t = M \cdot k + f_{k'}(r) \qquad\qquad (4)$$

where f and r denote a pseudorandom function and a randomness, respectively.

- Ver$_{\{k,k'\}}(M, t)$ → $\{0, 1\}$: outputs 1 if t is a valid tag, and 0 otherwise.

This Wegman-Carter MAC will be used in our scheme.

3.4 Orthogonal Keygen

The technique is proposed in [26] to generate a key such that it is orthogonal to all the augmented blocks. In a formal statement, given the set of augmented blocks $\{w_1, \cdots, w_m\}$, the algorithm outputs a key k such that $k \cdot w_i = 0$ for all $i = 1, \cdots, m$. The algorithm is given as follows.

    OrthogonalKeygen $(w_1, \cdots, w_m)$ → k: Let π denote the span of $w_1, \cdots, w_m \in \mathbb{F}_q^{z+m}$. Let M be the matrix in which each of the m augmented blocks is a row of M. $\text{rank}(M) = m$. Let π_M be the space spanned by the rows of M. The null space of M, denoted by $\pi_M^\perp$, is the set of all vectors $u \in \mathbb{F}_q^{z+m}$ such that $M \cdot u^T = 0$. For any $m \times (z + m)$ matrix, the rank-nullity theorem gives:

$$\text{rank}(M) + \text{nullity}(M) = z + m \tag{5}$$

where $\text{nullity}(M)$ is the dimension of $\pi_M^\perp$. And thus,

$$\dim(\pi_M^\perp) = (z + m) - m = z \tag{6}$$

Let $\{b_1, \cdots, b_z\} \in \mathbb{F}_q^{z(z+m)}$ be a basis of $\pi_M^\perp$ which can be found by solving $M \cdot u^T = 0$. Let f be a Pseudorandom function such that $f : \mathcal{K} \times [1, z] \to \mathbb{F}_q$. The key k is computed as:

- $r_i \leftarrow f(k_{PRF}, i) \in \mathbb{F}_q$ for $i \in \{1, \cdots, z\}$ and $k_{PRF} \in \mathcal{K}$.
- $k \leftarrow \sum_{i=1}^{z} r_i \cdot b_i \in \mathbb{F}_q^{z+m}$.

4   System Model

4.1   System Entities

The system model (Fig. 2) consists of the following three types of entities:

- *Data owner*: Data owner is a trusted entity who owns a data and wants to store the data in the servers. Before storing the data in the servers, the data owner encodes the data and uses his/her secret keys to compute tags for the data. The data owner will check the servers periodically. If a corrupted server is detected, he will repair the corruption using network coding.
- *User*: User is an untrusted entity who wants to retrieve the data of the data owner. The user is given keys by the data owner (not the secret keys of the data owner) to check the responses from the servers during data retrieval.
- *Servers*: Servers are the untrusted entities who store the data. The servers have responsibility to provide the proofs along with a partial data to the data owner (during the check and repair procedures) and to the user (during retrieve procedure).

4.2   System Requirements and Assumptions

- Only the data owner can compute the tags of the data using his/her secret keys. Although the user is given keys (which is different from the secret keys of the data owner) to check and to repair the servers, the user cannot compute the tags for the data.
- The user and the servers do not collude with each other.
- All the keys are transmitted via a secure channel.

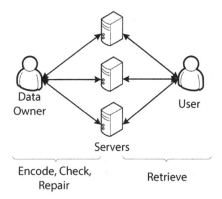

Fig. 2. The system model

5   Adversarial Model

5.1   Attacks from User

The user performs the following two attacks:

- The user searches the secret keys of the data owner via two ways: (i) brute force search from the key of the user, (ii) orthogonal keygen after retrieving the data.
- The user forges a tag for a *new* file block. Note that the user only forges a tag for a new file block because for an old file block, the tag is already computed by the data owner. Thus, forging a tag for an old file block is meaningless. The security from tag forgery of a new file block will be proved in Theorem 3 in Sect. 7.

5.2   Attacks from Servers

Response Replay Attack. This attack means that a malicious server reuses the correct response in the past check phase in order to save the computation cost, and is still able to pass the verification in the current check phase. For example:

- Epoch 1: the data owner sends a challenge Q to the server S_A. S_A responds $\{c_A, t_A\}$ where c_A and t_A denote the aggregated coded block and aggregated tag, respectively. The data owner verifies S_A by checking whether $t_A = c_A \cdot k_C$ where k_C denotes the secret key of the data owner. Suppose that the equality holds.
- Epoch 2: the data owner sends a challenge Q' to S_A. S_A reuses $\{c_A, t_A\}$ which are generated in the epoch 1 without computing another response for Q'. S_A still passes the verification $t_A = c_A \cdot k_C$.

Pollution Attack. This attack means that a malicious server responds a valid coded block to pass the check phase, but then provides an invalid coded block in the repair phase in order to prevent data recovery. For example:

- Encode: the data owner encodes the augmented blocks $\{w_1, w_2, w_3\}$ into six coded blocks:
  - $c_{11} = w_1$ and $c_{12} = w_2 + w_3$.
  - $c_{21} = w_3$ and $c_{22} = w_1 + w_2$.
  - $c_{31} = w_1 + w_3$ and $c_{32} = w_2 + w_3$.

  Then, $\{c_{11}, c_{12}\}$ are stored in the server S_1; $\{c_{21}, c_{22}\}$ are stored in the server S_2; and $\{c_{31}, c_{32}\}$ are stored in the server S_3.
- Check: the corrupted S_3 is detected.
- Repair: to repair S_3, the data owner requires S_1 and S_2 to provide their aggregated coded blocks. S_1 provides $c_1 = 1c_{11} + 1c_{12} = w_1 + w_2 + w_3$. Suppose S_2 injects a polluted block $c_2 = X$ which is an arbitrary value. The data owner computes two new coded blocks for the new server S_3': $c_{31}' = 1c_1 + 1c_2 = X + w_1 + w_2 + w_3$, and $c_{32}' = 1c_1 + 2c_2 = 2X + w_1 + w_2 + w_3$.

The number of unknowns is now $(m + 1)$ where m denotes the number of augmented blocks (in this example, $m = 4$ and the unknowns are X, w_1, w_2 and w_3). Therefore, the original file cannot be retrieved from any m or more coded blocks.

6   Our Proposed POR-2P Scheme

The notations used throughout our scheme are given as follows:

- $\mathcal{DO}$ denotes the data owner.
- $\mathcal{U}$ denotes the user.
- n denotes the number of servers.
- S_i denotes a server where $i \in \{1, \cdots, n\}$.
- F denotes the original file.
- m denotes the number of file blocks.
- $\mathbb{F}_q^z$ denotes the z-dimensional finite field of a prime order q.
- v_k denotes a file block where $k \in \{1, \cdots, m\}$.
- w_k denotes an augmented block of v_k where $k \in \{1, \cdots, m\}$.
- d denotes the number of coded blocks stored in a server.
- c_{ij} denotes a coded block where $i \in \{1, \cdots, n\}, j \in \{1, \cdots, d\}$.
- t_{ij} denotes the tag of c_{ij} where $i \in \{1, \cdots, n\}, j \in \{1, \cdots, d\}$.
- s denotes the number of spot checks where $1 \leq s \leq d$.
- S_r denotes a corrupted server.
- S_r' denotes a new server used to replace S_r.
- f denotes a pseudo-random function: $\{0, 1\}^* \times \{0, 1\}^\kappa \to \mathbb{F}_q$.

6.1 Setup

1. *Augmented blocks*: $\mathcal{DO}$ divides F into m file blocks $F = v_1||\cdots||v_m$. $v_k \in \mathbb{F}_q^z$ where $k \in \{1, \cdots, m\}$. $\mathcal{DO}$ creates m augmented blocks. Each augmented block has the following form:

$$w_k = (v_k, \overbrace{\underbrace{0, \cdots, 0, 1}_{k}, 0, \cdots, 0}^{m}) \in \mathbb{F}_q^{z+m} \tag{7}$$

2. *Keygen:* $\mathcal{DO}$ generates the following keys:
   - $k_{DO} \overset{rand}{\leftarrow} \mathbb{F}_q^{z+m}$.
   - $k_\phi \in \mathbb{F}_q^{z+m} \leftarrow$ OrthogonalKeygen$(w_1, \cdots, w_m)$. The property of k_ϕ is that it is orthogonal to each of $\{w_1, \cdots, w_m\}$. Formally, $k_\phi w_k = 0$ for all $k \in \{1, \cdots, m\}$.
   - $k_{PRF} \overset{rand}{\leftarrow} \mathbb{F}_q^\kappa$.

$\mathcal{DO}$ then computes:

$$k_U = k_{DO} + k_\phi \in \mathbb{F}_q^{z+m} \tag{8}$$

$\mathcal{DO}$ sends $\{k_U, k_{PRF}\}$ to $\mathcal{U}$. $\mathcal{DO}$ keeps $\{k_{DO}, k_\phi, k_{PRF}\}$.

6.2 Encode

1. $\mathcal{DO}$ computes nd coded blocks and nd tags as follows:
   For $\forall i \in \{1, \cdots, n\}, \forall j \in \{1, \cdots, d\}$:
   - $\mathcal{DO}$ generates m coefficients: $\alpha_{ijk} \overset{rand}{\leftarrow} \mathbb{F}_q$.
   - $\mathcal{DO}$ computes coded block:

$$c_{ij} = \sum_{k=1}^{m} \alpha_{ijk} \cdot w_k \in \mathbb{F}_q^{z+m} \tag{9}$$

   - $\mathcal{DO}$ computes tag:

$$t_{ij} = k_{DO} \cdot c_{ij} + f_{k_{PRF}}(i||j) \in \mathbb{F}_q \tag{10}$$

2. For $\forall j \in \{1, d\}$, $\mathcal{DO}$ sends $\{c_{ij}, t_{ij}\}$ to $\mathcal{S}_i$.

6.3 Check (spot Check)

1. $\mathcal{DO}$ generates the challenge Q as follows:
   - $\mathcal{DO}$ generates $s \overset{rand}{\leftarrow} \{1, \cdots, d\}$. s can be different for each server and each check time.
   - $\mathcal{DO}$ generates the challenge Q consisting of s pairs $(b_1, \beta_1), \cdots, (b_s, \beta_s)$ where $b_u \overset{rand}{\leftarrow} \{1, \cdots, d\}$ and $\beta_u \overset{rand}{\leftarrow} \mathbb{F}_q$ for $u \in \{1, \cdots, s\}$.
   - $\mathcal{DO}$ sends $Q = \{(b_1, \beta_1), \cdots, (b_s, \beta_s)\}$ to $\mathcal{S}_i$.

2. $\mathcal{S}_i$ responds $\mathcal{DO}$ as follows:
   - $\mathcal{S}_i$ combines coded blocks:

$$c_i = \sum_{u=1}^{s} \beta_u \cdot c_{ib_u} \in \mathbb{F}_q^{z+m} \tag{11}$$

   - $\mathcal{S}_i$ combines tags:

$$t_i = \sum_{u=1}^{s} \beta_u \cdot t_{ib_u} \in \mathbb{F}_q \tag{12}$$

   - $\mathcal{S}_i$ sends $\{c_i, t_i\}$ to $\mathcal{DO}$.
3. $\mathcal{DO}$ verifies $\mathcal{S}_i$ as follows:
   - $\mathcal{DO}$ computes:

$$t_i' = k_{DO}c_i + \sum_{u=1}^{s} \beta_u \cdot f_{k_{PRF}}(i||b_u) \tag{13}$$

   - $\mathcal{DO}$ checks whether the following equation holds. If it holds, $\mathcal{S}_i$ is healthy. Otherwise, $\mathcal{S}_i$ is corrupted.

$$t_i' = t_i. \tag{14}$$

The correctness of Eq. 14 is proved as follows:

Proof.
$t_i' = k_{DO}c_i + \sum_{u=1}^{s} \beta_u f_{k_{PRF}}(i||b_u)$ //because of Eq. 13
$\quad = \sum_{u=1}^{s} k_{DO}\beta_u c_{ib_u} + \sum_{u=1}^{s} \beta_u f_{k_{PRF}}(i||b_u)$ // because of Eq. 11
$\quad = \sum_{u=1}^{s} \beta_u(k_{DO}c_{ib_u} + f_{k_{PRF}}(i||b_u))$
$\quad = \sum_{u=1}^{s} \beta_u t_{ib_u}$ //because of Eq. 10 with $j = b_u$
$\quad = t_i$ //because of Eq. 12

6.4 Repair

When a corrupted server ($\mathcal{S}_r$) is detected, the new server ($\mathcal{S'}_r$) is used to replace $\mathcal{S}_r$.

1. $\mathcal{DO}$ performs as in the check phase until he gets enough d valid aggregated coded blocks (which are contained in the server responses), says, $R_c = \{c_{i_1}, \cdots, c_{i_d}\}$.
2. $\mathcal{DO}$ computes d coded blocks and d tags for $\mathcal{S}'_r$ as follows:
   - $\mathcal{DO}$ assigns d valid aggregated coded blocks as the new coded blocks of $\mathcal{S'}_r$: $(c_{r_1}, \cdots, c_{r_d}) \leftarrow (c_{i_1}, \cdots, c_{i_d})$.
   - $\mathcal{DO}$ computes new tags: $t_{rj} = c_{rj} \cdot k_U + f_{k_{PRF}}(r||j)$ where $j \in \{1, \cdots, d\}$.
3. $\mathcal{DO}$ sends $\{c_{rj}, t_{rj}\}$ to $\mathcal{S}'_r$ where $j \in \{1, \cdots, d\}$.

6.5 Retrieve

When $\mathcal{U}$ wants to retrieve F, firstly, he performs similarly to the check phase in order to collect enough m coded blocks. $\mathcal{U}$ then solves m file blocks and recovers F by concatenating all the file blocks. The difference between the check phase and the retrieve phase is that $\mathcal{DO}$ checks the servers using k_{DO} and k_{PRF} while in the retrieve phase, $\mathcal{U}$ checks the servers using k_U and k_{PRF}. Concretely, $\mathcal{U}$ performs as follows:

1. $\mathcal{U}$ generates the challenge Q as follows:
   - $\mathcal{U}$ generates $s \overset{rand}{\leftarrow} \{1, \cdots, d\}$.
   - $\mathcal{U}$ generates the challenge Q consisting of s pairs $(b_1, \beta_1), \cdots, (b_s, \beta_s)$ where $b_u \overset{rand}{\leftarrow} \{1, \cdots, d\}$ and $\beta_u \overset{rand}{\leftarrow} \mathbb{F}_q$ for $u \in \{1, \cdots, s\}$.
   - $\mathcal{U}$ sends $Q = \{(b_1, \beta_1), \cdots, (b_s, \beta_s)\}$ to $\mathcal{S}_i$.
2. $\mathcal{S}_i$ responds $\mathcal{U}$ as follows:
   - $\mathcal{S}_i$ combines coded blocks:

$$c_i = \sum_{u=1}^{s} \beta_u \cdot c_{ib_u} \in \mathbb{F}_q^{z+m} \tag{15}$$

   - $\mathcal{S}_i$ combines tags:

$$t_i = \sum_{u=1}^{s} \beta_u \cdot t_{ib_u} \in \mathbb{F}_q \tag{16}$$

   - $\mathcal{S}_i$ sends $\{c_i, t_i\}$ to $\mathcal{U}$.
3. $\mathcal{U}$ verifies $\mathcal{S}_i$ as follows:
   - $\mathcal{U}$ computes:

$$t_i' = k_U c_i + \sum_{u=1}^{s} \beta_u \cdot f_{k_{PRF}}(i||b_u) \tag{17}$$

   - $\mathcal{U}$ checks whether the following equation holds. If it holds, $\mathcal{S}_i$ is healthy; otherwise, $\mathcal{S}_i$ is corrupted.

$$t_i' = t_i. \tag{18}$$

The correctness of Eq. 18 is proved as follows:

Proof.
$t_i' = k_U c_i + \sum_{u=1}^{s} \beta_u f_{k_{PRF}}(i||b_u)$ //because of Eq. 17
$= (k_{DO} + k_\phi)c_i + \sum_{u=1}^{s} \beta_u f_{k_{PRF}}(i||b_u)$ //because of Eq. 8
$= (k_{DO} + k_\phi)\sum_{u=1}^{s} \beta_u c_{ib_u} + \sum_{u=1}^{s} \beta_u f_{k_{PRF}}(i||b_u)$ //because of Eq. 15
$= (k_{DO} + k_\phi)\sum_{u=1}^{s} \sum_{k=1}^{m} \beta_u \alpha_{ib_u k} w_k + \sum_{u=1}^{s} \beta_u f_{k_{PRF}}(i||b_u)$
　//because of Eq. 9 when replacing $j = b_u$
$= k_{DO} \sum_{u=1}^{s} \sum_{k=1}^{m} \beta_u \alpha_{ib_u k} w_k + \sum_{u=1}^{s} \beta_u f_{k_{PRF}}(i||b_u)$
　// because $k_\phi w_k = 0, \forall k \in \{1, \cdots, m\}$
$= k_{DO} \sum_{u=1}^{s} \beta_u c_{ib_u} + \sum_{u=1}^{s} \beta_u f_{k_{PRF}}(i||b_u)$ // because of Eq. 9 with $j = b_u$
$= \sum_{u=1}^{s} \beta_u (k_{DO} c_{ib_u} + f_{k_{PRF}}(i||b_u))$
$= \sum_{u=1}^{s} \beta_u t_{ib_u}$ // because of Eq. 10 with $b_u = j$
$= t_i$ // because of Eq. 16

$\square$

4. After collecting enough m aggregated coded blocks, $\mathcal{U}$ computes m augmented blocks $\{w_1, \cdots, w_m\}$ by using Gaussian elimination, then obtains m file blocks $\{v_1, \cdots, v_m\}$ which are contained in the first element of each augmented block. Finally, $\mathcal{U}$ recovers the original file as $F = v_1||\cdots||v_m$.

Access Control. In this part, we show that how POR-2P can address access control in retrieval process. Consider the scenario that $\mathcal{DO}$ owns multiple files and there are multiple users. Each user has a different access privilege to each file. To deal with this challenge, our main idea is that if $\mathcal{DO}$ wants a user to retrieve which files, $\mathcal{DO}$ will generate the key k_ϕ such that it is orthogonal to those files.

Concretely, suppose that $\mathcal{DO}$ owns h files: $\{F_1, \cdots, F_h\}$. Let x denote file index. Then, for each $x \in \{1, \cdots, g\}$, $\mathcal{DO}$ performs:

- Divide F_x into m blocks: $F_x = v_{x1}||\cdots||v_{xm}$.
- Create augmented blocks: $\{w_{x1}, \cdots, w_{xm}\}$.
- Compute coded blocks: $\{c_{xi1}, \cdots, c_{xid}\}$ for each $i \in \{1, \cdots, n\}$.
- Compute tags: $\{t_{xi1}, \cdots, t_{xid}\}$ for each $i \in \{1, \cdots, n\}$.

Suppose that there are h users $\{\mathcal{U}_1, \cdots, \mathcal{U}_h\}$ participating in the system. Suppose that $\mathcal{DO}$ allows $\mathcal{U}_y$ where $y \in \{1, \cdots, h\}$ to retrieve a subset of files: $\Gamma_y = \{F_{x_1}, \cdots, F_{x_r}\} \subseteq \{F_1, \cdots, F_h\}$. To enable this access control, $\mathcal{DO}$ manages the keys as follows:

- $k_{DO} \stackrel{rand}{\leftarrow} \mathbb{F}_q^{z+m}$.
- $k_{\phi_y} \in \mathbb{F}_q^{z+m} \leftarrow \mathsf{OrthogonalKeygen}(w_{x1}, \cdots, w_{xm})$ for all $x \in \{x_1, \cdots, x_r\}$. The property of k_{ϕ_y} is that it is orthogonal to all augmented blocks of the files which belong to Γ_y. Formally, $k_{\phi_y} w_{x1} = \cdots = k_{\phi_y} w_{xm} = 0$ for all $x \in \{x_1, \cdots, x_r\}$.
- $k_{PRF} \stackrel{rand}{\leftarrow} \mathbb{F}_q^\kappa$.

Then, $\mathcal{DO}$ sends $k_{U_y} = k_{DO} + k_{\phi_y}$ to $\mathcal{U}_y$. Note that k_{DO} and k_{PRF} are the same for all users, but only k_{ϕ_y} is different for each user according to which files that the user is allowed to retrieve.

7   Security Analysis

Before describing how the POR is secured from the attacks in the adversarial model, we give the data retrieval condition as follows.

Theorem 1. *F can be retrieved if in any epoch, at least m coded blocks are healthy.*

Proof. $F = v_1||\cdots||v_m$. Thus, to retrieve F, we view $v_1, \cdots, v_m$ as m unknowns that need to be solved. Because each coded block is computed from a linear combination of all m file blocks, to solve these m coded block, we need at least m coded blocks to make the linear coefficient matrix have full rank. □

7.1   Attacks from User

We consider the probability for $\mathcal{U}$ to search for the secret keys $\{k_{DO}, k_\phi\}$ of $\mathcal{DO}$.

Theorem 2. *Given k_U, $\{k_{DO}, k_\phi\}$ cannot be derived via the brute force search or orthogonal keygen.*

Proof. Because $k_U = k_{DO} + k_\phi \in \mathbb{F}_q^{z+m}$, the probability to find k_{DO} and k_ϕ via brute force search is $1/q^{z+m}$. If q is chosen large enough (i.e., 160 bits), the probability to find $\{k_{DO}, k_\phi\}$ is $1/(2^{160})^{(z+m)}$, which is negligible.

Besides the brute force search, $\mathcal{U}$ may search $\{k_{DO}, k_\phi\}$ as follows: after getting enough m coded blocks and retrieving all m augmented blocks, $\mathcal{U}$ runs the orthogonal keygen to find all basis vectors which are orthogonal to all m augmented blocks to obtain k_ϕ. Let $\{b_1, \cdots, b_z\}$ be the basis vectors found by $\mathcal{U}$ (as mentioned in the orthogonal keygen). k_ϕ is computed as: $k_\phi \leftarrow \sum_{i=1}^{z} r_i \cdot b_i \in \mathbb{F}_q^{z+m}$ where $r_i \in \mathbb{F}_q$ is randomly generated by a pseudo random function. Therefore, the probability for $\mathcal{U}$ to obtain k_ϕ is z/q. This means that $\mathcal{U}$ has to guess all z random r_i's to obtain k_ϕ. If q is chosen large enough (i.e., 160 bits), the probability to find k_ϕ is $z/2^{160}$, which is negligible. □

We now prove that $\mathcal{U}$ cannot compute the tag for any new file block. For the old file blocks, $\mathcal{U}$ does not have any purpose to compute the tags because the tags already exist (computed by $\mathcal{DO}$).

Theorem 3. *Given a new file block v_π ($v_\pi \neq v_1, \cdots, v_m$) and given the key $k_U = k_{DO} + k_\phi$, $\mathcal{U}$ cannot forge the tag for v_π.*

Proof. Given v_π, the new coded block is computed as:

$$c_{ij} = \sum_{k=1}^{m} \alpha_{ijk} w_k + \alpha_\pi w_\pi \in \mathbb{F}_q^{z+m} \qquad (19)$$

where $\alpha_\pi \xleftarrow{rand} \mathbb{F}_q$. Suppose that $\mathcal{U}$ tries to compute the tag for c_{ij} using k_U and k_{PRF} as follows:

$$
\begin{aligned}
t_{ij} &= k_U \cdot c_{ij} + f_{k_{PRF}}(i\|j) \in \mathbb{F}_q \\
&= (k_{DO} + k_\phi) \cdot c_{ij} + f_{k_{PRF}}(i\|j) \\
&= (k_{DO} + k_\phi)(\sum_{k=1}^{m} \alpha_{ijk} w_k + \alpha_\pi w_\pi) + f_{k_{PRF}}(i\|j) \\
&= k_{DO} \sum_{k=1}^{m} \alpha_{ijk} w_k + (k_{DO} + k_\phi)\alpha_\pi w_\pi + f_{k_{PRF}}(i\|j) \text{ //because } k_\phi w_k = 0
\end{aligned}
$$

Note that because only $\mathcal{DO}$ knowns k_ϕ, only $\mathcal{DO}$ can generate v_π such that $k_\phi v_\pi = 0$. In other words, if v_π is not generated by $\mathcal{DO}$ but another one (i.e., the user), $k_\phi v_\pi \neq 0$.

In the check phase, $\mathcal{DO}$ verifies the servers using k_{DO} and k_{PRF} with Eq. 14 as follows:

$$
\begin{aligned}
t_i' &= k_{DO}c_i + \sum_{u=1}^{s} \beta_u \cdot f_{k_{PRF}}(i||b_u) \\
&= \sum_{u=1}^{s} k_{DO}\beta_u c_{ib_u} + \sum_{u=1}^{s} \beta_u \cdot f_{k_{PRF}}(i||b_u) \\
&= \sum_{u=1}^{s} \beta_u(k_{DO}c_{ib_u} + f_{k_{PRF}}(i||b_u)) \\
&= \sum_{u=1}^{s} \beta_u(k_{DO}(\sum_{k=1}^{m} \alpha_{ib_u k}w_k + \alpha_\pi w_\pi) + f_{k_{PRF}}(i||b_u)) \\
&= \sum_{u=1}^{s} \beta_u(k_{DO}\sum_{k=1}^{m} \alpha_{ib_u k}w_k + k_{DO}\alpha_\pi w_\pi + f_{k_{PRF}}(i||b_u)) \\
t_i &= \sum_{u=1}^{s} \beta_u t_{ib_u} \\
&= \sum_{u=1}^{s} \beta_u(k_{DO}\sum_{k=1}^{m} \alpha_{ijk}w_k + (k_{DO}+k_\phi)\alpha_\pi w_\pi + f_{k_{PRF}}(i||j))
\end{aligned}
$$

// replace $t_{ib_u} = t_{ij}$ where $j = b_u$

It is clear that $t_i \neq t_i'$. Therefore, $\mathcal{U}$ cannot forge the tag for v_π. $\square$

7.2 Attacks from Servers

Response Replay Attack. Suppose the malicious server performing this attack is $\mathcal{S}_i$.

- Epoch 1: $\mathcal{DO}$ challenges S_i by $Q = \{(b_1, \beta_1), \cdots, (b_s, \beta_s)\}$. S_i responds a valid pair of $\{c_i, t_i\}$. $\mathcal{DO}$ verifies $t_i = k_{DO}c_i + \sum_{u=1}^{s} \beta_u \cdot f_{k_{PRF}}(i||b_u)$.
- Epoch 2: $\mathcal{DO}$ challenges S_i by $Q' = \{(b_1', \beta_1'), \cdots, (b_s', \beta_s')\}$. S_i reuses $\{c_i, t_i\}$, but cannot pass the verification because: $t_i \neq k_{DO}c_i + \sum_{u=1}^{s} \beta_u' \cdot f_{k_{PRF}}(i||b_u')$.

Thus, $\mathcal{S}_i$ cannot pass the verification with this attack. Similarly, in the retrieve phase, $\mathcal{U}$ also performs as the check phase using his keys k_U and k_{PRF}, $\mathcal{S}_i$ also cannot pass the verification with this attack.

Pollution Attack. Suppose that the malicious server S_i provides a polluted pair of $\{c_i, t_i\}$ to $\mathcal{DO}$ (in repair phase) or to $\mathcal{U}$ (in the retrieve phase). The key point here is that $\mathcal{DO}$ and $\mathcal{U}$ always check every provided response. S_i cannot pass the verification $t_i = k_{DO}c_i + \sum_{u=1}^{s} \beta_u \cdot f_{k_{PRF}}(i||b_u)$ (Eq. 14) and $t_i = k_U c_i + \sum_{u=1}^{s} \beta_u \cdot f_{k_{PRF}}(i||b_u)$ (Eq. 18) if c_i and t_i are not the independent linear combinations of the coded blocks and tags at the points: $\{b_1, \cdots, b_s\}$ using the coefficient $\{\beta_1, \cdots, \beta_s\}$.

8 Efficiency Analysis and Performance Evaluation

Efficiency Analysis. The efficiency comparison between the RDC-NC [20], NC-Audit [22], MD-POR [23] and POR-2P schemes is given in Table 1. The NC-Audit and MD-POR schemes support the public authentication which means that an entity called Third Party Auditor (TPA) is delegated the task of checking the servers by the data owner. The MD-POR has multiple data owners. For the fair comparison, we suppose that the check phase in the NC-Audit and MD-POR schemes is performed by the data owner, and we suppose that the MD-POR only has a single data owner.

Table 1. Comparison

		RDC-NC [20]	NC-Audit [22]	MDspsPOR [23]	POR-2P (proposal)
Encode phase	Comp. ($\mathcal{DO}$)	$O(mnd)$	$O(mnd)$	$O(m)$	$O(mnd)$
	Comp. (servers)	$O(1)$	$O(1)$	$O(mnd)$	$O(1)$
	Comm	$O(nd(\frac{\lceil F \rceil}{m}+m))$	$O(nd(\frac{\lceil F \rceil}{m}+m)+mnd)$	$O(mn(\frac{\lceil F \rceil}{m}+m))$	$O(nd(\frac{\lceil F \rceil}{m}+m)$
Check phase	Comp. ($\mathcal{DO}$)	$O(nds)$	$O(ns)$	$O(n)$	$O(n)$
	Comp. (servers)	$O(ndm)$	$O(ns)$	$O(nd)$	$O(ns)$
	Comm	$O(n(\frac{\lceil F \rceil}{m}+m))$	$O(n(\frac{\lceil F \rceil}{m}+m))$	$O(n(\frac{\lceil F \rceil}{m}+m))$	$O(n(\frac{\lceil F \rceil}{m}+m))$
Repair phase	Comp. ($\mathcal{DO}$)	$O(ld)$	$O(ld)$	$O(ld)$	$O(sd)$
	Comp. (servers)	$O(ld)$	$O(ld)$	$O(ld)$	$O(sd)$
	Comm	$O((l+d)(\frac{\lceil F \rceil}{m}+m))$	$O((l+d)(\frac{\lceil F \rceil}{m}+m)+ld)$	$O((l+d)(\frac{\lceil F \rceil}{m}+m))$	$O((s+d)(\frac{\lceil F \rceil}{m}+m))$
Retrieve phase	Comp. ($\mathcal{U}$)	N/A	N/A	N/A	$O(sm)+O(G)$
	Comp. ($\mathcal{DO}$)	$O(sm)+O(G)$	$O(sm)+O(G)$	$O(sm)+O(G)$	$O(sm)+O(G)$
	Comp. (servers)	$O(sm)$	$O(sm)$	$O(sm)$	$O(sm)$
	Comm	$O(|F|+m^2)$	$O(|F|+m^2)$	$O(|F|+m^2)$	$O(|F|+m^2)$

l denotes the number of healthy servers used in the RDC-NC, NC-Audit and MD-POR.
$O(G)$ denotes the complexity of the Gaussian elimination to solve m file blocks.
Comp. means computation.
Comm. means communication.
N/A means not applicable due to the lack of support.

Performance Evaluation. We evaluate the computation performance of the POR-2P scheme to show that it is applicable for a real system. A program written by Python 2.7.3 is executed using a computer with Intel Core i5 processor, 2.4 GHz, 4 GB of RAM, Windows 7 64-bit OS. The prime q is set to be 256 bits. The number of servers is set to be 10 ($n = 10$). The number of coded blocks stored in each server is set to be 20 ($d = 20$). The number of spot checks for each server is set to be a half of d ($s = d/2 = 10$). The size of each file block is set to be 2^{23} bits (1 MB). The experiment results are observed with four sets of computation performance: Fig. 3 (encode), Fig. 4 (check), Fig. 5 (repair), and Fig. 6 (retrieve), by varying the file size.

Figure 3 reveals that the computation time in the encode and init (splitting file) functions linearly increase while the keygen function is constant. If the file size is 1 GB, the computation time in the encode and init functions is roughly 8308.561 s and 1863.914 s, respectively. Figure 4 reveals that the computation time of the challenge, respond, and verify functions is constant. Figure 5 reveals that the computation time of the repair function is also constant. Figure 6 reveals that the computation time in the retrieve function is almost linear in user-side and is constant in server-side. If the file size is 1 GB, the computation time of retrieve function in user-side is roughly 2691.186 s.

Although the graphs of the encode, the init and the retrieve functions on data owner-side linearly increase with the file size, the encode and init phases are executed only one time in the beginning; and the retrieve phase is also executed very few. Meanwhile, the check and repair phases are executed very often during the system lifetime with a constant computation as showed in the graphs. The above results show that the POR-2P is very efficient and applicable in a real system.

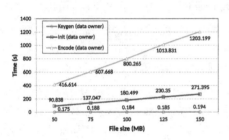

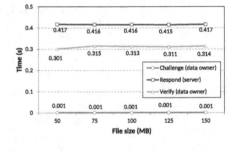

Fig. 3. Computation of encode phase   **Fig. 4.** Computation of check phase

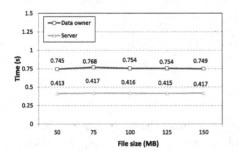

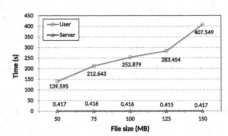

Fig. 5. Computation of repair phase   **Fig. 6.** Computation of retrieve phase

9   Conclusion and Future Work

This paper proposes the POR-2P to support the data provision-payment system in which the user can check and can retrieve the data using a symmetric key setting. The POR-2R can also deal with access control during retrieval process. The security analysis shows that the POR-2P can prevent the attacks from the user and the servers. Furthermore, the efficiency analysis and performance evaluation show that POR-2P is very applicable to a real system. Further work is investigated the implementation of the previous schemes.

References

1. Juels, A., Kaliski, B.: PORs: Proofs of retrievability for large files. In: Proceedings of 14th ACM Conference on Computer and Communications Security - CCS 2007, pp. 584–597 (2007)
2. Shacham, H., Waters, B.: Compact proofs of retrievability. In: Pieprzyk, J. (ed.) ASIACRYPT 2008. LNCS, vol. 5350, pp. 90–107. Springer, Heidelberg (2008)
3. Bowers, K., Juels, A., Oprea, A.: Proofs of retrievability: theory and implementation. In: Proceedings of Workshop on Cloud Computing Security - CCSW 2009, pp. 43–54 (2009)

4. Bolosky, W.J., Douceur, J.R., Ely, D., Theimer, M.: Feasibility of a serverless distributed file system deployed on an existing set of desktop PCs. In: Proceedings of ACM Conference on Measurement and Modeling of Computation Systems - SIGMETRICS 2000, pp. 34–43 (2000)
5. Curtmola, R., Khan, O., Burns, R., Ateniese, G.: MR-PDP: multiple-replica provable data possession. In: Proceedings of 28th Conference on Distributed Computing Systems, pp. 411–420 (2008)
6. Aguilera, M.K., Janakiraman, R., Xu, L.: Efficient fault-tolerant distributed storage using erasure codes, Technical report. Washington University in St. Louis (2004)
7. Bowers, K., Juels, A., Oprea, A.: HAIL: a high-availability and integrity layer for cloud storage. In: Proceedings of 16th ACM Conference on Computer and Communications Security - CCS 2009, pp. 187–198 (2009)
8. Shi, E., Stefanov, E., Papamanthou, C.: Practical dynamic proofs of retrievability. In: Proceedings of ACM SIGSAC Conference on Computer and Communications Security - CCS 2013, pp. 325–336 (2013)
9. Cash, D., Küpçü, A., Wichs, D.: Dynamic proofs of retrievability via oblivious RAM. In: Johansson, T., Nguyen, P.Q. (eds.) EUROCRYPT 2013. LNCS, vol. 7881, pp. 279–295. Springer, Heidelberg (2013)
10. Ahlswede, R., Cai, N., Li, S., Yeung, R.: Network information flow. IEEE Trans. Inf. Theor. 46(4), 1204–1216 (2000)
11. Li, S.Y.R., Yeung, R.W., Cai, N.: Linear network coding. IEEE Trans. Inf. Theor. 49(2), 371–381 (2003)
12. Dimakis, A., Godfrey, P., Wu, Y., Wainwright, M., Ramchandran, K.: Network coding for distributed storage systems. IEEE Trans. Inf. Theor. 56(9), 4539–4551 (2010)
13. Acedanski, S., Deb, S., Medard, M., Koetter, R.: How good is random linear coding based distributed networked storage? In: Workshop on Network Coding, Theory and Applications - NETCOD 2005 (2005)
14. Agrawal, S., Boneh, D.: Homomorphic MACs: MAC-based integrity for network coding. In: Abdalla, M., Pointcheval, D., Fouque, P.-A., Vergnaud, D. (eds.) ACNS 2009. LNCS, vol. 5536, pp. 292–305. Springer, Heidelberg (2009)
15. Cheng, C., Jiang, T.: An efficient homomorphic MAC with small key size for authentication in network coding. IEEE Trans. Comput. 62(10), 2096–2100 (2012)
16. Cheng, C., Jiang, T., Zhang, Q.: TESLA-based homomorphic MAC for authentication in P2P system for live streaming with network coding. IEEE J. Sel. Areas Commun. 31(9), 291–298 (2013)
17. Johnson, R., Molnar, D., Song, D., Wagner, D.: Homomorphic signature schemes. In: Preneel, B. (ed.) CT-RSA 2002. LNCS, vol. 2271, pp. 244–262. Springer, Heidelberg (2002)
18. Freeman, D.M.: Improved security for linearly homomorphic signatures: a generic framework. In: Fischlin, M., Buchmann, J., Manulis, M. (eds.) PKC 2012. LNCS, vol. 7293, pp. 697–714. Springer, Heidelberg (2012)
19. Li, J., Yang, S., Wang, X., Xue, X., Li, B.: Tree-structured Data Regeneration in Distributed Storage Systems with Network Coding. In: Proceedings of 29th Conference on Information Communications - INFOCOM 2010, pp. 2892–2900 (2010)
20. Chen, B., Curtmola, R., Ateniese, G., Burns, R.: Remote data checking for network coding-based distributed storage systems. In: Proceedings of ACM Cloud Computing Security Workshop - CCSW 2010, pp. 31–42 (2010)

21. Chen, H.C.H., Hu, Y., Lee, P.P.C., Tang, Y.: NCCloud: a network-coding-based storage system in a cloud-of-clouds. IEEE Trans. Comput. **63**(1), 31–44 (2014)
22. Le, A., Markopoulou, A.: NC-Audit: auditing for network coding storage. In: International Symposium on Network Coding - NetCod 2012, pp. 155–160 (2012)
23. Omote, K., Thao, T.P.: MD-POR: Multi-source and direct repair for network coding-based proof of retrievability. Int. J. Distrib. Sens. Network. (IJDSN) **2015**, 14 (2015). Article ID: 586720
24. Yan, W., Yang, M., Li, L., Fang, H.: Short signature scheme for multi-source network coding. Comput. Commun. **35**(3), 344–351 (2012)
25. Koetter, R., Medard, M.: An algebraic approach to network coding. IEEE/ACM Trans. Network. **11**(5), 782–795 (2003)
26. Le, A., Markopoulou, A.: On detecting pollution attacks in inter-session network coding. In: Proceedings of 31st IEEE Conference on Computer Communications - INFOCOM 2012, pp. 343–351 (2012)

A Single Key Scheduling Based Compression Function

Jiageng Chen[1], Rashed Mazumder[1(✉)], and Atsuko Miyaji[1,2,3]

[1] Japan Advanced Institute of Science and Technology, Ishikawa, Japan
{jg-chen,s1420213,miyaji}@jaist.ac.jp
[2] Japan Science and Technology Agency (JST) CREST, Saitama, Japan
[3] Graduate School of Engineering, Osaka University, Osaka, Japan

Abstract. A cryptographic hash is defined as a transformation of variable length-message into a fixed length value. The application of cryptographic hash is increasing day by day. In modern cryptography, it is now defined as "Swiss Army Knife of Cryptography" because of usage in the verify process of integrity for files or messages, verification of the password, file/data identifier, pseudo-random generation and key derivation. The cryptographic hash consists of a compression function, where compression function can be built by scratch or blockcipher. The blockcipher based hash is suitable for constrained device (WSN device) encryption because of direct hardware implementation of the blockcipher. The blockcipher hash can be categorized into (n, n) and $(n, 2n)$ [(block-length, key-length)]. A class of (n, n) is more suitable than the $(n, 2n)$ because of less power and memory utilization. There are some familiar schemes of (n, n) blockcipher hash such as MDC-2, MDC-4, MJH, Bart-12, MSR, where some schemes provide higher security bound and some are good for efficiency. The schemes of MDC-2, MDC-4, Bart, MSR need multiple key scheduling but the MJH needs single key scheduling. The proof technique of early mentioned schemes are based on the ideal cipher model (ICM), except the Bart and MJH. These two follows a model of the finite field multiplicative operation.

In this paper, we proposed a scheme of (n, n) blockcipher hash that satisfies a single key scheduling (KS = 1). The collision and preimage resistance of our scheme is bounded by $O(2^n)$ and $O(2^{2n})$. Our scheme follows three calls of blockcipher under the Davies Meyer (DM) mode. At first, we use the ICM proof technique. Later, we provide the weak cipher model (WCM) proof technique, which is more rigorous than the ICM.

Keywords: Ideal cipher model (ICM), Weak cipher model (WCM), Collision resistance (CR), Preimage resistance (PR), Efficiency rate (r)

1 Introduction

A cryptographic hash treats as an one way hash function, where literally it is impossible to backtrack [1–3]. It takes an arbitrary size of message as input

This study is partly supported by Grant-in-Aid for Scientific Research (C) (15K00183) and (15K00189).

C. Lambrinoudakis and A. Gabillon (Eds.): CRiSIS 2015, LNCS 9572, pp. 207–222, 2016.
DOI: 10.1007/978-3-319-31811-0_13

and provides a fixed length of message-digest/tag for an output [1–3]. There are many applications, which are based on this cryptographic tool. Usually, the cryptographic hash function has been used for creating small, fixed size of message digests so that the desire digest can play role as a proxy for a very large variable length-message in the digital signature scheme [1–3]. In modern cryptography, it is also used in message authentication code, pseudo-random number generator and key-derivation function [1–4].

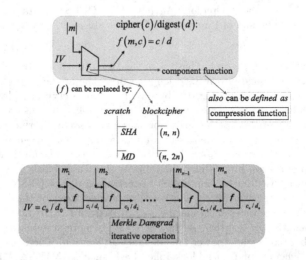

Fig. 1. Working scope of cryptographic hash [1–4, 17, 18]

The Merkle Damgrad iteration process has been used for building cryptographic hash where f is being used as compression function (Fig. 1) [5,6]. This f can be substituted by the scratch (SHA, MD) or blockcipher (AES, DES) [3,5,6]. The blockcipher is being used now more frequently because of vulnerability of the scratch based hash [3,7,8]. In the perspective of efficiency, the blockcipher (AES) is better choice than the SHA/MD in certain cases (10% less power consumption than the SHA-1) [2,9,10]. It is also suitable for constrained device encryption such as RFID-tag, wireless sensor network device. In respect of a hardware designer, it only needs to implement blockcipher for obtaining an encryption under a hash function [2,3,9,10,23,24,28].

In the early phase of blockcipher based cryptographic hash, the single block-length (SBL) blockcipher was the most common tool [1,2,11]. In SBL, the output and block-length is equal. Later, due to birthday type attack, it was required to provide a bigger output [1–3]. Finally, the double block-length (DBL) blockcipher takes the place of the SBL, where the output of the DBL is twice of the block-length [1–4]. There are two variants of DBL blockcipher such as (n, n) DBL and $(n, 2n)$ DBL. The (n, n) blockcipher is more suitable for encryption because of small key size [1–4,9,10].

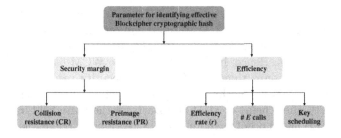

Fig. 2. Evaluation criteria of blockcipher hash [1–4,11]

Table 1. Existing research result of (n,n) blockcipher hash: "Security margin, proof technique"

	ICM		WCM		FFM	
	CR	PR	CR	PR	CR	PR
MDC-2 [13]	$\mathcal{O}(2^{n/2})$	$\mathcal{O}(2^n)$	-	-	-	-
MDC-4 [13]	$\mathcal{O}(2^{5n/8})$	$\mathcal{O}(2^{5n/4})$	-	-	-	-
MJH [13]	-	-	-	-	$\mathcal{O}(2^{n/2})$	$\mathcal{O}(2^n)$
Bart [13]	-	-	-	-	$\mathcal{O}(2^n)$	$\mathcal{O}(2^{3n/2})$
MSR [14]	$\mathcal{O}(2^{tn})$	$\mathcal{O}(2^{2tn})$	-	-	-	-
CIDM [31]	$\mathcal{O}(2^n)$	$\mathcal{O}(2^{2n})$	-	-	-	-

ICM: ideal cipher model
WCM: weak cipher model
FFM: finite field multiplicative operation

There are two basic parameters such as security bound and efficiency, which indicate the effectiveness of the blockcipher based cryptographic hash (Fig. 2) [1–4,11]. The collision resistance (CR) and preimage resistance (PR) are the two sub-parameters under the security margin. For the CR, it is hard to find a couple of message X and X' such that, $H(X) = H(X')|(X \neq X')$ [1]. It is needed to satisfy the requirements of CR and PR for any blockcipher based cryptographic hash [1–4]. The efficiency rate (r), number of blockcipher ($\# E$), number of key scheduling (KS) are extensions of efficiency parameter [1]. The efficiency rate is defined as division of message-size by the multiplication of the block size and the number of blockcipher call per iteration ($r = |m|/\#E \times n$) [1,3,4]. If the same key is being used in the blockcipher based hash for each iteration, then it is defined as single key scheduling (KS) [3,4,15,16]. Usually, it is normal practice to limit the value of $r, \#E,$ and KS as much as possible [1,3,4,12,15,16].

Now we are trying to address the issue of security proof technique, where the ideal cipher model (ICM) is the most common and easy applicable tool for a blockcipher cryptographic hash [17,18]. Under the ICM, the adversary has limited access capability (it can query two types of query) [17,18]. On the other hand, the weak cipher model (WCM) is more rigorous than the ICM [19,20]. The adversary has more freedom under the WCM, where adversary can make three types of query [19,20]. Hence, it is obvious that the WCM based security result will be better and tighter than the ICM based security result. The scheme of MDC-2, MDC-4, MSR follow the ideal cipher model proof technique [14,29,30]. On the contrary, the scheme of MJH and Bart use the finite field multiplicative operation (FFM) based proof technique [13,14]. As a proof technique, the FFM is good but due to finite field operation it increases the actual blockcipher cost [21].

Table 2. Existing research result of (n, n) blockcipher hash: "Based on Efficiency"

Scheme name	Compression function	Efficiency rate (r)	KS	($\#E$)
MDC-2 [13]	$3n \to 2n$	$1/2$	2	2
MDC-4 [13]	$3n \to 2n$	$1/4$	4	4
MJH [13]	$3n + c \to 2n$	$1/2$	1	2
Bart [13]	$3n \to 2n$	$1/3$	3	3
MSR [14]	$2n + tn \to 2n$	t	2	2
CIDM [31]	$3n \to 2n$	$1/3$	3	3

In Tables 1 and 2, we sketch out the existing research results of the (n, n) blockcipher cryptographic hash. According to the previous discussions and Tables 1 and 2, it can be addressed that there is a gap for making a new scheme, which can provide better security result under a single key scheduling. Additionally, the propose scheme will be secured under the both ICM and WCM based proof technique (Table 1).

Table 3. Comparison study of existing schemes and new scheme (Aspect: Security Proof)

Scheme name	ICM		WCM		FFM	
	CR	PR	CR	PR	CR	PR
NEW	$\mathcal{O}(2^n)$	$\mathcal{O}(2^{2n})$	$\mathcal{O}(2^n)$	$\mathcal{O}(2^n)$	-	-
MDC-2 [13]	$\mathcal{O}(2^{n/2})$	$\mathcal{O}(2^n)$	-	-	-	-
MDC-4 [13]	$\mathcal{O}(2^{5n/8})$	$\mathcal{O}(2^{5n/4})$	-	-	-	-
MJH [13]	-	-	-	-	$\mathcal{O}(2^{n/2})$	$\mathcal{O}(2^n)$
Bart [13]	-	-	-	-	$\mathcal{O}(2^{n/2})$	$\mathcal{O}(2^{3n/2})$
MSR [14]	$\mathcal{O}(2^{tn})$	$\mathcal{O}(2^{2tn})$	-	-	-	-
CIDM [31]	$\mathcal{O}(2^n)$	$\mathcal{O}(2^{2n})$	-	-	-	-

1.1   Contribution in the Research Field of (n, n) Blockcipher Hash

In this paper, we proposed a scheme of (n, n) blockcipher hash that satisfies a single key scheduling with better security bound (Tables 3 and 4). We use three calls of blockcipher through the Davies Meyer (DM) mode. The result of collision resistance and preimage resistance are $O(2^n)$ and $O\left(2^{2n}\right)$ under the ICM. Additionally, the proposed scheme is bounded by CR $= O(2^n)$ and PR $= O\left(2^n\right)$ under the WCM. The efficiency rate of proposed scheme is $1/3$.

1.2   Related Research for (n, n) Blockcipher Hash

The MSR scheme proposed in 2014 which can handle a fraction of message [14]. The security bound $\left(O\left(2^{tn}\right), O\left(2^{2tn}\right)\right)$ of MSR scheme is good but it needs double key scheduling (KS $= 2$). The scheme of Bart needs multiple key scheduling (KS $= 3$) but the security bound is better than the MSR [13,14]. The other two schemes of the MDC-2 and MDC-4 have lower security bound. Additionally, both of these schemes need multiple key scheduling [29,30]. Currently, the MJH is the only scheme that satisfies a single key scheduling but the security bound is less than the Bart and MSR [12,13]. For application, a blockcipher based hash depends on the security margin and efficiency. The ICM based schemes are less applicable because of strong assumption [19]. Under the WCM, the blockcipher is random but completely insecure as a blockcipher [19], which indicates that the WCM based scheme is more applicable in real life such as authentication, digital signature. Interestingly, above mentioned schemes are not secured under the WCM.

Table 4. Comparison study of existing schemes and new scheme (Aspect: Efficiency)

Scheme name	Compression function	(r)	KS	$(\#E)$	Operational mode
NEW	$3n \to 2n$	$1/3$	1	3	Semi-parallel
MDC-2 [13]	$3n \to 2n$	$1/2$	2	2	Parallel
MDC-4 [13]	$3n \to 2n$	$1/4$	4	4	Semi-Parallel
MJH [13]	$3n + c \to 2n$	$1/2$	1	2	Parallel
Bart [13]	$3n \to 2n$	$1/3$	3	3	Semi-Parallel
MSR [14]	$2n + tn \to 2n$	t	2	2	Parallel
MR [31]	$3n \to 2n$	$1/3$	3	3	Serial

In current cryptography, the applications of RFID tag, wireless sensor network, smart cards are enormous, where the main disadvantage of these devices are limited number of processor cycles and limited amount of working memory. That's why, the memory management of key schedule is vital. According to [32], if the key length is 128 bits then for key schedule, the storage will be needed

176 bytes. From [2], we can evaluate the requirement of total number gates for any scheme. For example, the MJH needs 21064 GE ($176 \times 8 \times 8 + 9800$). Now we can check for the Bart, where it needs 47,992 GE because of triple key scheduling ($11264 \times 3 + 14,200$) [2,32]. Our proposed scheme is semi-parallel and single key scheduling. It needs to store extra 128 bits for key storage and 256 bits for internal output storage. Therefore, the total number of required GE is 28,536 ($176 \times 8 \times 8 + 128 \times 8 + 256 \times 8 + 14,200$) [2,32].

1.3 Organization

In Sect. 2, we mention preliminaries and notations. Our NEW scheme is defined in Sect. 3. Next in Sect. 4, we provide a security proof of the proposed scheme. The summery and scope of future work will be mentioned in Sect. 5.

2 Preliminaries

2.1 Notations

In the Table 5, we mention the required notations and symbols for the definition and security proof of the proposed scheme.

Table 5. Important Notations

H^{NEW}: hash function	x_i, y_i: chaining value	$N=2^n$: domain size
$\mathcal{A}$: Adversary	Q: query	$\oplus$: ex-or operation
$\odot$: concatenate string operation	$\otimes$: truncate operation	x_0, y_0: initialization
$F^{E^{\text{NEW}}}$: compression function	m: message	$\mathcal{Q}$: query database

2.2 Blockcipher

A blockcipher is defined as a deterministic algorithm that can operate based on fixed-length set of data [19,20,22]. It is an application of symmetric cryptography. An (n, k) be blockcipher, where k, n means respectively key and block length. Assume that, $E : \{0,1\}^k \times \{0,1\}^n \rightarrow \{0,1\}^n$ be (n, k) blockcipher ($k, n > 0$). Then $Bl(n, k)$ be the set of all (n, k) blockciphers. There are two models such as ideal cipher model (ICM) and weak cipher model (WCM). In the ICM model, there are two types of query, where E is defined as forward query and selected randomly. The E^{-1} ($E^{-1}(c, k) = m$) is called backward query, where m, k, c are defined as message, key and ciphertext. Usually, the forward and backward query is known as encryption and decryption query. These two types of query will be asked by the adversary under the ICM. The adversary can make another extra query, which is defined as key disclosure query under the WCM model. The key disclosure is noted as E^k, where the query input are plaintext and ciphertext. In reply, adversary will get the key ($E^k(m, c) = k$) [17–20].

2.3   Security Definition

It is assumed that, the adversary $\mathcal{A}$ will be computationally unbounded, but it will be terminated if it finds a similar output for a couple of distinct input. If we use ICM proof technique, the adversary can make two types of query $\left(E, E^{-1}\right)$. On the other hand, the adversary will make three types of query $\left(E, E^{-1}, E^k\right)$ for the WCM based proof technique. We will provide both ICM and WCM based proof technique for our scheme.

2.4   Game for Collision Resistance (Under Compression Function)

An adversary $\mathcal{A}$ will access the blockcipher $Bl(n, k)$. The game is to find a collision for $H(m) = H(m') \,|\, m \neq m'$ under f. Therefore, the advantage of $\mathcal{A}$ will be:

$$\text{Adv}_f^{\text{comp}}(\mathcal{A}) = \Pr \left[\begin{array}{l} E^{\text{NEW}} \leftarrow Bl\,(n, k)\,;\,(x, y, z),\,(x', y', z') \leftarrow \mathcal{A}^{\text{ICM/WCM}}\,: \\ (x, y, z) \neq (x', y', z') \wedge f^{E^{\text{NEW}}}(x, y, z) = f^{E^{\text{NEW}}}(x', y', z') \end{array} \right]$$

Assume that, $x, y \,|\, (x_0, y_0 : \text{initial value})$ are the set of chaining values. Hence, for calculating the advantage, the maximum will be taken from all adversaries for $\text{Adv}_f^{\text{Comp}}(q) = \max_{\mathcal{A}} \left\{ \text{Adv}_f^{\text{Comp}}(\mathcal{A}) \right\}$, which can be occurred from at best q queries [17,18,26,27].

2.5   Game for Preimage Resistance (Under Compression Function)

The adversary $\mathcal{A}$ can access the blockcipher $(Bl\,(n, k))$ based oracle. It chooses randomly x', y' at the beginning point of query process. Now the advantage of $\mathcal{A}$ is to find a preimage a hit under f is:

$$\text{Adv}_f^{\text{Pre}}(\mathcal{A}) = \Pr \left[H^{\text{NEW}}(x, y, z) = (x', y') \right] \,|\, (z = \text{message})$$

The maximum will be taken from all adversaries for $\text{Adv}_f^{\text{Comp}}(q) = \max_{\mathcal{A}} \left\{ \text{Adv}_f^{\text{Comp}}(\mathcal{A}) \right\}$, which can be occurred from at best q queries [17,18, 26,27].

3   Definition of Proposed Scheme

In this section, we proposed a scheme of (n, n) blockcipher cryptographic hash as NEW (Fig. 3). It satisfies a single key scheduling (KS $= 1$). It is based on three calls of (n, n) blockcipher under the Davies Meyer mode (DM) (message goes as key input) [17,18]. The efficiency rate of our scheme is $1/3$.

Definition 1. Let, $E \in Bl\,(k, n)$ be the block cipher, where $(k, n) \in \{0, 1\}^n$ means key and block length. The compression function $F^{E^{\text{NEW}}}(H^{\text{NEW}})$:

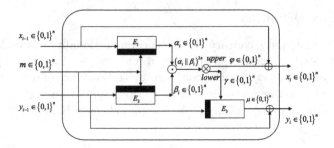

Fig. 3. Proposed New Scheme (for notation and symbol: Table 3)

$\{0,1\}^n \times \{0,1\}^n \times \{0,1\}^n \to \{0,1\}^{2n}$ contains of three blockciphers, defined as follows:

$$E_1 \leftarrow E_1 (m_i, x_{i-1}) = \alpha_i$$
$$E_2 \leftarrow E_2 (m_i, y_{i-1}) = \beta_i$$
$$E_3 \leftarrow E_3 (m_i, \gamma_i) = \mu_i$$
$$where,$$
$$x_i \leftarrow \varphi_i \oplus x_{i-1} \left| \varphi_i \leftarrow^{\otimes^{upper}} \{(\alpha_i || \beta_i)\} \right.$$
$$\gamma_i \leftarrow^{\otimes^{lower}} \{(\alpha_i || \beta_i)\} \qquad \qquad upper, lower \in \{0,1\}^n$$
$$y_i \leftarrow \mu_i \oplus y_{i-1}$$

Finally,

$$H^{\text{NEW}} (x_{i-1}, y_{i-1}, m_i)$$
$$= \begin{pmatrix} E_1 (x_{i-1}, m_i) || E_2 (y_{i-1}, m_i) \to^{\otimes} \varphi \oplus x_{i-1} \to x_i, \\ E_3 (\gamma_i, m_i) \to \mu \oplus y_{i-1} \to y_i \end{pmatrix}$$

4   Security Analysis of Proposed Scheme

Usually, the ICM is widely used for the security proof of blockcipher hash [12–14,29,30]. The WCM is better than the ICM for its weaker assumption [16,18–20]. The target of the adversary will be unique under the both security proof models. We assume that the adversary $\mathcal{A}$ can get access to the blockcipher $(Bl\,(n,k))$ oracle. It tries to find a collision under $H^{\text{NEW}} \left(F^{E^{\text{NEW}}} \right)$ through the following conditions (Table 6).

4.1   ICM Based Proof Technique

Collision Security Analysis. Under the ICM, the adversary $\mathcal{A}$ is allowed to make two types of query to the oracle of blockcipher $(Bl\,(n,k))$ such as forward and backward query. An adversary $\mathcal{A}$ can get ciphertext through forward query, where a backward query provides plaintext. The query is noted as $Q_i|i < q$. After

Table 6. Conditions of collision occurrence

Conditions $(x, y :$ chaining value, $x_0, y_0 :$ initial value, $m :$ message)
1. $(x_{i-1}, y_{i-1}, m_i), (x_{i'-1}, y_{i'-1}, m_{i'}) \| i' < i < q$
$H^{\text{NEW}}(x_{i-1}, y_{i-1}, m_i) = H^{\text{NEW}}(x_{i'-1}, y_{i'-1}, m_{i'})$
$\| (x_{i-1}, y_{i-1}, m_i) \neq (x_{i'-1}, y_{i'-1}, m_{i'})$
2. $(x_{i-1}, y_{i-1}, m_i) \| i < q$; $H^{\text{NEW}}(x_{i-1}, y_{i-1}, m_i) \to (x_i = y_i)$
3. $(x_{i-1}, y_{i-1}, m_i) \| i < q$; $H^{\text{NEW}}(x_{i-1}, y_{i-1}, m_i) = x_0, y_0$

each iteration, a query will be stored at $\mathcal{Q} \| (\mathcal{Q} \in Q_i, Q_{i+1}, .., Q_q) \wedge (1 < i \leq q)$, where query looks $Q \in (x, y, m)$ $[x, y, m =$ chaining value, message]. We will follow the certain conditions from Table 6 for finding collision hit under the ICM.

Theorem 1. *Let H^{NEW} be a blockcipher hash function consists of compression function $F^{E^{NEW}}$ (Definition 1 and Fig. 3). The task of the adversary $\mathcal{A}$ is to find collision through H^{NEW} after q queries. Therefore, the adversarial advantage will be bounded by:*

$$Adv_{H^{NEW}}^{coll}(q) \leq \frac{q^2 - 2q}{(2^n - 3q)^2}$$

Proof. The adversary $\mathcal{A}$ will ask to the blockcipher oracle until it doesn't get success. As for example, after i'-th query the query set looks $(Q_{i'} \in (x', y', m'))$. For next any iteration, there is a chance to find a query $(Q_i \in (x, y, m)) \| (i' < i)$ that produces the same output as the output of i' iteration. There are two more conditions for collision hit, which are available in the Table 6.

Condition-1. For the first condition, it needs two iterations of H^{NEW}. It means, the adversary $\mathcal{A}$ tries to find a collision (Table 6) for two different set of query. We assume that $Ev_{\text{condtion-1}}^{coll}$ be the event for finding a collision under the $H^{\text{NEW}} \left(F^{E^{\text{NEW}}} \right)$. Our scheme needs three calls of blockcipher per iteration by construction. Therefore, the collision probability for a event of $Ev_{\text{condition-1}}^{coll} \| (i' < i)$ will be:

$$\Pr[Ev_{\text{condition-1}}^{coll}] = \frac{i}{(2^n - 3i)(2^n - 3i)}$$

If $Ev_{\text{condition-1}}^{coll} \| (i' < i)$ be the event of finding a collision under the $F^{E^{\text{NEW}}}$, then the probability of collision events after q queries will be $\Pr[Ev_{\text{condition-1}}^{coll}] = \Pr[Ev_{3,\text{condtion-1}}^{coll} \vee Ev_{4,\text{condition-1}}^{coll} \vee \cdots \vee Ev_{q,\text{condition-1}}^{coll}]$.

$$= \sum_{i=3}^{q} \Pr[Ev_{i,\text{condition-1}}^{coll}] = \sum_{i=3}^{q} \frac{i}{(2^n - 3i)(2^n - 3i)} \leq \frac{(q-2)(q-3)}{(2^n - 3q)^2} \quad (1)$$

Condition-2. According to Table 6, there is a scope for collision hit within a single query. Let, $Ev_{\text{condition-2}}^{coll}$ be the event for finding a collision under the H^{NEW}

$\left(F^{E^{NEW}}\right)$, where three calls of blockcipher will be executed per iteration. Hence, the collision probability for the event of $Ev^{\text{coll}}_{\text{condition-2}}$ will be $\Pr\left[Ev^{\text{coll}}_{\text{condition-2}}\right] = \frac{1}{(2^n-3i)(2^n-3i)}$. The probability of collision events are:

$$\Pr[Ev^{\text{coll}}_{\text{condition-2}}] = \Pr[Ev^{\text{coll}}_{3,\text{condition-2}} \vee Ev^{\text{coll}}_{4,\text{condition-2}} \vee \cdots \vee Ev^{\text{coll}}_{q,\text{condition-2}}]$$

$$= \sum_{i=3}^{q} \Pr[Ev^{\text{coll}}_{i,\text{condtion-2}}] = \sum_{i=3}^{q} \frac{1}{(2^n-3i)(2^n-3i)} \leq \frac{(q-2)}{(2^n-3q)^2} \qquad (2)$$

Condition-3. We know for any blockcipher based hash (compression function), it needs initialization value. Let, there is a possibility for the adversary to get a collision under these initializing values at any stage of query process. We assume that $Ev^{\text{coll}}_{\text{condition-3}}$ be the event for finding a collision against the set of initialization value through $H^{NEW}\left(F^{E^{NEW}}\right)$. The collision probability for the event of $Ev^{\text{coll}}_{\text{condition-3}}$ will be:

$$\Pr[Ev^{\text{coll}}_{\text{condition-3}}] = \frac{2}{(2^n-3i)(2^n-3i)}$$

Therefore, the probability of collision events are:

$$\Pr[Ev^{\text{coll}}_{\text{condition-3}}] = \Pr[Ev^{\text{coll}}_{3,\text{condition-3}} \vee Ev^{\text{coll}}_{4,\text{condition-3}} \vee \cdots \vee Ev^{\text{coll}}_{q,\text{condition-3}}]$$

$$= \sum_{i=3}^{q} \Pr[Ev^{\text{coll}}_{i,\text{condition-3}}] = \sum_{i=3}^{q} \frac{2}{(2^n-3i)(2^n-3i)} \leq \frac{2(q-2)}{(2^n-3q)^2} \qquad (3)$$

Taking the values of 1, 2 and 3, Theorem 1 will be satisfied.

Preimage Security Analysis. The preimage resistance of the (n,n) blockcipher hash usually is bounded by $O(2^n)$ [3,4,12,13,15,23,29,30]. The probability of preimage hit comes from the set size of $1/(2^n-q)$ where the parameters are defined as $(2^n = \text{domain size})$ and $(q = \text{number of query})$ [3,17,18,25]. If the number of query goes to the equal value of 2^n, the denominator will be 0 and result will be useless. The above problem is first addressed by [25] in Asiacrypt 2011. Also authors of [25] provide a new technique for eliminating this problem as well as better preimage security bound. We will follow the proof technique of [25] for our scheme's security proof and implement according to our scheme's definition. We assume that a $\mathcal{A}$ be the adversary that can ask a set of pair-query to the blockcipher oracle. Initially, $\mathcal{A}$ picks the value of (x',y') randomly. The target of $\mathcal{A}$ is to find the probability for any iteration $(i \leq q)$, where $H^{NEW}(x,y,m) = \{(x',y')\}$.

Theorem 2. *Let $H^{NEW}(F^{E^{NEW}})$ be a double block length compression function and $\mathcal{A}$ be an adversary to find a preimage hit under the H^{NEW} after q queries. Then the advantage of adversary $\mathcal{A}$ will be bounded by:*

$$Adv^{pre}_{H^{NEW}}(q) \leq 8(q-2)^2 \Big/ (2^n-3q)^2 + \frac{4q^2}{2^{2n}}$$

Proof. According to the [25], we will take the concept of query classification. The query classification is classified as super query and normal query [25]. The normal query is based on adaptive query, where non-adaptive method is true for super query [3,25]. At first, adversary $\mathcal{A}$ will ask to the oracle adaptively until the size of database reaches into $N/2$. Then the rest of the queries provide to the adversary as free [25], where database size will be $N/2$. In the later half, the query will be asked non-adaptively. If the preimage hit occurs in the database of normal query, then it is defined as NormalQueryWin otherwise it is called SuperQueryWin [3,25]. Therefore, we need to find out the probability of hitting for NormalQueryWin and SuperQueryWin.

Condition-1. For NormalQueryWin, the adversary $\mathcal{A}$ will ask to the oracle through either forward or backward query. We assume that $\mathcal{A}$ makes a forward query. The result will be come from the set size $(N - 3i)/2$ (due to three calls of blockcipher). Therefore, the probability of the output (x_i, y_i) $(i \leq N/2)$ will be $2 \times 2/(N - 3i)$. Let, $Ev_{\text{condition-1}}^{\text{pre(forward)}}$ be the event of preimage hitting. Hence, the probability of preimage hitting events are $\Pr[Ev_{\text{condtion-1}}^{\text{pre(forward)}}] = \Pr[Ev_{3,\text{condtion-1}}^{\text{pre}} \vee Ev_{4,\text{condtion-1}}^{\text{pre}} \vee \ldots \vee Ev_{q,\text{condtion-1}}^{\text{pre}}].$

$$= \sum_{i=3}^{q} \Pr[Ev_{i,\text{condtion-1}}^{\text{pre(forward)}}] = \sum_{i=3}^{q} \frac{4}{(2^n - 3i)} \leq \frac{4(q-2)}{(2^n - 3q)} \tag{4}$$

For any forward query (encryption), there is a chance to occur a preimgae hit under the backward query (decryption). If $Ev_{\text{condition-1}}^{\text{pre(backward)}}$ be the event of preimage hit, then the probability will be:

$$\sum_{i=3}^{q} \Pr[Ev_{i,\text{condtion-1}}^{\text{pre(backward)}}] = \sum_{i=3}^{q} \frac{2}{(2^n - 3i)} \leq \frac{2(q-2)}{(2^n - 3q)} \tag{5}$$

From 4 and 5,

$$\Pr[\text{Condition-1}] = \frac{8(q-2)^2}{(2^n - 3q)^2} \tag{6}$$

Condition-2. For SuperQueryWin [3,25], the adversary $\mathcal{A}$ will pick the value of x_i, y_i non-adaptively from the super query database, where domain size is $N/2$. The sub conditions of condition-2 are as follows for either forward or backward query:

$$H^{\text{NEW}}(x_{i-1}, y_{i-1}) = (x_i, y_i) = (x'/y') \tag{7}$$

$$H^{\text{NEW}}(x_{i-1}, y_{i-1}) = (x_i, y_i) = (y'/x') \tag{8}$$

For 7, we assume that $Ev_{\text{condition-2}}^{\text{pre(forward)}}$ be the event of preimage hit. Then the probability of preimage hitting events are $\Pr[Ev_{\text{condtion-2}}^{\text{pre(forward)}}] = \Pr[Ev_{3,\text{condtion-2}}^{\text{pre}} \vee Ev_{4,\text{condtion-2}}^{\text{pre}} \vee \ldots \vee Ev_{q,\text{condtion-2}}^{\text{pre}}].$

$$= \sum_{i=3}^{q} \Pr[Ev_{i,\text{condtion-2}}^{\text{pre(forward)}}] = \sum_{i=1}^{q} \frac{2}{2^n} \leq \frac{2q}{2^n} \tag{9}$$

The result of 8 will be (as same explanation of 7):

$$\sum_{i=3}^{q} \Pr[Ev_{i,\text{condtion-2}}^{\text{pre(backward)}}] = \sum_{i=3}^{q} \frac{2}{2^n} \leq \frac{2q}{2^n} \tag{10}$$

Therefore, from 9 and 10,

$$\Pr[\text{Condition-2}] = \frac{4q^2}{2^{2n}} \tag{11}$$

Finally, adding 6 and 11, Theorem 2 will be satisfied.

4.2   WCM Based Proof Technique

Collision Security Analysis. The adversary $\mathcal{A}$ is allowed to make three types of query under the WCM. These are defined as forward, backward and key-disclosure query (E, E^{-1}, E^k). The query is noted as $Q_i | i < q$ and defined as $Q \in (x, y, m)$. The $\mathcal{Q} | ((\mathcal{Q} \in Q_i, Q_{i+1}, .., Q_q) \wedge (1 < i \leq q))$ be the query database, where after each iteration query has been stored.

Theorem 3. *Let H^{NEW} be a blockcipher based hash consists of a compression function FE^{NEW} (Definition 1 and Fig. 3) and $\mathcal{A}$ be an adversary to find a collision hit under the H^{NEW}. After q queries, the advantage of adversary $\mathcal{A}$ will be bounded by:*

$$Adv_{H^{NEW}}^{coll}(q) \leq \frac{3q^2 - 12q}{(2^n - 3q)^2}$$

Proof. The adversary $\mathcal{A}$ can make forward, backward and key-disclosure query under the WCM. In forward query, the adversary can ask for ciphertext through plaintext and key. A backward query returns the plaintext and key-disclosure query is responsible for the key. Under any j-th iteration, a query will be $Q_j \in \{x_{j-1}, y_{j-1}, m_j\}$. We assume there is another iteration $i | (j < i < q)$, where query looks $Q_i \in \{x_{i-1}, y_{i-1}, m_i\}$. For finding a collision under $Q_j \in \{x_{j-1}, y_{j-1}, m_j\}$ and $Q_i \in \{x_{i-1}, y_{i-1}, m_i\}$ the probable conditions are:

$$\begin{aligned} H^{NEW}(x_{j-1}, y_{j-1}, m_j) &= H^{NEW}(x_{i-1}, y_{i-1}, m_i) \\ \vee H^{NEW}(x_{j-1}, y_{j-1}, m_j) &= (x_0, y_0) | (x_{j-1}, y_{j-1}, m_j) \neq (x_{i-1}, y_{i-1}, m_i) \end{aligned} \tag{12}$$

Forward query. Under the forward query, we assume that $Ev_{\text{forward}}^{coll}$ be the event for finding a collision through $H^{NEW}\left(FE^{NEW}\right)$. Our scheme needs three calls of blockcipher per iteration by construction. According to 12, the collision probability for the event of $Ev_{\text{forward}}^{coll} | (j < i)$ will be:

$$\Pr[Ev_{\text{forward}}^{coll}] = \frac{i}{(2^n - 3i)(2^n - 3i)} + \frac{1}{(2^n - 3i)(2^n - 3i)}$$

If $Ev_{\text{forward}}^{\text{coll}}|(j < i)$ be the event for finding a collision under the $F^{E^{NEW}}$ for q pairs of queries. Then the probability of collision events are $\Pr[Ev_{\text{forward}}^{\text{coll}}] = \Pr[Ev_{3,\text{forward}}^{\text{coll}} \vee Ev_{4,\text{forward}}^{\text{coll}} \vee \ldots \vee Ev_{q,\text{forward}}^{\text{coll}}]$.

$$= \sum_{i=3}^{q} \Pr[Ev_{i,\text{forward}}^{\text{coll}}] = \sum_{i=3}^{q} \frac{i}{(2^n - 3i)(2^n - 3i)} + \frac{1}{(2^n - 3i)(2^n - 3i)} \leq \frac{q^2 - 4q + 3}{(2^n - 3q)^2}$$
(13)

Backward query. According to the 12 and same explanation of the forward query, the probability of backward query will be:

$$= \sum_{i=3}^{q} \Pr[Ev_{i,\text{backward}}^{\text{coll}}] = \sum_{i=3}^{q} \frac{i}{(2^n - 3i)(2^n - 3i)} + \frac{1}{(2^n - 3i)(2^n - 3i)} \leq \frac{q^2 - 4q + 3}{(2^n - 3q)^2}$$
(14)

Key-disclosure query. According to the 12 and same explanation of the forward query, the probability of key-disclosure will be:

$$= \sum_{i=3}^{q} \Pr[Ev_{i,\text{key-disclosure}}^{\text{coll}}] = \sum_{i=3}^{q} \frac{i}{(2^n - 3i)(2^n - 3i)} + \frac{1}{(2^n - 3i)(2^n - 3i)} \leq \frac{q^2 - 4q + 3}{(2^n - 3q)^2}$$
(15)

Adding the results of 13, 14 and 15, Theorem 3 will be satisfied.

Preimage Security Analysis. In preimage security analysis, adversary $\mathcal{A}$ randomly selects (x', y') at the beginning point of query process. Then it looks for the query-input of x, y, m, which can produce the output of $H^{NEW}(x, y, m)$ such that $H^{NEW}(x, y, m) = (x', y')$

Theorem 4. *Let H^{NEW} be a blockcipher based compression function and $\mathcal{A}$ be an adversary to find a preimage hit under the $H^{NEW}\left(F^{E^{NEW}}\right)$ after q pairs of queries. Hence, the advantage of $\mathcal{A}$ will be bounded by:*

$$Adv_{H^{NEW}}^{pre}(q) \leq \frac{2q - 4}{(2^n - 3q)^2}$$

Proof. The adversary $\mathcal{A}$ can make forward, backward or key-disclosure query for finding the following condition:

$$H^{NEW}(x, y, m) = (x', y'), \text{where } (i < q)$$
(16)

Forward query. Under the forward query, we assume that $Ev_{\text{forward}}^{pre}$ be the event for finding a preimage hit through the $H^{NEW}\left(F^{E^{NEW}}\right)$. According to the 16, the preimage hit probability will be:

$$\Pr[Ev_{\text{forward}}^{pre}] = \frac{2}{(2^n - 3i)(2^n - 3i)}$$

If $Ev^{pre}_{forward}|(i < q)$ be the event for finding a preimage hit through $F^{E^{NEW}}$ for q pairs of queries. Then the probability of preimage hitting events are $\Pr[Ev^{pre}_{forward}] = \Pr[Ev^{pre}_{3,forward} \vee Ev^{pre}_{4,forward} \vee \ldots \vee Ev^{pre}_{q,forward}]$.

$$= \sum_{i=3}^{q} \Pr[Ev^{pre}_{i,forward}] = \sum_{i=3}^{q} \frac{2}{(2^n - 3i)(2^n - 3i)} \leq \frac{2q - 4}{(2^n - 3q)^2} \qquad (17)$$

Backward query. As same explanation of the forward query, the probability of backward query will be:

$$= \sum_{i=3}^{q} \Pr[Ev^{pre}_{i,backward}] = \sum_{i=3}^{q} \frac{2}{(2^n - 3i)(2^n - 3i)} \leq \frac{2q - 4}{(2^n - 3q)^2} \qquad (18)$$

Key-disclosure query. The probability of the key-disclosure query will be:

$$= \sum_{i=3}^{q} \Pr[Ev^{pre}_{i,key-disclosure}] = \sum_{i=3}^{q} \frac{2}{(2^n - 3i)(2^n - 3i)} \leq \frac{2q - 4}{(2^n - 3q)^2} \qquad (19)$$

Adding the results of 17, 18 and 19, Theorem 4 will be satisfied.

5   Conclusion

In this paper, we proposed an (n,n) blockcipher based hash (compression function) that satisfies a single key scheduling. We use both the ICM and WCM technique for providing security proof. The result of the CR and PR security bound under the ICM are $O(2^n)$ and $O(2^{2n})$. For the WCM, our scheme is bounded by $CR = O(2^n)$ and $Pr = O(2^n)$. Our proposed scheme follows three calls of blockcipher, where it operates in nature of semi-serial. Actually the calling of blockcipher, operational mode are also key factors in respect of efficiency of blockcipher hash. Still there are few works are pending such as reducing the number of blockcipher call and propose a complete parallel scheme. Our scheme's security bound is proved under the Davies Meyer mode of PGV [17,18]. Therefore, there is a chance to provide a new scheme which will be secured under any mode of PVG [17,18].

References

1. Menezes, A.J., van Oorschot, P.C., Vanstone, S.A.: Handbook of Applied Cryptography, 5th edn. CRC Press, Boca Raton (2001)
2. Bogdanov, A., Leander, G., Paar, C., Poschmann, A., Robshaw, M.J.B., Seurin, Y.: Hash functions and RFID tags: mind the gap. In: Oswald, E., Rohatgi, P. (eds.) CHES 2008. LNCS, vol. 5154, pp. 283–299. Springer, Heidelberg (2008)
3. Fleischmann, E., Forler, C., Lucks, S., Wenzel, J.: Weimar-DM: a highly secure double-length compression function. In: Susilo, W., Mu, Y., Seberry, J. (eds.) ACISP 2012. LNCS, vol. 7372, pp. 152–165. Springer, Heidelberg (2012)

4. Hirose, S.: Some plausible constructions of double-block-length hash functions. In: Robshaw, M. (ed.) FSE 2006. LNCS, vol. 4047, pp. 210–225. Springer, Heidelberg (2006)

5. Dodis, Y., Ristenpart, T., Shrimpton, T.: Salvaging merkle-damgård for practical applications. In: Joux, A. (ed.) EUROCRYPT 2009. LNCS, vol. 5479, pp. 371–388. Springer, Heidelberg (2009)

6. Coron, J.-S., Dodis, Y., Malinaud, C., Puniya, P.: Merkle-damgård revisited: how to construct a hash function. In: Shoup, V. (ed.) CRYPTO 2005. LNCS, vol. 3621, pp. 430–448. Springer, Heidelberg (2005)

7. Wang, X., Lai, X., Feng, D., Chen, H., Yu, X.: Cryptanalysis of the hash functions MD4 and RIPEMD. In: Cramer, R. (ed.) EUROCRYPT 2005. LNCS, vol. 3494, pp. 1–18. Springer, Heidelberg (2005)

8. Wang, X., Yin, Y.L., Yu, H.: Finding collisions in the full SHA-1. In: Shoup, V. (ed.) CRYPTO 2005. LNCS, vol. 3621, pp. 17–36. Springer, Heidelberg (2005)

9. Kaps, J.-P., Sunar, B.: Energy comparison of AES and SHA-1 for ubiquitous computing. In: Zhou, X., Sokolsky, O., Yan, L., Jung, E.-S., Shao, Z., Mu, Y., Lee, D.C., Kim, D.Y., Jeong, Y.-S., Xu, C.-Z. (eds.) EUC Workshops 2006. LNCS, vol. 4097, pp. 372–381. Springer, Heidelberg (2006)

10. Lee, J., Kapitanova, K., Son, S.H.: The price of security in wireless sensor networks. ELSEVIER Comput. Netw. **54**(17), 2967–2978 (2010)

11. Lai, X., Massey, J.L.: Hash functions based on block ciphers. In: Rueppel, R.A. (ed.) EUROCRYPT 1992. LNCS, vol. 658, pp. 55–70. Springer, Heidelberg (1993)

12. Lee, J., Stam, M.: MJH: a faster alternative to MDC-2. In: Kiayias, A. (ed.) CT-RSA 2011. LNCS, vol. 6558, pp. 213–236. Springer, Heidelberg (2011)

13. Mennink, B.: Optimal collision security in double block length hashing with single length key. In: Wang, X., Sako, K. (eds.) ASIACRYPT 2012. LNCS, vol. 7658, pp. 526–543. Springer, Heidelberg (2012)

14. Miyaji, A., Rashed, M., Tsuyoshi, S.: A new (n, n) blockcipher based hash function for short messages. In: IEEE, ASIAJCIS, 978-1-4799-5733, pp. 56–63 (2014)

15. Lee, J., Kwon, D.: The security of Abreast-DM in the ideal cipher model. IEICE Trans. **94**(A(1)), 104–109 (2011)

16. Lee, J., Stam, M., Steinberger, J.: The collision security of Tandem-DM in the ideal cipher model. In: Rogaway, P. (ed.) CRYPTO 2011. LNCS, vol. 6841, pp. 561–577. Springer, Heidelberg (2011)

17. Black, J.A., Rogaway, P., Shrimpton, T.: Black-box analysis of the Block-cipher-based Hash-function constructions from PGV. In: Yung, M. (ed.) CRYPTO 2002. LNCS, vol. 2442, pp. 320–335. Springer, Heidelberg (2002)

18. Black, J.A., Rogaway, P., Shrimpton, T., Stam, M.: An analysis of the blockcipher-based hash functions from PGV. J. Cryptology **23**, 519–545 (2010)

19. Hirose, S., Kuwakado, H.: Collision resistance of hash functions in a weak ideal cipher model. IEICE Trans. **95**(A(1)), 251–255 (2012)

20. Liskov, M.: Constructing an ideal hash function from weak ideal compression functions. In: Biham, E., Youssef, A.M. (eds.) SAC 2006. LNCS, vol. 4356, pp. 358–375. Springer, Heidelberg (2007)

21. Özen, O., Stam, M.: Another glance at double-length hashing. In: Parker, M.G. (ed.) Cryptography and Coding 2009. LNCS, vol. 5921, pp. 176–201. Springer, Heidelberg (2009)

22. Shannon, C.E.: Communication theory of secrecy systems. Bell Syst. Tech. J. **128-4**, 656–715 (1949)

23. Nandi, M., Lee, W.I., Sakurai, K., Lee, S.-J.: Security analysis of a 2/3-rate double length compression function in the black-box model. In: Gilbert, H., Handschuh, H. (eds.) FSE 2005. LNCS, vol. 3557, pp. 243–254. Springer, Heidelberg (2005)

24. Lee, J., Hong, S., Sung, J., Park, H.: A new double-block-length hash function using feistel structure. In: Park, J.H., Chen, H.-H., Atiquzzaman, M., Lee, C., Kim, T., Yeo, S.-S. (eds.) ISA 2009. LNCS, vol. 5576, pp. 11–20. Springer, Heidelberg (2009)

25. Armknecht, F., Fleischmann, E., Krause, M., Lee, J., Stam, M., Steinberger, J.: The preimage security of double-block-length compression functions. In: Lee, D.H., Wang, X. (eds.) ASIACRYPT 2011. LNCS, vol. 7073, pp. 233–251. Springer, Heidelberg (2011)

26. Joux, A.: Multicollisions in iterated hash functions. Application to cascaded constructions. In: Franklin, M. (ed.) CRYPTO 2004. LNCS, vol. 3152, pp. 306–316. Springer, Heidelberg (2004)

27. Gauravaram, P., Kelsey, J.: Linear-XOR and additive checksums don't protect damgård-merkle hashes from generic attacks. In: Malkin, T. (ed.) CT-RSA 2008. LNCS, vol. 4964, pp. 36–51. Springer, Heidelberg (2008)

28. Kuwakado, H., Hirose, S.: Hashing mode using a lightweight blockcipher. In: Stam, M. (ed.) IMACC 2013. LNCS, vol. 8308, pp. 213–231. Springer, Heidelberg (2013)

29. Brachtl, B.O., Coppersmith, D., Hyden, M.M., Matyas Jr., S.M., Meyer, C.H.W., Oseas, J., Pilpel, S., Schilling, M.: Data authentication using modification detection codes based on a public one-way encryption function. U. S. Patent, # 4,908,861, March 1990

30. Fleischmann, E., Forler, C., Lucks, S.: The collision security of MDC-4. In: Mitrokotsa, A., Vaudenay, S. (eds.) AFRICACRYPT 2012. LNCS, vol. 7374, pp. 252–269. Springer, Heidelberg (2012)

31. Miyaji, A., Rashed, M.: A new (n, n) blockcipher based hash function: apposite for RFID tag. Smart Innovation Syst. Technol. **33**, 519–528 (2015)

32. Joan, D., Vincent, R.: The Design of Rijndael, AES-The Advanced Encryption Standard. Springer Press, Heidelberg (2002). ISBN 978-3-662-04722-4

Attacks and Security Measures

Security Issue of WirelessHART Based SCADA Systems

Lyes Bayou[1]([✉]), David Espes[2], Nora Cuppens-Boulahia[1],
and Frédéric Cuppens[1]

[1] Télécom Bretagne-LabSTICC,
2 Rue de la Châtaigneraie, Césson Sévigné, France
lyes.bayou@telecom-bretagne.eu
[2] University of Western Brittany - LabSTICC, Brest, France

Abstract. The security of Supervisory Control and Data Acquistition systems (SCADA) has become these last years, a major worldwide concern. Indeed, several incidents and cyber-attacks stressed the emergency to make more efforts to secure these systems which manage important economical infrastructures. The increasing use of wireless sensors also brings their security vulnerabilities. Therefore, several communication protocols were developed to meet real time and security requirements needed by this kind of systems. WirelessHART is the first approved international standard for industrial wireless devices. It implements several mechanisms to ensure hop-by-hop and end-to-end security. However, despite these mechanisms, it remains possible for an attacker to conduct an attack against such wireless networks. In this paper, we give the first description of a Sybil attack specially tailored to target WirelessHART based SCADA systems. This attack can lead to harmful consequences such as disturbing the infrastructure functioning, interrupting it or more again causing its destruction (overheating of a nuclear reactor).

1 Introduction

Nowadays, the security of Supervisory Control and Data Acquisition systems (SCADA) has become a major issue. Indeed, these systems are used to manage complex industrial facilities such as water supply, energy grid, pipeline, etc. Generally they are deployed in a large area and depend on data collected from a set of remote sensors. Most of times these systems have a great importance considering the role they play in the national economy.

Managing security threats targeting these systems is a problem of vital importance for the company's long-range strategy. An attack can have either an outside or an inside origin. An outsider attacker does not have any knowledge about secrets (passwords, keys, etc.) used to protect the network. The outsider can have several profiles. It can be a State targeting a strategic facilities (case of the worm Stuxnet [1] which targeted the Iranian nuclear plants), a terrorist group, a hacktivist with political or ideological motivations like Anonymous or Greenpeace, or just cybercriminals wanting to make profits. Unlike an outside attacker,

© Springer International Publishing Switzerland 2016
C. Lambrinoudakis and A. Gabillon (Eds.): CRiSIS 2015, LNCS 9572, pp. 225–241, 2016.
DOI: 10.1007/978-3-319-31811-0_14

an insider one has access to some secrets. She can be for example an unsatisfied employee or a contractor. This kind of attackers has enough knowledge to bypass some security features. A famous example of an inside attack against an industrial control system is the attack on Maroochy Shire Council's sewage control system in Australia [2]. In January 2000, over a three-month period, an ex-employee caused the flooding of the grounds of a nearby hotel, a park, and a river with a million liters of sewage. He was motivated by convincing the company to hire him again to solve these dysfunctions [3]. The most important lesson learned from this case is that to conduct its attack, the ex-employee just used a laptop computer and a radio transmitter.

Indeed, the increasing use of wireless connections due to their flexibility and easy deployment, management and maintenance also brings new security challenges. Therefore, it becomes obvious that additionally to real-time requirement, any communication protocol used in these systems must ensure the availability and the integrity of data collected from these sensors. Several communication protocols were specially developed to meet this requirement in terms of time, availability, and security. The most important are ZigBee Pro [4], WirelessHART [5], and ISA 100.11 [6].

Among these protocols, WirelessHART is the first international approved standard. Developed by HART Communication Foundation, it aims to provide a reliable and secure wireless communication for industrial process automation. It uses a time-synchronized, self-organized and self-healing mesh architecture to provide a reliable and real-time communication. It is included in version 7 of the HART standard, released in 2007, and was approved as an IEC 62591 standard in 2010. These characteristics make WirelessHART the leading standard of all communication protocols, installed in more than 30 million devices worldwide [5].

In this paper, we give the first description of a Sybil attack specially tailored to target a WirelessHART network. This attack can cause harmful damages to the facility by disconnecting partially or entirely the wireless sensors from the SCADA system. Indeed, although WirelessHART implements several mechanisms to ensure hop-by-hop and end-to-end security, it remains possible to an attacker to conduct a Sybil attack which can isolate a large number of sensors from the network. Conducted against a real facilities, such attack can disturb deeply its functioning and can lead to stop it or more again induce its destruction.

Sybil attack was first described by Douceur in [7]. He shows that in the absence of a central identification authority that checks correspondence between entity and identity, a malicious entity can present multiple identities. Sybil attack was initially described for peer-to-peer networks, however it can be applied to any network's type. Karlof and Wagner point out in [8] that sybil attacks can be used against routing algorithms in sensor networks to reduce significantly the effectiveness of redundancy schemes. In [9] Newsome and al. analyze sybil attacks in sensor networks and establish a classification of different forms of attacks (Direct vs Indirect communications, Fabricated vs Stolen identities, Simultaneous vs Non-simultaneous). They also examine how it can be used to attack several types of protocols in WSN such as distributed storage, routing, data aggregation, voting, fair resource allocation and misbehavior detection algorithms.

We organized the paper as follows. Section 2 presents an overview of studies about the security of wireless sensor networks used in industrial environment, especially those dedicated to WirelessHART. Section 3 describes WirelessHART security mechanisms. In Sect. 4 we present Sybil Disconnect Attack against WirelessHART networks. We analyze in Sect. 5 Sybil Attack threats on the Wireless Sensor Networks. The proposed solution is presented in Sect. 6. The conclusion and future works of our paper are presented in Sect. 7.

2 Related Works

SCADA systems are facing security challenges they were not initially designed to deal with. This is mainly due to the increasing interconnections between the factory floor and the corporate networks and the move from the use of proprietary owned communication standards to open international standards [10]. But there are differences between SCADA and traditional IT networks. Stouffer and al. summarize some of them in [11]. The most significant ones are that SCADA systems operate continuously with little down time, they are designed to meet high performances in terms of reliability and safety, and they are expected to work for 10 or 15 years long. For these reasons traditional security mechanisms used in IT must be adapted before deploying them in SCADA systems. In literature we find that researchers focus on applying intrusions detection systems and firewalls in SCADA environment [12,13], and treat only the wired part of the network. For example, most proposed IDS focus on wired communication protocols such as Modbus [14] or DNP3 [15].

We find only few studies on the security of wireless sensor networks used in industrial environment. Coppolino and al. propose in [16] an architecture for an intrusion detection system for critical information infrastructures using wireless sensor network. Their solution is a hybrid approach combining misuse and anomaly based techniques. In the same way, there are few numbers of studies dedicated to WirelessHART and even less to its security. Mostly these studies show the performances of this protocol by evaluating its capabilities to operate in an industrial environment and its capacity to meet real-time requirement [17–19]. Other studies make comparison between WirelessHART and its principal competitors [20,21] such as ZigBee Pro and ISA 100.11.

In [22] Raza and al. discuss the strengths and the weaknesses of security mechanisms and analyze them against the well known threats in the wireless sensor networks. They conclude that WirelessHART is strong enough to be used in the industrial process control environment and specifically they state that Sybil attacks are almost impossible in this kind of networks. Alcazar and Lopez identify in [20] vulnerabilities and threats in ZigBee PRO, WirelessHART and ISA100.11.a. They analyze in detail the security features of each of these protocols. For them, Sybil attacks are hardly ever launched in WirelessHART since it offers strong authentication capabilities before and after deployment. However, they recommend to add a rekeying process to WirelessHART to enforce its resilience to sniffing attacks and thereby key disclosure. We must also note that these studies are based on the specifications of the standard without conducting any tests. Roosta and al. describe in [23] a model-based intrusion detection system for WirelessHART sensor networks. This IDS models normal behavior of the different wireless devices and detects attacks when there is a deviation from the model. However, this kind of IDS can be bypassed with attacks based on the use of features deviated from their initial use.

3   WirlessHART Security

WirelessHART [5] was developed to provide reliable and secure communications for industrial process automation requirement. It allows to build a time-synchronized, self-organized and self-healing mesh network of wireless sensors. In particular, security is one of its important features. Therefore, it implements several mechanisms to ensure data confidentiality, authenticity and integrity in hop-by-hop and end-to-end transmissions.

The hop-by-hop transmission security is provided by the Data Link Layer (DLL) using a cryptographic key called "Network Key" shared by all devices part of the wireless network. It defends against attackers who are outside the network and do not share its secret (Outside attacker). The end-to-end security is provided by the Network Layer (NL) using a cryptographic key called "Session Key" known only by the two communicant devices. It defends against attackers who may be on the network path between the source and the destination (Inside attacker).

The Network Manager is one of the important device in a WirelessHART network. It is responsible for the overall management, scheduling, and optimization of the wireless network. It generates and maintains all of the routing information and also allocates communication resources. Along with it there is also the Security Manager which is responsible for the generation, storage, and management of cryptographic keys. These two devices can be implemented in one entity.

3.1   Security at Data Link Layer

To ensure hop-by-hop security a keyed Message Integrity Code (MIC) is implemented in Data Link Layer. In WirelessHART each Data Link Protocol Data Unit (DLPDU) is authenticated by the sending device using a cryptographic key shared by all devices part of the network. Therefore, before processing any received DLPDU, a device must check the MIC to verify the identity of the sending device. We must note that the DLPDU itself is not enciphered but authenticated by a four-byte MIC generated with CCM* mode (Combined Counter with CBC-MAC (corrected)) using the AES-128 block cipher. Each device is configured with two kinds of cryptographic keys: the well-known key and the network key. The well-known key is used in Advertisement DLPDU and joining process. It is identical for all devices and has a built in value. The network key is used for all other DLPDUs. It is supplied by the Network Manager to a device, when it joins the network.

3.2   Security at Network Layer

The network layer uses also a keyed Message Integrity Code (MIC) for the authentication of the Network Protocol Data Unit (NPDU). Additionally, it is used to encrypt and decrypt the NPDU payload. The end-to-end security is session oriented, it provides a private and secure communication between a pair of network devices. Each session is defined by a dedicated 128-bits cryptographic key and a message counter which defends against replay attacks. It is also used to form the nounce used to generate the MIC.

Four sessions are set up as soon as any device joins the network. They allow the transmission of sensing data from a device to the Network Manager, and the transmission of commands from the Network Manager to a field device. Each communication can be done in a unicast or a broadcast mode. In addition, each device has a join session which cannot be deleted. The Join_key is the only key that can be written directly by connecting to the device's maintenance port. It can also be written by the network manager. All other keys are distributed by the Network Manager.

4   Sybil Attack in WirelessHART Network

4.1   Data Link Protocol Data Unit (DLPDU) Structure

The common structure of a WirelessHART DLPDU, illustrated in Fig. 1, is:

Fig. 1. WirelessHART DLPDU structure

- A header: indicating the source and destination addresses, the type of the DLPDU, its priority and the type of the network key used for the generation of the MIC (Message Integrity Code).
- The DLPDU payload which depends on the type of the packet.
- A footer composed of a Keyed Message Integrity Code (MIC) calculated on the header and the payload, and a Cyclic Redundancy Check (CRC16) used for error detection.

In WirelessHART there are five (05) DLPDU types:

1. Data DLPDU: encapsulates packets from the NL in transit to their final destination device. The network layer is the source and the destination for all Data DLPDUs;
2. Ack DLPDU: is the immediate link level response to receipt of the source device's transmission DLPDU;

3. Keep-alive DLPDU: used for maintaining connections between neighboring devices;
4. Advertise DLPDU: used for providing information to neighboring devices trying to join the network;
5. Disconnect DLPDU: used to inform neighboring devices that the device is leaving the network.

Ack, Advertise, Keep-Alive and Disconnect DLPDUs are generated and consumed in Data Link Layer and are not propagated to the network layer or forwarded through the network.

4.2   Disconnect DLPDU

According to WirelessHART standard [5] a device can either be disconnected by the Network Manager or disconnect himself or simply die. In the first case, the Network Manager sends a disconnect command (960) to the device, whereas in the second case the device sends a Disconnect DLPDU to inform its neighbors that it is leaving the network. This DLPDU is originated in the data link layer and secured by the Network Key. It is transmitted in the first available link as shown in Fig. 2(a).

When a Disconnect DLPDU is received by a device, it removes the sending device from its neighbor list, and deletes all links connecting to the sending device. (see Fig. 2(b)). Also, the neighbors indirectly inform the network manager with health reports (i.e. periodic statistics transmitted to the Network Manager by each device about its neighbors) about the device disconnection. The Network Manager updates device's routing tables to forward packets through other routes and reallocates disconnected device's resources (ex.: slots). By that, the disconnected device has not anymore any allocated resources and shall go through a complete rejoin sequence. The overall message exchange is summarized in Fig. 3.

4.3   Disconnect Sybil Attack

As described in Sect. 3, in WirelessHART communication security is ensured by two cryptographic keys. The Network Key which defends against outsider attacks and the Session Key which defends against insider attacks. The use of these keys, aim to provide an in-deep defense against wireless security threats. We describe here a harmful attack requiring only the known of the Network Key and using disconnect DLPDU.

A disconnect attack is a sybil attack in which an attacker spoof the identity of a legitimate device by forging fake Disconnect DLPDU and setting the source address to the targeted device's address. As a result the targeted device will be disconnected from the network since its device neighbors will remove it from their tables. This attack is based on the fact that the disconnect DLPDU is originated in the data link layer and all devices in the network share the same key (Network Key) for generating and validating the Message Integrity Code (MIC) in the DLL.

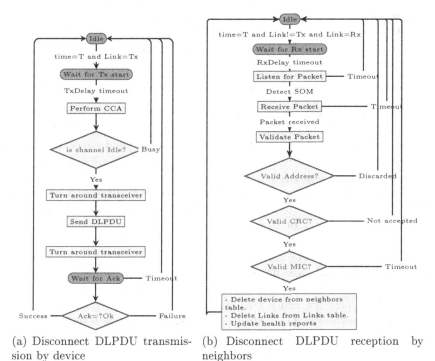

(a) Disconnect DLPDU transmission by device

(b) Disconnect DLPDU reception by neighbors

Fig. 2. Disconnect DLPDU processing

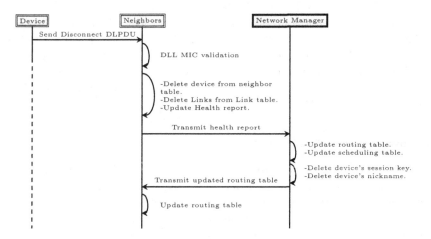

Fig. 3. Disconnect message exchange sequence

To perform a Disconnect Sybil Attack, an attacker needs to collect some information about the targeted device: the short and long address of the device; and mainly find a slot to send out the disconnect packet. We assume that the attacker knows the Network Key but not the session key of the targeted device.

4.4 Collecting Information About the Target Device

In order to gather needed information about targeted device, the attacker should listen awhile to the packets forwarded throughout the network. By this, it will obtain needed information such as the short and the long address of the targeted device and also synchronize itself with the network current time. Indeed, these information are not enciphered in exchanged messages.

WirelessHART uses Time Division Multiple Access (TDMA) and Channel hopping to control access to the medium. Each communication between two devices occurs in one slot of 10 ms. Only one packet is transmitted in one slot from the sender to the receiver which has to reply with an acknowledgment packet in the same slot. The 2.4 GHz band is divided into 16 channels numbered from 11 to 26 (channel 26 is not used). So, each slot is identified by a number called Absolute Slot Number (ASN) indicating the count of slots elapsed since the start of the network and a channel offset. As all communication occur in predefined slots established by Network Manager, attacker need to find the right slot within it can send out the Disconnect packet to the target neighbors. This can be done in several way, such as:

- if the attacker is a legitimate device, it will receive its own schedule from the Network Manager and by that it will know if the targeted device will perform a broadcast transmission and at which frequency.
- the attacker can use the retry slot to send out the disconnect packet to target's neighbors one by one. Indeed, the Network Manager when allocating normal slot for data transmission, also allocates a retry slot. This slot is used only when the transmission in the normal one failed. Otherwise, it will not be used.
- in our scenario we send the disconnect DLPDU to the parent of the target device using the join link dedicated to the reception of the join request from new devices. Information about this link are periodically transmitted in the Advertisement DLPDU of the target device parent.

4.5 Sybil Attack Implementation

For validating our attack, we implement our own WirelessHART simulator based on OMNeT++ [24]. OMNeT++ is a discrete event, extensible, modular, C++ based simulation library and framework, for building network simulators. It includes extensions for real-time simulation, network emulation, database integration, and several other functions. We also use INETMANET [25] a fork of the INET Framework, which adds a number of experimental features and protocols, mainly for mobile ad-hoc networks.

We implement an entirely automated sybil attack in which a legitimate device usurps the identity of another device by forging a fake Disconnect DLPDU and setting the nickname (short address) of the target device as the source address of the forged DLPDU.

The implementation of the malicious device is based on the implementation of WirelessHART device one. Initially, the malicious device acts as a normal device. When triggered, it enters a search mode in which it waits for getting an Advertisement from the parent of the targeted device. When done, it will use the join link of the parent device to send to it the forged Disconnect DLPDU. At the reception of this DLPDU, the parent device validates it with the Network Key and processes it by removing the sending device from its neighbors table and also all links related to this device. By so, the targeted device is automatically disconnected from the network since it has not anymore any connection with its parent and has to go through the entire join procedure. The attack is summarized in Fig. 4.

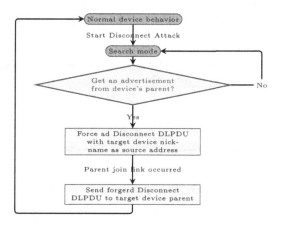

Fig. 4. Sybil disconnect attack

5   Sybil Attack Threats Analysis

To conduct our simulation, we build a wireless network composed of one Network Manager and ten wireless devices as shown in Fig. 5(a). We start the simulation by initiating the network: the Network Manager begins to send Advertisement DLPDU and wireless devices enter joining procedure. Each time a new device joins the network, it will start to send sensing data at a periodic time of 4 s and advertisement DLPDU. Figure 5(b) illustrates the global topology of the wireless network as seen by the Network Manager.

We restart the simulation and we launch the Sybil Disconnect Attack at T = 800 s. The device with nickname 0x0003 is configured to be the "malicious"

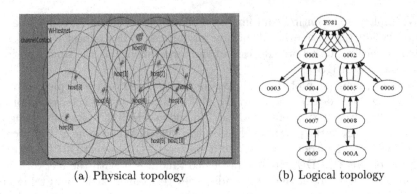

(a) Physical topology   (b) Logical topology

Fig. 5. Simulation network topology

device and the device with nickname 0x0004 will be the "target" device. The "parent" device will be the device with nickname 0x0001. According to Fig. 6(b), in normal case the Network Manager receives sensing data from target device at a fixed frequency of 4 s. In Fig. 6(b) we can see that just after the attack was launched, the Network Manager stops to receive data from target node. Figure 7(b) shows that the data send success rate for target node falls quickly from 100 % to 0 % immediately after the attack was conducted.

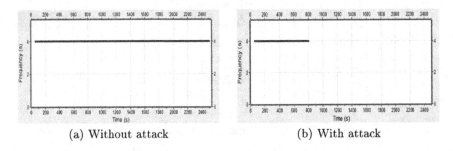

(a) Without attack   (b) With attack

Fig. 6. Data sensing time arrival to Network Manager frequency from target device

Comparatively to Fig. 7(a) in (b) we can see clearly that the target device is completely disconnected from the network and even if it continues to try to send its own packets or to forward packets received from its children devices, the success rate is 0 %. So by disconnecting a device we disconnect also its children (devices 0x0007 and 0x000A in this case).

In Fig. 8 we variate the position of the target device to show the impact of the Disconnect Attack on the network charge. We can see that the decrease of the network load is directly correlated with the number of hops to reach the Network Manager and the number of its children. Consequently, an attack on a device situated at two hops (see Fig. 8(b)) decreases the network load by almost 37 %,

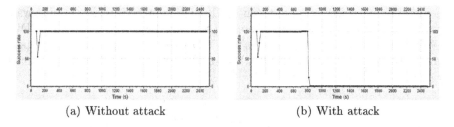

Fig. 7. Data send success rate for target node

an attack against a device situated at three hops (see Fig. 8(c)) decreases the network charge by 29 % and an attack against a device at four hops decrease it by 16 % (see Fig. 8(d)). As expected, more the target device is near the Network Manager more the impact of the attack on the network load is significant. Indeed, this is due to the number of its children.

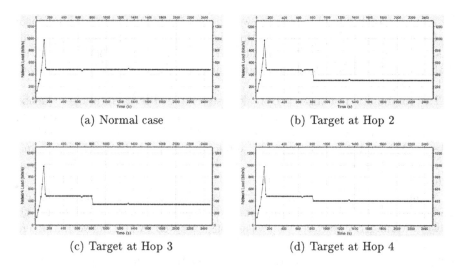

Fig. 8. Network load in byte "before and after attack"

Table 1 indicates the time spent by a malicious node in search mode and also the total attack duration from the beginning of the search mode to the sent of the Disconnect DLPDU. The duration of the attack depends on the size of the management superframe (used for commands transmission and reception). In our simulation, it is set to 200 slots (2 s). And also advertisement DLPDU sending frequency (set to 4 s).

In the general case, T_{adv} the time to get an advertisement depends on its frequency sending: $MAX(T_{adv}) = 15 \times F_{sending\_adv}$ where $F_{sending\_adv}$ is the frequency of sending advertisement and 15 is the number of used channels.

When the attacker gets an advertisement DLPDU from the parent, it must wait at worst the duration of the superframe to send the forged disconnect DLPDU. So, $MAX(T_{total\_attack}) = 15 \times F_{sending\_adv} + S$ where S is the size of the super-frame. In our case, we get $MAX(T_{adv}) = 4\,\text{s}$ (Advertisement are sent on channel 11) and $MAX(T_{total\_attack}) = 4 + 2 = 6\,\text{s}$

Table 1. Attack duration

Target	Search mode duration (s)			Total attack duration (s)		
	Avg	Min	Max	Avg	Min	Max
Device 0004	2	0.01	3.99	4.58	2.01	5.96

6   Proposed Solution

Disconnect attack uses two security weaknesses in the WirlessHART protocol: the implementation of a critical feature, i.e. Disconnect DLPDU, in the Data Link Layer. Probably, the Disconnect DLPDU is a feature inherited from the IEEE 802.15.4-2006 standard [26]; and the use of a shared secret key in the Data Link Layer.

The combination of these two weaknesses can lead to harmful consequences on network behavior: disturbing routing protocol, isolating a group of nodes, etc.

In order to mitigate such attacks, we should prohibit the use of critical features in DLL and move them to the application layer. Indeed, AL Commands are secured by a Session key known only by the field device and the Network Manager.

As illustrated in Fig. 9(a), a field device sends a Disconnect Command instead of a Disconnect DLPDU. The Command is forwarded through the network to the Network Manager. Figure 9(b) shows actions executed by the Network Manager when receiving a Disconnect Command. It deciphers the network layer payload using the session key and after authenticating the sender, it updates routing tables and reallocates sending resources. In that way, the attacker will not be able to spoof the identity of any other device as it does not know the secret key shared by both of them. The overall message exchange is summarized in Fig. 10.

We analyze the impact of the solution on the overall functioning of the network. For that, we analyze two parameters: the network overload and time elapsing between the disconnection of a device and when the Network Manager is informed of it.

In the case of the disconnect DLPDU the disconnecting device sends one packet of 22 bytes to its neighbors. When send_health_report_timer (set by default to 15 min) elapsed each neighbor will report to Network Manager the list of devices present in its neighborhood. By this, the Network Manager will deduce that a device has disconnected. Health reports are application level commands

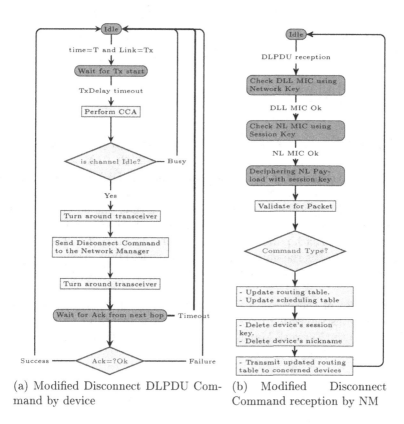

(a) Modified Disconnect DLPDU Command by device

(b) Modified Disconnect Command reception by NM

Fig. 9. Modified Disconnect Command processing

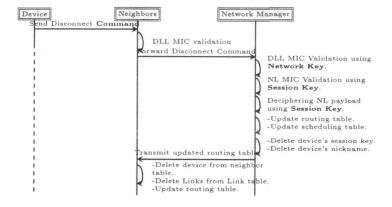

Fig. 10. Modified disconnect message exchange sequence

Table 2. Network overload by number of hops.

Number of hops	Disconnect DLPDU (Bytes)	Disconnect Command (Bytes)
2	174	72
3	326	144
4	478	216

encapsulated in packets of 127 bytes and forwarded to the Network Manager hop-by-hop. The cost of the transmission is: $cost = 22 + (N - 1) \times (127 + 25)$ where 25 bytes is the size of the acknowledgment DLPDU and N is the number of hops from disconnecting device to the Network Manager.

However, if the disconnecting device has more than one parent the Network Manager needs to know about the device disconnection to wait till it receive all health reports from each parent. So then, the total cost is $cost = 22 + \sum_{i=1}^{M}(N_i) \times (127 + 25)$ where M is the number of neighbor devices that disconnecting device is not the parent and N_i is the number of hops from each device to the Network Manager.

For the case of the use of a disconnect Command, a packet of 47 bytes is sent from the disconnecting device to its parent neighbor and then forwarded hop-by-hop to the Network Manager. $cost = N \times (47 + 25)$ where 25 bytes is the size of the acknowledgment DLPDU (Table 2).

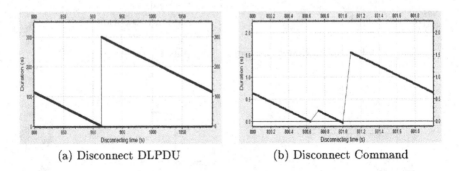

(a) Disconnect DLPDU   (b) Disconnect Command

Fig. 11. Time duration before the NM is informed about a device disconnection

For the second parameter, we variate the time when a device disconnects and we report time elapsed before the Network Manager is informed about the disconnection. Figure 11 illustrates that the time elapsed before the Network Manager is informed about the disconnection of a device in the case of the use of the disconnect DLPDU (Fig. 11(a)) is significantly bigger than the one elapsed in the case of the use of the disconnect Command (Fig. 11(b)). Indeed, disconnect Command is forwarded directly, hop-by-hop, each time a slot is available from the disconnecting device to the Network Manager. In the other case the information is transmitted to the Network Manager by the neighbors of the disconnecting device in their health reports which sending frequency is set by default to 15 min. Therefore, the average time in the case of using disconnect DLPDU will be 7,5 min. In our simulation we set this frequency to 5 min (300 s) and even with this three times high sending frequency of health reports we get big values (Max = 300 s, Avg = 150 s) comparatively to the case of using disconnect command (Max = 1.5 s, Avg = 0.67 s).

7   Conclusion and Future Works

We have described in this work a serious security issue in WirelessHART, the leading standard for wireless sensor networks used in SCADA systems. We demonstrate that an insider attacker can cause harmful disturbance to the network. We also give a fully-automated way to take advantage of this weakness to isolate partially or more again totally the wireless sensors from the SCADA network. The conducted tests confirm the feasibility of this attack and its dangerous potentiality. They demonstrate that this attack is easily conducted and do not require any additional means. Moreover the time to collect needed information to launch the attack is significantly short.

On another hand, we do not consider some mechanisms provided by WirelessHART such as route redundancy and retry mechanisms which allow to switch from one route to another one when the destination is unreachable. This can be done as a future work either by disconnecting the target device from each of its parents one by one or by adopting a reversed approach, by usurping the identity of each parent and sending fakes disconnect DLPDUs to the target device.

References

1. Falliere, N., Murchu, L.O., Chien, E.: W32. stuxnet dossier. White paper, Symantec Corp., Security Response, vol. 5 (2011)
2. Slay, J., Miller, M.: Lessons learned from the maroochy water breach. In: Goetz, E., Shenoi, S. (eds.) Critical Infrastructure Protection, Post-Proceedings of the First Annual IFIPWorking Group 11.10 International Conference on Critical Infrastructure Protection. IFIP, vol. 253, pp. 73–82. Springer, USA (2007)
3. Cárdenas, A.A., Roosta, T., Sastry, S.: Rethinking security properties, threat models, and the design space in sensor networks: a case study in SCADA systems. Ad Hoc Netw. 7(8), 1434–1447 (2009)
4. ZigBee Alliance: ZigBee Pro. http://www.zigbee.org
5. HART Communication Foundation: WirelessHART. http://www.hartcom.org
6. Wireless System for Automation: ISA100. http://www.isa.org
7. Douceur, J.R.: The sybil attack. In: Druschel, P., Kaashoek, M.F., Rowstron, A. (eds.) IPTPS 2002. LNCS, vol. 2429, pp. 251–260. Springer, Heidelberg (2002)
8. Karlof, C., Wagner, D.: Secure routing in wireless sensor networks: attacks and countermeasures. Ad Hoc Netw. 1(2–3), 293–315 (2003)

9. Newsome, J., Shi, E., Song, D.X., Perrig, A.: The sybil attack in sensor networks: analysis and defenses. In: Ramchandran, K., Sztipanovits, J., Hou, J.C., Pappas, T.N. (eds.) Proceedings of the Third International Symposium on Information Processing in Sensor Networks, IPSN, pp. 259–268. ACM, USA (2004)

10. Igure, V.M., Laughter, S.A., Williams, R.D.: Security issues in SCADA networks. Comput. Secur. **25**(7), 498–506 (2006)

11. Stouffer, K.A., Falco, J.A., Scarfone, K.A.: SP 800–82. Guide to industrial control systems (ICS) security. Technical report, National Institute of Standards and Technology, Gaithersburg, MD, United States (2011)

12. Larkin, R.D., Lopez Jr., J., Butts, J.W., Grimaila, M.R.: Evaluation of security solutions in the SCADA environment. SIGMIS Database **45**(1), 38–53 (2014). http://dx.doi.org/10.1145/2591056.2591060

13. Tabrizi, F.M., Pattabiraman, K.: A model-based intrusion detection system for smart meters. In: 15th International IEEE Symposium on High-Assurance Systems Engineering, HASE 2014, Miami Beach, FL, USA, 9–11 January 2014, pp. 17–24. IEEE Computer Society (2014)

14. Huitsing, P., Chandia, R., Papa, M., Shenoi, S.: Attack taxonomies for the modbus protocols. IJCIP **1**, 37–44 (2008)

15. Fovino, I.N., Carcano, A., Murel, T.D.L., Trombetta, A., Masera, M.: Modbus/DNP3 state-based intrusion detection system. In: 24th IEEE International Conference on Advanced Information Networking and Applications, AINA, pp. 729–736. IEEE Computer Society, Australia (2010)

16. Coppolino, L., D'Antonio, S., Romano, L., Spagnuolo, G.: An intrusion detection system for critical information infrastructures using wireless sensor network technologies. In: 2010 5th International Conference on Critical Infrastructure (CRIS), pp. 1–8, September 2010

17. Han, S., Zhu, X., Mok, A.K., Chen, D., Nixon, M.: Reliable and real-time communication in industrial wireless mesh networks. In: 17th IEEE RTAS, pp. 3–12. IEEE Computer Society, USA (2011)

18. Kim, A.N., Hekland, F., Petersen, S., Doyle, P.: When HART goes wireless: understanding and implementing the wirelesshart standard. In: Proceedings of 13th IEEE International Conference on Emerging Technologies and Factory Automation, ETFA, Hamburg, Germany, pp. 899–907. IEEE (2008)

19. Song, J., Han, S., Mok, A., Chen, D., Lucas, M., Nixon, M.: Wirelesshart: applying wireless technology in real-time industrial process control. In: Real-Time and Embedded Technology and Applications Symposium, RTAS 2008, pp. 377–386, IEEE, April 2008

20. Alcaraz, C., Lopez, J.: A security analysis for wireless sensor mesh networks in highly critical systems. IEEE Trans. Syst. Man Cybern. Part C **40**(4), 419–428 (2010)

21. Petersen, S., Carlsen, S.: Wirelesshart versus ISA100.11a: the format war hits the factory floor. Ind. Electron. Mag. IEEE **5**(4), 23–34 (2011)

22. Raza, S., Slabbert, A., Voigt, T., Landernäs, K.: Security considerations for the wirelesshart protocol. In: Proceedings of 12th IEEE International Conference on Emerging Technologies and Factory Automation, ETFA, pp. 1–8. IEEE, Spain (2009)

23. Roosta, T., Nilsson, D.K., Lindqvist, U., Valdes, A.: An intrusion detection system for wireless process control systems. In: IEEE 5th International Conference on Mobile Adhoc and Sensor Systems, MASS, pp. 866–872. IEEE, USA (2008)
24. OMNeT++. http://www.omnetpp.org/
25. InetManet. https://github.com/aarizaq/inetmanet-2.0
26. IEEE 802.15.4-2006: Standard for local and metropolitan area networks-part 15.4: Low-Rate Wireless Personal Area Networks (LR-WPANs). http://www.ieee.org

Attack Volume Model: Geometrical Approach and Application

Gustavo Gonzalez Granadillo$^{(\boxtimes)}$, Grégoire Jacob, and Hervé Debar

Institut Mines-Télécom, Télécom SudParis, CNRS UMR 5157 SAMOVAR,
9 rue Charles Fourier, 91011 Evry, France
{gustavo.gonzalez_granadillo,gregoire.jacob,
herve.debar}@telecom-sudparis.eu

Abstract. The sophistication and efficiency of current attacks makes the detection and mitigation process a very difficult task for security analysts. Research in information security has always focused on the effects of a given attack over a particular target and the methodologies to evaluate and select countermeasures accordingly. Multiple attack scenarios are hardly considered concurrently to assess the risk and propose security solutions. This paper proposes a geometrical model that represents the volume of attacks and countermeasures based on a three-dimensional coordinate system (i.e. user, channel, and resource). The CARVER methodology is used to give an appropriate weight to each entity composing the axes in the coordinate system. These weights represent the criticality of the different system entities. As a result, volumes are related to risks, making it possible to determine the magnitude and coverage of each attack and countermeasure within a given system.

Keywords: Attack volume · Multiple attacks · Security impact · CARVER · Response actions

1 Introduction

Threat mitigation is complex; a major part of this complexity is due to the fact that attacks are often divided into multiple stages, possibly distributed across multiple sources. Most of the approaches to mitigate current attacks consider one attack at a time [5,9] by evaluating each step of the attack and proposing security solutions to either stop it or decrease its severity. However, very little effort is dedicated to studying and analyzing the effects of multiple attacks over a given target.

Current research focuses on approaches to detect such attacks and demonstrate their robustness and the difficulty in their mitigation [1,3]. Most of these works propose approaches to detect multiple attacks but few of them propose a methodology to react against them.

In this paper, we propose a representation of each attack in a three-dimensional coordinate system (i.e. user, channel, and resource). The same coordinates include also system assets and potential countermeasures. The axes of the

© Springer International Publishing Switzerland 2016
C. Lambrinoudakis and A. Gabillon (Eds.): CRiSIS 2015, LNCS 9572, pp. 242–257, 2016.
DOI: 10.1007/978-3-319-31811-0_15

coordinate system are complementary to each other, and their projection results into a parallelepiped with a corresponding volume in our system. The CARVER methodology [14] gives an appropriate weight to each entity composing the axes in our coordinate system based on 6 criteria (i.e., criticality, accessibility, recuperability, vulnerability, effect, and recognizability), making it possible to assign more impact to critical assets.

In addition, we compute the union and intersection of the different volumes (i.e. system, attacks, and countermeasures) by using geometrical operations, making it possible to determine the impact of multiple attacks arriving simultaneously on the system and the effects of implementing multiple countermeasures as a reaction strategy.

The rest of the paper is structured as follows: Sect. 2 introduces the state of the art on attack surface. Section 3 describes our proposed model and details the different types of volumes considered in the approach, as well as the system dimensions. Section 4 discusses the volume construction of the entities composing our geometrical model. Section 5 details the geometrical approach to compute the union and intersection of multiple volumes. Section 6 depicts a scenario with two attacks to show the applicability of the model. Related works are presented in Sect. 7. Finally, conclusions and perspective for future work are presented in Sect. 8.

2   Attack Surface

The attack surface is a model that measures quantitatively the level of exposure of a given system (i.e., the reachable and exploitable vulnerabilities existing on the system) [15].

Operating Systems Attack Surface: According to Howard et al. [7,8], the attack surface of an operating system is the union of code, interfaces, services, protocols, and practices available to users. The model determines whether one version of a system is more secure than another by assessing the system's attackability,(i.e., likelihood that it will be successfully attacked). The authors describe a system's attack surface over three abstract dimensions: targets & enablers, channels & protocols, and access rights. As a result, the larger the attack surface, the more likely the system is to be attacked.

Software Systems Attack Surface: Manadhata et al. [13] propose to systematically measure the attack surface of a software system (e.g., IMAP server, FTP daemons, Operating Systems) based on the analysis of its source code, through three dimensions: methods, channels, and data. Not all resources are part of the attack surface, nor all of them contribute equally to the attack surface measurement. As a result, given two systems, it is possible to compare their attack surface measurements to indicate, along each of the three dimensions, whether one is more secure than the other with respect to the attack surface metric.

Other Attack Surface Approaches: Gruschka and Jensen [6] propose a taxonomy based on the notion of attack surfaces in cloud computing scenarios. Six attack vectors are identified: (1) A service instance towards a user, (2) A user instance towards a service, (3) A cloud system towards a service instance, (4) A service instance towards a cloud system, (5) A cloud system towards a user, (6) A user towards a cloud system.

Petajasoja et al. [16] analyze a system's attack surface using the Common Vulnerability Scoring System (CVSS). The approach compares the system behavior with previously undetermined interactions and transient attack surfaces. After the attack vectors are identified, the CVSS base scores is used to prioritize the attack surface interfaces. As a result, it is possible to identify the most critical interfaces and prioritize the test effort.

Microsoft has recently realized an attack surface analyzer tool [4] that identifies changes made to an operating system attack surface by the installation of new software. A pre-released version of Microsoft Windows Vista was examined to determine the external security exposure and to identify the changes on components in the networking stack, network services, and core protocols. Such changes are enumerated and their effect on the external security of the system is analyzed.

3   Our Geometrical Model: Attack Volume

We propose to extend the surface model into a volume model that represents systems, attacks and countermeasures in a three dimensional coordinate system considering the user account, channel, and resource dimensions.

The three axes are bounded by the size of the system. The volume encompassed by the three axes represents the maximum risk at which the system is exposed, and corresponds to the system volume. Inside this volume, we define sub-volumes that correspond to the attacks and/or countermeasures applied on the system.

3.1   Volume Definition

A volume is the three-dimensional space enclosed by some closed boundary. We study 3 types of volumes: the system volume (the maximal space susceptible to attacks), the attack volume (part of the system volume that is compromised or threatened), and the countermeasure volume (part of the system volume that is protected by a given countermeasure).

System Volume (SV): It represents the maximal space a given system (e.g. S1) is exposed to attackers. This volume includes tangible assets (e.g., PCs, mobile phones, network components, etc.), as well as intangible assets (e.g., confidential information, business reputation, etc.) that are vulnerable to known and unknown threats. Each of these assets are represented in the system volume as user accounts, channels, and/or resources.

Attack Volume (AV): Within the complete system volume exposed to attackers (including all possible vulnerable resources of the given system), we concentrate on a given attack to identify the portion of the volume being targeted based on the vulnerabilities it can exploit. These vulnerabilities are related to all the dimensions that comprise the system volume (i.e. user accounts, channels, and resources).

Countermeasure Volume (CV): The countermeasure volume represents the level of action that a security solution has on a given system. In other words, the countermeasure volume is the percentage of the system volume that is covered and protected by a given countermeasure. An attack is covered by a countermeasure if their volumes overlap. The countermeasure can exceed the attack volume and cover part of the system that is not affected by the attack.

3.2   System Dimensions

We identified three main dimensions that contribute directly to the execution of a given attack: User account (subject), Resource (object), and Channel (the way to execute actions, e.g. connect, read, write, etc.). This latter is represented as the transitions between subjects and objects. For instance, in order to access a web-server (object) of a given organization, a user (subject) connects to the system by providing his/her login and password (action). Please note that these notions are very similar to traditional security policy models, e.g. RBAC [12].

User Account: A user account is a unique identifier for a user in a given system that allows him/her to connect and interact with the system's environment (i.e. super administrator, system administrator, standard user, guest, internal user, or nobody).

Channel: In order to have access to a particular resource, a user must use a given channel. A channel can be an IP address, a port number, a protocol, a password, or any other method used to access a particular resource in the system. Each organization must define the way its users connect to the system and have access to the organization's resources. In this paper we select IP addresses and port numbers as the corresponding channels for our model.

Resource: A resource is either a physical component (e.g. host, server, printer) or a logical component (e.g. files, records, database) of limited availability within a computer system. We defined 2 levels of privileges (i.e. kernel, user), and 7 level of transitions (i.e. read, write, execute, and their combinations), and we assigned numerical values based on their characteristics.

Each axis entity is assigned a weighting factor (discussed in Sect. 4) depending on the contribution of each entity to the calculation of the corresponding volume. This weighting factor corresponds to the criticality of each entity represented on the axis. For example, an admin user will be represented by a longer segment on the *User account* axis than a standard user.

3.3   Volume Calculation

The projection of the three axis in our coordinate system generates a parallelepiped in three dimensions. The volume of a parallelepiped is the product of the area of its base 'A' and its height 'h'. The base is any of the six faces of the geometric figure, whereas the height is the perpendicular distance between the base and the opposite face.

The volume calculation requires the computation of the contribution of each axis represented in the coordinate system. The axis contribution is determined as the sum of the product of each set of axis type entities (e.g., user account type, port class, resource type, etc.) by its associated weighting factor. For instance, in order to compute the contribution of the user account dimension (Co_{Acc}) in the calculation of the volume of system S_1 we count all similar elements (E) that belong to the same user account type (e.g., system admin, standard user, guest, etc.), and we multiply the resulting figure by its associated weighting factor (WF discussed in Sect. 4), as shown in Eq. 1.

$$Co_{Acc}(S_1) = (Count(E \in sup\_admin(S_1)) \times WF(sup\_admin)) +$$
$$(Count(E \in sys\_admin(S_1)) \times WF(sys\_admin)) + (Count(E \in std\_user(S_1))$$
$$\times WF(std\_user)) + (Count(E \in int\_user(S_1)) \times WF(int\_user)) +$$
$$(Count(E \in guest(S_1)) \times WF(guest)) \tag{1}$$

The remaining of this section details the calculation of the different volumes defined in Sect. 3.1.

3.3.1   System Volume (SV) Calculation

Consider a system S, which is a vector composed of three kind of entities: a set of user accounts (Acc), a set of IP address and open ports (Ip-Port), and the system's resource (Res). The volume of system S is represented by the vector $\langle Co_{Acc}(S), Co_{Ip-Port}(S), Co_{Res}(S) \rangle$. The system volume is calculated as the product of the axes contribution to the system (S), as shown in Eq. 2.

$$SV(S) = \prod_{AXES} Co_{Axis}(S) \tag{2}$$

3.3.2   Attack Volume (AV) Calculation

Consider A as a given attack, $SV_{Acc}(A)$ as the A's account-based volume, $SV_{Ip-Port}(A)$ as the A's channel-based volume, and $SV_{Res}(A)$ as the A's resource-based volume. The volume of attack A is represented by the vector: $\langle Co_{Acc}(A), Co_{Ip-Port}(A), Co_{Res}(A) \rangle$. The attack volume is calculated as the product of the axes contribution to the attack (A), as shown in Eq. 3.

$$AV(A) = \prod_{AXES} Co_{Axis}(A) \tag{3}$$

The coverage (Cov) of a given attack (A) respect to a given system (S) is a value that ranges between zero and one. Such coverage is computed as the ratio between the attack volume overlapping with the system volume $(AV(A \cap S))$ and the system volume $(SV(S))$, as shown in Eq. 4:

$$Cov(A/S) = \frac{AV(A \cap S)}{SV(S)} \tag{4}$$

Where $AV(A \cap S)$ represents the volume that results from the elements of system (S) that are compromised by attack (A)

3.3.3   Countermeasure Volume (CV) Calculation

Consider a given countermeasure C, a set of user accounts as the attack vector 'Acc', a set of IP address and ports as the attack vector 'Ip-Port', and the system's resource as the attack vector 'Res'. The volume of countermeasure C is represented by the vector: $\langle Co_{Acc}(C), Co_{Ip-Port}(C), Co_{Res}(C) \rangle$. The countermeasure volume is calculated as the product of the axes contribution to the countermeasure (C), as shown in Eq. 5.

$$AV(C) = \prod_{AXES} Co_{Axis}(C) \tag{5}$$

The coverage (Cov) of a given countermeasure (C) respect to a given attack (A) is a value that ranges from zero to one. Such coverage is calculated as the ratio between the countermeasure volume overlapping with the attack volume $(CV(C \cap A))$ and the attack volume $(AV(A))$, as shown in Eq. 6:

$$Cov(C/A) = \frac{CV(C \cap A)}{AV(A)} \tag{6}$$

Where $AV(C \cap A)$ represents the volume that results from the elements of attack (A) that are mitigated by countermeasure (C). From Eq. 6, the higher the ratio, the greater the mitigation level.

4   Unit Volume Construction

Each axis contributes differently in the volume calculation. This contribution represents the impact of a given entity in the execution of an attack. Following the CARVER methodology [14], we assign a weighting factor to each entity represented in our coordinate system based on the analysis of six criteria (i.e., criticality, accessibility, recuperability, vulnerability, effect, and recognizability). The remaining of the section details this methodology and the intra-dimension normalization.

4.1   Carver Methodology

Norman [14] proposes a methodology to measure the priority of each element in a given system, based on the following factors:

- **Criticality (C):** measures the impact that an asset has on carrying out the organization's mission. A target is said to be critical when its destruction or damage has a significant impact on production or service. Criticality depends on several factors such as: time (e.g., the speed at which the impact of a target affects operations), quality (e.g., the level of damage caused to output, production or service), surrogate (e.g., effect in the output, production or service), relativity (e.g., number of targets, position, relative value).
- **Accessibility (A):** refers to the ability and means to communicate or interact with a system, use system resources to handle information, gain knowledge of the information the system contains, or control system components and functions [10].
- **Recuperability (R):** measures the time that a target needs to replace, repair, or bypass destruction or damage. Recuperability varies with the available sources and type of targeted components.
- **Vulnerability (V):** is a weakness in an information system, system security procedures, internal controls, or implementation that can be exploited or triggered by a threat source [10]. A target is vulnerable if the operational element has the means and expertise to successfully attack the target.
- **Effect (E):** measures all significant impact (whether desired or not), at the target and beyond, that may result once the selected target is attacked.
- **Recognizability (R):** is the degree to which a target can be recognized by an operational element. Factors such as the size and complexity of the target, the existence of distinctive signatures, the presence of masking or camouflage influence the level of recognizability of a given target.

The methodology assigns numerical values on a scale of 1 to 10 to each considered factor and places them in a decision matrix. The sum of the values indicate the severity of a given dimension.

4.2   Intra-dimension Normalization

Each category within the axis contributes differently to the volume calculation. The weighting factor corresponds to the severity of a given category based on CARVER. The remaining of this section details the weighting factor assigned to each category of the coordinate system's dimensions.

4.2.1   User Accounts
We define six categories of user accounts (i.e., super administrator, system administrator, standard user, guest, internal user, and nobody). Each user account category has an associated weighting factor that corresponds to the CARVER analysis, as shown in Table 1.

4.2.2   Channels
We defined five categories of port numbers: Class 1 (well known and widely used ports, e.g., 20, 25, 80); Class 2 (well known and not widely used ports,

Table 1. Intra-dimension weighting factor

	Dimension	C	A	R	V	E	R	Total	WF
User Account	Super Admin (sup_admin)	10	9	8	10	10	9	56	5
	System Admin (sys_admin)	8	8	7	9	8	7	47	4
	Standard User (std_user)	6	7	6	7	7	5	38	3
	Internal User (int_user)	4	5	4	6	5	5	29	2
	Guest (guest)	3	3	2	5	4	2	19	1
	Nobody (nobody)	1	1	1	1	1	1	6	0
IP-Port	Class 1	10	9	8	8	7	8	50	4
	Class 2	8	7	6	5	5	6	39	3
	Class 3	7	8	5	7	5	6	38	3
	Class 4	3	2	3	4	3	5	20	1
	Class 5	2	1	1	3	1	1	9	0
	Public	8	7	5	7	6	5	37	3
	Private	5	1	4	3	4	3	20	1
	Reserved/ Special purpose	2	1	3	1	1	1	9	0
Resource	Kernel & R-W-X	10	10	9	9	9	9	56	5
	Kernel & W-X/R-X/R-W	8	9	9	9	7	8	50	4
	Kernel & R/W/X	6	7	7	8	7	5	40	3
	User & R-W-X	5	5	7	7	6	6	36	3
	User & W-X/R-X/R-W	5	5	6	5	4	5	30	2
	User & W/X	3	3	5	3	2	3	19	1
	User & R	1	2	2	1	1	3	10	0

e.g., 46, 50, 56); Class 3 (registered official ports that are used by multiple applications, e.g., 1109, 1550, 2082); Class 4 (registered official ports and not widely used, e.g., 1024, 49151); and Class 5 (private ports, e.g., from 49152 to 65635). We also defined three categories of IP addresses (i.e., Public, Private, and Reserved/special purpose). Each port and IP category has been assigned a weighting factor that correspond to the CARVER analysis, as presented in Table 1.

The resulting IP-Port couple is then represented as the sequence of affected IP address, followed by the active port numbers in ascending order (e.g., IP_1, IP_2,..., IP_n, $Port_1$, $Port_2$,..., $Port_n$).

4.2.3 Resources

We assigned a weight to each resource based on the effort to obtain the access rights and privileges associated to a given resource, as shown in Table 1. The index that results from the division between the Privilege (PR) value and the Transition (TR) value (i.e., $\frac{PR}{TR}$) represents the level of access assigned to a given resource on the system.

5 Volume Union and Intersection

The calculation of the Attack Volume (AV) for multiple attacks requires the identification of their union and intersection. The union of two or more attack volumes ranges from the sum of the individual attack volumes minus their intersection in its lower bound, to the sum of the individual volumes in its upper bound (Eq. 7). The intersection of two or more attack volumes ranges from zero in its lower bound, to the minimum volume of the group of attacks in its upper bound (Eq. 8).

$$AV(A_1 \cup ... \cup A_n) \in \left[\sum_{i=1}^{n} AV(A_i) - \sum_{i,j=1}^{n} AV(A_i \cap A_j), \quad \sum_{i=1}^{n} AV(A_i) \right] \quad (7)$$

$$AV(A_1 \cap ... \cap A_n) \in [0, \quad min(AV(A_1), ..., AV(A_n))] \quad (8)$$

Two cases can be distinguished in the calculation of the volume union and intersection: joint and disjoint volumes.

5.1 Disjoint Volumes

The volume of one attack is disjoint from another attack volume if they have no elements in common. For instance, given two attacks (A_1, A_2), Attacks A_1 and A_2 are *disjoint* if their combined volume has no element in common, therefore, the attack volume of the union is calculated as the sum of their individual volumes, and the attack volume of the intersection is equal to 0, as shown in Eq. 9.

$$iff \ A_1 \cap A_2 = \varnothing \begin{cases} AV(A_1 \cup A_2) = AV(A_1) + AV(A_2) \\ AV(A_1 \cap A_2) = 0 \end{cases} \quad (9)$$

5.2 Joint Volumes

The Volume of one attack is partially or totally covered by another attack if they share some or all of their elements. For instance, given two attacks (A_1, A_2), Attacks A_1 and A_2 are *joint* if their combined volume has at least one element in common, therefore, the attack volume of the union is calculated as the sum of their individual volumes minus their intersection, and the attack volume of the intersection is calculated as the sum of their individual volumes minus their union, as shown in Eq. 10.

$$iff \ A_1 \cap A_2 \neq \varnothing \begin{cases} AV(A_1 \cup A_2) = AV(A_1) + AV(A_2) - AV(A_1 \cap A_2) \\ AV(A_1 \cap A_2) = AV(A_1) + AV(A_2) - AV(A_1 \cup A_2) \end{cases} \quad (10)$$

Given two attacks (A_1, A_2), *Attack A_1 is a subset of Attack A_2* if the volume of A_1 is a subset of the volume of A_2 ($AV(A_1) \subseteq AV(A_2)$), therefore, the attack volume of the union is equal to the attack volume of the bigger attack, and the attack volume of the intersection is equal to the attack volume of the smaller attack, as shown in Eq. 11.

$$iff \ A_1 \subseteq A_2 \begin{cases} AV(A_1 \cup A_2) = AV(A_2) \\ AV(A_1 \cap A_2) = AV(A_1) \end{cases} \quad (11)$$

Given two attacks (A_1, A_2), *Attacks A_1 and A_2 have the same volume* if Attack A_1 is a subset of Attack A_2 and Attack A_2 is a subset of Attack A_1, therefore, the attack volumes of the union and the intersection are the same as their individual attack volumes (Eq. 12).

$$iff\ A_1 \subseteq A_2 \wedge A_2 \subseteq A_1 \rightarrow AV(A_1 \cup A_2) = AV(A_1 \cap A_2) = AV(A_1) = AV(A_2) \tag{12}$$

Considering two attack volumes (i.e., $AV(A_1) = (Co_{Acc}(A_1), Co_{Ip-Port}(A_1), Co_{Res}(A_1))$; $AV(A_2) = (Co_{Acc}(A_2), Co_{Ip-Port}(A_2), Co_{Res}(A_2))$, the attack volume intersection is calculated as the sum of all elements 'E' that are included in both set of volumes times their corresponding weighting factor, as shown in Eq. 13.

$$AV(A_1 \cap A_2) = \prod Co_{Vec}(A_1 \cap A_2) \tag{13}$$

Where:

$$Co_{Vec}(A_1 \cap A_2) = Co_{Acc}(A_1 \cap A_2) \times Co_{Ip-Port}(A_1 \cap A_2) \times Co_{Res}(A_1 \cap A_2)$$

$$Co_{Acc}(A_1 \cap A_2) = \sum_{i=0}^{n}(E_i \times WF(E_i) \mid E_i \in A_1 \wedge E_i \in A_2)$$

$$Co_{Ip-Port}(A_1 \cap A_2) = \sum_{i=0}^{n}(E_i \times WF(E_i) \mid E_i \in A_1 \wedge E_i \in A_2)$$

$$Co_{Res}(A_1 \cap A_2) = \sum_{i=0}^{n}(E_i \times WF(E_i) \mid E_i \in A_1 \wedge E_i \in A_2)$$

From the previous equations, 'E' represents the elements associated to each attack dimension (i.e., IP address, channel, and resource) that are compromised during the execution of a given attack; 'n' represents the maximal number of elements 'E'; and 'WF(E_i)' corresponds to the weighting factor of the element E_i as proposed in Sect. 4.

5.3 Dimension-Based Volume Calculation

The calculation of the attack volume union and intersection based on a given dimension derives Eqs. 14 and 15.

$$Co_{Axis}(A_1 \cup A_2) = Co_{Axis}(A_1) + Co_{Axis}(A_2) - Co_{Axis}(A_1 \cap A_2) \tag{14}$$

$$Co_{Axis}(A_1 \cap A_2) = \sum_{E \in Axis_1 \cap Axis_2} WF(E) \tag{15}$$

Given two attacks (A_1, A_2), a set of elements $A=\{E_1, E_2, ...E_n\}$ that are targeted by A_1 in this dimension, and a set of elements $B=\{E_a, E_b, ...E_x\}$ that are targeted by A_2, the contribution of the union to the volume is calculated as the sum of each individual volumes minus their intersection. The intersection of both attacks is calculated as the sum of the elements that belong to both dimensions (A, B) times their corresponding weighting factor.

For instance, given two attacks (A_1, A_2), a set of user accounts $UA_1 = \{Acc_1, Acc_2, ...Acc_n\}$ that are targeted by A_1, and a set of user accounts $UA_2 = \{Acc_a, Acc_b, ...Acc_x\}$ that are targeted by A_2, the volume intersection of both attacks based on the user account dimension is calculated as the elements that belong to both set of user accounts (UA_1, UA_2) times their corresponding weighting factor, as shown in Eq. 16.

$$
\begin{aligned}
Co_{Acc}(A_1 \cap A_2) = {} & Count(sup\_admin \in UA_1 \wedge UA_2) \times WF(sup\_admin) \\
& + Count(sys\_admin \in UA_1 \wedge UA_2) \times WF(sys\_admin) \\
& + Count(std\_user \in UA_1 \wedge UA_2) \times WF(std\_user) \\
& + Count(int\_user \in UA_1 \wedge UA_2) \times WF(int\_user) \\
& + Count(guest \in UA_1 \wedge UA_2) \times WF(guest) \quad (16)
\end{aligned}
$$

6 Use Case: Multiple Attacks

We model a department of a Telecommunication educational institution with 65 user accounts, 255 public IP addresses, and 12 open ports (class 1 ports). The main types of resources shared by this institution are servers, workstations, and printers. Table 2 summarizes the information about resources, channels and user accounts for the studied system. The *range* column shows the list of affected entities for each category, the *description* column details the type of entity, the N column displays the total number of entities per category, the WF column shows the weighting factor value assigned to each category of entities, and the *Coordinate* column shows the initial and final position of the entity within the coordinate system.

Table 2. Entities information

Dimension	Range	Description	N	WF	Coordinate
Resource	R1:R150	School servers	150	5	0:750
	R151:R215	Dept. workstations	65	3	750:945
	R216:R255	School printers	40	2	945:1025
Channel	Ch1:Ch255	Public IP	255	3	0:765
	Ch256:Ch267	Port Class 1	12	4	765:813
User Account	U1:U25	Standard user	25	3	0:75
	U26:U59	Internal user	34	2	76:143
	U60:U65	Guest	6	1	144:149

Note that each entity represents a segment in one axis of the coordinate system (with an initial and final position). For instance, resource *R1* (i.e., server with WF = 5) is represented as the segment 0:5 in the resource axis; channel

Ch1 (i.e., public IP with WF = 3) is represented as the segment 0:3 in the channel axis; and user *U1* (standard user, with WF = 3) is represented as the segment 0:3 in the user account axis. An event on these three entities originates a parallelepiped with the following coordinates (RCU (5,3,3)).

6.1 Attack Scenario

The school department has been targeted with two sophisticated malware attacks. Attack A_1 (i.e., Conficker) is a computer worm targeting the Microsoft Windows operating system, which uses flaws in Windows software and dictionary attacks on administrator passwords to propagate while forming a botnet [11]. The attack targeted all department workstations (i.e., R151:R215), all school printers (i.e., R216:R255), 105 public IP addresses (i.e., Ch151:Ch255), and all user accounts (i.e., U1:U65).

Attack A_2, (i.e., Zeus), occurs simultaneously in the system. Students are prompted to install a malware called Zeus [2], after clicking a link appearing in their Facebook accounts. The malware sits dormant on the system until users access their bank account, at which point it makes a copy of their user-names and passwords. Zeus targets all the school servers (R1:R150), all department workstations (R151:R215), 227 IP addresses (i.e., Ch1:Ch215 & Ch256:Ch267), and all user accounts (i.e., U1:U65).

Figure 1(a) and (b) show the graphical representation of the individual attacks A_1 and A_2 respectively within system S. Note that A_1 is represented by one parallelepided (red), whereas A_2 is composed of two parallelepipeds (green).

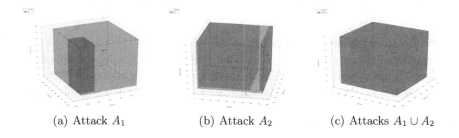

(a) Attack A_1 (b) Attack A_2 (c) Attacks $A_1 \cup A_2$

Fig. 1. Graphical representations of attacks A_1 and A_2 within system S (Color figure online)

Figure 1(c) depicts the graphical representation the combined attack $A_1 \cup A_2$ within system S. Please note that the union of both attacks cover a much wider volume than if attacks were treated individually. In this case, the combined volume of $A_1 \cup A_2$ totally covers the system volume.

6.2   Countermeasure Analysis

Several countermeasures are proposed to react over the Conficker and Zeus attacks [2,11]. In this paper we will analyze the five most common solutions for these malware attacks.

C1 Signature procedures: Create signatures for matching against the shell-code pattern and use them with IDS/IPS (e.g., Snort)

C2 Change Policies: Make all shares "read-only", trojans easily spread via shares

C3 Anti-virus/malware: Download and install antivirus/antimalware on all the machines of the network

C4 OS Patches: Download and install patches for windows (e.g., KB95-8644, KB95-7097, KB95-8687) on all machines

C5 Firewall rules: Block access to a list of IP and domains by using a proxy server (e.g., Squid)

Using Eqs. 3, and 9, we compute the volume of attack A_1 and A_2 respectively. The volume of the combined attack $A_1 \cup A_2$ is calculated using Eq. 10. In addition, Eqs. 2 and 5 are used to compute the volume of the system and countermeasures respectively. For instance, the system volume is calculated as follows:

$Co_{Res} = [(150 \times 5) + (65 \times 3) + (40 \times 2)] = 1{,}025$ units
$Co_{Ch} = [(255 \times 3) + (12 \times 4)] = 813$ units
$Co_{Acc} = [(25 \times 3) + (34 \times 2) + (6 \times 1)] = 149$ units
$V(S) = Co_{Res} \times Co_{Ch} \times Co_{Acc} = 124{,}165{,}425$ units^3

Figure 2 shows the graphical representation of the individual and combined countermeasures vs. the combined attack $A_1 \cup A_2$ within system S

6.2.1   Countermeasure Coverage

Each countermeasure is represented as a parallelepiped that covers a set of user accounts, channels and resources from the system S. Such coverage represents only a portion of the combined attack (i.e., Conficker + Zeus). Table 3 summarizes the information about the attacks and countermeasures studied in the system with their coordinate values. These latter result out of the product of the entity number and its associated weighting factor. For instance, there are 255 resources in the system, out of which we have 150 servers (WF = 5), 65 workstations (WF = 2), and 40 printers (WF = 2). The total system coordinate goes from 0 to 1025 (i.e., $(150 \times 5) + (65 \times 4) + (40 \times 2)$).

From Table 3, COV represents the coverage of a given entity (e.g., S, A_2, C_4) with respect to the combined attack $A_1 \cup A_2$. Such coverage is calculated using Eqs. 4 and 6. Results show that the combined attack covers 100 % of system 'S'. However, none of the countermeasures covers 100 % of the combined attack volume.

In addition, the individual application of any of the countermeasures represents a partial mitigation of the combined attack, that in the best of the cases reaches 73 % (countermeasure C_4) of the total risk, meaning that part of the attack is not treated at all.

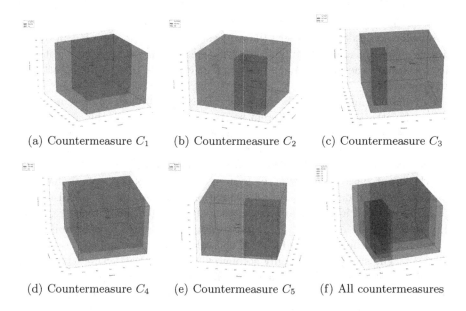

(a) Countermeasure C_1 (b) Countermeasure C_2 (c) Countermeasure C_3

(d) Countermeasure C_4 (e) Countermeasure C_5 (f) All countermeasures

Fig. 2. Graphical representation of countermeasures vs attacks within system S

Table 3. System, attack and countermeasure Information

	Resource	Coord.	Channel	Coord.	User	Coord.	Volume (units^3)	COV
S	R1:R255	0:1025	Ch1:Ch267	0:813	U1:U65	0:149	124,165,425	1.00
A_1	R151:R255	750:1025	Ch151:Ch255	450:765	U1:U65	0:149	12,907,125	0.10
A_2	R1:R215	0:945	Ch1:Ch215 & Ch256:Ch267	0:645 & 765:813	U1:U65	0:149	97,577,865	0.79
C_1	R1:R150	0:750	Ch1:Ch150	0:450	U1:U65	0:149	50,287,500	0.41
C_2	R151:R255	750:1025	Ch151:Ch255	450:765	U1:U65	0:149	12,907,125	0.10
C_3	R151:R215	750:945	Ch151:Ch215	450:645	U1:U65	0:149	5,665,725	0.05
C_4	R1:R215	0:945	Ch1:Ch215	0:645	U1:U65	0:149	90,819,225	0.73
C_5	R151:R255	750:945	Ch151:Ch267	450:813	U1:U65	0:149	10,546,965	0.08

The attack volume model is therefore, a useful tool in the selection of counter-measures based on their level of coverage. Combining this parameter with a cost sensitive metric will provide a complete overview of the financial and technical impact of attacks and countermeasures.

7   Related Work

Measuring the attack surface has been initially proposed by Howard et al. [7,8]. Our approach differs from Howard's in two aspects: First, the attack surface approach does not provide a systematic method to assign weights to the attack vectors. We provide a weighting factor to each element composing our coordinate system based on a multi-criteria methodology. Second, the surface model focuses on measuring the attack surface of operating systems. The work does not consider an analysis of other software systems. Our approach is suitable to be implemented in any kind of system, regardless of its nature, making it possible to compare the measurements of different elements (i.e., systems, attacks, countermeasures).

Manadhata et al. [13], has been, so far, the only approach to systematically measure the attack surface of different software. We differ from this approach in several aspects: (1) Manadhata's methodology cannot be applied in the absence of source code. Our approach, in contrast, does not require a source code to be implemented. We perform the volume evaluation based on a geometrical analysis of the input data from our three system's dimensions (i.e. users, channels, resources). (2) The damage potential estimation includes only technical impact (e.g., privilege elevation). Our approach considers several other criteria (e.g., criticality, accessibility, recuperability, vulnerability, effect, and recongizability) in the estimation of the weighting factor of each element composing the coordinate system. (3) The surface model only compares the level of attackability between two similar systems; no attempt has been made to compare the attack surface of different system environments. Our model compares the level of attackability between two or more systems, regardless of their nature (i.e., comparing the coverage volume of an anti-virus, a firewall, and an IPS on the system). (4) The surface model does not allow the security administrator to evaluate the impact of multiple attacks occurring simultaneously in a given system. Our approach can be used to evaluate the impact of multiple and complex attack scenarios.

8   Conclusion and Future Work

In this paper we introduced the attack volume as an improvement of the attack surface model proposed by Howard et al. [8] and Manadhata et al. [13]. Based on the several limitations derived by the implementation of the attack surface model, we propose an approach to model the information retrieved by a URI into a three-dimensional coordinate system (i.e., user, channel, and resource).

We propose a weighting factor, based on the CARVER methodology, to assign a weight on each axis according to six criteria (i.e. criticality, accessibility, recuperability, vulnerability, effect and recognizability). As a result, we are able to establish a direct connection between volumes and risks (e.g. big volume equals high risk). The figure that results from the projection of the 3 axis represents a parallelepiped, whose volume is then compared with other volumes on the system. Countermeasures are selected based on their coverage with respect to the attack volume.

Future work will concentrate in integrating other axes (e.g., time, attacker's capability, contexts) into the coordinate system, which may result in a variety of geometrical figures (e.g., hypercube) that are not initially considered in the calculation of the attack volume. In addition, we will consider to relate volume units with monetary values in order to determine the financial impact of multiple attacks and countermeasures. This transformation will provide the rules that security organizations could use to charge their clients according to the desired risk level.

Acknowledgements. The research in this paper has received funding from the Information Technology for European Advancements (ITEA2) within the context of the ADAX Project (Attack Detection and Countermeasure Simulation), and the PANOPTESEC project, as part of the Seventh Framework Programme (FP7) of the European Commission (GA 610416).

References

1. Agarwal, P., Efrat, A., Ganjugunte, S., Hay, D., Sankararaman, S., Zussman, G.: Network vulnerability to single, multiple and probabilistic physical attacks. In: Military Communications Conference (2010)

2. Baumhof, A., Shipp, A.: Zeus P2P advancements and MitB attack vectors. Technical report, ThreatMetrix Labs Public Report (2012)

3. Fan, J., Gierlichs, B., Vercauteren, F.: To infinity and beyond: combined attack on ECC using points of low order. In: Preneel, B., Takagi, T. (eds.) CHES 2011. LNCS, vol. 6917, pp. 143–159. Springer, Heidelberg (2011)

4. Fisher, D.: Microsoft releases attack surface analizer tool (2012). http://threatpost. com/en_us/blogs/microsoft-releases-attack-surface-analyzer-tool-080612

5. Granadillo, G.G., Belhaouane, M., Débar, H., Jacob, G.: Rori-based countermeasure selection using the orbac formalism. Int. J. Inf. Secur. **13**(1), 63–79 (2014)

6. Gruschka, N.: Attack surfaces: a taxonomy for attacks on cloud services. In: 3rd International Conference on Cloud Computing. IEEE (2010)

7. Howard, M.: Mitigate security risks by minimizing the code you expose to untrusted users. MSDN Mag. (2004)

8. Howard, M., Pincus, J., Wing, J.M.: Measuring relative attack surfaces. In: Lee, D.T., Shieh, S.P., Tygar, J.D. (eds.) Computer Security in the 21st Century, pp. 109–137. Springer, Heidelberg (2005)

9. Kheir, N., Cuppens-Boulahia, N., Cuppens, F., Debar, H.: A service dependency model for cost-sensitive intrusion response. In: Gritzalis, D., Preneel, B., Theoharidou, M. (eds.) ESORICS 2010. LNCS, vol. 6345, pp. 626–642. Springer, Heidelberg (2010)

10. Kissel, R.: Glossary of key information security terms. National Institute of Standards and Technologies, U.S. Department of Commerce (2011)

11. Kriegisch, A.: Detecting conficker in your network. Technical report, CERT White Paper (2009)

12. Li, N., Tripunitara, M.: Security analysis in role-based access control. ACM Trans. Inf. Syst. Secur. **9**(4), 391–420 (2006)

13. Manadhata, P., Wing, J.: An attack surface metric. IEEE Trans. Softw. Eng. **37**, 371–386 (2010)

14. Norman, T.L.: Risk Analysis and Security Countermeasure Selection. CRC Press, Taylor and Francis Group, Boca Raton (2010)

15. Northcutt, S.: The attack surface problem. In: SANS technology Institute Document (2011)

16. Petajasoja, S., Kortti, H., Takanen, A., Tirila, J.: IMS threat and attack surface analysis using common vulnerability scoring system. In: 35th IEEE Annual Computer Software and Applications Conference Workshops (2011)

An Intensive Analysis of Security and Privacy Browser Add-Ons

Nikolaos Tsalis[1](✉), Alexios Mylonas[2], and Dimitris Gritzalis[1]

[1] Information Security and Critical Infrastructure Protection
(INFOSEC) Laboratory, Department of Informatics,
Athens University of Economics and Business,
76 Patission Ave., 10434 Athens, Greece
{ntsalis, dgrit}@aueb.gr
[2] Faculty of Computing, Engineering and Sciences,
Staffordshire University, Beaconside, Stafford ST18 0AD, UK
alexios.mylonas@staffs.ac.uk

Abstract. Browsers enable the user to surf over the Internet and access web sites that may include social media, email service, etc. However, such an activity incorporates various web threats (e.g. tracking, malicious content, etc.) that may imperil the user's data and any sensitive information involved. Therefore, web browsers offer pre-installed security controls to protect users from these threats. Third-party browser software (i.e. add-ons) is also available that enhances these pre-installed security controls, or substitutes them. In this paper, we examine the available security controls that exist in modern browsers to reveal any gaps in the offered security protection. We also study the available security and privacy add-ons and observe whether the above mentioned gaps (i.e. when a security control is unavailable) are covered or need to be revisited.

Keywords: Web browser security · Privacy · Add-ons · User protection · Malware · Phishing · Controls

1 Introduction

Web browsing activities (e.g. e-commerce, online banking, social media, etc.) are accompanied by web threats that pose a direct risk towards the user, such as phishing attacks, malicious software, tracking sensitive information etc. [1]. When a user selects one of the popular web browsers (i.e. Apple Safari, Google Chrome, Internet Explorer, Mozilla Firefox or Opera) it is important to make that choice based on the features each browser provides (e.g. appearance, speed, usability, etc.). Among them there should be the available security controls provided by all modern browsers (e.g. malware/phishing protection, do-not-track service, etc.).

Pre-installed security controls aim to protect the user from web threats. Moreover, browsers offer additional software, namely add-ons, which extend the functionality of browsers. Add-ons are focused on categories, such as *accessibility, news & weather, photos, productivity, social*, etc. One of them (that exists in some of the browsers) is *security and/or privacy*, which includes add-ons that aim to offer additional security/privacy mechanisms to the user. However, add-ons are based on a community of developers and do not have the same popularity in the different browser ecosystems. As a result, some add-ons that are valuable at protecting users' security and privacy (e.g. NoScript) are not available in some of the browsers (e.g. Internet Explorer).

In this context, our work provides a comprehensive analysis of the availability of security and/or privacy controls, which are pre-installed in modern browsers. In addition, we survey the available security and/or privacy add-ons of each browser and examine whether they cover the identified gaps of the browsers' controls, when one or more security controls are not offered. Our work reveals that browsers differentiate a lot concerning both the availability of the provided security controls and the corresponding add-ons.

The rest of the paper is structured as follows. Section 2 presents the related work. Section 3 includes the methodology of our research. Section 4 depicts the results of our findings. Section 5 includes a discussion of the results and Sect. 6 consists of our conclusions.

2   Related Work

In this paper we examine the security and privacy protection that is offered by the add-ons of the most popular desktop browsers. Former literature has examined the availability of controls in the above mentioned browsers (e.g. Safari, Chrome, etc.). Our previous work [2] surveyed the availability and manageability of the available pre-installed security controls of modern browsers, in both desktop and mobile devices. This work expands our previous one.

Botha et al. in [3] provide a simple comparison of the availability of security options in Internet Explorer 7 and Internet Explorer Mobile (for Windows Mobile 6 Professional Ed.). Furthermore, [4] focuses on the visibility of security indicators in smartphones. Carlini et al. performed a security review of 100 Google Chrome's extensions, which resulted in 70 located vulnerabilities across 40 of the total extensions examined [5].

In addition, [6] proposed a privacy preserving mechanism called "SpyShield", which enhances spyware protection by detecting malicious add-ons, that aim to monitor sensitive information. The authors tested the above mentioned mechanism on the Internet Explorer browser.

Kapravelos et al. in [7] presented similar work that focused on detecting malicious behavior of browser extensions. Such an approach included monitoring the execution phase of such extensions in correlation with the corresponding network activity, in order to detect any anomalies.

Lastly, the authors in [8] analyzed 25 of the most popular Firefox's extensions. They have found that 88 % of them need less than the full set of the available privileges and they have proposed a novel extension system that enforces the least privilege principle.

3 Methodology

3.1 Security and Privacy Controls

The scope of our analysis includes the popular browsers for Windows desktops, i.e. Chrome (v. 41), Firefox (v. 36), Internet Explorer 11, Opera (v. 27), and Safari (v. 5.1.7). Table 1 includes the popularity of each browser, until March 2015 [9]:

Table 1. Browsers user base

Browser	User base (%)
Chrome	63.7 %
Firefox	22.1 %
Internet Explorer	7.7 %
Safari	3.9 %
Opera	1.5 %

The browsers were installed in a workstation running Windows 7, which is the most commonly used operating system (52.3 %) [9]. Then, we enumerated the browsers graphical interfaces and any available hidden menus (e.g. *"about:config"* in Firefox) in order to collect which security controls are offered in each browser.

3.2 Security and Privacy Add-Ons

We visited each browser's add-on repository, so as to identify the available security and privacy add-ons. To this end, we visited the add-on repository of Safari [10], Chrome [11], Internet Explorer [12], Firefox [13] and Opera [14] and enumerated their add-ons. Then, we grouped the add-ons' categories and mapped each add-on to one category, based on the add-ons functionality (i.e. services and features offered). Some add-ons have been grouped in more than one categories, as they provide multiple functionality. For the mapping of the add-ons functionality we used the following taxonomy[1]:

1. **Content filtering:** Block content (advertisements, cookies, images, pop-ups, etc.)
2. **Parental control:** Includes traffic filters to block websites containing inappropriate material[2]
3. **Passwords:**
   a. **Generators:** Generation of strong passwords
   b. **Managers:** Creation of a master password and password management

---

[1] Categories marked with 1, 2, 3... are the 1st level categories, while those marked with a, b, c... are the 2nd level categories (i.e. sub-categories).

[2] Apart from the parental control functionality, since such sites often include malware, this control can protect users' security and privacy.

4. **Plain proxy:** Simple proxy without any encryption included
5. **Privacy:** Privacy protection add-ons (e.g. privacy settings manager)
6. **Protection from rogue websites:**
   a. **Antivirus blacklists:** Websites providing online antivirus scans of files for malicious software (e.g. Virus Total [15])
   b. **Malware blacklists:** Websites providing blacklists blocking malicious content (e.g. MalwareDomains [16])
   c. **Phishing blacklists:** Websites providing blacklists blocking phishing attacks (e.g. PhishTank [17])
   d. **Reputation blacklists:** Websites providing blacklists blocking pages based on their reputation (e.g. Web Of Trust [18])
   e. **Sandbox:** Analysis of downloaded files for malicious software (e.g. Dr. Web LinkChecker [19])
7. **Third-party software management:** Blocking third-party software (e.g. Flash, Java, JavaScript, etc.)
8. **Tracking:** Blocking website(s) that track user's online behavior
   a. **Social Media (SM) redirection:** Blocking the visited website from redirecting the user to a social media website
9. **Traffic encryption via proxy:** Proxy that encrypts user's traffic.

4 Results

4.1 Revisiting Pre-installed Security Controls

In our previous work [2], we examined the availability and manageability of security controls offered by popular smartphone and desktop browsers. The availability of those controls is re-examined to highlight any changes that may exist in the latest browsers' versions. The results of our work are summarized in Table 2, using the following notation: (i) ☒ is used when the security control is not offered whereas (ii) ■ is used when the browser offered the security control. Also, the following acronyms are used for the browsers: AS = Apple Safari, GC = Google Chrome, IE = Internet Explorer, MF = Mozilla Firefox and OP = Opera.

Opera modified three of its controls in its latest version: the *"master password"* and the *"SSL/TLS version selection"* controls, both of which were available in the past and are now removed. While, the same browser altered one of the available controls of this category, i.e. the *"manually update extensions"* control, which was not available in the past. Also, Chrome added a *"master password"*, which was previously unavailable. Finally, Firefox no longer provides the reporting control for rogue websites and Opera removed both *"modify user-agent"* and *"website checking"* controls.

The last two rows of Table 2 include the amount of unavailable controls in each browser from a total of 32 controls, and the percentage of those, respectively. Indicatively, Safari did not implemented 34.4 % of the surveyed controls, while Firefox offered the majority of the controls that are examined herein.

The availability of a control does not offer, though, any guarantees regarding the security offered. The scope of this paper does not include the accuracy or precision of

Table 2.   Availability of controls (n = 32)

Browsers	AS	GC	IE	MF	OP
Content controls					
Block cookies	■	■	■	■	
Block images	■	■	■	■	
Block pop-ups	■	■	■	■	
Privacy controls					
Block location data	■	■	■	■	
Block referrer	☒	■	☒	■	☒
Block third-party cookies	■	■	■	■	
Enable DNT	■	■	■	■	
History manager	■	■	■	■	
Private browsing	■	■	■	■	
Browser management controls					
Browser update	☒	■	■	■	
Certificate manager	■	■	■	■	
Master password	☒	■	☒	■	☒
Proxy server	■	■	■	■	
Search engine manager	■	■	■	■	
SSL/TLS version selection	☒	☒	■	■	☒
Task manager	☒	■	☒	☒	
Third-party software controls					
Auto update extensions	■	■	■	■	
Auto update plugins	☒	☒	☒	☒	☒
Disable extension	■	■	■	■	
Disable Java	■	■	■	■	
Disable JavaScript	■	■	■	■	
Disable plugin	■	■	■	■	
External plugin check	☒	☒	☒	■	☒
Manually update extensions	■	■	☒	■	
Manually update plugins	☒	■	☒	■	☒
Web browsing controls					
Certificate warning	■	■	■	■	
Local blacklist	☒	■	■	■	
Malware protection	■	■	■	■	
Modify user-agent	■	■	■	■	☒
Phishing protection	■	■	■	■	
Report rogue Website	☒	☒	■	☒	
Website checking	☒	☒	■	☒	☒
☒ =	11	5	7	4	8
% =	34.4%	15.65%	21.9%	12.5%	25%

these controls. However, the relevant literature has explored this area. For instance the authors in [20–22] evaluated phishing and malware protection controls provided by popular mobile browsers in Android and iOS and desktop browsers in Windows.

4.2   Survey of Browsers Add-Ons

The amount of security and/or privacy add-ons offered by each browser, up to April 2015, is depicted in Table 3. We tested only a subset of the add-ons offered by Chrome (65) and Firefox (65), based on user popularity, so as to end up with almost the same amount of tested add-ons in all browsers. All the available add-ons, that were included in the rest of the browsers, were tested. Thus, we examined a total of 227 add-ons. The list of the examined add-ons is available in the paper's Appendix. Chrome did not offer a specific category, so we found relevant add-ons with the use of specific keywords for each of the proposed categories (e.g. privacy, tracking, passwords, etc.). The add-ons were selected again based on user popularity.

Table 3.   Available security/privacy add-ons per browser

Browser	Security and/or privacy add-ons
Safari	38
Chrome	N/A[a]
Internet Explorer	7
Firefox	1327
Opera	52

[a]GC does not group security add-ons in one category, which so the total number of security add-ons is unknown.

The mapping between the available categories and the add-ons is not one-to-one, as some add-ons offer mechanisms for more than one of the categories. Moreover, the tests were conducted from January to April 2015 therefore it is possible that some add-ons might have been altered (e.g. deleted or added).

Figures 1, 2, 3, 4 and 5 summarize the results regarding the security/privacy add-ons that were found in each category[3]. Each figure indicates the percentage of the total security/privacy add-ons, in each browser. The sum the percentages of security/privacy add-ons in Figs. 1, 2, 3, 4 and 5 might exceeds 100 %, since one add-on may belong in more than one category, based on the features it offers (e.g. tracking protection and a proxy service). Additionally, Table 4 (see Appendix) depicts the add-ons of each category provided by surveyed browsers and the names of the examined add-ons are included in the Appendix.

---

[3] 2nd level categories (e.g. password manager, etc.) are included in Table 4 of the Appendix, and not depicted in this section.

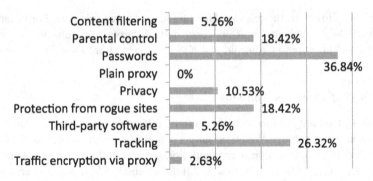

Fig. 1. Available add-ons in Safari (n = 38)

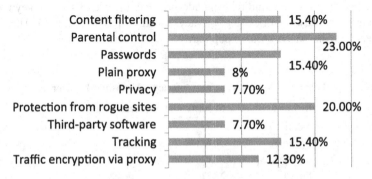

Fig. 2. Available add-ons in Chrome (n = 65)

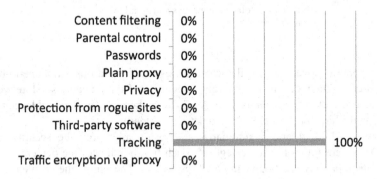

Fig. 3. Available add-ons in Internet Explorer (n = 7)

5   Discussion

5.1   Revisiting Pre-installed Security Controls

Our analysis showed that all browsers provide the content controls, while the second category (i.e. privacy controls) does not include the "block referrer" control in the

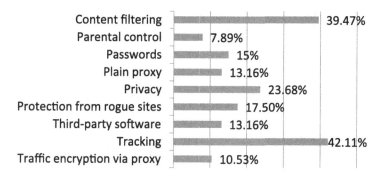

Fig. 4. Available add-ons in Firefox (n = 65)

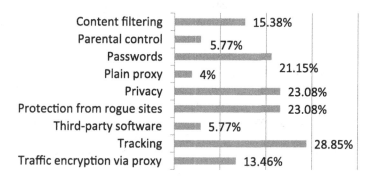

Fig. 5. Available add-ons in Opera (n = 52)

majority of the tested browsers. Thus, the HTTP value in the header is most of the times transmitted and can be collected by malicious entities that aim to track users.

Browser management controls were not available in the majority of the browsers. More specifically, most of the browsers did not support the use of a master password, the selection of the SSL/TLS version and a task manager. None of them offered an auto-update function for the included plugins, while most of them failed to provide manual updates or external checks for those plugins. These are important in terms of acquiring the latest updates, which often include security patches.

Only a few browsers offered reporting rogue websites, although IE was the only one to provide a website checking control. Such an approach is clearly a major drawback, in terms of not offering a checking service for possible rogue websites and so, the user is exposed to malicious sites.

In the rest of this section, we discuss the security gaps in terms of non implemented controls, that were found in each browser:

Safari: As summarized in Table 2, 34.4 % of the surveyed controls were not implemented, and thus AS does not offer an adequate level of security. From those controls, the most critical are summarized as follows: the browser lacks a master password service and thus the user cannot manage the installed passwords in the browser.

Table 4. Number of add-ons in each browser (n = 227)

1st level	2nd level	AS	GC	IE	MF	OP
Content filtering	–	7	15	0	17	18
Parental control	–	2	10	0	4	53
Passwords	–	14	10	0	6	41
	Generators	4	6	0	4	20
	Managers	14	7	0	5	32
Plain proxy	–	0	5	0	6	12
Privacy	–	4	5	0	10	30
Protection from rogue websites	–	7	13	0	8	39
	Antivirus	2	3	0	3	10
	Malware	4	5	0	3	17
	Phishing	4	2	0	2	11
	Reputation	2	7	0	3	17
	Sandbox	2	3	0	3	8
Third-party software	–	2	5	0	6	15
Tracking	–	10	10	7	17	53
	SM redirection	3	0	0	0	5
Traffic encryption via proxy	–	1	8	0	5	20
Total		**38**	**65**	**7**	**65**	**52**

Also, there is no blacklist mechanism available to filter websites based on reputation, and no reporting services if the user wants to check a visited website regarding its legitimacy. In addition, there is no SSL/TLS version selection option available, and as a result the user cannot upgrade the mechanism to its latest version.

Chrome: We had similar results to Safari. Once more, there is lack of SSL/TLS version selection and no reporting or checking mechanisms regarding the websites visited by the user. Thus, the user is unable to check a visited website whether it is malicious or not.

Internet Explorer: It does not offer a master password service and the option to block the referrer. Moreover, there were not available controls regarding the manual update of the browser's features (i.e. extensions and plugins). Finally, the user cannot use an external source to check the included plugins, a feature that is currently offered only by MF.

Firefox: As summarized in Table 2, Firefox provides the highest number of available controls. In addition, its community offers the highest amount of available add-ons, regarding security and/or privacy (i.e. 1327, April 2015). The only security limitation of Firefox's was the absence a reputation based mechanism to filter the visited websites, as discussed in the Safari browser.

Opera: It was the second less secure browser (after IE) with regards to the availability of security controls. Almost all of the unavailable controls were similar to the AS, except the "modify user-agent" control, which was not provided by Opera.

5.2   Survey of Add-Ons

The analysis revealed that all browsers except for GC and IE offered a 1st level categorization dedicated for security and or privacy add-ons. More specifically, Safari provided *Security*, Firefox and Opera provided *Privacy & Security*. Chrome and IE did not, and as a result we manually searched for the security and privacy add-ons. This confusing structure/organization of add-ons may result in confusing the users when searching for any useful (with respect to the provided security) add-on. For example, Chrome classified a popular add blocker add-on (i.e. AdBlock Plus [23]) in the "search & browsing tools" category, which does not encourage the user to install the application.

Additionally, none of the browsers offered a 2nd level categorization (e.g. passwords, malware protection, VPNs, etc.). Such approach, could be proven beneficial for users, since they could be searching for specific add-ons only in.

All of the browsers provided an adequate description of each add-on, except Safari, which only provided a short paragraph. Thus, the user had to visit the developer's website to find additional information regarding the add-on(s).

In the rest of this subsection, we discuss the results of our analysis, concerning the available add-ons in each browser's repository:

Safari: As Fig. 1 depicts, Safari's community clearly covers almost every one of the surveyed categories. Its main focus is two-fold: offering password services for password generation and management (36.84 %), and protecting the user from tracking (26.32 %). These two pose as the community's highest priorities. Note that the first category was one the browser's gap, in terms of unavailable controls. Next, Safari's add-ons focus in website filtering protection, i.e. parental control and rogue sites' filtering (both at 18.42 %). Thus, they protect the user from visiting websites that contain malicious or offensive content that covers the second security gap as well. The other categories were partially covered by Safari's community, with the highest being the "privacy" category (10.53 %) and the lowest being the "plain proxy", which is not covered.

Chrome: According to Fig. 2, Chrome provides add-ons in each of the surveyed categories, thus, satisfied the unavailable controls that we have been identified in this work. More specifically, the browser's community focuses on offering parental control services (23 %) and rogue sites filtering mechanisms (20 %), therefore succeeding in protecting the user against malicious websites. Moreover, Chrome offers add-ons that provide the user with content blocking mechanisms, password services and tracking blocking services (all with a 15.4 % availability). This suggests that the Chrome community considers those services almost as equal of importance as the highest priorities, as discussed above. All the other categories, were partially covered by Chrome's community, with the highest being the "traffic encryption via proxy" category reaching 12.3 %, while the rest of the categories have a 7.7 % availability. Note that this applies only to the current tested subset, which includes a part of the most popular add-ons of the browser, based on user popularity.

Internet Explorer: Internet Explorer offers only 7 security and/or privacy add-ons. All of them focus on tracking protection and, thus, all the categories that are not covered by the browser's controls, are unprotected by the offered add-ons as well. As a result, Internet Explorer's add-ons fail to provide the unavailable security and/or privacy protection.

Firefox: According to Fig. 4, Firefox browser fully covers not only the unavailable controls, but the total categories (and sub-categories) of the add-ons. More specifically, the browser's highest priorities are tracking protection (42.11 %) and content filtering services (39.47 %). As a result, the user is able to block both tracking websites that aim in accessing sensitive information and content elements (e.g. pop-ups) that could either annoy or harm the user (e.g. phishing content). Also, all the other categories are again adequately covered, while varying from 23.68 % (privacy) to 7.89 % (parental control). Overall, Firefox succeeds in offering almost a full set of both controls and add-ons regarding the surveyed categories.

Opera: Despite the controls' unavailability, Opera offered a variety of add-ons regarding all the tested categories. Four categories clearly pose as Opera's main focus: tracking blocking services (28.85), privacy and protection from rogue sites (both at 23.08 %) and password services (21.15 %). The rest of categories were partially covered by Opera's community, with the highest being the "content filtering" category reaching 15.38 % and the lowest being the "plain proxy" one, which is located at 3.85 %. Overall, Opera may not offer a complete set of security and privacy controls, but such a feature is clearly covered by the browser's community regarding the available add-ons.

Overall availability of add-ons

Figure 6 summarizes the above. It reveals the overall focus of the community that provides security-oriented add-ons in the browser ecosystem.

As Fig. 6 suggests, *"tracking"* and *"content filtering"* categories include 25 % of the most popular, security-oriented add-ons. This suggests that the highest priority in the browsing ecosystem is enhancing the protection of the user from malicious entities who aim to violate users' privacy. In parallel, the community aims to offer filtering services for content elements (i.e. cookies, advertisements, images and pop-ups), which could either create annoyance or include malicious software (e.g. phishing, scam) that harm the user.

After that, there are the *"passwords"* and *"protection from rogue websites"* categories, which hold 19.34 % and 18.4 % respectively. The former category includes password oriented services, i.e. *managers* (15.1 %) and *generators* (9.43 %), and covers the identified gap, since almost all modern web browsers (except Firefox) do not offer such a control. The latter, includes protection based on\against: *malware* (8.02 %), *reputation* (8.02 %), *phishing* (5.19 %) *antivirus* (4.72 %) and *sandbox* (3.77 %). Such services aim in protecting the user from malicious websites.

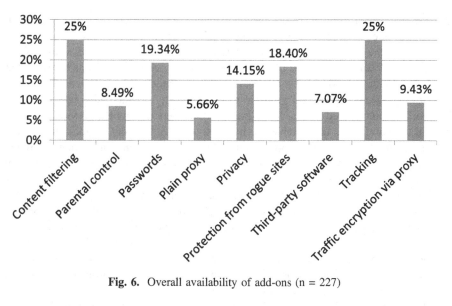

Fig. 6. Overall availability of add-ons (n = 227)

The *"privacy"* category includes privacy oriented contents (e.g. autofill forms, cache, location, etc.). Those can either be blocked or cleared (e.g. cache cleaner), so as not to be monitored by an unauthorized entity. This category includes 14.15 % of the surveyed add-ons.

The remaining four categories are located just below 10 %. More specifically, in descending order: *traffic encryption via proxy* (9.43 %), *parental control* (8.49 %), *third-party software* (7.07 %) and *plain proxy* (5.66 %). The first and last category reveal the need to use a proxy service to either access any region protected content, or hide user's identity for tracking protection. The *"parental control"* category includes website filtering to block any inappropriate material[4]. Finally, the last surveyed category (i.e. *third-party software*) allows the management (i.e. blocking, enabling) of third-party software: flash, java, javascript, etc., in order to protect the user from services that are not built-in the browser, since malicious content may be included.

6   Conclusions

The paper provides a comprehensive analysis of the available security and privacy controls that are pre-installed in popular desktop web browsers. It also provided a comparative evaluation of the availability of security-oriented add-ons in each desktop browser. This paper extends our previous work [2] and examines the security controls (both, pre-installed and third-party add-ons) that are available in modern desktop browsers.

---

[4] Pornographic or gambling material.

We analyzed a total of 32 pre-installed security-oriented controls and found that Firefox provided the majority of them (i.e. 84.4 %). Safari offered only 65.6 % of the controls and the availability of the controls in the rest of the browsers varied (from approx. 71–85 %). The analysis of the available security-oriented add-ons revealed that Firefox and Chrome provided a plethora of security and/or privacy oriented add-ons. The other browsers had in total approximately 50 security-oriented add-ons only, while Internet Explorer offered only seven. Almost all browsers (except IE) provided add-ons that fill the gap for the unavailable pre-installed security controls. In addition, already existing controls (e.g. malware protection, master password, etc.) are enhanced by the availability of add-ons, if the user chooses not to only trust the browser's built-in mechanisms.

The analysis reveals that web browsers can enhance the grouping of the available security-oriented add-ons. That holds true as all browsers, except GC and IE, offered only a 1st level categorization. The absence of this add-on grouping hinders users' searches for add-ons that enhance their security. However, none of the browsers offered additional subgroups (2nd level categorization), which could further enhance user's search results when looking for a specific subcategory of an add-on (e.g. password generators). In this work, we provide such a taxonomy of add-on categories.

Our analysis focuses on the availability of security oriented controls. However, their performance is not in the scope of this paper. Another limitation of our work is that new security controls and add-ons may be added to browsers or the popularity of the addons might change. While, some add-ons could include security features even if they were not categorized as security and/or privacy add-ons and thus were out of scope. Also, in Chrome and Firefox only the 65 most popular add-ons, in order to have a consistent comparison with the rest browser that had only approximately 35 addons on average. In future work we plan to extend our work by increasing the number of addons that have been surveyed, as well as measure the effectiveness and performance of security controls (pre-installed and addons). Also we plan to include in our analysis the mobile counterparts of the analyzed browsers.

Appendix

Apple Safari. 1Password, AdBlock Lite, Adblock Plus, Adguard AdBlocker, Avatier Single Sign-On (SSO), Blur, Bonafeyed, Cognisec Workspace Application Helper, Cryptocat, Cryptonify, DisableGoogleRedirect, Dr.Web LinkChecker, Facebook Disconnect, Ghostery, Google Disconnect, HyprKey Authenticator, Incognito, JavaScript Blocker, Keeper - Password and Data Vault, LastPass, Mitto Password Manager, MyPermissions Cleaner, PoliceWEB.net, Redirector, RoboForm Online, SafariSGP, Safe In Cloud, SafeSurf, Search Virustotal.com, Security Plus, SID, Teddy ID Password Manager, Total Defense TrafficLight, TrafficLight, Twitter Disconnect, uBlock, URLFilter, WOT.

Google Chrome. 1Password, AdBlock, Adblock Plus, Adblock Plus Pro, Adblock Super, Ad-blocker for Gmail, Adguard AdBlocker, Adult Blocker, Avast Online

Security, AVG Do Not Track, AVG PrivacyFix, Bitdefender QuickScan, Blockfilter| The Advanced Adult Filter, Blocksi Web Filter, Blur, Browsec, Cache Killer, Clear Cache, Clear Cache Shortcut, CommonKey Team Password Manager, Cookie Manager, CyberGhost VPN, Deadbolt Password Generator, Do Not Track, DotVPN, Dr. Web Anti-Virus Link Checker, EditThisCookie, eSafely, Falcon Proxy, FlashControl, FreeMyBrowser, Ghostery, Hide Images, HTTPS Everywhere, iNetClean porn filter - protect your family, LastPass, Parental Control App, Parental Controls & Web Filter from MetaCert, Passter Password Manager, Password Hasher Plus, PasswordBox, Privacy Badger, Privacy Guardr, Privacy manager, Proxy Auto Auth, Proxy Era, Proxy Helper, Proxy SwitchyOmega, Proxy SwitchySharp, ScriptBlock, ScriptSafe, Secure Downloader, Secure Passwords, Security Plus, Simple JavaScript Toggle, Simply Block Ads!, StopItKids parental control, Strong Password Generator, Swap My Cookies, Vanilla Cookie Manager, VTchromizer, WebFilter Pro, Webmail Ad Blocker, YouDeemIt - Parental Advice System, ZenMate Security & Privacy VPN.

Internet Explorer. EasyList Standard, EasyPrivacy, Indonesian EasyList, PrivacyChoice - all companies, PrivacyChoice - Block companies without NAI, Stop Google Tracking, TRUSTe.

Mozilla Firefox. Ad Killer, Adblock Edge, AdBlock for Firefox, AdBlock Lite, Adblock Plus, Adblock Plus Pop-up Addon, Advanced Cookie Manager, anonymoX, Anti-Porn Pro, Autofill Forms, AutoProxy, AVG Do Not Track, BetterPrivacy, Bitdefender QuickScan, BlockSite, Bluhell Firewall, Blur, BugMeNot, Censure Block, Clear Console, Click&Clean, Cookie Monster, Cookies Manager+, Disable Anti-Adblock, Disconnect, Dr.Web LinkChecker, DuckDuckGo Plus, Empty Cache Button, Facebook Disconnect, FB Phishing Protector, Flash Block, Flash Control, friGate, Ghostery, Google Privacy, Google search link fix, Hide My Ass! Web Proxy, JavaScript Deobfuscator, KeeFox, LastPass Password Manager, Lightbeam for Firefox, McAfee Security Scan Plus detection, Modify Headers, Multifox, NO Google Analytics, NoScript Security Suite, Password Exporter, Private Tab, ProCon Latte Content Filter, ProxTube - Unblock YouTube, Public Fox, QuickJava, RefControl, RequestPolicy, Saved Password Editor, Self-Destructing Cookies, SSL Version Control, Stealthy, Strict Pop-up Blocker, Tamper Data, User Agent Overrider, Web of Trust, WorldIP, YesScript, ZenMate Security & Privacy VPN.

Opera. Ghostery, ZenMate, WOT, LastPass, Dr.Web Link Checker, DotVPN, HTTPS Everywhere, History Eraser, Avira Browser Safety, Browsec, Disconnect, CyberGhost VPN, Blur, AVG PrivacyFix, VPN.S HTTP Proxy, MyPermissions Cleaner, HideMy Ass, PasswordBox, Adult Blocker, Google Analytics Opt-out, Cryptocat, History On/Off, RoboForm Lite Password Manager, μMatrix, Location Guard, Blocksi, SingleClick Cleaner, Security Plus, SimpleClear, Facebook Redirect Fixer, Stop-it, SafeBrowser, Show passwords, Local pass store, BlocksiLite, Show Password, Cobra Online Security ATD, Disconnect Privacy Icons, Cookie Jar, IvlogSafe, Blockfilter, KANOPE, Google Safe Browsing, Filter request headers, Twitter Redirect Fixer, PasswordMaker Pro, Certified Messages, Floodwatch, vPass, Limitlesslane, LogMote, PreferSafe.

References

1. Securelist.com: Financial cyber threats in 2014: Things changed - Securelist (2015). http://securelist.com/analysis/kaspersky-security-bulletin/68720/financial-cyber-threats-in-2014-things-changed/. Accessed 10 Apr 2015
2. Mylonas, A., Tsalis, N., Gritzalis, D.: Evaluating the manageability of web browsers controls. In: Accorsi, R., Ranise, S. (eds.) STM 2013. LNCS, vol. 8203, pp. 82–98. Springer, Heidelberg (2013)
3. Botha, R., Furnell, S., Clarke, N.: From desktop to mobile: examining the security experience. Comput. Secur. 28(3–4), 130–137 (2009)
4. Amrutkar, C., Traynor, P., van Oorschot, P.C.: Measuring SSL indicators on mobile browsers: extended life, or end of the road? In: Gollmann, D., Freiling, F.C. (eds.) ISC 2012. LNCS, vol. 7483, pp. 86–103. Springer, Heidelberg (2012)
5. Carlini, N., Felt, A., Wagner, D.: An evaluation of the google chrome extension security architecture. In: 21st USENIX Conference on Security, USA (2012)
6. Li, Z., Wang, X.-F., Choi, J.Y.: SpyShield: preserving privacy from spy add-ons. In: Kruegel, C., Lippmann, R., Clark, A. (eds.) RAID 2007. LNCS, vol. 4637, pp. 296–316. Springer, Heidelberg (2007)
7. Kapravelos, A., Grier, C., Chachra, N., Kruegel, C., Vigna, G., Paxson, V.: Hulk: eliciting malicious behavior in browser extensions. In: 23rd USENIX Security Symposium (USENIX Security 2014). USENIX Association, USA (2014)
8. Barth, A., Felt, A.P., Saxena, P., Boodman, A.: Protecting browsers from extension vulnerabilities. In: 17th Network and Distributed System Security Symposium (NDSS 2010), USA (2009)
9. W3schools.com: Browser Statistics (2015). http://www.w3schools.com/browsers/browsers_stats.asp. Accessed 10 Apr 2015
10. Extensions.apple.com: Apple - Safari - Safari Extensions Gallery (2015). https://extensions.apple.com/. Accessed 10 Apr 2015
11. Chrome.google.com: Chrome Web Store (2015). https://chrome.google.com/webstore/category/extensions. Accessed 10 Apr 2015
12. Internet Explorer Gallery (2015). http://www.iegallery.com/PinnedSites. Accessed 10 Apr 2015
13. Addons.mozilla.org: Add-ons for Firefox (2015). https://addons.mozilla.org/en-US/firefox/. Accessed 10 Apr 2015
14. Opera add-ons (2015). https://addons.opera.com/en/. Accessed 10 Apr 2015
15. Virustotal.com: VirusTotal - Free Online Virus, Malware and URL Scanner (2015). https://www.virustotal.com/. Accessed 10 Apr 2015
16. Malwaredomains.com: DNS-BH – Malware Domain Blocklist (2015). http://www.malwaredomains.com/. Accessed 25 Apr 2015
17. Phishtank.com: PhishTank|Join the fight against phishing (2015). https://www.phishtank.com/. Accessed 25 Apr 2015
18. Ltd. W: Safe Browsing Tool|WOT (Web of Trust) (2015). In: Mywot.com. https://www.mywot.com/. Accessed 25 Apr 2015
19. LinkChecker, D.: Dr.Web LinkChecker (2013). In: Addons.mozilla.org. https://addons.mozilla.org/en-US/firefox/addon/drweb-anti-virus-link-checker/?src=search. Accessed 25 Apr 2015
20. Virvilis, N., Tsalis, N., Mylonas, A., Gritzalis, D.: Mobile devices: a phisher's paradise. In: 11th International Conference on Security and Cryptography (SECRYPT 2014), pp. 79–87. ScitePress, Austria

21. Virvilis, N., Mylonas, A., Tsalis, N., Gritzalis, D.: Security busters: web browser security vs. rogue sites. Comput. Secur. **52**, 90–105 (2015)
22. Tsalis, N., Virvilis, N., Mylonas, A., Apostolopoulos, A., Gritzalis, D.: Browser blacklists: a utopia of phishing protection. In: Security and Cryptography (2015)
23. Chrome.google.com: Adblock Plus (2015). https://chrome.google.com/webstore/detail/adblock-plus/afkdehgifkgjdcdlbfkjnmaeagepfbgp?hl=en. Accessed 25 Apr 2015

MBotCS: A Mobile Botnet Detection System Based on Machine Learning

Xin Meng[✉] and George Spanoudakis

Department of Computer Science, City University London, London, UK
{xin.meng.1, g.e.spanoudakis}@city.ac.uk

Abstract. As the use of mobile devices spreads dramatically, hackers have started making use of mobile botnets to steal user information or perform other malicious attacks. To address this problem, in this paper we propose a mobile botnet detection system, called MBotCS. MBotCS can detect mobile device traffic indicative of the presence of a mobile botnet based on prior training using machine learning techniques. Our approach has been evaluated using real mobile device traffic captured from Android mobile devices, running normal apps and mobile botnets. In the evaluation, we investigated the use of 5 machine learning classifier algorithms and a group of machine learning box algorithms with different validation schemes. We have also evaluated the effect of our approach with respect to its effect on the overall performance and battery consumption of mobile devices.

Keywords: Android · Mobile botnet · Security · Machine learning

1 Introduction

Recently, the use of mobile devices such as smartphones and tablets has increased impressively. According to Cisco, 497 million new mobile devices and connections were sold in 2014 [9]. Other recent reports forecast that mobile-cellular subscriptions will be more than 7bn by the end of 2015 [21]. Market reports also show that since 2012 Google's Android operating system has overtaken other smartphone operating systems and accounted for more than 80 % share of market in 2014. Along with the growth in the use of mobile devices, there have also been a growing number of mobile malware systems, often in the form of mobile botnets. According to KASPERSKY [8], a mobile botnet is defined as a collection of applications, which are connected through a network and communicate with each other and a remote server (known as the "botmaster") in order to perform orchestrated attacks (e.g., remotely executed commands, information stealing, SMS dispatching). According to [8], 148,778 mobile malware applications had been detected at the end of 2013 and nearly 62 % of them were part of mobile botnets. The first mobile botnet was an iPhone botnet, known as *iKee.B* [17], which was traced back in 2009. *iKee.B* was not a particularly harmful botnet because iOS is a closed system. Unlike it, Android, which is an open system, has become a major target for mobile botnet creators. *Geinimi* was the first Android botnet that was discovered in 2010 [37]. Other Android botnets include *Android.Troj.mdk*, i.e., a Trojan found in more than 7,000 apps that has infected more than a 1 m mobile

© Springer International Publishing Switzerland 2016
C. Lambrinoudakis and A. Gabillon (Eds.): CRiSIS 2015, LNCS 9572, pp. 274–291, 2016.
DOI: 10.1007/978-3-319-31811-0_17

users in China, and *NotCompatible.C*, i.e., a Trojan targeting protected enterprise networks [27]. Research on mobile botnets (see [16] for related surveys) has looked at device specific botnet detection [22] as well as mobile botnet implementation principles and architectures for creating mobile botnets [11, 34].

In this paper, we describe a proactive approach for detecting unknown mobile botnets that we have implemented for Android devices. Our approach is based on the analysis of traffic data of Android mobile devices using machine learning (ML) techniques and can be realised through an architecture involving traffic monitors and controllers installed on them. The use of ML for detecting mobile botnets has, to the best of our knowledge, also been explored in [12]. However, this study has had some methodological ambiguities. These were related to the exact data set used and, most importantly, to whether the trained ML algorithms were tested against traffic generated by previously unseen botnets or upon a traffic set involving new traffic from botnets that were also used to generate traffic in the training set. Furthermore, to the best of our knowledge, so far there has been no implementation of ML detectors running on the mobile device itself neither any evaluation of the impact that this would have on the mobile device (the study in [12] focused on evaluating the performance of the detector learning process).

The experimental study that we report in this paper has been aimed to overcome the above limitations and investigate a number of additional factors, notably: (a) the merit of aggregate ML classifiers, (b) the sensitivity of the detection capability of ML detectors on different types of botnet families, and (c) the actual cost of using ML detectors on mobile devices in terms of execution efficiency and battery consumption. Furthermore, our study has been based on a mobile botnet detection system that we implemented and deployed on a mobile device.

The rest of this paper is organised as follows. Section 2 reviews related work. Section 3 describes the architecture of MBotCS. Section 4 presents the design of our experiments and Sect. 5 gives an analysis of the results obtained from them. Finally, Sect. 6 outlines conclusions and plans for future work.

2 Related Work

Existing research has focused on detecting general types of mobile malware and mobile botnets. Research on general types of mobile malware is more extensive than research on mobile botnets. In the following, we review these two strands of research, separately.

2.1 Special Mobile Botnet Detection Techniques

Mobile botnet detection has been studied by Vural et al. [31, 32]. In [31], the authors propose a detection technique based on network forensics and give a list of fuzzy metrics for building SMS (short message service) behavior profiles to use in detection. This approach was improved by introducing detection based on artificial immune system principles in [32]. Another system, which can perform dynamic behavioral analysis of Android malware automatically, is *Copper-Droid* [18].

Seo et al. [22] have developed a static analysis tool, called *DroidAnalyser*, to identify potential vulnerabilities of Android apps and root exploits. This tool processes mobile behaviour in two stages: (a) it checks them against suspicious signatures and (b) it searches app code using pre-fixed keywords. Using (a) and (b), *DroidAnalyser* can provide warnings before installing an application on a mobile device. However, it cannot detect malware infection from runtime behaviour. Other detection systems, which are based static analysis, include *SandDroid* [30] and *MobileSandbox* [26].

2.2 General Mobile Malware Detection Techniques

Some of the methods generated for the detection of general mobile malware, can also detect some of the mobile botnets. A monitor of Symbian OS and Windows Mobile smartphone that extracts features for anomaly detection has, for example, been used to monitor logs and detect normal and infected traffic in [21]. However, this system does not run on a mobile device itself.

The approach in [2] includes a static analysis system for analysing Android market applications and uses automated reverse engineering and refactoring of binary application packages to mitigate security and privacy threats driven by security preferences of the user. The approach is based on a probabilistic diffusion scheme using device usage patterns [1]. The *Android Application Sandbox* [4] has also been used for both static and dynamic analysis on Android programs and for detecting suspicious applications automatically based on the collaborative detection [20]. This assumes that if the neighbours of a device are infected, the device itself is likely to be infected.

Zhou et al. [35] have developed an approach for detecting "piggybacked" Android applications (i.e., applications that contain destructive payloads or malware code) using: (a) *a module decoupling technique* that partitions the source code of an application into primary and non-primary modules and (b) a *feature fingerprint technique* that extracts various semantic features (from primary modules) and converts them into feature vectors. They have collected more than 1,200 malware samples of Android malware families and characterised them systematically using these techniques.

Shabtai et al. [23] proposed a knowledge-based approach for detecting known classes of Android mobile malware based on temporal behavior patterns. The basic idea is to train a classifier to detect different types of applications based on application features. This approach has been implemented in *Andromaly* [24], and was subsequently improved with Knowledge-based Temporal Abstractions (KBTA) [25]. KBTAs were used to derive context-specific interpretations of applications from timed behavior data.

3   MBotCS System

MBotCS is based on the architecture shown in the left part of Fig. 1. As shown in the figure, MBotCS has 4 main components: the *traffic data pre-processor*, *machine learning analyser* (ML analyser), *user interface* and the *training dataset*. It also uses *tPacketCapture* [29] and *Gsam Battery Monitor* [28] to capture mobile traffic and monitor the mobile battery consumption, respectively. All the traffic passing through the mobile device is captured by *tPacketCapture* and stored in the *pcap* file on the SDcard of mobile device. The *traffic data pre-processor* reads the *pcap* file periodically and converts any incremental data in it into the standard structure file for the *ML analyser*. The *ML analyser* trains the classifiers by the *training dataset* and classifies the captured traffic in real-time as infected or normal. Traffic classifications are shown on the *user interface*, warning the users to block suspicious applications (i.e., applications that generated traffic classified as infected). The ML analyser is re-trained dynamically when new traffic exceeds a given threshold. Users get warnings through a GUI shown in the right part of Fig. 1.

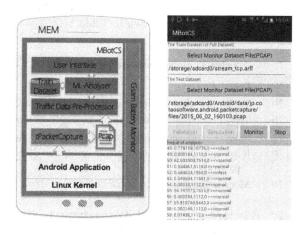

Fig. 1. The overall architecture and the GUI of MBotCS

4 Methodological Setup of the Experiments

The implementation of MBotCS has been used in an initial set of experiments that were carried out to evaluate: (1) the accuracy of the classifications produced by it, and (2) its performance in terms of energy consumption and execution time on Android devices. In this section, we describe the methodological set up of these experiments, whilst their results are presented in Sect. 5.

The experiments involved 3 steps: (1) the capture of mobile device traffic for further analysis (*traffic capture*), (2) the generation of the data set for training and testing the traffic analyser (*dataset generation*), and (3) the experimental use of different ML classifier algorithms as the basis for training the traffic analyser (*classifier analysis*).

4.1 Traffic Capture

The mobile device used in the experiments was a Samsung Note 1st generation (GT-I9228) running Android version 4.1.2 (i.e., *Jelly Bean*). Jelly Bean is the most frequently used version of Android with more 50 % of installations in November 2014 [14]. To avoid interference of other applications, the mobile device used for the experiment was reset to the default Android OS settings before the experiments started.

To collect traffic data, we deployed 12 normal applications and 163 mobile botnet malware applications, grouped into 10 different families. The normal applications that we used were: Chrome, Gmail, Maps, Facebook, Twitter, Feedly, YouTube, Messenger, Skype, PlayNewsstand, Flipboard, and MailDroid. These applications were selected due to their popularity. Also to be certain about their genuineness, all of them were downloaded from the Android Official APP Store (Google Play). The botnet malware applications were selected from the *MalGenome* project [36], according to their level of pandemic risk. MalGenome has collected more than 1200 Android malware applications. The vast majority of these applications (>90 %) are botnets. The botnet malware families that we used are shown in Table 1.

Table 1. Botnet malware families

Malware family	No	Description
1. AnserverBot	20	Trojan that aims to remote control users' cellphones.
2. BaseBridge	20	Trojan attempting to send premium-rate SMS messages.
3. DroidDream	12	It hijacks applications and controls the UI and performs commands.
4. DroidKung Fu3	20	It forwards information to remote server and downloads additional payload.
5. DroidKung Fu4	20	More sophisticated version of DroidKungFu.
6. Geinimi	20	Trojan that opens a back door and transmits information to remote server.
7. GoldDream	20	Trojan that steals information from Android devices.
8. KMin	2	Trojan attempting to send information to a remote server.
9. Pjapps	20	Trojan that opens a back door and retrieves commands from servers.
10. Plankton	9	It forwards information to server and downloads files.

4.2   Dataset Generation

To generate the experimental traffic data, we created two different set ups of the mobile device. The first set up (*set up A*) contained only normal applications. The second set up (*set up B*) contained both normal applications and malware. A device with each of these two set-ups was used to generate traffic, over a 24-h trial period. Over the 24-h period, in the case of *set up A* we carried out 120 transactions using only the normal applications of the set up. The same transactions were also executed at exactly the same time in the trial period of *set up B*, which also lasted 24 h. Our assumption behind this experimental design was that, whilst using the normal applications of *set up B* to carry out the 120 transactions, the mobile botnet malware families that were part of the set up would also be activated by themselves or by their bot master and would generate infected traffic. This assumption was correct as we discuss below.

To capture raw traffic data from the mobile device, we used *tPacketCapture* and stored it in the *pcap* file. The captured *pcap* file was processed to generate a structured dataset for further analysis. In particular, the traffic data in the *pcap* file were processed to extract features that we considered important for the classifier analysis phase, namely the *Source IP Address, Destination IP Address, Protocol, Frame Duration, UDP Packet Size, TCP Packet Size, Stream Index*[1] [7] *and the HTTP Request URL*. To extract these features we used *TShark* [33].

The packet traffic data that were obtained from this step were further processed in order to label them as "normal" or "infected". This step was performed by a script that we developed to compare the mixed traffic file generated by set up B with normal traffic file generated by set up A. More specifically, to label the different packets in the traffic of set up A and set up B, we considered three features of the packets: the *Source IP Address*, the *Destination IP Address* and the used *Protocol*. The set of legitimate (i.e., non-infected) combinations of values of these features was established by analysing the normal traffic data generated from set up A first. These combinations were subsequently expanded further through combinations with legitimate public IP addresses taken from Google Public IP address [13]. Based on this, we generated a three feature pattern-matching library, an extract of which is shown in Table 2. Subsequently, every packet in the mixed traffic generated by set up B was compared with the patterns in the library. If the packet had a combination of values for Source IP Address, Destination IP Address, and Protocol matching a pattern in the library, it was labeled as "normal". Otherwise, it was labeled as "infected".

Table 2. Pattern-matching library

Normal Pattern			Public IP Address Pattern		
Source IP	Destination IP	Protocol	Source IP	Destination IP	Protocol
10.8.0.1	74.125.71.100	6		216.239.32.0	
74.125.71.100	10.8.0.1	6		216.239.32.1	
10.8.0.1	74.125.71.95	6		2.14.192.0	
.....	.....	.....		.....	

Subsequently, we combined the packets with the labels and exported them in *csv* format (a universal dataset format). Furthermore, as TCP traffic is a stream-oriented protocol (i.e., TCP packets are part of instances of integrated communication between a client and a server, known as streams), we also grouped the individual packets into streams, following TCP. This process yielded two separate data sets: (a) the *packet dataset* and (b) the *stream dataset*. The grouping of packets into streams was based on a flag in TCP packets called *Stream Index*, which indicates the communication stream that each packet belongs to. Thus, an element in the stream dataset was formed by assembling all the packets, which had the same stream index. Streams were labeled as

---

[1] Stream index is a number applied to each TCP conversation seen in the traffic file.

"infected" if they had at least one packet within them that had been labeled as "infected", and "normal" otherwise.

A preliminary analysis of the datasets generated by the two set ups indicated that all *domain name system* (DNS) packets, which used the *user datagram protocol* (UDP) had been labeled as normal. Hence, UDP traffic was excluded from further analysis and the training phase focused on TCP traffic only. This was plausible as botnets involve a series of communications between the bot master and the mobile botnets that is based on TCP traffic [6]. Following the packets and stream labeling, the features used for training were: Packets/Stream Frame Duration, Packets/Stream Packet Size, and Arguments Number in HTTP Request URL. Overall, the traffic capture and labeling process produced two datasets for the 3rd phase of our experiments (i.e., the classifier analysis phase): (1) the TCP packets dataset, which included 13652 infected packets and 20715 normal packets; and (2) TCP stream dataset, which included 1043 infected streams and 563 normal streams.

4.3   Classifier Analysis

To analyse the traffic data in the third phase of our experiments, we used 5 supervised machine learning algorithms and a group of machine learning box algorithms. The implementations of these algorithms that use were the ones of WEKA [15], i.e., the open source machine learning analysis toolkit. The algorithms that we used were:

- *Naïve Bayes:* Naïve Bayes is a family of probabilistic classifiers based on applying Bayes' theorem. This family assumes that the features of the data items to be classified are strongly independent [19].
- *Decision Tree (J48):* J48 is a Java implementation of C4.5, i.e., a decision tree based classifier [3].
- *K-nearest neighbour (KNN):* The k-nearest neighbour (KNN) is a non-parametric classifier algorithm. In KNN, an object is assigned to the class that is the most frequent amongst its k nearest neighbours [10].
- *Neural Network (MNN):* Neural network classification algorithms are used in classification problems characterised by a large number of inputs parameters with unknown relationships [5]. Although in our datasets we had a rather small number of packet/stream features, neural networks were used in the interest of completeness. The specific algorithm that we used was the multi-layer perceptron.
- *Support Vector Machine (SMO):* Support Vector Machine is a supervised associated learning algorithm, using Platt's sequential minimal optimization (SMO).

In addition to single algorithms, we used *ML boxing*, a technique where classifications of the individual ML algorithms are aggregated in order to improve the accuracy of results. More specifically, we used three aggregation methods:

- *ML-BOX (AND):* In this aggregate classifier, an instance of the dataset was classified as infected if ALL the individual classifiers indicated it as infected. Otherwise, the instance was classified as normal.

- *ML-BOX (OR):* In this aggregate classifier, an instance of the dataset was classified as infected if AT LEAST ONE the individual classifiers indicated it as infected. Otherwise, the instance was classified as normal.
- *ML-BOX (HALF):* In this aggregate classifier, an instance of the dataset was classified as infected if MORE THAN HALF of the individual classifiers indicated it as infected. Otherwise, the instance was classified as normal.

ML boxing was used to aggregate: (a) the results of all individual classifiers and (b) the results of only J48 and KNN as these algorithms outperformed the rest in the single algorithm based classifications. In the following, we will refer to the outcomes of (a) as "ML-BOX (.)" and the results of (b) as "ML-BOX+(.)". In the case of ML-BOX +(HALF), if the J48 and KNN algorithms classified the instance of dataset in the same class, ML-BOX+(HALF) generated the same common classification. When J48 and KNN were in disagreement, ML-BOX+(HALF) generated a classification based on the outcome of the 3 remaining classifiers only.

To validate the experimental training results, we used 3 validation schemes based on *K-fold cross validation* and *10 % split validation*.

K-fold cross validation is a common technique for estimating the performance of a ML classifier. According to it, in a learning training involving m training examples, the examples are initially arranged in random orders and then they are divided into k folds. A classifier is then trained with examples in all folds but fold $i(i = 1 \dots k)$, and its outcomes are tested using the examples in fold i. Following this training-testing process, the classification error of a classifier is computed by $E = \left(\sum_{i=1 \dots K} n_i \right) / m$ where n_i is the number of the wrongly classified examples in fold i and m is the number of training examples. Based on this scheme, we used 90-10 % 10-fold and 50-50 % 2-fold cross validation, which are two typical validation approaches in ML. Split validation is simpler as it divides the training dataset into two parts, one part containing data used only for training and another part containing data used only for testing. In 90-10 % split validation, 90 % of the data are selected as training dataset and 10 % as the test dataset.

The analysis of the performance of classifiers was also based on two different formulations of the training and test data sets. In the first formulation (*experiment 1*), both the training and the test data sets could include data from the same malware family, although the two data sets were disjoint. Hence, in this experiment, classifiers could have been trained with instances of traffic from a malware family that they needed to detect. In the second formulation (*experiment 2*), the training and test data sets were restricted to include only data from different malware families. Hence, in this experiment, the classifiers were tested on totally unknown malware families (i.e., malware families whose infected data traffic had not been considered at all in the training phase).

5   Experimental Results

5.1   Basic Observations

To evaluate and compare the results arising in the different experiments, we used three performance measures: the *True Positive Rate* (TPR), the *False Positive Rate*

(FPR) and *Precision*. These measures are used typically for the evaluation of ML based classification and are defined as follows:

$$\text{True Positive Rate: TPR} = \text{TP}/(\text{TP}+\text{FN})(\text{aka Recall}) \tag{1}$$

$$\text{False Positive Rate: FPR} = \text{FP}/(\text{TN}+\text{FP}) \tag{2}$$

$$\text{Precision} = \text{TP}/(\text{TP}+\text{FP}) \tag{3}$$

In the above formulas, *True positive* (TP) is the number of normal data that were correctly classified by an ML algorithm; *True negative* (TN) is the number of infected data that were correctly classified by an ML algorithm; *False positive* (FP) is the number of normal data that were incorrectly classified as infected by an ML algorithm; and *False negative* (FN) is the number of infected data that were incorrectly classified as normal by an ML algorithm.

Experiment 1. As discussed in Sect. 4, all the UDP protocol traffic in the dataset was labeled normal and was filtered out in the subsequent analysis. Thus, the attributes that we used in the experiment were *frame duration, TCP packet size* and *the number of arguments in the HTTP requests URL*. Also classifications were performed separately for the stream and packet data sets using all basic classifier algorithms. Hence, we carried out 30 groups of basic algorithm experiments (5 classifier algorithms × 3 validation schemes × 2 data sets) and 18 groups of ML-BOX experiments (6 box algorithms × 3 validation schemes × 1 data set).

The results of the experiments for the atomic and aggregate classifiers from experiment 1 are shown in Table 3. The table shows the recall, precision and FPR measures for stream and packet data separately and for different validation set ups (90-10 % 10-fold validation, 50-50 % 2-fold validation, and 10-90 % split validation). The main overall observation from Table 3 was that the results in the case of packet level traffic were not encouraging and that the results for stream traffic were considerably better.

This could be explained as follows. In TCP communication, the server and client should make a connection by a 3-way handshake, then send transfer data (payload packets) in fragments to stay below a maximum transmission unit (MTU). Also for each data transfer, the receiver sends an acknowledgement signal packet (ACK signal). Finally, the initiator sends a FIN signal packet to end the communication. In our experiments, data of normal and infected applications were labeled by the source and destination IP address of each traffic instance. In the case of the packet dataset, there was a large number of FIN and ACK packets labeled as "infected" due to the used IP addresses. The remaining features of these packets, however, were similar to FIN and ACK packets labeled as "normal". Thus, the classifiers could not distinguish between them. In the case of the stream dataset, however, FIN and ACK packets were grouped into single streams and hence their own characteristics did not feature prominently in the training and testing data sets. Hence, the classifiers were not misled by these signal packets in cases where they had the same features as payload packets and, consequently, the performance of the stream dataset was better than that of the packet dataset.

Table 3. Results of experiment 1

Algorithms			90%-10% 10-fold cross-validation			50%-50% 2-fold cross-validation			10%-90% split dataset		
			Recall	FPR	Precision	Recall	FPR	Precision	Recall	FPR	Precision
Naïve Bayesian	Packet	Infect	0.031	0.006	0.760	0.030	0.006	0.750	0.609	0.006	0.994
		Normal	0.994	0.969	0.609	0.994	0.970	0.608	0.994	0.391	0.609
	Stream	Infect	0.064	0.028	0.788	0.096	0.043	0.781	0.938	0.827	0.645
		Normal	0.972	0.936	0.391	0.957	0.904	0.395	0.173	0.062	0.635
J48 Tree	Packet	Infect	0.335	0.066	0.769	0.344	0.077	0.746	0.198	0.041	0.763
		Normal	0.934	0.665	0.680	0.923	0.656	0.681	0.959	0.802	0.644
	Stream	Infect	0.908	0.276	0.842	0.870	0.307	0.821	0.881	0.398	0.780
		Normal	0.724	0.092	0.829	0.693	0.130	0.766	0.602	0.119	0.760
MNN	Packet	Infect	0.183	0.161	0.428	0.455	0.404	0.426	0.909	0.807	0.427
		Normal	0.839	0.817	0.609	0.596	0.545	0.624	0.193	0.091	0.761
	Stream	Infect	0.877	0.752	0.654	0.946	0.826	0.650	0.982	0.913	0.633
		Normal	0.248	0.123	0.556	0.174	0.054	0.667	0.087	0.018	0.750
KNN	Packet	Infect	0.455	0.154	0.660	0.461	0.177	0.632	0.479	0.210	0.602
		Normal	0.846	0.545	0.702	0.823	0.539	0.698	0.790	0.521	0.696
	Stream	Infect	0.893	0.216	0.870	0.887	0.248	0.853	0.800	0.230	0.848
		Normal	0.784	0.107	0.818	0.752	0.113	0.804	0.770	0.200	0.706
SVM	Packet	Infect	0.012	0.003	0.726	0.012	0.003	0.726	0.013	0.003	0.733
		Normal	0.997	0.988	0.605	0.997	0.988	0.605	0.997	0.987	0.604
	Stream	Infect	0.998	0.966	0.626	0.997	0.969	0.625	0.999	0.983	0.620
		Normal	0.034	0.002	0.917	0.031	0.003	0.870	0.017	0.001	0.909
ML-BOX(AND)	Stream	Infect	0.053	0.011	0.887	0.036	0.008	0.884	0.679	0.150	0.884
		Normal	0.946	0.487	0.751	0.992	0.964	0.389	0.850	0.321	0.612
ML-BOX(OR)	Stream	Infect	0.996	0.969	0.625	0.996	0.958	0.627	0.998	0.954	0.637
		Normal	0.053	0.011	0.887	0.042	0.004	0.871	0.046	0.002	0.929
ML-BOX(HALF)	Stream	Infect	0.941	0.349	0.813	0.936	0.340	0.817	0.945	0.670	0.703
		Normal	0.941	0.349	0.813	0.660	0.064	0.864	0.330	0.055	0.782
ML-BOX+(AND)	Stream	Infect	0.845	0.129	0.914	0.835	0.148	0.902	0.759	0.173	0.880
		Normal	0.947	0.382	0.801	0.852	0.165	0.761	0.827	0.241	0.672
ML-BOX+(OR)	Stream	Infect	0.947	0.382	0.801	0.945	0.410	0.789	0.891	0.460	0.764
		Normal	0.845	0.129	0.914	0.590	0.055	0.870	0.540	0.109	0.746
ML-BOX+(HALF)	Stream	Infect	0.939	0.359	0.814	0.847	0.205	0.900	0.856	0.426	0.782
		Normal	0.939	0.165	0.922	0.795	0.153	0.704	0.574	0.144	0.691

Focusing on stream traffic only, Table 4 shows the average recall, TPR and precision across for the two validation schemes with the best outcome (i.e., the 90-10 and 50-50 k-fold validation) in the case of infected traffic, and the relative ranking of each algorithm given the each of the evaluation measures. In the case of KNN, for example, the table shows ".870/1" under precision for the 90-10 validation scheme. This means that the precision of KNN was .870 for the 90-10 scheme and that this algorithm was ranked 1st amongst the atomic algorithms. The results show a mixed picture. In particular, KNN and J48 were the best two atomic algorithms in terms of precision; KNN and J48 were the best two atomic algorithms in terms of recall; and Naïve Bayesian and KNN were the best two atomic algorithms in terms of FPR. The outcome was the same in the case of precision and FPR for the 50-50 % scheme but in this case the ranking of atomic algorithms changed for recall (SVM still turned out as best but was followed by MNN).

The results of aggregated algorithms were in general better than those of atomic algorithms in this experiment. In particular, the ML-BOX(OR) and ML-BOX+(OR) algorithms produced the best recall for infected traffic (i.e., about 99 % and 95 %, respectively) for both validation schemes. In terms of precision and FPR, the best two algorithms were ML-BOX+(AND) and ML-BOX(AND), albeit the different order of their ranking under each of these measures. ML-BOX(OR) and ML-BOX+(OR)

Table 4. Ranking of algorithms for infected stream traffic in Experiment 1

Classifier Split	Precision (ave)		FPR (ave)		Recall (ave)	
	90-10	50-50	90-10	50-50	90-10	50-50
Naïve Bayesian	.788/3	.781/3	.028/1	.043/1	.064/5	.096/5
J48 Tree	.842/2	.821/2	.276/3	.307/3	.908/2	.870/3
MNN	.654/5	.650/5	.752/4	.826/4	.877/4	.946/2
KNN	.870/1	.853/1	.216/2	.248/2	.893/3	.887/4
SVM	.626/4	.625/4	.966/5	.969/5	.998/1	.997/1
ML-BOX(AND)	.887/2	.884/3	.011/1	.008/1	.053/6	.036/6
ML-BOX(OR)	.625/6	.627/6	.969/6	.958/6	.996/1	.996/1
ML-BOX(HALF)	.813/4	.817/4	.349/3	.340/4	.941/3	.936/3
ML-BOX+(AND)	.914/1	.902/1	.129/2	.148/2	.845/5	.835/5
ML-BOX+(OR)	.801/5	.789/5	.382/5	.410/5	.947/2	.945/2
ML-BOX+(HALF)	.814/3	.900/2	.359/4	.205/3	.939/4	.847/4

yielded a higher recall than the individual algorithms because they classified as infected the union of the streams classified as such by any of these algorithms (i.e., a superset of all the sets of infected streams returned by the individual algorithms). ML-BOX(AND) and ML-BOX+(AND) yielded a higher precision than individual algorithms as they classified as infected the intersection of the streams that were classified as such by these algorithms (i.e., a subset of all the sets of infected streams returned by the individual algorithms).

Comparing the results across different validation schemes, the results in terms of precision and FPR in the case of 90-10 % 10-fold validation were better than those of the 50-50 % 2-fold validation for most algorithms, although no notable differences amongst these two schemes were observed for recall.

Experiment 2. The second experiment focused on assessing the capability of classifiers to detect totally unknown mobile botnet malware. To do so, we partitioned the infected stream dataset into different subsets containing only data from the individual mobile botnet malware families. This produced 9 sets of infected data coming from all families in Table 1 except from family 8 which did not produce any infected data. The 9 sets of infected data were mixed with a random selection of 10 % of normal stream data to formulate an infected family data set. Subsequently, we used ~90-10 % 10-fold validation by selecting data streams from 8 families and testing it on the remaining 1 family and ~50-50 % 2-fold validation by selecting data streams from 5 families and testing it on the remaining 4 families.

The results of experiment 2 in terms of recall, TPR and precision are shown in Tables 5 and 6. Table 5 shows the average recall, TPR and precision across all families for the two splits and the relative ranking of each algorithm given the relevant measure (in the case of J48 for example the table shows ".665/1" under precision for the 90-10 scheme meaning that the precision of J48 was .665 and that this algorithm was ranked 1st amongst the atomic algorithms). Table 6 shows the results for each of the individual malware families as produced in the 90-10 scheme.

Table 5. Ranking of algorithms for infected stream traffic in Experiment 2

Classifier	Precision (ave)		FPR (ave)		Recall (ave)	
	90-10	50-50	90-10	50-50	90-10	50-50
Naïve Bayesian	.606/3	.693/2	.030/1	.158/1	.116/5	.190/5
J48 Tree	.665/1	.756/1	.204/2	.222/2	.567/4	.530/3
MNN	.544/4	.544/5	.783/4	.680/4	.886/2	.727/2
KNN	.617/2	.656/3	.276/3	.336/3	.583/3	.511/4
SVM	.529/5	.555/4	.957/5	.900/5	.988/1	.927/1
ML-BOX(AND)	.735/1	.741/1	.008/1	.031/1	.088/6	.089/6
ML-BOX(OR)	.529/6	.582/6	.957/6	.935/5	.988/1	.976/1
ML-BOX(HALF)	.637/5	.674/5	.345/4	.398/4	.718/3	.613/3
ML-BOX+(AND)	.662/2	.735/2	.119/2	.148/2	.396/5	.388/5
ML-BOX+(OR)	.640/3	.691/4	.360/5	.410/6	.753/2	.704/2
ML-BOX+(HALF)	.638/4	.694/3	.342/3	.344/3	.716/4	.602/4

The main observations drawn from experiment 2 are:

(i) The precision, recall and FPR of all classifiers (both the atomic and the aggregated ones) dropped w.r.t experiment 1, as it can be seen by contrasting the recall and precision figures for the 90-10 and 50-50 cross validation column for stream data in Table 3 with the corresponding figures in Table 5. The drop was more significant in the case of recall.

(ii) The cross validation with the 50-50 slit generated better outcomes than the 90-10 split in terms of precision, recall and FPR for all algorithms. This was probably due to over fitting, as in the 90-10 scheme we found recall to correlate positively with the training-to-test data set size (TTTS) ratio and precision to correlate with TTTS negatively: the correlation coefficients were 0.41 for TTTS/Recall, and −0.90 for TTTS/Precision.

(iii) Results were poor for all families with a low number (<50) of infected streams (i.e., families 3, 5, 6, 7). Generally, recall

(iv) The algorithms J48 and Naïve Bayesian have had the best performance in terms of precision and FPR amongst the atomic algorithms in the 90-10 and 50-50 scheme. However, their performance in terms of recall was not so good (0.567 and 0.116, respectively). In terms of recall, the best performers amongst single algorithms were SVM and MNN. However, both these algorithms had low precision and high FRP rates.

(v) ML-BOX (AND) and ML-BOX+(AND) have had the best performance in terms of precision and FPR amongst the aggregate (box) algorithms in the 90-10 and 50-50 schemes. However, their performance in terms of recall was not poor (0.088 and 0.396, respectively). In terms of recall, the best performers amongst box algorithms were ML-BOX(OR) and ML-BOX+(OR). However, only ML-BOX +(OR) appeared to have acceptable precision and FPR rate.

(vi) Recall and FPR were found to correlate positively with the size of the infected data set of a family and precision was found to correlate negatively with it.

Table 6. Recall/FUR/Precision for individual botnet families (90-10 scheme)

Malware Family	1 (187 infect streams)			2 (181 infect streams)			3 (7 infect streams)		
Measures	Recall	FPR	Precision	Recall	FPR	Precision	Recall	FPR	Precision
Naive Bayesian	0.059	0.03	0.846	0.05	0.03	0.818	0.571	0.03	0.667
J48 Tree	0.636	0.152	0.922	0.403	0.182	0.859	0.714	0.242	0.238
MNN	0.695	0.53	0.788	0.994	0.864	0.759	1	0.864	0.109
KNN	0.642	0.288	0.863	0.768	0.242	0.897	0.857	0.303	0.231
SVM	1	0.955	0.748	1	0.955	0.742	1	0.97	0.099
ML-BOX(AND)	0.032	0	1	0.028	0.015	0.833	0.571	0.015	0.8
ML-BOX(OR)	1	0.955	0.748	1	0.955	0.742	1	0.97	0.099
ML-BOX(HALF)	0.658	0.227	0.891	0.796	0.318	0.873	0.857	0.424	0.176
ML-BOX+(AND)	0.556	0.136	0.92	0.376	0.121	0.895	0.714	0.136	0.357
ML-BOX+(OR)	0.722	0.303	0.871	0.796	0.303	0.878	0.857	0.409	0.182
ML-BOX+(HALF)	0.658	0.227	0.891	0.796	0.303	0.878	0.857	0.409	0.182
Malware Family	4 (205 infect streams)			5 (55 infect streams)			6 (10 infect streams)		
Measures	Recall	FPR	Precision	Recall	FPR	Precision	Recall	FPR	Precision
Naive Bayesian	0.054	0.03	0.846	0.018	0.03	0.333	0.2	0.03	0.5
J48 Tree	0.639	0.182	0.916	0.145	0.227	0.348	0.6	0.258	0.261
MNN	0.917	0.788	0.783	0.745	0.848	0.423	0.9	0.848	0.138
KNN	0.561	0.227	0.885	0.418	0.212	0.622	0.8	0.303	0.286
SVM	0.995	0.955	0.764	1	0.955	0.466	0.9	0.955	0.125
ML-BOX(AND)	0.01	0	1	0	0.015	0	0.1	0.015	0.5
ML-BOX(OR)	0.995	0.955	0.764	1	0.955	0.466	0.9	0.955	0.125
ML-BOX(HALF)	0.795	0.288	0.896	0.364	0.348	0.465	0.8	0.409	0.229
ML-BOX+(AND)	0.4	0.121	0.911	0.145	0.091	0.571	0.6	0.152	0.375
ML-BOX+(OR)	0.8	0.288	0.896	0.418	0.348	0.5	0.8	0.409	0.229
ML-BOX+(HALF)	0.785	0.288	0.894	0.364	0.348	0.465	0.8	0.409	0.229
Malware Family	7 (38 infect streams)			9 (117 infect streams)			10 (243 infect streams)		
Measures	Recall	FPR	Precision	Recall	FPR	Precision	Recall	FPR	Precision
Naive Bayesian	0.026	0.03	0.333	0.06	0.03	0.778	0.004	0.03	0.333
J48 Tree	0.763	0.242	0.644	0.607	0.152	0.877	0.593	0.197	0.917
MNN	0.974	0.727	0.435	0.752	0.727	0.647	1	0.848	0.813
KNN	0.447	0.303	0.459	0.667	0.303	0.796	0.086	0.303	0.512
SVM	1	0.955	0.376	1	0.955	0.65	1	0.955	0.794
ML-BOX(AND)	0.026	0	1	0.026	0.015	0.75	0	0	0
ML-BOX(OR)	1	0.955	0.376	1	0.955	0.65	1	0.955	0.794
ML-BOX(HALF)	0.842	0.394	0.552	0.692	0.333	0.786	0.654	0.364	0.869
ML-BOX+(AND)	0.342	0.136	0.591	0.41	0.045	0.941	0.025	0.136	0.4
ML-BOX+(OR)	0.868	0.409	0.55	0.863	0.409	0.789	0.654	0.364	0.869
ML-BOX+(HALF)	0.842	0.394	0.552	0.692	0.333	0.786	0.654	0.364	0.869

5.2 Performance

Although the performance of mobile devices has improved significantly in recent years, their computing and energy capabilities are still limited. Therefore, a system deployed on a mobile device should be designed to minimize the demand of such resources. Hence, in our experiments we should also evaluate the execution time and battery consumption of MBotCS. The mobile device used in this evaluation was a GT-I9228 with 1440 MHz CPU clock, 1 GB of RAM and battery of 2500 mAh. MBotCS, tPacketCapture, and Gsam Battery Monitor had been installed on it. Then we made a random selection of 10 botnet applications and 10 normal applications of those indicated in Sect. 4.1 and run the evaluation experiment for 12 h. The set up of the experiment involved the following sequence of steps:

(1) Charged fully the battery of the mobile device and installed all the applications.
(2) Launched the Gsam Battery Monitor, tPacketCapture and MBotCs applications.
(3) Launched the normal and infected applications mentioned above and run 5 min for each application to simulate user behaviours, and the remaining experiment time keep the mobile device on standby.
(4) Gathered and analysed results.
(5) A comparison experiment was performed for a time period of the same length on the following day. The set up was identical to the initial experiment (i.e., we went through steps (1)–(4) except that we did not deploy MBotCS.

Results - Battery Consumption: The graphs of battery consumption in percentage terms and battery temperature during the experiment is shown in Fig. 2. According to the figure, the battery consumption was not affected significantly by the use of MBotCS. In particular, the use of MBotCS consumed 0.5 % of the total battery usage of the device during the period of its deployment. Of this, 0.2 % was the battery usage caused by tPacketCapture. These figures show that MBotCS has had a very low energy effect on the battery consumption of the device.

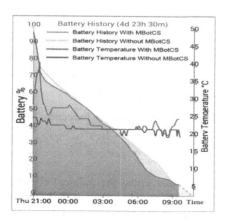

Fig. 2. Battery consumption

Execution Time: When activated, MBotCS checks the *pcap* file periodically, and if new traffic is captured, it scans and analyses it. In these scans, the scan sequence number (*sq*) is recorded. Using the J48, KNN and ML-BOX+(HALF) classifiers in the ML-Analyser, we recorded the number of streams (N^{sq}) in the new traffic and the total execution time (T^{sq}) for analysing the new traffic. Figure 3 shows the average execution times for the three classifiers, computed by the formula $T_{ave}^{sq} = \sum_{i=0}^{sq} T^{sq} / \sum_{i=0}^{sq} N^{sq}$ (the average for sequence number 100, for instance, is the average of execution time of a classifier over all stream instances from 1 to 100). The figure also shows the fitted curves for the average execution times of these algorithms.

The results show that the average execution time of J48 across all executions was 1.216 s with a standard deviation of 0.228 and the average of KNN across all executions was 11.562 s with a standard deviation of 1.779. The average of ML-BOX+(HALF) across all executions was 11.387 s with a standard deviation of 1.087. A t-test check showed the statistical significance of the observed differences between the average execution times of J48 and KNN at $\alpha = 0.05$ $(p-value = 2.701 \; E - 91 \ll 0.05)$, confirming that J48 have had better performance than KNN.

Also, the average execution time of different classifiers remained almost constant with respect to the processed number of streams performance, as shown by the curves fitted on execution times in Fig. 3. This indicates the capability of MBotCS to produce a reasonably fast detection/response once the ML-Analyser has been trained.

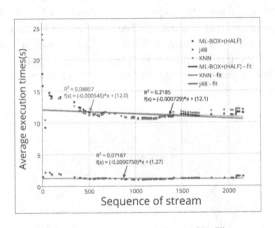

Fig. 3. The ML-Analyser Execution Time

5.3   Discussion

Regarding the observed differences across the different classifier algorithms, it should be noted that a relevant factor is the total number of streams in the stream dataset. This number was not very high (even though we captured a large number of individual packets). Also a statistical analysis of the values of the features in the dataset showed that these values did not have a normal distribution. Furthermore, features were not independent (e.g., the TCP size depends on the arguments of an HTTP request). For datasets with such characteristics, certain classifier algorithms such as the Naïve Bayesian classifier are not suitable (as NB requires the features in the dataset to be independent and have normally distributed values). The main threats to the validity of the outcomes of our experiments are summarised below:

(1) All the traffic was captured on only one mobile device, so contingency factors of hardware and software might have not been fully accounted for (e.g., disconnections from the network, crashes of applications due to insufficient memory).
(2) In general, there is an active period for every malware application. Some botnets may change the botmaster server or go through updates of the malicious code in the infected applications. None of these was reflected in the traffic that we considered.
(3) The availability of a bot master could not be guaranteed in our experiments. Therefore, the considered botnets may have further interactions that were not captured in the traffic that we used.
(4) The size of the stream dataset used in the experiments was relatively small and therefore the observed results need to be confirmed by larger experiments.

6   Conclusions and Future Work

In this paper, we have presented MBotCS, a mobile botnet detection system implemented for Android mobile devices that uses machine learning to detect traffic generated by mobile botnet malware.

To evaluate the feasibility of this approach for mobile botnet detection, we carried out a series experiments. These experiments have shown promise in detecting botnets. Detection was more effective in cases where the ML classifiers had been trained using traffic of a given botnet (albeit different from the traffic used in the test) than in cases where ML classifiers had to detect totally unknown botnets. The experiments also showed that detection was more effective for stream traffic than for packet traffic and that aggregate (box) ML algorithms were more effective than atomic algorithms. They also showed significant differences between the execution times of different ML algorithms on the mobile device and low battery consumption, which is a prerequisite for the feasibility of the approach on mobile devices.

Currently, we are investigating the possibility of analysing traffic across networks of mobile devices (as opposed to single devices) and traffic between botnets and the system software of the device to see if we get any performance gains. We are also planning more extensive experimental evaluations with larger data sets. Finally, we want to explore the use of unsupervised classification and contrast its outcomes with supervised classification, and investigate the reasons underpinning the differences in the performance of the basic ML algorithms.

The datasets that we used for the experiments reported in this paper, and the scripts for their generation are available from: http://emx2.co.uk/mbotcs/.

References

1. Alpcan, T., Bauckhage, C., Schmidt, A.-D.: A probabilistic diffusion scheme for anomaly detection on smartphones. In: Samarati, P., Tunstall, M., Posegga, J., Markantonakis, K., Sauveron, D. (eds.) WISTP 2010. LNCS, vol. 6033, pp. 31–46. Springer, Heidelberg (2010)
2. Batyuk, L., Herpich, M.: Using static analysis for automatic assessment and mitigation of unwanted and malicious activities within Android applications. In: 2011 6th International Conference Malicious Unwanted Software, pp. 66–72 (2011)
3. Bhargava, D., et al.: Decision tree analysis on j48 algorithm for data mining. Int. J. Adv. Res. Comput. Sci. Softw. Eng. 3(6), 1114–1119 (2013)
4. Bläsing, T., et al.: An android application sandbox system for suspicious software detection. In: Proceedings of the 5th IEEE International Conference on Malicious and Unwanted Software, pp. 55–62 (2010)
5. Boland, M.V., Murphy, R.F.: A neural network classifier capable of recognizing the patterns of all major subcellular structures in fluorescence microscope images of HeLa cells. Bioinformatics 17(12), 1213–1223 (2001)
6. Braun, L., Münz, G., Carle, G.: Packet sampling for worm and botnet detection in TCP connections. In: Proceedings of the 2010 IEEE/IFIP Network Operations and Management Symposium, NOMS 2010, pp. 264–271 (2010)
7. Chappell, L.A., Combs, G.: Wireshark 101: Essential Skills for Network Analysis. Protocol Analysis Institute, Chappell University, San Jose (2013)
8. Funk C., Garnaeva M.: Kaspersky security bulletin (2013). https://securelist.com/analysis/kaspersky-security-bulletin/58265/kaspersky-security-bulletin-2013-overall-statistics-for-2013
9. Cisco: Cisco visual networking index: Global mobile data traffic forecast update, 2014–2019. Tech. report (2015). http://www.cisco.com/en/US/solutions/collateral/ns341/ns525/ns537/ns705/ns827/white_paper_c11-520862.html
10. Cunningham, P., Delany, S.J.: k-nearest neighbour classifiers. In: Multiple Classifier Systems, pp. 1–17 (2007)
11. Eslahi, M., Salleh, R., Anuar, N.B.: MoBots: a new generation of botnets on mobile devices and networks. In: 2012 International Symposium on Computer Applications and Industrial Electronics, pp. 262–266 (2012)
12. Feizollah, A., et al.: A study of machine learning classifiers for anomaly-based mobile botnet detection. Malays. J. Comput. Sci. 26(4), 251–265 (2014)
13. Google: Google IP address ranges. https://support.google.com/a/answer/60764?hl=en. Accessed June 2015
14. Google: Dashboards. https://developer.android.com/about/dashboards/index.html. Accessed June 2015
15. Hall, M., et al.: The WEKA data mining software: an update. ACM SIGKDD Explor. Newsletter 11(1), 10–18 (2009)
16. Kalige, E., Burkey, D.: A case study of Eurograbber: How 36 million euros was stolen via malware. Versafe (White paper) (2012)
17. Porras, P., Saïdi, H., Yegneswaran, V.: An analysis of the iKee.B iPhone Botnet. In: Schmidt, A.U., Russello, G., Lioy, A., Prasad, N.R., Lian, S. (eds.) MobiSec 2010. LNICST, vol. 47, pp. 141–152. Springer, Heidelberg (2010)
18. Reina, A., Fattori, A., Cavallaro, L.: A system call-centric analysis and stimulation technique to automatically reconstruct android malware behaviors. In: EuroSec, April 2013
19. Rish, I.: An empirical study of the naive Bayes classifier. In: IJCAI 2001 Workshop on Empirical Methods in Artificial Intelligence, vol. 3, no. 22, pp. 41–46 (2001)

20. Schmidt, A.D., et al.: Static analysis of executables for collaborative malware detection on android. In: IEEE International Conference on Communications 2009, pp. 1–5 (2009)
21. Schmidt, A.D., et al.: Monitoring smartphones for anomaly detection. Mob. Netw. Appl. **14** (1), 92–106 (2009)
22. Seo, S.H., Gupta, A., Sallam, A.M., Bertino, E., Yim, K.: Detecting mobile malware threats to homeland security through static analysis. J. Netw. Comput. Appl. **38**, 43–53 (2014)
23. Shabtai, A., Kanonov, U., Elovici, Y.: Detection, alert and response to malicious behavior in mobile devices: knowledge-based approach. In: Kirda, E., Jha, S., Balzarotti, D. (eds.) RAID 2009. LNCS, vol. 5758, pp. 357–358. Springer, Heidelberg (2009)
24. Shabtai, A., et al.: "Andromaly": a behavioral malware detection framework for android devices. J. Intell. Inf. Syst. **38**(1), 161–190 (2012)
25. Shahar, Y.: A framework for knowledge-based temporal abstraction. Artif. Intell. **90**(1), 79–133 (1997)
26. Spreitzenbarth, M., et al.: Mobile-sandbox: having a deeper look into android applications. In: 28th Annual ACM Symposium on Applied Computing, pp. 1808–1815. ACM (2013)
27. Strazzere, T.: The new not compatible: Sophisticated and evasive threat harbors the potential to compromise enterprise networks. https://blog.lookout.com/blog/2014/11/19/notcompatible/. Accessed June 2015
28. Tanner, G.: Gsam battery monitor. https://play.google.com/store/apps/details?id=com.gsamlabs.bbm&hl=en_GB. Accessed June 2015
29. Taosoftware: tpacketcapture. https://play.google.com/store/apps/details?id=jp.co.taosoftware.android.packetcapture. Accessed June 2015
30. Team, B.R., et al.: Sanddroid: an APK analysis sandbox. Xi'an jiaotong university (2014). http://sanddroid.xjtu.edu.cn/. Accessed June 2015
31. Vural, I., Venter, H.: Mobile botnet detection using network forensics. In: Berre, A.J., Gómez-Pérez, A., Tutschku, K., Fensel, D. (eds.) FIS 2010. LNCS, vol. 6369, pp. 57–67. Springer, Heidelberg (2010)
32. Vural, I., Venter, H.S.: Combating mobile spam through botnet detection using artificial immune systems. J. UCS **18**(6), 750–774 (2012)
33. Wireshark: The wireshark network analyzer 1.12.2. https://www.wireshark.org/docs/man-pages/tshark.html. Accessed June 2015
34. Xiang, C., et al.: Andbot: towards advanced mobile botnets. In: 4th USENIX Conference on Large-Scale Exploits and Emergent Threats. USENIX Association (2011)
35. Zhou, W., et al.: Fast, scalable detection of "piggybacked" mobile applications. In: 3rd ACM Conference on Data and application security and privacy - CODASPY 2013, p. 185 (2013). http://dl.acm.org/citation.cfm?doid=2435349.2435377
36. Zhou, Y., Jiang, X.: Dissecting android malware: characterization and evolution. In: IEEE Symposium on Security and Privacy (SP 2012), pp. 95–109. IEEE (2012)
37. Zorz, Z.: Android trojan with botnet capabilities found in the wild. http://www.net-security.org/malware_news.php?id=1577. Accessed June 2015

Toward Securing MANET Against
the Energy Depletion Attack

Aida Ben Chehida Douss[✉], Ryma Abassi, and Sihem Guemara El Fatmi

Higher School of Communication, Sup'Com,
University of Carthage Tunis, Tunis, Tunisia
{bechehida.aida,ryma.abassi,sihem.guemara}@supcom.rnu.tn

Abstract. A Distributed Denial of Service (DDoS) attacks are used
by malicious nodes in order to flood a victim node with large data
flows. When the victim is a communication node, these attacks aim to
damage network performances by reducing its resources such as bandwidth (bandwidth depletion attack), computing power (processor depletion attack) and energy (energy depletion attack). Due to their proper
characteristics (wireless and dynamic topologies, low battery life, etc.),
Mobile Ad hoc NETworks (MANETs) are more vulnerable than other
networks and their damages can quickly became very serious. Moreover,
for such networks, the energy depletion attack is obviously the most common because it makes nodes unable to process legitimate requests and
traffic. It follows that for MANETs, for which such attack can be completely disabling, it is better to prevent this type of attack rather than
reacting after its occurrence. The aim of this paper fits into the previous strategy: it proposes as a first part, a security mechanism preventing
energy depletion attack which ties up the residual energy of a victim
MANET node making it unable to process legitimate requests and consequently the needed service. The environment on which the proposition
is made uses the delegation concept and extends a recently proposed
reputation based clustering MANET environment organizing the network into clusters with elected cluster heads (CHs) and detecting and
isolating malicious nodes. The second part of this paper concerns the formal specification of the proposed mechanism based on a certain number
of constraints and its verification using adequate algorithms.

Keywords: MANET · Security · Energy depletion attack · Delegation ·
Specification · Verification

1 Introduction

A Mobile ad hoc network (MANET) is a spontaneous network that can be established without the aid of any fixed infrastructure or central administration. This
means that all its nodes act simultaneously as host and router and take part
in its discovery and maintenance of routes [9]. Because of MANET characteristics and loopholes such as limited bandwidth, memory and battery power, it is

© Springer International Publishing Switzerland 2016
C. Lambrinoudakis and A. Gabillon (Eds.): CRiSIS 2015, LNCS 9572, pp. 292–306, 2016.
DOI: 10.1007/978-3-319-31811-0_18

very hard to achieve security and consequently make them vulnerable to several attacks. One of these attacks is distributed denial-of-service (DDoS).

DDoS are attacks where multiple systems act together and target a single victim [2]. The target node is temporarily flooded with an extremely large volume of packets making it unavailable and saturating the communication bandwidth and victim node resources so that the valid communication cannot be kept and network performances are greatly deteriorated. DDoS attacks can be grouped into three broad scenarios [3]: (1) energy depletion attack designed to send continuously bogus packets to a node with the intention of consuming the victim's battery energy and preventing other nodes from communicating with this latter, (2) storage and processing resources attack which target memory, storage space, or CPU of the service provider and (3) bandwidth depletion attack designed to flood the victim with unwanted traffic preventing by the fact legitimate traffic from reaching it.

Having that energy is an important resource in MANET; we are interested in this paper by energy depletion attack in such environment.

The main contribution of this paper is then, the definition of a security mechanism used for energy depletion prevention in MANET. This proposition is two-folds. First, a delegation based mechanism preventing energy depletion attack in MANET is introduced. Second, an adequate formalization and verification are achieved.

The proposed delegation mechanism is built over a reputation based clustering MANET environment detecting malicious nodes and isolating them based on their reputation values. The whole environment was built upon a mobility based clustering approach organizing MANET into clusters with one-hop members and elected cluster-heads (CHs). In such network, attackers will often target CHs. Hence, our proposition is to associate to each CH with a delegation process allowing the transfer of its functionalities to one of its cluster member when its residual energy reaches a minimum threshold.

The formal specification of the proposed delegation process is presented based on some constraints such as monotonicity, permanence, totality, level of delegation, agreement, multiple delegations and revocation. The whole delegation process is then verified using adequate algorithms.

The rest of this paper is organized as follow: Sect. 2 recalls some existing works dealing with DDoS attacks in MANET. In Sect. 3, the recently proposed reputation based clustering MANET environment is presented. Section 4 focuses on the energy depletion attack basics. Section 5 is concerned with the novel energy depletion attack prevention mechanism. In Sect. 6, the formalization of the proposed delegation process using some constraints is presented. A verification of the delegation process is given in Sect. 7. Finally, Sect. 8 concludes this paper.

2   Related Works

Recently, DDoS attacks issue has received considerable attention by researches in the MANET community. This kind of attack is used by malicious nodes in order to flood a victim node with large data flows. In this section, we are interested by existing works dealing with DDoS attacks in MANET. In [4], authors proposed an intrusion prevention system against DDoS attacks, so the network gets more secure through attacks and detect malicious node and malicious behavior through the intrusion prevention system (IPS). In this paper, authors proposed a scheme in MANET's security issues which is related to routing protocols. This work is done through network simulator-2 (NS-2) and it is used to measure the network performance. This paper applies Intrusion Prevention system so that network can become totally secure from attack and it can also detect malicious node and activity through IPS and it can detect via Intrusion Detection System. This scheme can also be used for detecting DoS.

Authors proposed in [5], a method for determining intrusion or misbehave in MANETs using intrusion detection system. This method protects the network from DDoS attacks by proposing a new defense mechanism which consists of a Flow Monitoring Table (FMT) for all mobile nodes. The table contains the following parameters: sender id, receiver id, protocol type, transport info, event time, node coordinate axis and application layer info. According to these parameters, the behavior of the network in normal case, in DDoS attack and in IDS case are analyzed. First, the normal profile is created. Second, the attack is described in which an attacker node is created to send unwanted packet to the neighboring node. Third, the IDS checks the normal and abnormal behavior of the network according to parameters. In this paper NS-2 is used to analyze TCP at normal time and DDoS time, IDS case, routing load, packet delivery ratio and analysis of packet sends and receives. The simulation results conclude that the IDS 99.9 % recoverable.

S.A. Arunmozhi and Y. Venkataramani [6] have proposed the Flow Monitoring (FMON) scheme for MANETs that is resistant to the Reduction of Quality (RoQ) attack. RoQ attack is a new style of DDoS attack which is difficult to detect. RoQ attacks throttle the TCP throughput heavily and reduce the QoS to end systems gradually rather than refusing the clients from the services completely. The proposed defend mechanism consists of a flow monitoring table (FMT) at each node to identify the attackers. If the channel continues to be congested because some sender nodes do not reduce their sending rate, it can be found by the destination using the updated FMT. Once the attackers are identified, all packets from those nodes will be blocked. Simulation results show that the proposed scheme achieves higher throughput and packet delivery ratio with reduced packet drop for legitimate users.

In this paper, we are interested by energy depletion attack targeting the reputation based clustering MANET environment. This is achieved through the proposition of a delegation based mechanism preventing this type of attack by avoiding the loss of the CH role as well as its replacement by a malicious node.

3   A Reputation Based Clustering MANET Environment

Recently, we proposed a reputation based clustering MANET environment [7] securing routing process by detecting malicious nodes and isolating them.

This environment is based on two main components. The first component MCA (Mobility-based Clustering Approach) [8], is based on two main phases: (1) the setting-up phase that organizes MANET into clusters with one-hop members and elected Cluster-Heads (CH). The election of CHs is made based on a weight calculated according to the residual energy and the mobility. The elected CH should have the smallest weight. (2) The maintenance phase that maintains the organization of the network in the presence of mobility. It adapts clusters following network topology changes i.e. node addition, displacement or failure.

The second component TMCA (Trust MCA) [7] is built upon MCA. TMCA detects and isolates malicious routing behaviors based on CHs direct observations as well as alerts exchanged between them. Four modules were specified into the TMCA scheme.

1. The monitoring module supervising member behaviors based on the Watchdog mechanism. The CH may detect two kinds of events: (1) a positive event i.e. the member node forwards the packet and do not modifies it, (2) a negative event i.e. the member node don't forward the packet or modifies it.
2. The reputation module updating members' reputations according to the events detected by the monitoring module.
3. The isolation module isolates misbehaving member nodes whose reputation values falls below a minimum value equal to -3.
4. The identity recognition module assessing alerts sources exchanged between CHs.

Let us note that these modules are implemented in all nodes in the network but are activated only for elected CHs. Moreover, a rehabilitation mechanism was also used to rehabilitate malicious node having well behaved for a given period of time.

The proposed reputation based clustering MANET environment was formalized in a recent work using a formal specification language called SCMSL (Secured Clustered MANET Specification Language) [9]. A validation process based on automated systems through the use of inference systems was also built in order to prove the security policy consistency and completeness.

4   Energy Depletion Attack Basics

In this section, we present the energy depletion attack modeling in a clustered MANET as well as its impact in such environment.

4.1   Energy Depletion Attack Modeling and Assumptions

There are certain attack models we are not addressing in this paper. Therefore, we made the following assumptions:

- The considered attack target is a MANET organized into clusters with one-hop members and elected CHs. Each CH uses the modules explained in Sect. 3 to monitor its cluster members' behavior.

– At least, two nodes have to cooperate to achieve the energy depletion attack. If only one node performs the attack, its own energy will be depleted.
– Only member nodes can achieve such attack whereas actives CHs are assumed to be safe i.e. cannot behave maliciously to perform the energy depletion attack.

4.2 Energy Depletion Attack Impact

Let us recall that in this paper, we focus on energy depletion attack in which two or more member nodes collaborate to disturb the TMCA process.

To perform the energy depletion attack, malicious member nodes periodically flood their CH with a relatively large number of data or control packets. This will deplete the CH's residual energy and make it unavailable. All cluster members belonging to this CH will be aware about this failure and will use the MCA maintenance phase to elect the novel CH between the member nodes. The elected member node should have the lowest weight i.e. should be stable with a low relative mobility and with enough residual energy.

In fact, cluster members exchange periodically *Weight* messages containing their combined weight calculated through two parameters: Mobility and residual energy. Once a member node detects the failure of its CH, it compares its weight with its cluster members' weights. If it has the lowest weight among its cluster member, it considers itself as CH and informs the rest of the cluster members by sending a CH message. Else, it simply waits for this message from another member node. Hence, a malicious member node can become CH and decreases honest member nodes' reputation values in order to discard them from communications or increases malicious member nodes reputations to prevent them from being isolated.

Let us consider the network depicted by Fig. 1a and composed by eleven nodes organized into three clusters with three elected CHs: 7, 9 and 10. We assume that member nodes 5 and 1 are malicious and perform the energy depletion attack. Such as depicted by Fig. 1a, malicious member nodes flood their CH with a large number of packets. The CH 9's residual energy will be depleted, thus one of the member nodes will become CH. If for instance member node 1 is elected as CH (Fig. 1b), the cluster will be managed by a malicious node.

5   Proposed Prevention Mechanism Against Energy Depletion Attack

In this section, the main contribution of this paper is presented. It concerns the energy depletion attack prevention by avoiding the loss of the CH role as well as its replacement by a malicious node.

In order to prevent the energy depletion attack and to limit the potential consequences of such attack, a delegation process is proposed allowing the CH to delegate its functionalities to one of its cluster member when its residual energy reaches a minimum threshold. Let us recall that delegation [10] is the

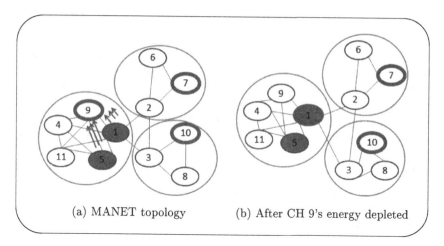

(a) MANET topology   (b) After CH 9's energy depleted

Fig. 1. Energy depletion attack impact

process allowing a node to share or transfer its functionalities. Using delegation, a node (the *delegator*) will be able to give its functionalities to another node (the *delegatee*) when it is no longer able to perform them. For our concern, delegation process is used to allow the transfer of the CHs functionalities to one of its members when it is not able to perform them anymore.

The proposed energy depletion attack prevention mechanism is based on the following properties:

- Once the CH's energy reaches a minimum threshold, it delegates its functionalities to one of its cluster member through an election process.
- To ensure security, the chosen member node should have the highest reputation value and the lowest weight.
- Each CH maintains a reputation table containing members' reputation values and weights as well as a *CH_list* with CHs' identifiers.
- The proposed prevention mechanism is built upon two phases: (1) the initialization phase to choose the *delegatee* member node and (2) the notification phase to inform the *delegatee* and other cluster members about the identity of the new CH.

In the following the two phases are detailed.

5.1   The Initialization Phase

Initialization is the first phase in the proposed prevention mechanism. It is triggered when the residual energy of a given CH reaches a minimum threshold. In this case, the CH calculates for each member node a combined value (CV_i) using the member node's reputation value metric (rp_value_i) and its weight (W_i) from the reputation table by the following formula (1).

$$CV_i = \alpha_1(rp\_value_i) + \alpha_2(W_i) \tag{1}$$

Where α_1 and α_2 are the weights and $\alpha_1 + \alpha_2 = 1$.

The elected member node is then the node having the highest combined value and consequently the most honest and stable member node as well as the one having the highest energy value. Having that malicious nodes spend more energy than other members to perform the energy depletion attack, they will not be selected as CH.

When more than one cluster member has the same CV value, the chosen one is the node having the highest identifier. This assumption was made in order to avoid a blocking situation during the CH election.

Algorithm 1 depicts the initialization procedure using the following notations:

- i, the current node executing the procedure.
- $Member\_ID$, a member node identifier.
- $Cluster_i$, the set of member nodes in i's cluster.
- rp_value_i, i's reputation value.
- $Weight\_Value_i$, i's weight value.
- CV_i, i's combined value.
- rp_table_i: i's reputation table.
- rt_table_i: i's routing table.
- $Send_j\ Msg\ ()$, node i sends to node j a message Msg.

Algorithm 1. Initialization procedure

BEGIN

       IN (rp_table_i)

       FOR EACH Member_ID $\in$ $Cluster_i$

       $CV_{\text{Member\_ID}} = \alpha_1\ rp\_value_{\text{Member\_ID}} + \alpha_2\ Weight\_Value_{\text{Member\_ID}}$

       SELECT Member_ID /

       $CV_{\text{Member_ID}} = $ MAX $(CV_x)\ \forall\ x \in Cluster_i$

       IF{Member_ID} THEN

           BEGIN

           SELECT d $\in$ {Member_ID} /

           ID_value(d) = MAX (ID_value (d_i))

           END

END

5.2   The Notification Phase

Once the initialization phase performed, the CH unicasts a delegation request through the Del_REQ message to the chosen member node including its identifier and the *delegatee*'s identifier. When the member node receives this message and accepts the delegation request, it replies with the Del_REP message including its identifier. Upon receiving this message, the CH shares its reputation table with the new CH and notifies its cluster members as well as other CHs in the network about the identity of the new CH using the Del_NOTIF message. This message includes old and new CHs identities. These messages are defined in Table 1.

Algorithm 2 depicts the notification procedure.

Table 1. Exchanged messages and notation

Message	Meaning
Del_REQ (CH_ID, New_CH_ID)	Notifies the selected member that it was chosen to be the new CH
Del_REP (New_CH_ID)	Notifies CH that the selected member node agrees to be CH
Del_NOTIF (CH_ID, New_CH_ID)	Notifies cluster member about the new chosen CH identity

---

Algorithm 2. Notification procedure

BEGIN

    Send$_d$ (Del_REQ (i, d))

        IF (Receive$_d$ Del_REP (d)) **THEN**

            BEGIN

            Share (rp_table (i, d))

            Send$_{Clusteri, CH\_list}$ (Del_NOTIF (i, d))

            END

        ELSE Wait (Del_Timer)

            IF (Del_Timer is expired)

            THEN

            BEGIN

            rp_value$_d$ = −3

            Blacklist$_i$ = Blacklist$_i$ ∪ {d}

            Send$_{Clusteri, CH\_list}$ (ALERT (i, 0, d))

            rt_table$_i$:= rtable$_i$ / {d}

            END

END

Let us note that if the CH does not receive a Del_REP message from the chosen member node during a fixed time Del_timer, the following actions are triggered:

- Setting the member's reputation value to −3 and blacklisting it.
- Informing cluster members and other CHs (using ALERT message) about this non cooperative node and considering it as malicious.
- Deleting all paths including the malicious node from the routing table.
- Performing the initialization phase to select a new member.

Once the notification phase performed, each CH receiving the Del_NOTIF message (notifying about the new chosen CH d), adds the node d into its *CH_list*.

Let us note that the proposed delegation process has another beneficial effect. It improves network performances and maintains also clusters' stability by avoiding the re-invocation of the clustering approach in case of CH failure or when the CH is obliged to create a new cluster with a new coming node like explained in our recent work in the MCA maintenance phase.

6 Delegation Modeling

The first step towards verification process is a formal specification. Hence, we present in this section a formal specification of the proposed delegation process.

We then summarize the delegation constraints such as introduced in the literature and apply them in our delegation based environment.

6.1 Delegation Basics

Let us recall that delegation is the process whereby a user without any administrative prerogatives obtains the ability to grant some authorizations such as introduced in [10]. In order to propose a complete framework dealing with delegation, we identify the main delegation constraints [11]. These latter comprise monotonicity, permanence, totality, levels of delegation, multiple delegation, agreement and revocation.

In the following, the delegation rule is modeled; the delegation constraints are presented and are applied in our delegation based environment.

6.2 Delegation Rule Modeling

We propose to model the delegation rule delg as follows:

$$Event \rightarrow delg\ (Delegator,\ Delegatee,\ Constraint)$$

Where:

- *event* is the trigger of the delegation process. In our context, delegation is triggered in two cases: (1) when the CH's energy falls below a given threshold $Energy_{Min}$ or (2) in the MCA maintenance phase, when the CH is obliged to create a new cluster with a new coming node.
- *delegator* represents the subject initiating the delegation process. In our context the *delegator* is the CH.
- *delegatee* represents the delegation beneficiary. In our delegation process, the *delegatee* is one of the *delegator*'s member nodes.
- *constraint* is used to precise *delegatee*'s constraints needed in order to be elected as new CH. In our context, the *delegatee* should have the maximum combined value CV to become CH.

The previous rule is then used as follows:

$$(Energy\ (CH) < Energy_{min}) \vee New\_coming\_node \rightarrow delg\ (CH,\ Member\_node,\ Max\ (CV_{member\_node}))$$

Let us note that $\wedge$ and $\vee$ represent respectively the logical operators AND, and OR.

The proposed delegation rule indicates that when the residual energy of a CH falls below a minimum threshold $Energy_{min}$ or when it is obliged to create a new cluster with a new coming node, the CH delegates its functionalities to one of its cluster member. The chosen member node should have the maximum combined value CV.

6.3 Definition of Delegation Constraints

The following Table 2 summarizes the delegation constraints such as applied in our delegation based environment.

7 Delegation Constraints Verification

In this section, we first formally define the delegation constraints presented above then we propose adequate algorithms in order to verify these constraints.

7.1 Non-monotonic Constraint Verification

Formally, a non-monotonic delegation constraint is defined as follows:

$$\exists (CH\_old, CH\_new) / CH\_old \notin CH\_list \\ \wedge \; CH\_old \in Cluster\_Members\_list \\ (CH\_new)$$

Where CH_old represents the *delegator* and CH_new the *delegatee*. CH_list contains all CHs' identifiers in the network and $Cluster\_Members\_list$ contains all cluster members belonging to a given CH.

As depicted in Algorithm 3, when the CH_old no longer belongs to the CH_list and if it becomes a member node in the CH_new's cluster (belongs to the CH_new's $Cluster\_Members\_list$), the delegation is non-monotonic.

Algorithm 3. Monotonicity verification procedure

$\exists \, (CH\_old, CH\_new$e$)$
$\quad\quad\quad$**IF** $CH\_old \notin$ CH_list
$\quad\quad\quad$**AND** $CH\_old \in$ Cluster_Members_list (CH_new)
$\quad\quad\quad$**THEN** Non-monotonic delegation verified

7.2 Permanent Constraint Verification

Formally, a permanent delegation constraint is defined as follows:

$$\forall \, t, \forall \, c \in C, \exists \, CH \in CH\_list \, / \, is\_CH \, (CH, \, c)$$

Where t represents the current time, C the clusters' set and c a given cluster. $is\_ch(CH,c)$ means that CH is the cluster-head of the cluster c.

As depicted in Algorithm 4, permanence is verified if there is only one CH belonging to the CH_list in each cluster c.

Algorithm 4. Permanence verification procedure

$\forall \, t, \forall \, c \in C$
$\quad\quad\quad$**IF** $\exists$ CH $\in$ CH_list
$\quad\quad\quad$**AND** is_CH (CH, c)
$\quad\quad\quad$**THEN** Permanent delegation verified

Table 2. Delegation constraints

Constraint	Definition	Choice

Monotonicity	Precises the state of the *delegator* after the delegation process.
	
	  – Non-monotonic: the *delegator* loses its functionalities.
	  – Monotonic: the *delegator* maintains its functionalities.
		Non-monotonic: The CH will not be able to operate and to manage the cluster before the delegation process.

Permanence	Precises the types of delegation in terms of their time duration.
	
	  – Permanent: another user permanently replaces the delegating user.
	  – Temporary: delegation is time limited
		Permanent: Once a CH delegates its functions, there is no specification of the time.

Totality	Precises how completely the permissions are delegated.
	
	  – Total: delegation of all the functions to the delegated node.
	  – Partial: only subsets of the delegated functions are delegated.
		Total: The CH delegates all its permissions and functions to the chosen member node.

Levels of delegation	Defines whether or not each delegation can be further delegated and how many times.
	
	  – Single-step: not allow the delegation to be further delegated.
	  – Multi-step: allows the *delegatee* to further delegate its delegated functions to a third user, and so on.
		Multi-step: Once the energy of the new *delegatee* reaches the minimum energy, it can delegate its functions to another cluster member.

Multiple delegation	Precises the number of *delegatees* to whom a *delegator* can delegate the same right at any given time.
	
	  – Multiple:a *delegator* delegates its functions to more than one *delegatee*.
	  – Not multiple:a *delegator* delegates its functions to only one *delegatee*.
		Not multiple: A CH has to delegate its functions to only one cluster member.

Agreements	Precises the delegation protocol between the *delegator* and the *delegatee*.
	
	  – Bilateral: delegation is accepted by both the *delegator* and the *delegatee*.
	  – Unilateral: is a one-way decision.
		Bilateral:
		
		  – The delegation should be accepted by the chosen node. If the *delegatee* does not accept, its reputation will be decreased.

Revocation	Represents the process by which a *delegator* can take away the privileges that it delegated.	We are not concerned with revocation.

7.3   Total Constraint Verification

A delegation process is total if the CH delegates all its functions to the chosen member node. The *delegator* loses then, its CH's role and becomes a member node and consequently, the *delegatee* should be the unique CH in the cluster. Formally, a total delegation constraint is defined as follows:

$$\exists (CH\_old, CH\_new) \mathbin{/} CH\_old \mathrel{!=} CH\_new$$
$$\wedge CH\_old \notin CH\_list$$
$$\wedge\ CH\_old \in Cluster\_Members\_list\ (CH\_new)$$

As depicted in Algorithm 5, given a *CH_old* delegating its role to a *CH_new*, if the *CH_new* is different from the *CH_old* and if the *CH_old* loses its CH's role after the delegation process i.e. it no longer belongs to the *CH_list* as it becomes member node in the *CH_new*'s *Cluster_Members_list*, the total constraint is verified.

Algorithm 5. Totality verification procedure

FOR EACH (*CH_old, CH_new*)
       IF *CH_old* != *CH_new*
       AND *CH_old* ∉ CH_list
       AND *CH_old* ∈ Cluster_Members_list (*CH_new*)
       THEN Total delegation verified

7.4   Multi-step Constraint Verification

A delegation process is multi-step if the new CH (the *delegatee*) is allowed to further delegate its delegated role to a third user, and so on. Formally, a multi-step delegation constraint is defined as follows:

$$\forall (CH\_new, m \in Cluster\_members\_list$$
$$(CH\_new)) \mathbin{/}$$
$$Energy\ (CH\_new) < Energy_{min} \rightarrow Delegate$$
$$(CH\_new, m)$$

Where *Energy(CH_new)* represents the *CH_new*'s residual energy and *Delegate (CH_new, m)* means that *CH_new* delegates its functions to the member node *m*.

As depicted in Algorithm 6, whenever the residual energy of a given *delegatee* reaches $Energy_{min}$, it delegates its functions to a new CH (one of its member *m*).

Algorithm 6 of delegation verification procedure

∀ *CH_new*,m ∈ Cluster_Members_list (*CH_new*)
       IF Energy(*CH_new*)<Energy$_{min}$
       AND Delegate (*CH_new*, m)
       THEN Multi-step delegation verified

7.5 Not-multiple Delegation Constraint Verification

Formally, a not-multiple delegation constraint is defined as follows:

$$\forall t, \forall\ c \in C,\ \exists!\ CH \in CH\_list\ /\ is\_CH\ (CH, c)$$

The not-multiple delegation constraint verification procedure is summarized by Algorithm 7: since a CH delegates its functions to only one cluster member, hence, at each instant t, each cluster is managed by a unique CH.

Algorithm 7. Multiple verification procedure

$\forall\ t, \forall\ c \in C$

    IF $\exists!$ CH $\in$ CH_list

    AND is_CH (CH, c)

    THEN Permanent delegation verified

7.6 Bilateral Delegation Constraint Verification

A bilateral delegation constraint is verified if the delegation is accepted by both the *delegator* and the *delegatee*. Formally, a bilateral delegation constraint is defined as follows:

$$\exists(CH\_old,\ CH\_new)\ /\ Delegate\ (CH\_old, CH\_new) \\ \wedge\ Accept\_Delegation\ (CH\_new)$$

The bilateral delegation constraint verification procedure is summarized in Algorithm 8. When a *CH_old* delegates its functions to one of its cluster member *CH_new* and this delegation is accepted by *CH_new*, then the bilateral delegation constraint is verified.

Algorithm 8. Agreement constraint verification procedure

$\exists\ (CH\_old,\ CH\_new)$

    IF Delegate $(CH\_old,\ CH\_new)$

    AND Accept_Delegation (CH_new)

    THEN Bilateral delegation verified

---

8 Conclusion

MANET is an infrastructure less network due to its capability of operating without the support of any fixed infrastructure. Because of its characteristics, MANET has no clear line of defense so it is accessible to both legitimate network users and malicious attackers. In the presence of malicious nodes, one of the main challenges in MANET is to design a robust security solution that can prevent it from various DDOS attacks. Network resources such as bandwidth (bandwidth depletion attack), computing power (processor depletion attack) and energy (energy depletion attack) are mostly the victims of DDoS attacks.

Having that energy is an important resource in MANET; the main contribution of this paper is then two-folds. First, we proposed a delegation-based mechanism preventing energy depletion attack which deplete victim node's residual energy and make it unavailable. The proposed mechanism is built over a recently proposed reputation based clustering MANET environment organizing the network into clusters with one-hop members and elected cluster-heads (CHs) and detecting malicious member nodes and isolating them. This mechanism prevents energy depletion attack performed by some member nodes against CHs. Hence, the proposition associates to each CH with a delegation process allowing it to transfer its functions to one of its cluster member once its residual energy reaches a minimum threshold. The chosen member node is the most honest and stable node as well as the one having the highest energy value. Second, a formal specification of the proposed mechanism based on a certain number of constraints is proposed and verified using adequate algorithms.

In future works, we intend implementing this mechanism and assessing the performance of our scheme by applying it in a real distributed and dynamic environment.

References

1. Kaushik, S., Kaushik, M.: Analysis of MANET security, architecture and assessment. Int. J. Electron. Comput. Sci. Eng. (IJECSE) **1**(2), 787–793 (2012). ISSN 2277–1956
2. Geetika, N.K.: Detection and prevention algorithms of DDOS attack in MANETs. Int. J. Adv. Res. Comput. Sci. Softw. Eng. **3**(8), 61–65 (2013)
3. Chhabra, M., Gupta, B., Almomani, A.: A novel solution to handle DDOS attack in MANET. J. Inf. Secur. **4**(3), 165–179 (2013)
4. Sinha, S.K., Singh, R.K., Pandey, K.K., Sahu, M.K.: Distributed denial of service attack prevention using critical link method in MANET. Int. J. Adv. Res. Comput. Sci. Electron. Eng. (IJARCSEE) **2**(3), 325 (2013)
5. Ahirwal, R., Mahour, L.: Analysis of DDoS attack effect and protection scheme in wireless mobile ad-hoc networks. Int. J. Comput. Sci. Eng. (IJCSE) **4**(6), 1164 (2012)
6. Arunmozhi, S.A., Venkataramani, Y.: A flow monitoring scheme to defend reduction-of-quality (RoQ) attacks in mobile ad-hoc networks. Inf. Secur. J. Global Perspect. **19**(5), 263–272 (2010)
7. Ben Chehida Douss, A., Abassi, R., Guemara El Fatmi, S.: A reputation-based clustering mechanism for MANET routing security. In: Proceedings of the 8th International Conference on Availability, Reliability and Security (ARES), Regensburg, Germany, September 2013
8. Ben Chehida Douss, A., Abassi, R., Guemara El Fatmi, S.: Towards the definition of a mobility-based clustering environment for MANET. In: Proceedings of the Ninth International Conference on Wireless and Mobile Communications (ICWMC), Nice, France, August 2013

9. Ben Chehida Douss, A., Abassi, R., Guemara El Fatmi, S.: A model for specification and validation of a trust management based security scheme in a MANET environment. In: Proceedings of the 4th International Workshop on Security of Mobile Applications (IWSMA), ARES, Toulouse, France, August 2015
10. Abassi, R., Guemara El Fatmi, S.: Dealing with delegation in a trust-based MANET. In: Proceedings of the IEEE 20th International Conference on Telecommunications (ICT) (2013)
11. Abassi, R., Guemara El Fatmi, S.: Delegation management modeling in a security policy based environment. In: Symbolic Computation in Software Science (SCSS) (2012)

Author Index

Printed in the United States
By Bookmasters